THE CENTENARY BURNS

After JOHN FAED

A COTTAGE HOME

THE POETRY OF
ROBERT BURNS

Edited by

W. E. HENLEY AND T. F. HENDERSON

With Numerous Illustrations

VOLUME IV

AMS PRESS
NEW YORK

Reprinted from the edition of 1896-97, Edinburgh and London
First AMS EDITION published 1970
Manufactured in the United States of America

International Standard Book Number:
Complete set: 0-404-01250-7
Volume 4: 0-404-01254-X

Library of Congress Card Catalog Number: 78-113567

AMS PRESS, INC.
NEW YORK, N.Y. 10003

EDITORS' PREFACE

Our aims in this Edition of the poetry of Burns were outlined in the Preface to our First Volume. Now that our work is done, it may be meet to touch on them with a certain particularity.

(1.) One, the first, was a classic text; and this was only to be achieved by exhaustively collating all the available versions, whether printed or holograph. After careful inquiry and research access was got to such a mass of MSS., including many not hitherto utilised, that this Centenary Edition may fairly claim to be regarded as a complete lexicon of the text of Burns's verse. Not only, in effect, is that text established and authenticated, but also a list is given of all important variations, with the authority for each. A mere rag-bag of anonymous and second-hand differences is a plain incitement to bewilderment and error. But an ordered and authenticated register supplies the sole means of testing the selected text, at the same time that it is of no small value as a guide to the Poet's methods.

(2.) For the exact and adequate understanding of the Bard we thought it right to give the history, so far as known, and the local setting of his every several piece, together with an explanation of his chief allusions—many among them of the most fleeting kind. In this connexion we hazarded the remark that Burns was 'what is called a local poet,' and that, to make sure of his being comprehended and appreciated, 'the safer as well as the more serviceable course' was rather 'to err on the score of too much commentary than on that of not enough.' The mere suggestion that the singer of Montgomerie's Peggy and the 'proper young belles' of Mauchline, the satirist of Auld and Fisher and Russell, the champion of Gavin Hamilton, the correspondent of Davie Sillar and Rankine and Lapraik—the Burns, in fact, who

claimed with pride to be the peculiar Bard of
Coila—was 'local' in any sense whatever, has
given, it seems, unpardonable offence—not, of
course, to the intelligent Scot, but—to certain
Scotsmen who, it would appear, are bent on
making Burns the pretext for and the buried
treasure in a whole dust-yard, a sort of Harmony-
Jail, of parochial 'fittons, figments, and leasings.'
These have not scrupled, in accounting for our
very necessary statement, to ascribe to us the
most discreditable motives: so that we have even
been accused of the deliberate design to bejape
and belittle the Poet we were professing to
illustrate. Again, one 'serious Burns student'
has assured the world, or such of it as he
could reach, that our 'gibes against the Poet's
parochialism' have covered us with 'obloquy.'
As matter of fact, no finer eulogy could be
passed on Burns, no nobler tribute paid his
gift, than is contained in the demonstration
that, though 'the satirist and singer of a parish,'
he appeals to 'a world-wide public': since he
must of necessity command such an audience by
virtue of intrinsic splendour and innate magnifi-

cence and in despite of local and peculiar accidents.

(3.) For the Southron reader, still more essential to the understanding of Burns was a full and sufficient glossary. This, for convenience, is made marginal—as it were a running translation of the text; but in the case of certain words the explanation is relegated to the Notes. In this volume there is added a complete Glossarial Index, which, by means of quotations, will guide the reader, it is hoped, to an exacter appreciation of meanings and shades of meaning than the isolated exhibition of a marginal equivalent could do. For divers references to English Poets in the Glossarial Index we are indebted to Mr. W. J. Craig, Editor of *The Oxford Shakespeare*.

(4.) We have done our utmost to define and determine the relations of Burns to the past: for the very sufficient reasons (*a*) that no great poet was ever more directly 'the product of immediate and remote forebears' than Burns, or more entirely and conspicuously the product of a certain school, and (*b*) that in him the school aforesaid culminated. Here, again, we have been credited with a desire to achieve the 'depreciation' of Burns, with an endeavour to lessen his position as 'a great lyric poet,' with the will to 'change his place in the estimation of the world.' To all which it is enough to reply that the worst unfriends to Burns and Burns's fame are those who would see the man other than he was and establish his reputation on a basis of falsehood. Facts, he said—

> 'Facts are chiels that winna ding
> An' daurna be disputed';

and to qualify an honest attempt at the discovery and elucidation of facts as an insult to his memory is surely a culmination of burlesque in argument. A reputation falsely founded demoralises those who accept it for the living truth; for a man can never be rightly known nor properly understood till he is set in his true perspective, and the amount of his debt to his ancestors is more or less exactly estimated. In this thought we have spent our labour and our time. If we be mistaken, then so much the worse for us. But, unless we be mistaken, then so much the worse—not for Burns: whose qualities are immortal: but—for those who insist on reading him for merits which he has not, and on reverencing him for virtues to which he laid no claim.

W. E. H.
T. F. H.

LONDON, 20*th July* 1897

CONTENTS

MISCELLANEOUS SONGS

	PAGE
A RUINED FARMER	1
MONTGOMERIE'S PEGGY	3
THE LASS OF CESSNOCK BANKS	3
THO' FICKLE FORTUNE	6
RAGING FORTUNE	7
MY FATHER WAS A FARMER	8
O, LEAVE NOVÉLS	11
THE MAUCHLINE LADY	12
ONE NIGHT AS I DID WANDER	12
THERE WAS A LAD	13
WILL YE GO TO THE INDIES, MY MARY	15
HER FLOWING LOCKS	16
THE LASS O' BALLOCHMYLE	16
THE NIGHT WAS STILL	18
MASONIC SONG	19
THE BONIE MOOR-HEN	20
HERE'S A BOTTLE	21
THE BONIE LASS OF ALBANIE	22
AMANG THE TREES	23
THE CHEVALIER'S LAMENT	24
YESTREEN I HAD A PINT O' WINE	25
SWEET ARE THE BANKS	27

CONTENTS

	PAGE
YE FLOWERY BANKS	28
CALEDONIA	29
YOU'RE WELCOME, WILLIE STEWART	31
WHEN FIRST I SAW	32
BEHOLD THE HOUR (FIRST SET)	34
HERE'S A HEALTH TO THEM THAT'S AWA	35
AH, CHLORIS	37
PRETTY PEG	37
MEG O' THE MILL (SECOND SET)	38
PHILLIS THE FAIR	39
O SAW YE MY DEAR, MY PHILLY	40
'TWAS NA HER BONIE BLUE E'E	41
WHY, WHY TELL THY LOVER	42
THE PRIMROSE	42
O, WERT THOU IN THE CAULD BLAST	43

INTERPOLATIONS

YOUR FRIENDSHIP	44
FOR THEE IS LAUGHING NATURE	44
NO COLD APPROACH	44
ALTHO' HE HAS LEFT ME	45
LET LOOVE SPARKLE	45
AS DOWN THE BURN	45

IMPROBABLES

ON ROUGH ROADS	46
ELEGY ON STELLA	46
POEM ON PASTORAL POETRY	50
ON THE DESTRUCTION OF DRUMLANRIG WOODS	53
THE JOYFUL WIDOWER	55
WHY SHOULD WE IDLY WASTE OUR PRIME	57

CONTENTS

	PAGE
THE TREE OF LIBERTY	58
TO A KISS	62
DELIA (AN ODE)	63
TO THE OWL	64
THE VOWELS (A TALE)	66
ON THE ILLNESS OF A FAVOURITE CHILD	67
ON THE DEATH OF A FAVOURITE CHILD	68

ADDENDUM TO

MALLY'S MEEK	69

BIBLIOGRAPHICAL . . . 73

NOTES :—

MISCELLANEOUS SONGS

A RUINED FARMER	81
MONTGOMERIE'S PEGGY	82
THE LASS OF CESSNOCK BANKS	82
THO' FICKLE FORTUNE	83
RAGING FORTUNE	84
MY FATHER WAS A FARMER	84
O, LEAVE NOVÉLS	84
THE MAUCHLINE LADY	84
ONE NIGHT AS I DID WANDER	85
THERE WAS A LAD	85
WILL YE GO TO THE INDIES, MY MARY	86
HER FLOWING LOCKS	86
THE LASS O' BALLOCHMYLE	87
THE NIGHT WAS STILL	88
MASONIC SONG	88
THE BONIE MOOR-HEN	89

CONTENTS

NOTES:—*Continued.*

	PAGE
HERE'S A BOTTLE	90
THE BONIE LASS OF ALBANIE	90
AMANG THE TREES	91
THE CHEVALIER'S LAMENT	92
YESTREEN I HAD A PINT O' WINE	92
SWEET ARE THE BANKS	94
YE FLOWERY BANKS	94
CALEDONIA	94
YOU'RE WELCOME, WILLIE STEWART	95
WHEN FIRST I SAW	95
BEHOLD THE HOUR (FIRST SET)	96
HERE'S A HEALTH TO THEM THAT'S AWA	96
AH, CHLORIS	98
PRETTY PEG	98
MEG O' THE MILL (SECOND SET)	99
PHILLIS THE FAIR	99
O, SAW YE MY DEAR, MY PHILLY	99
'TWAS NA HER BONIE BLUE E'E	100
WHY, WHY TELL THY LOVER	100
THE PRIMROSE	100
O, WERT THOU IN THE CAULD BLAST	102

INTERPOLATIONS

YOUR FRIENDSHIP	103
FOR THEE IS LAUGHING NATURE	103
NO COLD APPROACH	103
ALTHO' HE HAS LEFT ME	104
LET LOOVE SPARKLE	104
AS DOWN THE BURN	104

CONTENTS

IMPROBABLES

	PAGE
ON ROUGH ROADS	104
ELEGY ON STELLA	105
POEM ON PASTORAL POETRY	105
ON THE DESTRUCTION OF DRUMLANRIG WOODS	106
THE JOYFUL WIDOWER	106
WHY SHOULD WE IDLY WASTE OUR PRIME	107
THE TREE OF LIBERTY	107
TO A KISS	107
DELIA (AN ODE)	107
TO THE OWL	108
THE VOWELS (A TALE)	108
ON THE ILLNESS OF A FAVOURITE CHILD	108
ON THE DEATH OF A FAVOURITE CHILD	108

ADDENDUM TO

MALLY'S MEEK	108
INDEX OF TITLES TO VOLUME IV.	109
GLOSSARIAL INDEX	115
GENERAL INDEX	177
OF TITLES, FIRST LINES, ETC.	
INDEX OF PERSONS AND PLACES	217
LIFE: GENIUS: ACHIEVEMENT	231
BY W. E. HENLEY.	
INDEX TO ESSAY	343

LIST OF ILLUSTRATIONS

A Cottage Home . (*coloured*)	*Frontispiece*
	AT PAGE
A Ruined Farmer	2
Farm of Lochlea . . (*coloured*)	8
Burns and Highland Mary (*coloured*)	28
Here's a Health to Them that's Awa .	34
The Lea Rig . . (*coloured*)	40
The House in which Burns died . .	72
Burns at an Evening Party at Lord Monboddo's House . (*coloured*)	80
The Birthplace of Burns . . .	96
Mrs. Burns and her Grandchild . .	104
Early Draft of 'Scots Wha Hae' .	108
Interior of the Birthplace of Burns .	232
Alloway Kirk with Burns Monument .	248
Lincluden	280
St. Michael's Churchyard, Dumfries .	328

MISCELLANEOUS SONGS

A RUINED FARMER

I

The sun he is sunk in the west,
All creatures retirèd to rest,
While here I sit, all sore beset
      With sorrow, grief, and woe:
And it's O fickle Fortune, O!

II

The prosperous man is asleep,
Nor hears how the whirlwinds sweep;
But Misery and I must watch
      The surly tempests blow:
And it's O fickle Fortune, O!

III

There lies the dear Partner of my breast,
Her cares for a moment at rest!
Must I see thee, my youthful pride,
      Thus brought so very low?—
And it's O fickle Fortune, O!

IV

There lie my sweet babies in her arms;
No anxious fear their little hearts alarms;
But for their sake my heart does ache,
      With many a bitter throe:
And it's O fickle Fortune, O!

V

I once was by Fortune carest,
I once could relieve the distrest;
Now life's poor support, hardly earn'd,
      My fate will scarce bestow:
And it's O fickle Fortune, O!

VI

No comfort, no comfort I have!
How welcome to me were the grave!
But then my wife and children dear—
      O, whither would they go!
And it's O fickle Fortune, O!

VII

O, whither, O, whither shall I turn,
All friendless, forsaken, forlorn?
For in this world Rest or Peace
      I never more shall know:
And it's O fickle Fortune, O!

Etching by WILLIAM HOLE

A RUINED FARMER

"O, whither, O, whither shall I turn,
   All friendless, forsaken, forlorn?
For in this world Rest or Peace
     I never more shall know,
  And it's O fickle Fortune, O!"

MONTGOMERIE'S PEGGY

I

Altho' my bed were in yon muir,   *yonder*
   Amang the heather, in my plaidie,
Yet happy, happy would I be,
   Had I my dear Montgomerie's Peggy.

II

When o'er the hill beat surly storms,
   And winter nights were dark and rainy,
I'd seek some dell, and in my arms
   I'd shelter dear Montgomerie's Peggy.

III

Were I a Baron proud and high,
   And horse and servants waiting ready,
Then a' 'twad gie o' joy to me—   *'twould give*
   The sharin't with Montgomerie's Peggy.   *sharing it*

THE LASS OF CESSNOCK BANKS

I

On Cessnock banks a lassie dwells,
   Could I describe her shape and mien!
Our lasses a' she far excels—
   An' she has twa sparkling, rogueish een!   *eye*

THE LASS OF CESSNOCK BANKS

II

She's sweeter than the morning dawn,
    When rising Phœbus first is seen,
And dew-drops twinkle o'er the lawn—
    An' she has twa sparkling, rogueish een!

III

yonder   She's stately like yon youthful ash,
slopes   That grows the cowslip braes between,
    And drinks the stream with vigour fresh—
        An' she has twa sparkling, rogueish een!

IV

She's spotless like the flow'ring thorn
    With flow'rs so white and leaves so green,
When purest in the dewy morn—
    An' she has twa sparkling, rogueish een!

V

Her looks are like the vernal May,
    When ev'ning Phœbus shines serene,
While birds rejoice on every spray—
    An' she has twa sparkling, rogueish een!

VI

Her hair is like the curling mist,
    That climbs the mountain-sides at e'en,
When flow'r-reviving rains are past—
    An' she has twa sparkling, rogueish een!

VII

Her forehead's like the show'ry bow,
  When gleaming sunbeams intervene,
And gild the distant mountain's brow—
  An' she has twa sparkling, rogueish een!

VIII

Her cheeks are like yon crimson gem,
  The pride of all the flowery scene,
Just opening on its thorny stem—
  An' she has twa sparkling, rogueish een!

IX

Her teeth are like the nightly snow,
  When pale the morning rises keen,
While hid the murm'ring streamlets flow—
  An' she has twa sparkling, rogueish een!

X

Her lips are like yon cherries ripe,
  That sunny walls from Boreas screen:
They tempt the taste and charm the sight—
  An' she has twa sparkling, rogueish een!

XI

Her teeth are like a flock of sheep
  With fleeces newly washen clean,
That slowly mount the rising steep—
  An' she has twa sparkling, rogueish een!

XII

Her breath is like the fragrant breeze,
  That gently stirs the blossom'd bean,
When Phœbus sinks behind the seas—
  An' she has twa sparkling, rogueish een!

XIII

Her voice is like the ev'ning thrush,
  That sings on Cessnock banks unseen,
While his mate sits nestling in the bush—
  An' she has twa sparkling, rogueish een!

XIV

But it's not her air, her form, her face,
  Tho' matching Beauty's fabled Queen:
'Tis the mind that shines in ev'ry grace—
  An' chiefly in her rogueish een!

THO' FICKLE FORTUNE

I

Tho' fickle Fortune has deceived me
  (She promis'd fair, and perform'd but ill),
Of mistress, friends, and wealth bereaved me,
  Yet I bear a heart shall support me still.

II

I'll act with prudence as far as I'm able;
  But if success I must never find,
Then come, Misfortune, I bid thee welcome—
  I'll meet thee with an undaunted mind!

RAGING FORTUNE

I

O, RAGING Fortune's withering blast
  Has laid my leaf full low!
O, raging Fortune's withering blast
  Has laid my leaf full low!

II

My stem was fair, my bud was green,
  My blossom sweet did blow;
The dew fell fresh, the sun rose mild,
  And made my branches grow.

III

But luckless Fortune's northern storms
  Laid a' my blossoms low!
But luckless Fortune's northern storms
  Laid a' my blossoms low!

MY FATHER WAS A FARMER

I

My father was a farmer upon the Carrick border, O,
And carefully he bred me in decency and order, O.
He bade me act a manly part, though I had ne'er a farthing, O,
For without an honest, manly heart no man was worth regarding, O.

II

Then out into the world my course I did determine, O:
Tho' to be rich was not my wish, yet to be great was charming, O.
My talents they were not the worst, nor yet my education, O—
Resolv'd was I at least to try to mend my situation, O.

III

In many a way and vain essay I courted Fortune's favour, O:
Some cause unseen still stept between to frustrate each endeavour, O.
Sometimes by foes I was o'erpower'd, sometimes by friends forsaken, O,
And when my hope was at the top, I still was worst mistaken, O.

FARM OF LOCHLEA

MY FATHER WAS A FARMER

IV

Then sore harass'd, and tir'd at last with Fortune's vain delusion, O,
I dropt my schemes like idle dreams, and came to this conclusion, O:—
The past was bad, and the future hid; its good or ill untrièd, O,
But the present hour was in my pow'r, and so I would enjoy it, O.

V

No help, nor hope, nor view had I, nor person to befriend me, O;
So I must toil, and sweat, and broil, and labour to sustain me, O!
To plough and sow, to reap and mow, my father bred me early, O:
For one, he said, to labour bred was a match for Fortune fairly, O.

VI

Thus all obscure, unknown, and poor, thro' life I'm doom'd to wander, O,
Till down my weary bones I lay in everlasting slumber, O.
No view nor care, but shun whate'er might breed me pain or sorrow, O,
I live to-day as well's I may, regardless of to-morrow, O!

VII

But, cheerful still, I am as well as a monarch in a palace, O,
Tho' Fortune's frown still hunts me down, with all her wonted malice, O:
I make indeed my daily bread, but ne'er can make it farther, O,
But, as daily bread is all I need, I do not much regard her, O.

VIII

When sometimes by my labour I earn a little money, O,
Some unforeseen misfortune comes gen'rally upon me, O:
Mischance, mistake, or by neglect, or my good-natur'd folly, O—
But, come what will, I've sworn it still, I'll ne'er be melancholy, O.

IX

All you who follow wealth and power with unremitting ardour, O,
The more in this you look for bliss, you leave your view the farther, O.
Had you the wealth Potosi boasts, or nations to adore you, O,
A cheerful, honest-hearted clown I will prefer before you, O!

O, LEAVE NOVÉLS

I

O, leave novéls, ye Mauchline belles—
  Ye're safer at your spinning-wheel!
Such witching books are baited hooks
  For rakish rooks like Rob Mossgiel.

II

Your fine *Tom Jones* and *Grandisons*
  They make your youthful fancies reel!
They heat your brains, and fire your veins,
  And then you're prey for Rob Mossgiel.

III

Beware a tongue that's smoothly hung,
  A heart that warmly seems to feel!
That feeling heart but acts a part—
  'Tis rakish art in Rob Mossgiel.

IV

The frank address, the soft caress
  Are worse than poisoned darts of steel:
The frank address and politesse
  Are all finesse in Rob Mossgiel.

THE MAUCHLINE LADY

I

<small>[Notes]</small>

<small>went; rode</small>

When first I came to Stewart Kyle,
  My mind it was na steady:
Where'er I gaed, where'er I rade,
  A mistress still I had ay.

II

But when I came roun' by Mauchline toun,
  Not dreadin anybody,
My heart was caught, before I thought,
  And by a Mauchline lady.

ONE NIGHT AS I DID WANDER

One night as I did wander,
  When corn begins to shoot,
I sat me down to ponder
  Upon an auld tree-root:

<small>past</small>
<small>hastened</small>
<small>cooed</small>

Auld Ayr ran by before me,
  And bicker'd to the seas;
A cushat crooded o'er me,
  That echoed through the trees.

THERE WAS A LAD

Chorus

Robin was a rovin boy,
    Rantin, rovin, rantin, rovin,   *roystering*
Robin was a rovin boy,
    Rantin, rovin Robin!

I

THERE was a lad was born in Kyle,   *[Notes]*
But whatna day o' whatna style,   *what*
I doubt it's hardly worth the while
    To be sae nice wi' Robin.

II

Our monarch's hindmost year but ane   *one*
Was five-and-twenty days begun,   *[Notes]*
'Twas then a blast o' Janwar' win'   *January wind*
    Blew hansel in on Robin.   *[Notes]*

III

The gossip keekit in his loof,   *glanced; palm*
Quo' scho:—'Wha lives will see the proof,   *Quoth she*
This waly boy will be nae coof: *thumping; dolt*
    I think we'll ca' him Robin.

IV

<small>above</small>
<small>to</small>

'He'll hae misfortunes great an' sma',
But ay a heart aboon them a'.
He'll be a credit till us a':
We'll a' be proud o' Robin!

V

<small>every</small>
<small>kind</small>
<small>Commend me to</small>

'But sure as three times three mak nine,
I see by ilka score and line,
This chap will dearly like our kin',
So leeze me on thee, Robin!

VI

<small>sir</small>
<small>make; aspread</small>
<small>faults; worse</small>

'Guid faith,' quo' scho, 'I doubt you, stir,
Ye gar the lasses lie aspar;
But twenty fauts ye may hae waur—
So blessins on thee, Robin!'

Chorus

Robin was a rovin boy,
Rantin, rovin, rantin, rovin,
Robin was a rovin boy,
Rantin, rovin Robin!

WILL YE GO TO THE INDIES, MY MARY

I

Will ye go to the Indies, my Mary,
    And leave auld Scotia's shore?
Will ye go to the Indies, my Mary,
    Across th' Atlantic roar?

II

O, sweet grows the lime and the orange,
    And the apple on the pine;
But a' the charms o' the Indies
    Can never equal thine.

III

I hae sworn by the Heavens to my Mary,
    I hae sworn by the Heavens to be true,
And sae may the Heavens forget me,
    When I forget my vow!

IV

O, plight me your faith, my Mary,
    And plight me your lily-white hand!
O, plight me your faith, my Mary,
    Before I leave Scotia's strand!

THE LASS O' BALLOCHMYLE

V

We hae plighted our troth, my Mary,
  In mutual affection to join;
And curst be the cause that shall part us!
  The hour and the moment o' time!

HER FLOWING LOCKS

I

Her flowing locks, the raven's wing,
  Adown her neck and bosom hing. *hang*
How sweet unto that breast to cling,
  And round that neck entwine her!

II

Her lips are roses wat wi' dew— *wet*
  O, what a feast, her bonie mou!
Her cheeks a mair celestial hue,
  A crimson still diviner!

THE LASS O' BALLOCHMYLE

I

'Twas even: the dewy fields were green,
  On every blade the pearls hang, *hung*
The zephyr wanton'd round the bean,
  And bore its fragrant sweets alang,

In ev'ry glen the mavis sang,
　All Nature list'ning seem'd the while,
　　Except where greenwood echoes rang
　　Amang the braes o' Ballochmyle.　　　heights

II

With careless step I onward stray'd,
　My heart rejoic'd in Nature's joy,
When, musing in a lonely glade,
　A maiden fair I chanc'd to spy.
　　Her look was like the Morning's eye,
　　Her air like Nature's vernal smile.
　　Perfection whisper'd, passing by :—
'Behold the lass o' Ballochmyle!'

III

Fair is the morn in flowery May,
　And sweet is night in autumn mild,
When roving thro' the garden gay,
　Or wand'ring in the lonely wild;
　　But woman, Nature's darling child—
　　There all her charms she does compile
　　Even there her other works are foil'd
By the bonie lass o' Ballochmyle.

IV

O, had she been a country maid,
　And I the happy country swain,
Tho' shelter'd in the lowest shed
　That ever rose on Scotia's plain,

Thro' weary winter's wind and rain
With joy, with rapture, I would toil,
And nightly to my bosom strain
The bonie lass o' Ballochmyle!

V

Then Pride might climb the slipp'ry steep,
Where fame and honours lofty shine,
And thirst of gold might tempt the deep,
Or downward seek the Indian mine!
Give me the cot below the pine,
To tend the flocks or till the soil,
And ev'ry day have joys divine
With the bonie lass o' Ballochmyle.

THE NIGHT WAS STILL

I

The night was still, and o'er the hill
The moon shone on the castle wa',
The mavis sang, while dew-drops hang
Around her on the castle wa':

hung

II

Sae merrily they danc'd the ring
Frae eenin' till the cock did craw,
And ay the o'erword o' the spring
Was :—'Irvine's bairns are bonie a'!'

evening;
crow
refrain;
tune

MASONIC SONG

I

YE sons of old Killie, assembled by Willie
    To follow the noble vocation,
Your thrifty old mother has scarce such another
    To sit in that honorèd station!
I've little to say, but only to pray
    (As praying's the *ton* of your fashion).
A prayer from the Muse you well may excuse
    ('Tis seldom her favourite passion):—

II

'Ye Powers who preside o'er the wind and the tide,
    Who markèd each element's border,
Who formèd this frame with beneficent aim,
    Whose sovereign statute is order,
Within this dear mansion may wayward Contention
    Or witherèd Envy ne'er enter!
May Secrecy round be the mystical bound,
    And brotherly Love be the centre!'

THE BONIE MOOR-HEN

Chorus

<small>advise</small> I rede you, beware at the hunting, young men!
I rede you, beware at the hunting, young men!
Take some on the wing, and some as they spring,
<small>cautiously</small> But cannily steal on a bonie moor-hen.

I

<small>mown</small> The heather was blooming, the meadows were mawn,
<small>went; one</small> Our lads gaed a-hunting ae day at the dawn,
O'er moors and o'er mosses and monie a glen:
At length they discovered a bonie moor-hen.

II

Sweet-brushing the dew from the brown heather bells,
Her colours betray'd her on yon mossy fells!
Her plumage outlustred the pride o' the spring,
And O, as she wanton'd sae gay on the wing,

III

Auld Phœbus himsel', as he peep'd o'er the hill,
In spite at her plumage he tryèd his skill:
<small>height</small> He level'd his rays where she bask'd on the brae—
His rays were outshone, and but mark'd where she lay!

HERE'S A BOTTLE

IV

They hunted the valley, they hunted the hill,
The best of our lads wi' the best o' their skill·
But still as the fairest she sat in their sight,
Then, whirr! she was over, a mile at a flight.

Chorus

I rede you, beware at the hunting, young men!
I rede you, beware at the hunting, young men!
Take some on the wing, and some as they spring,
But cannily steal on a bonie moor-hen.

HERE'S A BOTTLE

*There's nane that's blest of human kind
But the cheerful and the gay, man.*

I

HERE's a bottle and an honest man!
    What wad ye wish for mair, man?   *more*
Wha kens, before his life may end,
    What his share may be o' care, man?

II

Then catch the moments as they fly,
    And use them as ye ought, man!
Believe me, Happiness is shy,
    And comes not ay when sought, man!

THE BONIE LASS OF ALBANIE

I

<small>sad; extremely</small>
My heart is wae, and unco wae,
  To think upon the raging sea,
That roars between her gardens green
  An' the bonie lass of Albanie.

II

This noble maid's of royal blood,
  That rulèd Albion's kingdoms three;
But O, alas for her bonie face!
  They hae wranged the lass of Albanie.

III

In the rolling tide of spreading Clyde
  There sits an isle of high degree,
<small>[Notes]</small>
And a town of fame, whose princely name
  Should grace the lass of Albanie.

IV

But there is a youth, a witless youth,
  That fills the place where she should be
We'll send him o'er to his native shore,
  And bring our ain sweet Albanie!

V

Alas the day, and woe the day!
<small>gained the prize</small>
  A false usurper wan the gree,
Who now commands the towers and lands,
  The royal right of Albanie.

VI

We'll daily pray, we'll nightly pray,
  On bended knees most fervently,
That the time may come, with pipe and drum
  We'll welcome hame fair Albanie.

AMANG THE TREES

I

Amang the trees, where humming bees
  At buds and flowers were hinging, O,   *hanging*
Auld Caledon drew out her drone,   *[Notes]*
  And to her pipe was singing, O.
'Twas Pibroch, Sang, Strathspeys and Reels—
  She dirl'd them aff fu' clearly, O,   *rang*
When there cam' a yell o' foreign squeels,
  That dang her tapsalteerie, O!   *knocked; head over heels*

II

Their capon craws an' queer 'ha, ha's,'   *[Notes]*
  They made our lugs grow eerie, O.   *ears; frightened*
The hungry bike did scrape and fyke,   *swarm; make ado*
  Till we were wae and weary, O.   *disgusted*
But a royal ghaist, wha ance was cas'd   *[Notes]; ghost*
  A prisoner aughteen year awa,   *eighteen*
He fir'd a Fiddler in the North,
  That dang them tapsalteerie, O!

THE CHEVALIER'S LAMENT

I

The small birds rejoice in the green leaves returning,
  The murmuring streamlet winds clear thro' the vale,
The primroses blow in the dews of the morning,
  And wild scatter'd cowslips bedeck the green dale:
    But what can give pleasure, or what can seem fair,
    When the lingering moments are number'd by care?
      No flow'rs gaily springing,
      Nor birds sweetly singing
    Can soothe the sad bosom of joyless despair!

II

The deed that I dar'd, could it merit their malice,
  A king and a father to place on his throne?
His right are these hills, and his right are those valleys,
  Where the wild beasts find shelter, tho' I can find none!
    But 'tis not my suff'rings thus wretched, forlorn—
    My brave gallant friends, 'tis your ruin I mourn!
      Your faith prov'd so loyal
      In hot bloody trial,
    Alas! can I make it no better return?

YESTREEN I HAD A PINT O' WINE *Last night*

I

Yestreen I had a pint o' wine,
    A place where body saw na;   *nobody saw*
Yestreen lay on this breast o' mine
    The gowden locks of Anna.

II

The hungry Jew in wilderness
    Rejoicing o'er his manna
Was naething to my hiney bliss   *honey*
    Upon the lips of Anna.

III

Ye monarchs take the East and West
    Frae Indus to Savannah:
Gie me within my straining grasp   *Give*
    The melting form of Anna!

IV

There I'll despise Imperial charms,
    An Empress or Sultana,
While dying raptures in her arms
    I give and take wi' Anna!

V

<small>Each ; go</small>

Awa, thou flaunting God of Day!
Awa, thou pale Diana!
Ilk Star, gae hide thy twinkling ray,
When I'm to meet my Anna!

VI

Come, in thy raven plumage, Night
(Sun, Moon, and Stars, withdrawn a'),
And bring an Angel-pen to write
My transports with my Anna!

POSTSCRIPT

I

<small>such;
mustn't</small>

The Kirk an' State may join, and tell
To do sic things I maunna:
The Kirk an' State may gae to Hell,
And I'll gae to my Anna.

II

<small>without</small>

She is the sunshine o' my e'e,
To live but her I canna:
Had I on earth but wishes three,
The first should be my Anna.

SWEET ARE THE BANKS

I

Sweet are the banks, the banks o' Doon,
    The spreading flowers are fair,
And everything is blythe and glad,
    But I am fu' o' care.
Thou'll break my heart, thou bonie bird,
    That sings upon the bough!
Thou minds me o' the happy days   *reminds*
    When my fause Luve was true.
Thou'll break my heart, thou bonie bird,
    That sings beside thy mate,
For sae I sat, and sae I sang,
    And wist na o' my fate!

II

Aft hae I rov'd by bonie Doon,
    To see the woodbine twine,
And ilka bird sang o' its luve,   *each*
    And sae did I o' mine.
Wi' lightsome heart I pu'd a rose   *plucked*
    Upon its thorny tree,
But my fause luver staw my rose,   *stole*
    And left the thorn wi' me.
Wi' lightsome heart I pu'd a rose
    Upon a morn in June,
And sae I flourish'd on the morn,
    And sae was pu'd or noon.   *before*

YE FLOWERY BANKS

I

Ye flowery banks o' bonie Doon,
    How can ye blume sae fair?
How can ye chant, ye little birds,
    And I sae fu' o' care?

II

Thou 'll break my heart, thou bonie bird,
    That sings upon the bough:
Thou minds me o' the happy days *[reminds]*
    When my fause Luve was true!

III

Thou 'll break my heart, thou bonie bird,
    That sings beside thy mate:
For sae I sat, and sae I sang,
    And wist na o' my fate!

IV

Aft hae I rov'd by bonie Doon
    To see the woodbine twine,
And ilka bird sang o' its luve, *[each]*
    And sae did I o' mine.

After JOHN FAED

BURNS AND HIGHLAND MARY

V

   Wi' lightsome heart I pu'd a rose
     Frae aff its thorny tree,   *From off*
   And my fause luver staw my rose,   *stole*
     But left the thorn wi' me.

CALEDONIA

I

There was on a time, but old Time was then young,
   That brave Caledonia, the chief of her line,
From some of your northern deities sprung
   (Who knows not that brave Caledonia's divine?).
From Tweed to the Orcades was her domain,
   To hunt, or to pasture, or do what she would.
Her heav'nly relations there fixèd her reign,
   And pledged her their godheads to warrant it good.

II

A lambkin in peace but a lion in war,
   The pride of her kindred the heroine grew.
Her grandsire, old Odin, triumphantly swore:—
   'Whoe'er shall provoke thee, th' encounter shall rue!'
With tillage or pasture at times she would sport,
   To feed her fair flocks by her green rustling corn;
But chiefly the woods were her fav'rite resort,
   Her darling amusement the hounds and the horn.

III

Long quiet she reign'd, till thitherward steers
    A flight of bold eagles from Adria's strand.
Repeated, successive, for many long years,
    They darken'd the air, and they plunder'd the land.
Their pounces were murder, and horror their cry;
    They 'd conquer'd and ravag'd a world beside.
She took to her hills, and her arrows let fly—
    The daring invaders, they fled or they died!

IV

[Notes] The Cameleon-Savage disturb'd her repose,
    With tumult, disquiet, rebellion, and strife.
Provok'd beyond bearing, at last she arose,
    And robbed him at once of his hopes and his life.
The Anglian Lion, the terror of France,
    Oft, prowling, ensanguin'd the Tweed's silver flood,
But, taught by the bright Caledonian lance,
    He learnèd to fear in his own native wood.

V

The fell Harpy-Raven took wing from the north,
    The scourge of the seas, and the dread of the shore;
The wild Scandinavian Boar issued forth
    To wanton in carnage and wallow in gore;
O'er countries and kingdoms their fury prevail'd,
    No arts could appease them, no arms could repel;
But brave Caledonia in vain they assail'd,
[Notes]   As Largs well can witness, and Loncartie tell.

VI

Thus bold, independent, unconquer'd, and free,
  Her bright course of glory for ever shall run,
For brave Caledonia immortal must be,
  I'll prove it from Euclid as clear as the sun:—
Rectangle-triangle, the figure we'll chuse;
  The upright is Chance, and old Time is the base,
But brave Caledonia's the hypothenuse;
  Then, *ergo*, she'll match them, and match them always!

YOU'RE WELCOME, WILLIE STEWART

Chorus

You're welcome, Willie Stewart!
  You're welcome, Willie Stewart!
There's ne'er a flower that blooms in May,
  That's half sae welcome's thou art!

I

Come, bumpers high! express your joy!
  The bowl we maun renew it—   must
The tappet hen, gae bring her ben,   go; [Notes]
  To welcome Willie Stewart!

WHEN FIRST I SAW

II

May foes be strong, and friends be slack!
Ilk action, may he rue it!
May woman on him turn her back,
 That wrangs thee, Willie Stewart!

Each
wrongs

Chorus

You're welcome, Willie Stewart!
 You're welcome, Willie Stewart!
There's ne'er a flower that blooms in May,
 That's half sae welcome's thou art!

WHEN FIRST I SAW

Chorus

She's aye, aye sae blithe, sae gay,
 She's aye sae blithe and cheerie,
She's aye sae bonie, blithe and gay,
 O, gin I were her dearie!

I

When first I saw fair Jeanie's face,
 I couldna tell what ail'd me:
My heart went fluttering pit-a-pat,
 My een they almost fail'd me.

She's aye sae neat, sae trim, sae tight,
    All grace does round her hover!
Ae look depriv'd me o' my heart,
    And I became her lover.

II

Had I Dundas's whole estate,
    Or Hopetoun's wealth to shine in;
Did warlike laurels crown my brow,
    Or humbler bays entwining;
I'd lay them a' at Jeanie's feet,
    Could I but hope to move her,
And, prouder than a belted knight,
    I'd be my Jeanie's lover.

III

But sair I fear some happier swain,
    Has gain'd my Jeanie's favour.
If so, may every bliss be hers,
    Though I maun never have her!   *must*
But gang she east, or gang she west,   *go*
    'Twixt Forth and Tweed all over,
While men have eyes, or ears, or taste,
    She'll always find a lover.

Chorus

She's aye, aye sae blithe, sae gay,
    She's aye sae blithe and cheerie,
She's aye sae bonie, blithe and gay,
    O, gin I were her dearie!

BEHOLD THE HOUR

FIRST SET

I

Behold the hour, the boat, arrive!
    My dearest Nancy, O, farewell!
Sever'd frae thee, can I survive,
    Frae thee whom I hae lov'd sae well?

II

Endless and deep shall be my grief,
    Nae ray of comfort shall I see,
But this most precious, dear belief,
    That thou wilt still remember me.

III

Along the solitary shore,
    Where flitting sea-fowl round me cry,
Across the rolling, dashing roar,
    I'll westward turn my wistful eye.

IV

'Happy thou Indian grove,' I'll say,
    'Where now my Nancy's path shall be!
While thro' your sweets she holds her way,
    O, tell me, does she muse on me?'

Sir GEORGE HARVEY

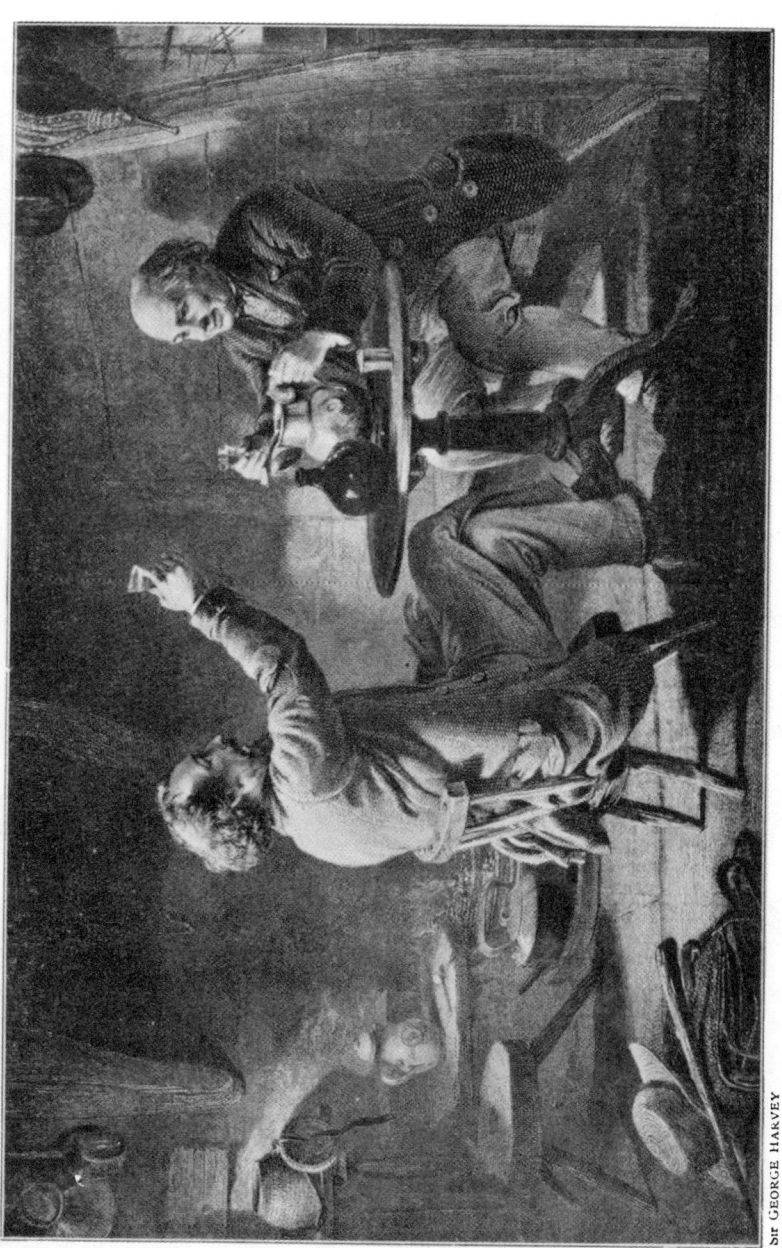

HERE'S A HEALTH TO THEM THAT'S AWA

"Here's a health to them that's awa,
    Here's a health to them that's awa!
And wha winna wish guid luck to our cause,
    May never guid luck be their fa'!

It's guid to be merry and wise,
    It's guid to be honest and true,
It's guid to support Caledonia's cause,
    And bide by the buff and the blue."—*Verse i.*

HERE'S A HEALTH TO THEM THAT'S AWA

I

Here's a health to them that's awa,
    Here's a health to them that's awa!
And wha winna wish guid luck to our cause,   *will not*
    May never guid luck be their fa'!   *lot*
It's guid to be merry and wise,   [Notes]
    It's guid to be honest and true,
It's guid to support Caledonia's cause
    And bide by the buff and the blue.   *stand*

II

Here's a health to them that's awa,
    Here's a health to them that's awa!
Here's a health to Charlie, the chief o' the clan,   [Notes]
    Altho' that his band be sma'!
May Liberty meet wi' success,
    May Prudence protect her frae evil!
May tyrants and Tyranny tine i' the mist   *be lost*
    And wander their way to the Devil!

III

Here's a health to them that's awa,
    Here's a health to them that's awa!
Here's a health to Tammie, the Norlan' laddie,   [Notes]
    That lives at the lug o' the Law!

Here's freedom to them that wad read,
  Here's freedom to them that would write!
There's nane ever fear'd that the truth should be heard
  But they whom the truth would indite!

indict

IV

Here's a health to them that's awa,
  An' here's to them that's awa!
Here's to Maitland and Wycombe! Let wha does na like 'em
  Be built in a hole in the wa'!
Here's timmer that's red at the heart,
  Here's fruit that is sound at the core,
And may he that wad turn the buff and blue coat
  Be turn'd to the back o' the door!

timber

V

Here's a health to them that's awa,
  Here's a health to them that's awa!
Here's Chieftain M'Leod, a chieftain worth gowd,
  Tho' bred amang mountains o' snaw!
Here's friends on baith sides o' the Firth,
  And friends on baith sides o' the Tweed,
And wha wad betray old Albion's right,
  May they never eat of her bread!

gold

AH, CHLORIS

I

Ah, Chloris, since it may not be
  That thou of love wilt hear,
If from the lover thou maun flee,   *must*
  Yet let the friend be dear!

II

Altho' I love my Chloris mair
  Than ever tongue could tell,
My passion I will ne'er declare—
  I'll say, I wish thee well.

III

Tho' a' my daily care thou art,
  And a' my nightly dream,
I'll hide the struggle in my heart,
  And say it is esteem.

PRETTY PEG

I

As I gaed up by yon gate-end,   *went;*
  When day was waxin weary,   *yonder road-*
Wha did I meet come down the street
  But pretty Peg, my dearie?

II

    Her air so sweet, her shape complete,
      Wi' nae proportion wanting—
    The Queen of Love could never move
      Wi' motion mair enchanting!

III

    With linkèd hands we took the sands
      Down by yon winding river;
    And O! that hour, and shady bow'r,
      Can I forget it? Never!

MEG O' THE MILL

SECOND SET

I

<small>got</small>

<small>dolt; hoard of money</small>

    O, KEN ye what Meg o' the mill has gotten?
    An' ken ye what Meg o' the mill has gotten?
    She's gotten a coof wi' a claute o' siller,
    And broken the heart o' the barley miller!

II

<small>gallows-worthy; dwarf</small>

    The miller was strappin, the miller was ruddy,
    A heart like a lord, and a hue like a lady.
    The laird was a widdifu', bleerit knurl—
    She's left the guid fellow, and taen the churl!

III

The miller, he hecht her a heart leal and loving. — offered
The laird did address her wi' matter more moving:
A fine pacing-horse wi' a clear, chainèd bridle, — bright
A whip by her side, and a bonie side saddle!

IV

O, wae on the siller—it is sae prevailing! — woe; potent
And wae on the love that is fixed on a mailen! — farm
A tocher's nae word in a true lover's parl, — dowry; speech
But gie me my love and a fig for the warl! — world

PHILLIS THE FAIR

I

While larks with little wing
   Fann'd the pure air,
Viewing the breathing Spring,
   Forth I did fare.
Gay, the sun's golden eye
Peep'd o'er the mountains high;
'Such thy bloom,' did I cry—
   'Phillis the fair!'

II

In each bird's careless song,
   Glad, I did share;
While yon wild flowers among,
   Chance led me there.

40 O SAW YE MY DEAR, MY PHILLY

    Sweet to the opening day,
    Rosebuds bent the dewy spray;
    'Such thy bloom,' did I say—
        'Phillis the fair!'

III

    Down in a shady walk
        Doves cooing were;
    I mark'd the cruel hawk
        Caught in a snare.
    So kind may Fortune be!
    Such make his destiny,
    He who would injure thee,
        Phillis the fair!

O SAW YE MY DEAR, MY PHILLY

I

    O, saw ye my Dear, my Philly?
    O, saw ye my Dear, my Philly?
    She's down i' the grove, she's wi' a new love,
will not   She winna come hame to her Willy.

II

    What says she my Dear, my Philly?
    What says she my Dear, my Philly?
know   She lets thee to wit she has thee forgot,
    And for ever disowns thee, her Willy.

After J. ARCHER

THE LEA-RIG

"Gie me the hour o' gloamin' grey—
It makes my heart sae cheery, O,
To meet thee on the lea-rig,
My ain kind dearie, O!"
—*Verse iii.*

III

O, had I ne'er seen thee, my Philly!
O, had I ne'er seen thee, my Philly!
As light as the air, and fause as thou's fair,
Thou's broken the heart o' thy Willy.

'TWAS NA HER BONIE BLUE E'E

I

'Twas na her bonie blue e'e was my ruin:
Fair tho' she be, that was ne'er my undoin.
'Twas the dear smile when naebody did mind us,
'Twas the bewitching, sweet, stoun glance o' kind- *stolen*
ness!

II

Sair do I fear that to hope is denied me,   *Sore*
Sair do I fear that despair maun abide me;   *must*
But tho' fell Fortune should fate us to sever,
Queen shall she be in my bosom for ever.

III

Chloris, I'm thine wi' a passion sincerest,
And thou hast plighted me love o' the dearest,
And thou 'rt the angel that never can alter—
Sooner the sun in his motion would falter!

WHY, WHY TELL THY LOVER

I

Why, why tell thy lover
Bliss he never must enjoy?
Why, why undeceive him,
And give all his hopes the lie?

II

O, why, while Fancy, raptur'd, slumbers,
'Chloris, Chloris,' all the theme,
Why, why wouldst thou, cruel,
Wake thy lover from his dream?

THE PRIMROSE

I

Dost ask me, why I send thee here
The firstling of the infant year:
This lovely native of the vale,
That hangs so pensive and so pale?

II

Look on its bending stalk, so weak,
That, each way yielding, doth not break,
And see how aptly it reveals
The doubts and fears a lover feels.

III

Look on its leaves of yellow hue
Bepearl'd thus with morning dew,
And these will whisper in thine ears :—
'The sweets of loves are wash'd with tears.'

O, WERT THOU IN THE CAULD BLAST

I

O, WERT thou in the cauld blast
  On yonder lea, on yonder lea,
My plaidie to the angry airt,   *quarter*
  I 'd shelter thee, I 'd shelter thee.
Or did Misfortune's bitter storms
  Around thee blaw, around thee blaw,
Thy bield should be my bosom,   *shelter*
  To share it a', to share it a'.

II

Or were I in the wildest waste,
  Sae black and bare, sae black and bare,
The desert were a Paradise,
  If thou wert there, if thou wert there.
Or were I monarch of the globe,
  Wi' thee to reign, wi' thee to reign,
The brightest jewel in my crown
  Wad be my queen, wad be my queen.

INTERPOLATIONS

YOUR FRIENDSHIP

I

Your friendship much can make me blest—
  O, why that bliss destroy?
Why urge the only, one request
  You know I will deny?

II

Your thought, if Love must harbour there,
  Conceal it in that thought,
Nor cause me from my bosom tear
  The very friend I sought.

FOR THEE IS LAUGHING NATURE

For thee is laughing Nature gay,
For thee she pours the vernal day:
For me in vain is Nature drest,
While Joy's a stranger to my breast.

NO COLD APPROACH

No cold approach, no alter'd mien,
  Just what would make suspicion start,
No pause the dire extremes between:
  He made me blest—and broke my heart.

ALTHO' HE HAS LEFT ME

Altho' he has left me for greed o' the siller,　　*money*
  I dinna envy him the gains he can win :　　*do not*
I rather wad bear a' the lade o' my sorrow　　*would ; load*
  Than ever hae acted sae faithless to him.　　*have*

LET LOOVE SPARKLE

Let loove sparkle in her e'e,
Let her lo'e nae man but me :
That's the tocher guid I prize,　　*dower*
There the luver's treasure lies.

AS DOWN THE BURN　　*brook*

As down the burn they took their way,
  And thro' the flowery dale ;
His cheek to hers he aft did lay,
  And love was ay the tale,
With :—' Mary, when shall we return,
  Sic pleasure to renew ? '　　*such*
Quoth Mary :—' Love, I like the burn,
  And ay shall follow you.'

IMPROBABLES

ON ROUGH ROADS

I'm now arriv'd—thanks to the Gods!—
  Through pathways rough and muddy:
A certain sign that makin' roads
  Is no this people's study.
Yet, though I'm no wi' scripture cramm'd,
  I'm sure the Bible says
That heedless sinners shall be damn'd,
  Unless they mend their ways.

ELEGY ON STELLA

I

Strait is the spot, and green the sod,
  From whence my sorrows flow;
And soundly sleeps the ever dear
  Inhabitant below.

II

Pardon my transport, gentle shade,
  While o'er the turf I bow!
Thy earthly house is circumscrib'd,
  And solitary now!

III

Not one poor stone to tell thy name
    Or make thy virtues known!
But what avails to thee—to me—
    The sculpture of a stone?

IV

I'll sit me down upon this turf,
    And wipe away this tear.
The chill blast passes swiftly by,
    And flits around thy bier.

V

Dark is the dwelling of the dead,
    And sad their house of rest:
Low lies the head by Death's cold arm
    In awful fold embraced.

VI

I saw the grim Avenger stand
    Incessant by thy side;
Unseen by thee, his deadly breath
    Thy lingering frame destroy'd.

VII

Pale grew the roses on thy cheek,
    And wither'd was thy bloom,
Till the slow poison brought thy youth
    Untimely to the tomb.

VIII

Thus wasted are the ranks of men—
    Youth, health, and beauty fall!
The ruthless ruin spreads around,
    And overwhelms us all.

IX

Behold where, round thy narrow house,
    The graves unnumber'd lie!
The multitude, that sleep below,
    Existed but to die.

X

Some with the tottering steps of Age
    Trod down the darksome way;
And some in Youth's lamented prime,
    Like thee, were torn away.

XI

Yet these, however hard their fate,
    Their native earth receives:
Amid their weeping friends they died,
    And fill their fathers' graves.

XII

From thy lov'd friends, when first thy heart,
    Was taught by Heaven to glow,
Far, far remov'd, the ruthless stroke
    Surpris'd, and laid thee low.

XIII

At the last limits of our Isle,
  Wash'd by the western wave,
Touch'd by thy fate, a thoughtful Bard
  Sits lonely on thy grave!

XIV

Pensive he eyes, before him spread,
  The deep, outstretch'd and vast.
His mourning notes are borne away
  Along the rapid blast.

XV

And while, amid the silent dead,
  Thy hapless fate he mourns,
His own long sorrows freshly bleed,
  And all his grief returns.

XVI

Like thee, cut off in early youth
  And flower of beauty's pride,
His friend, his first and only joy,
  His much-lov'd Stella died.

XVII

Him, too, the stern impulse of Fate
  Resistless bears along,
And the same rapid tide shall whelm
  The Poet and the Song.

XVIII

The tear of pity, which he shed,
    He asks not to receive:
Let but his poor remains be laid
    Obscurely in the grave!

XIX

His grief-worn heart with truest joy
    Shall meet the welcome shock;
His airy harp shall lie unstrung
    And silent on the rock.

XX

O my dear maid, my Stella, when
    Shall this sick period close,
And lead the solitary Bard
    To his belov'd repose?

POEM ON PASTORAL POETRY

I

HAIL, Poesie! thou Nymph reserv'd!
In chase o' thee, what crowds hae swerv'd

Frae common sense, or sunk enerv'd
        'Mang heaps o' clavers! *nonsense*
And och! o'er aft thy joes hae starv'd *sweethearts*
        'Mid a' thy favours!

II

Say, Lassie, why thy train amang,
While loud the trump's heroic clang,
And sock or buskin skelp alang *spank*
        To death or marriage,
Scarce ane has tried the shepherd-sang *one*
        But wi' miscarriage?

III

In Homer's craft Jock Milton thrives;
Eschýlus' pen Will Shakespeare drives;
Wee Pope, the knurlin, till him rives *dwarf; tugs*
        Horatian fame;
In thy sweet sang, Barbauld, survives
        Even Sappho's flame!

IV

But thee, Theocritus, wha matches?
They're no herd's ballats, Maro's catches! *shepherd's ballads*
Squire Pope but busks his skinklin patches *small*
        O' heathen tatters!
I pass by hunders, nameless wretches, *hundreds*
        That ape their betters.

52 POEM ON PASTORAL POETRY

V

<small>fine; learning</small> In this braw age o' wit and lear,
Will nane the Shepherd's whistle mair
Blaw sweetly in its native air
    And rural grace,
And wi' the far-fam'd Grecian share
    A rival place?

VI

<small>youth</small> Yes! there is ane—a Scottish callan!
<small>forward</small> There's ane! Come forrit, honest Allan!
<small>cower; porch</small> Thou need na jouk behint the hallan,
<small>fellow</small>   A chiel sae clever!
<small>[Notes]</small> The teeth o' Time may gnaw Tantallan,
    But thou's for ever.

VII

<small>perfection</small> Thou paints auld Nature to the nines
In thy sweet Caledonian lines!
<small>golden</small> Nae gowden stream thro' myrtles twines,
    Where Philomel,
While nightly breezes sweep the vines,
    Her griefs will tell:

VIII

<small>daisied; brooklet</small> In gowany glens thy burnie strays,
<small>clothes</small> Where bonie lasses bleach their claes,

DRUMLANRIG WOODS

Or trots by hazelly shaws and braes   woods;
    Wi' hawthorns gray,   slopes
Where blackbirds join the shepherd's lays
    At close o' day.

IX

Thy rural loves are Nature's sel':
Nae bombast spates o' nonsense swell,   floods
Nae snap conceits, but that sweet spell   smart
    O' witchin love,
That charm that can the strongest quell,
    The sternest move.

ON THE DESTRUCTION OF DRUMLANRIG WOODS

I

As on the banks of winding Nith
  Ae smiling simmer morn I stray'd,   One
And traced its bonie holms and haughs,   low-lying grounds
  Where linties sang, and lammies play'd,   linnets; lambs
I sat me down upon a craig,   rock
  And drank my fill o' fancy's dream,
When from the eddying deep below
  Up rose the Genius of the Stream.

II

	Dark like the frowning rock his brow,
	And troubled like his wintry wave,
sighs	And deep as sughs the boding wind
	Amang his caves the sigh he gave.
	' And come ye here, my son,' he cried,
birchen	'To wander in my birken shade?
	To muse some favourite Scottish theme,
	Or sing some favourite Scottish maid?

III

not long since	'There was a time, it's nae lang syne,
	Ye might hae seen me in my pride,
	When a' my banks sae bravely saw
	Their woody pictures in my tide;
	When hanging beech and spreading elm
	Shaded my stream sae clear and cool;
	And stately oaks their twisted arms
	Threw broad and dark across the pool;

IV

glancing	' When, glinting thro' the trees, appear'd
above	The wee white cot aboon the mill,
fireside smoke	And peaceful rose its ingle reek,
	That, slowly curling, clamb the hill.
	But now the cot is bare and cauld,
shelter	Its leafy bield for ever gane,
stunted birch	And scarce a stinted birk is left
alone	To shiver in the blast its lane.'

THE JOYFUL WIDOWER

V

'Alas!' quoth I, 'what ruefu' chance
   Has twin'd ye o' your stately trees?   *deprived*
Has laid your rocky bosom bare?
   Has stripp'd the cleeding aff your braes?   *clothing; slopes*
Was it the bitter eastern blast,
   That scatters blight in early spring?
Or was 't the wil'fire scorch'd their boughs?   *lightning*
   Or canker-worm wi' secret sting?'

VI

'Nae eastlin blast,' the Sprite replied—   *eastern*
   'It blaws na here sae fierce and fell,
And on my dry and halesome banks
   Nae canker-worms get leave to dwell:
Man! cruel man!' the Genius sigh'd,
   As through the cliffs he sank him down:
'The worm that gnaw'd my bonie trees,
   That reptile wears a Ducal crown.'

THE JOYFUL WIDOWER

I

I MARRIED with a scolding wife
   The fourteenth of November:
She made me weary of my life
   By one unruly member.

THE JOYFUL WIDOWER

Long did I bear the heavy yoke,
   And many griefs attended,
But to my comfort be it spoke,
   Now, now her life is ended!

II

We liv'd full one-and-twenty years
   A man and wife together.
At length from me her course she steer'd
   And gone I know not whither.
Would I could guess, I do profess:
   I speak, and do not flatter,
Of all the women in the world,
   I never would come at her!

III

Her body is bestowèd well—
   A handsome grave does hide her.
But sure her soul is not in Hell—
   The Deil would ne'er abide her!
I rather think she is aloft
   And imitating thunder,
For why?—Methinks I hear her voice
   Tearing the clouds asunder!

WHY SHOULD WE IDLY WASTE OUR PRIME

I

Why should we idly waste our prime
   Repeating our oppressions?
Come rouse to arms! 'Tis now the time
   To punish past transgressions.
'Tis said that Kings can do no wrong—
   Their murderous deeds deny it,
And, since from us their power is sprung,
   We have a right to try it.
Now each true patriot's song shall be:—
'Welcome Death or Libertie!'

II

Proud Priests and Bishops we'll translate
   And canonize as Martyrs;
The guillotine on Peers shall wait;
   And Knights shall hang in garters.
Those Despots long have trode us down,
   And Judges are their engines:
Such wretched minions of a Crown
   Demand the people's vengeance!
To-day 'tis *theirs*. To-morrow we
Shall don the Cap of Libertie!

III

The Golden Age we'll then revive:
    Each man will be a brother;
In harmony we all shall live,
    And share the earth together;
In Virtue train'd, enlighten'd Youth
    Will love each fellow-creature;
And future years shall prove the truth
    That Man is good by nature:
Then let us toast with three times three
The reign of Peace and Libertie!

THE TREE OF LIBERTY

I

HEARD ye o' the Tree o' France,
    And wat ye what's the name o't?
Around it a' the patriots dance—
    Weel Europe kens the fame o't!
It stands where ance the Bastile stood—
    A prison built by kings, man,
When Superstition's hellish brood
    Kept France in leading-strings, man.

wot

THE TREE OF LIBERTY

II

Upo' this tree there grows sic fruit, *such*
    Its virtues a' can tell, man:
It raises man aboon the brute, *above*
    It mak's him ken himsel', man!
Gif ance the peasant taste a bit, *If*
    He's greater than a lord, man,
And wi' the beggar shares a mite
    O' a' he can afford, man.

III

This fruit is worth a' Afric's wealth:
    To comfort us 'twas sent, man,
To gie the sweetest blush o' health,
    And mak' us a' content, man!
It clears the een, it cheers the heart, *eyes*
    Mak's high and low guid friends, man,
And he wha acts the traitor's part,
    It to perdition sends, man.

IV

My blessings ay attend the chiel, *fellow*
    Wha pitied Gallia's slaves, man,
And staw a branch, spite o' the Deil, *stole*
    Frae 'yont the western waves, man! *beyond*
Fair Virtue water'd it wi' care,
    And now she sees wi' pride, man,
How weel it buds and blossoms there,
    Its branches spreading wide, man.

V

    But vicious folk ay hate to see
        The works o' Virtue thrive, man.
    The courtly vermin's bann'd the tree,
        And grat to see it thrive, man!   *wept*
    King Louis thought to cut it down,
        When it was unco sma', man;   *very*
    For this the watchman crack'd his crown,
        Cut aff his head and a', man.

VI

    A wicked crew syne, on a time,   *then*
        Did tak' a solemn aith, man,   *oath*
    It ne'er should flourish to its prime—
        I wat they pledg'd their faith, man!   *wot*
    Awa they gaed wi' mock parade,   *went*
        Like beagles hunting game, man,
    But soon grew weary o' the trade,
        And wish'd they'd been at hame, man.

VII

    Fair Freedom, standing by the tree,
        Her sons did loudly ca', man.
    She sang a sang o' Liberty,
        Which pleas'd them ane and a', man.
    By her inspir'd, the new-born race
        Soon drew the avenging steel, man.
    The hirelings ran—her foes gied chase,   *gave*
        And bang'd the despot weel, man.

VIII

Let Britain boast her hardy oak,
    Her poplar, and her pine, man!
Auld Britain ance could crack her joke,
    And o'er her neighbours shine, man!
But seek the forest round and round,
    And soon 'twill be agreed, man,
That sic a tree can not be found
    'Twixt London and the Tweed, man.

IX

Without this tree alake this life
    Is but a vale o' woe, man,
A scene o' sorrow mix'd wi' strife,
    Nae real joys we know, man;
We labour soon, we labour late,
    To feed the titled knave, man,
And a' the comfort we're to get,
    Is that ayont the grave, man.   *beyond*

X

Wi' plenty o' sic trees, I trow,
    The warld would live in peace, man.
The sword would help to mak' a plough,
    The din o' war wad cease, man.
Like brethren in a common cause,
    We'd on each other smile, man;
And equal rights and equal laws
    Wad gladden every isle, man.

TO A KISS

XI

<small>Woe befall the fellow</small> Wae worth the loon wha wadna eat
  Sic halesome, dainty cheer, man!
I 'd gie the shoon frae aff my feet,
  To taste the fruit o't here, man!
<small>Then</small> Syne let us pray, Auld England may
  Sure plant this far-famed tree, man;
And blythe we 'll sing, and herald the day
  That gives us liberty, man.

TO A KISS

I

Humid seal of soft affections,
  Tend'rest pledge of future bliss,
Dearest tie of young connections,
  Love's first snow-drop, virgin kiss!

II

Speaking silence, dumb confession,
  Passion's birth and infant's play,
Dove-like fondness, chaste confession,
  Glowing dawn of brighter day!

III

Sorrowing joy, adieu's last action,
  Ling'ring lips—no more must join!
Words can never speak affection,
  Thrilling and sincere as thine!

DELIA

AN ODE

I

Fair the face of orient day,
    Fair the tints of op'ning rose:
But fairer still my Delia dawns,
    More lovely far her beauty blows.

II

Sweet the lark's wild-warbled lay,
    Sweet the tinkling rill to hear:
But, Delia, more delightful still
    Steal thine accents on mine ear.

III

The flower-enamoured busy bee
    The rosy banquet loves to sip;
Sweet the streamlet's limpid lapse
    To the sun-brown'd Arab's lip:

IV

But, Delia, on thy balmy lips
    Let me, no vagrant insect, rove!
O, let me steal one liquid kiss!
    For O! my soul is parch'd with love!

TO THE OWL

I

Sad bird of night, what sorrow calls thee forth,
    To vent thy plaints thus in the midnight hour?
Is it some blast that gathers in the north,
    Threat'ning to nip the verdure of thy bow'r?

II

Is it, sad owl, that Autumn strips the shade,
    And leaves thee here, unshelter'd and forlorn?
Or fear that Winter will thy nest invade?
    Or friendless Melancholy bids thee mourn?

III

Shut out, lone bird, from all the feather'd train,
    To tell thy sorrows to th' unheeding gloom,
No friend to pity when thou dost complain,
    Grief all thy thought, and solitude thy home,

IV

Sing on, sad mourner! I will bless thy strain,
    And pleas'd in sorrow listen to thy song.
Sing on, sad mourner! To the night complain,
    While the lone echo wafts thy notes along.

TO THE OWL

V

Is Beauty less, when down the glowing cheek
    Sad, piteous tears in native sorrows fall?
Less kind the heart when anguish bids it break?
    Less happy he who lists to Pity's call?

VI

Ah no, sad owl! nor is thy voice less sweet,
    That Sadness tunes it, and that Grief is there?
That Spring's gay notes, unskill'd, thou can't repeat,
    That Sorrow bids thee to the gloom repair!

VII

Nor that the treble songsters of the day,
    Are quite estranged, sad bird of night, from thee!
Nor that the thrush deserts the evening spray,
    When darkness calls thee from thy reverie!

VIII

From some old tower, thy melancholy dome,
    While the gray walls and desert solitudes
Return each note, responsive to the gloom
    Of ivied coverts and surrounding woods:

IX

There hooting, I will list more pleased to thee,
    Than ever lover to the nightingale,
Or drooping wretch, oppress'd with misery,
    Lending his ear to some condoling tale!

THE VOWELS
A TALE

'Twas where the birch and sounding thong are ply'd,
The noisy domicile of pedant pride;
Where Ignorance her darkening vapour throws,
And Cruelty directs the thickening blows !
Upon a time, Sir A B C the great,
In all his pedagogic powers elate,
His awful chair of state resolves to mount,
And call the trembling Vowels to account.

First enter'd A, a grave, broad, solemn wight,
But, ah ! deform'd, dishonest to the sight !
His twisted head look'd backward on his way,
And flagrant from the scourge he grunted, *ai !*

Reluctant, E stalk'd in ; a piteous case,
The justling tears ran down his honest face !
That name, that well-worn name, and all his own,
Pale, he surrenders at the tyrant's throne !
The Pedant stifles keen the Roman sound
Not all his mongrel diphthongs can compound ;
And next the title following close behind,
He to the nameless, ghastly wretch assign'd.

The cobwebb'd gothic dome resounded, Y !
In sullen vengeance, I disdain'd reply :
The Pedant swung his felon cudgel round,
And knock'd the groaning vowel to the ground !

ILLNESS OF A FAVOURITE CHILD

In rueful apprehension enter'd O,
The wailing minstrel of despairing woe:
Th' Inquisitor of Spain the most expert,
Might there have learnt new mysteries of his art.
So grim, deform'd, with horrors entering, U
His dearest friend and brother scarcely knew!

As trembling U stood staring all aghast,
The Pedant in his left hand clutch'd him fast,
In helpless infants' tears he dipp'd his right,
Baptiz'd him *eu*, and kick'd him from his sight.

ON THE ILLNESS OF A FAVOURITE CHILD

I

Now health forsakes that angel face.
   Nae mair my dearie smiles.
Pale sickness withers ilka grace,   every
   And a' my hopes beguiles.

II

The cruel Powers reject the prayer
   I hourly mak' for thee:
Ye Heavens! how great is my despair
   How can I see him die!

ON THE DEATH OF A FAVOURITE CHILD

I

O, sweet be thy sleep in the land of the grave,
   My dear little angel, for ever!
For ever?—O no! let not man be a slave,
   His hopes from existence to sever!

II

Though cold be the clay, where thou pillow'st thy head
   In the dark, silent mansions of sorrow,
The spring shall return to thy low, narrow bed,
   Like the beam of the day-star to-morrow.

III

The flower-stem shall bloom like thy sweet seraph form
   Ere the spoiler had nipt thee in blossom,
When thou shrank frae the scowl of the loud winter storm,
   And nestled thee close to that bosom.

DEATH OF A FAVOURITE CHILD

IV

O, still I behold thee, all lovely in death,
  Reclined on the lap of thy mother,
When the tear-trickle bright, when the short stifled breath
  Told how dear ye were ay to each other.

V

My child, thou art gone to the home of thy rest,
  Where suffering no longer can harm thee :
Where the songs of the Good, where the hymns of the Blest
  Through an endless existence shall charm thee !

VI

While he, thy fond parent, must sighing sojourn
  Through the dire desert regions of sorrow,
O'er the hope and misfortune of being to mourn,
  And sigh for this life's latest morrow.

ADDENDUM TO
MALLY'S MEEK

Her yellow hair, beyond compare,
  Comes tumbling down her swan-white neck,
And her twa eyes, like stars in skies,
  Would keep a sinking ship frae wreck !

NOTES

W. H. BARTLETT

THE HOUSE IN WHICH BURNS DIED, DUMFRIES

BIBLIOGRAPHICAL

MORE than half the verse of Burns was published posthumously; more than a third of it without his sanction. He was especially 'unthrifty of his sweets': bestowing them on all and sundry, as if he had been denied the privilege of publication in any other form. Much of his work was in the strictest sense occasional: written 'by way of *vive la bagatelle*' on window-panes, in albums, in volumes, in letters to friends. He never dreamed, or not until the very last, that the world would cherish any curiosity about these fugitives; and death came to him ere the chance of sifting gold from dross in a final Edition. Thus, his unrealised estate (so to speak) was not only of peculiar bulk: it was also of many qualities, and it was variously dispersed among a crowd of owners; so that he provided the gull with no defence against the gullcatcher—he left the credulous wholly unarmed and unprepared against the contrivances of them that would deceive. Again, he was accustomed to jot down from recitation, or to copy from letters, or from odd volumes, such lines, such stanzas, or such whole pieces as took his fancy; and more often than not he left his sources undenoted. Withal, he would despatch songs got in this way—with or without retouches—for publication, especially in Johnson's *Museum*; and, inasmuch as he signed not all those envoys which were his own, the task of separating false from true is one of very considerable difficulty. Often the probabilities are our only guides; and in these cases we have summarised the evidence, and taken that direction in which the balance seemed to incline. In others, any sort of evidence is of the scantest; and what there is has been made scanter still by the carelessness—or the romantic humour, to call it by no worse a name—of such Editors as Allan Cunningham, Hogg and Motherwell, and Robert Chambers. The chief exemplar in the other sense is certainly Scott Douglas: who, though he seems to have prepared himself for the work of editing Burns by resolutely declining to read any one else, was zealous in his quest of MS. authorities, and, had he known something of literature, and been less given to putting on what Mr. Pope calls 'a foolish face of praise' over any and every thing his author wrote, might have gone far to establish a sound tradition in the matter of text. But such a tradition was scarce indicated ere it succumbed to sentimentalism and pretence; the old, hap-hazard, irresponsible convention still holds its own; and Editions professing to give the 'complete text,' the 'true text,' the 'best text,' and the like, continue to be issued, which set forth an abundance of proof that they are based,—some wholly, all mainly—on the battered, jog-trot hack-authorities of the prime.

Certain pieces in our present Volume are described as 'Improbables.' In our judgment, few or none of them can justly be credited to Burns; and to consider the quality of nearly all is to perceive, and very clearly, that, partial as his Editors were to the use of such epithets as 'God-gifted,' and 'heaven-inspired,' and the like, there was no rubbish so poor but they found it good enough to father on the god of their idolatry. As regards ascriptions known for spurious, it will suffice to refer to the more notable among them in this place. The song, *Farewell to Ayrshire*, published in Johnson's *Museum* [No. 517 : 'Written by R. Burns'], and beginning, 'Scenes of Woe and Scenes of Pleasure,' is recognised for the work of Robert Gall (1776-1801). Gall, too, is responsible for *Now Bank and Brae*, an unsigned number in Johnson (No. 521), which, because it celebrates the 'bonny blink o' Mary's e'e,' Editor after Editor has persisted in regarding as a

BIBLIOGRAPHICAL 75

tribute to Mary Campbell. Two other songs, with 'Mary' as the heroine—*Powers Celestial* [alternative words to No. 460 in Johnson; Unsigned] and *Could Aught of Song* [No. 493 in Johnson: 'Written for this work by R. Burns']—were sent by R. Burns to the *Museum*, as the holographs in the Hastie Collection show; but both must have been transcribed by R. Burns from an *Edinburgh Magazine* for 1774. Yet a fourth on the same distracting theme, entitled, *Burns's Lament for Mary*, and beginning, 'O'er the Mist-Clouded Cliffs of the Lone Mountains Straying,' was scandalously ascribed to Burns by its real author, one John Burtt, schoolmaster in Kilmarnock, who sent it to *The Ayr Advertiser* in 1814. Again, the thing called *Evan Banks*, published in Johnson [No. 500 : 'Written for this work by Robert Burns'] and also in the first Currie (1800), but omitted from the second and later Editions, was written by Helen Maria Williams, who appears to have communicated it to Burns for insertion in the *Museum*. Other numbers in Johnson foisted on the Bard are *Will Ye Go and Mary, Katie* (No. 459), which is found in *The Charmer* (1782) and other books, and on which Burns made a few verbal changes; *The Auld Man, He Cam O'er the Lea* (No. 416); and a set of *Galla Water* (No. 125) originally published in Herd (1776) of which Burns changed but two lines:—(1) 'I aften kiss her till I'm wearie,' to 'The mair I kiss she's ay my deary'; and (2) 'That gar'd her greet till she was weary,' to 'That cost her mony a blirt and blearie.' The fragment, *Leezie Lindsay*, in Johnson (No. 434), was communicated by Burns; but although he described it as old, and promised additions which he never wrote, he has been credited, not only with the antique itself but also, with the several modern versions. Another false get, *Sheilah O'Neil*, first laid at his door in one of the tracts 'printed by Chapman and Lang for Stewart and Meikle,' and included in Cunningham (1834) and other Editions, is the brat of Sir Alexander Boswell. Then, *To Thee, Lov'd*

Nith, published in Cromek's *Reliques* (1808), was written by Maria Riddell; while *The Merry Ploughman* :—

> 'As I was wand'ring ae morning in Spring,
> I heard a young ploughman sae sweetly to sing;
> And as he was singing these words he did say,
> There's nae life like the ploughman's in the month o' sweet May,' *etc.*:—

though found by Cromek in Burns's hand, and therefore published in the *Reliques* (whence it has crept—and still continues creeping—into Edition after Edition), is part of an old stall-ballad, *The Ploughman's Glory*, which we have found in two different Edinburgh chaps, of 1776 and 1778 respectively. Last of all, a second set of *My Nanie, O* (see Vol. i. p. 413):—

> 'Red rolls the Nith 'tween bank and brae,
> Mirk is the night and rainie,' *etc.*:—

which found its way into Richards and Co.'s Edition (1821), has Romantic Movement' writ large all over it, and is now claimed for Allan Cunningham.

Several fragments published by Cunningham (1834), and still included in Editions of repute, are mere excerpts from *The Merry Muses*, torn from their context, and beggared of piquancy and significance; others, as *Donald Brodie*, are demonstrably not the work of Burns at all. Songs, too, from the same precious collection, with other indecent rhymes by Burns, have been ingeniously, but disingenuously, 'purified' for many Editions. But in this of ours the rule has been to print *verbatim* or not at all.

Among pieces other than lyrical, let it suffice to name the *Epitaph on the Poet's Daughter*, 'Here Lies a Rose, a Blooming Rose,' *etc.*, which Burns, if it were found in his hand, must have copied from Shenstone; *Before I Saw Clarinda's Face* and *The Hermit of Aberfeldy*, both communicated to Hogg and Motherwell's Edition by Peter Buchan, and both the work of a very humble poetaster, whether Buchan or another; the lines, *To My Bed*, which were published in Chambers (1838), and had already appeared in *The Gentleman's Magazine* for May 1759, as well as in *The Muses' Mirror* (1783); and the ballad, *Katherine Jaffray* (Aldine Edition, 1834, from a Burns holograph), which is found in the Herd MS. For spurious additions to genuine numbers, see our several Prefatory Notes.

With reference to the verses on *The Duchess of Gordon's Reel Dancing*, published in our Second Volume, p. 61, it has been pointed out that Burns repudiated their authorship in a letter to *The Star*, dated April 13th. But, in estimating the worth of his repudiation, there are important facts to consider. (1) He affirmed that he himself had not seen the copy of *The Star* containing these particular verses, and knew no more of the matter than what a friend of his 'from having slightly glanced over the paper could recollect.' (2) The verses—whether his or not—having been published without his sanction, he might think himself—as in less urgent circumstances others, including Sir Walter, have thought themselves—warranted in doing his utmost, even to the extent of flat denial, to disassociate himself from them. For their publication, not only was totally unauthorised by him but also, was calculated to injure his prospects. But (3) Peter Stuart, the Editor of *The Star*, carefully refrained—a notable circumstance—either from apologising to Burns or from accepting his repudiation. He stood utterly neutral:—'The Printer,' he wrote, 'feels himself exceedingly proud of the receipt of the following letter of a very ingenious Poet, whose productions were the delight and admiration of every reader of taste. The Printer believes that the best mode of answering the author's intention is by publication of his sentiments on a subject which appears interesting to his reputation.' (4) Besides the communication in *The Star*, Burns sent a private note to Peter Stuart, in which he, not only begged the insertion of the public letter as a favour but also, offered to make insertion worth Stuart's while. This is shown by (*a*) an Editorial Note at the foot of the letter:—'The Printer has the happiness of flattering himself with an assurance of the future correspondence of Mr. Burns, the sublime flights and inspiration of whose muse must raise the reputation of the first print'; and by (*b*) part of a letter to Alexander Cunningham, first published by us in Vol. i. p. 447:—'So sent them to Stuart as a bribe,' *etc.* (5) The rhymes we attribute to Burns might very well have been written in a drunken moment—he was sometimes partly oblivious, as he confessed, of stuff produced in such circumstances; they do him no discredit either as man or as poet; whilst certain others jocularly attributed to him in *The Star*, and probably concocted in the office, are mere caricature, and are plainly meant to be no more. (6) The fact that to *The Star* he had meanwhile sent an anonymous ode *On the Defeated Regency Bill* (Vol. ii. p. 159), may have given him some uneasiness, for that piece was despatched *before* he knew of the appearance of the lampoon on the Duchess of Gordon—not *after*, as we had believed; but in any case, on the supposition that the lampoon was a forgery, he adopted a strangely timid attitude towards the offending print. (7) Although he might not have known, when he wrote to *The Star*, that it was the first to print the lampoon, and was in fact the *fons et origo* of the whole 'calumny,' he must soon afterwards have learned as much from a note in reply to a letter of his in *The London Gazetteer*; but, instead of showing any resentment, he remained on the friendliest terms with Stuart while *The Star* existed. (8) There is no evidence of further intercourse between him and the Duchess of Gordon.

The chief 'calumny,' in fact, was the original statement in *The Star* (27th March 1789), that Burns, 'the ploughing poet,' had 'made this elegant stanza' on the Duchess of Gordon's appearance at an Edinburgh ball:—

> 'She was the mucklest of them aw,
> Like Saul she stood the Tribes aboon:
> Her goon was whiter than the snaw,
> Her face was redder than the moon.'

This lampoon (in which, by the way, the 'aw' for 'a'' of the first line is pure Anglo-Scots) was copied into *The London Gazetteer* of the 28th March. There Burns read it, and thereupon he (10th April) sent the Editor of that print an indignant denial of its ascription to himself. The Editor referred him to 'the Printer of *The Star*,' from which journal the stanza was literally copied into the *Gazetteer*; and further, pretended to inform him that the Duchess of Gordon, 'with much difficulty,' and 'by the industry and penetration of Lord Fife,' had already discovered that the author of the *jeu d'esprit* was, not the ploughing poet but, the 'Right Honourable the Treasurer of the Navy' (*i.e.* Harry Dundas). How the Duchess came to communicate her discovery to an Editor still so inimical as to affirm the lines to be 'certainly not so dull as Mr. Burns insinuates' was (naturally) left in darkness: the whole thing being (in fact) an elaborate pleasantry at the expense of (*a*) Dundas and (*b*) Her Grace of Gordon. Dundas's strong northern accent, and the 'Scotticisms with which his speeches abounded,' are said by Wraxall to have had a strangely ludicrous effect; and his diction is imitated in *The Rolliad* in a mock Probationary Ode for the laureateship:—

    'Hoot! hoot awaw!
    Hoot! hoot awaw!
  Ye lawland Bards! Who are ye aw?
  What are your sangs! What aw your lair to boot?
  Vain are your thoughts the prize to win,
  Sae dight your gobs, and stint your senseless din.
    Hoot hoot awaw! hoot! hoot!' *etc.*:—

the author of which was quite clever enough to have written the original Anglo-Scots lampoon in *The Star*. Another point in the *Gazetteer* joke lay in the veiled, but notorious, jealousy between Dundas and the Duchess of each other's influence with Pitt. But if, as has been argued (with immense solemnity), Dundas did really concoct the libel, and did really send it to an Opposition print, how could a scandal of such enormity sink so entirely into oblivion that only now was it recoverable in the interests of a down-trodden Bard! In truth, the business is a mare's nest of the first magnitude: one so monstrous large, indeed, that we feel constrained to apologise for abolishing a perennial joy to the simple, happy Common Burnsite, by stating, in so many words, what it is. We should have refrained from pricking the bubble, but for the fact that a poor, dead party jest has been used to prop the very grandiloquent theory that Pitt's Naval Treasurer cherished so intimate an enmity against a certain Miraculous Would-Be Exciseman, that, being himself a Tory and a Minister, he seduced a friend of the Would-Be Exciseman's, who was also Editor of an Opposition print, into a conspiracy designed (1) to hold the Duchess of Gordon and the Miraculous Would-Be up to public ridicule; (2) to embroil the Miraculous *etc.* with the Duchess of Gordon; and (3) to degrade the Duchess of Gordon in the sight of the Prime Minister, to the end that he would no more tolerate her approach!

In sober earnest, the case is thus resumed:—(1) 'If the Gordon pasquil was really written by "the great dispenser of patronage in Scotland," it must be regarded as indicating the reverse of respect for the character of Burns, who is represented as the "ploughing poet," fond of women and whisky'—(which, as we know, he was *not*)—'and capable of ridiculing a patroness in verse'—(which, for Maria Riddell had offended him, and the Duchess of Gordon had not, it is monstrous to suppose he ever could have been). And (2) 'In any case, the newspaper incident must have given Burns a strong impression that Henry Dundas was no warm friend or admirer of his, and would not facilitate his rapid promotion.' (1) The true reply to a set of inferences of this temper is that Dundas had never read either *For A' That* or *Thou Ling'ring Star*; that he knew not Highland Mary from Bonie Jean; that he recked not of Burns Anniversaries, and had not so much as carved the haggis at a Burns Club Dinner; and that,

Key to the Picture of BURNS at an evening Party at Lord Monboddo's.

1. Burns
2. Miss Burnett
3. Duchess of Gordon
4. Earl of Glencairn
5. Dr Blacklock
6. Dr John Moore
7. Dr Hugh Blair
8. Revd John Skinner
9. William Tyler of Woodhouselee
10. Mrs Bruce of Clackmanan
11. Mrs Dunlop of Dunlop
12. William Smellie
13. George Thomson Esq.
14. President Dundas
15. Lord Monboddo
16. Captain Grose
17. Duguld Stewart
18. Dr Adam Ferguson
19. Principal Robertson.

BURNS AT AN EVENING PARTY AT LORD MONBODDO'S HOUSE

JAMES EDGAR

being thus lamentably ignorant, he took no pains to secure his reputation with posterity by providing preferment for a greater than Homer and Shakespeare, who was also independent enough to think with the Whigs, and withal so admirably honest that he disdained to dissemble his opinions ! But, to take at least the second of these inferences seriously :—(1) Either Dundas wrote or contrived the lampoon or he did not, and Burns believed it or he did not; and if Dundas had nothing to do with the lampoon, then the grandiloquent theory vanishes into space, whether Burns believed, or did not believe, in Dundas's writing or contriving. (2) Demonstrably Burns, though a Scotsman, was not a Burnsite, and stood in no need of a certain surgical operation. (3) Two years after the event, Burns states that he never saw the name of Dundas in the newspapers but his heart felt 'straitened for room' in his bosom; but he gives a quite different reason for the straitening, and doesn't so much as refer to the outrage done on him by the Naval Treasurer. And (4) *The Star* was a party journal; Burns, anxious for advancement as he was, would still be meddling with politics from a party point of view; he insisted on contributing to *The Star*; and his 'rapid promotion' was pretty certainly made impossible by his contributions.

MISCELLANEOUS SONGS

A RUINED FARMER

CHAMBERS, 1852. Made to the tune, *Go From My Window, Love, Do*. For the privilege of inspecting the original MS. we are indebted to Mr. W. Nelson, Edinburgh.

Probably written during the crisis of William Burness his difficulties at Mount Oliphant :—'The farm proved a ruinous bargain; and to clench the curse, we fell into the hands of a factor, who sat for the picture I have drawn of one in my *Tale of Two Dogs*' (R. B. in Autobiographical Letter).

MONTGOMERIE'S PEGGY

CROMEK (1808). Inscribed in the *First Common Place Book*, September 1785, where it is described as 'done, something in imitation of the manner of a noble old Scottish Piece, called *M'Millan's Peggy.*' It is set to the tune, *Galla Water*.

'My Montgomerie's Peggy was my deity for six or eight months. She had been bred, tho' as the world says, without any just pretence for it, in a style of life rather elegant. But as Vanburgh says in one of his comedies, my "damn'd Star found me out" there too, for though I began the affair, merely in a *gaité de cœur*, or, to tell the truth, what would scarcely be believed, a vanity of showing my parts in courtship, particularly my abilities at a *billet doux*, which I always piqu'd myself upon, made me lay siege to her; and when, as I always do in my foolish gallantries, I had battered myself into a very warm affection for her, she told me, one day, in a flag of truce, that her fortress had been for some time before the rightful property of another; but with the greatest friendship and politeness, she offered me every alliance, except actual possession' (R. B.). Mrs. Begg stated that the girl was housekeeper at Coilfield House.

THE LASS OF CESSNOCK BANKS

CROMEK (1808) in an imperfect form: 'From the oral communication of a lady residing in Glasgow.' Reprinted in the Aldine Edition (1839) from an original MS. Tune, *If He Be a Butcher Neat and Trim*. As Cromek's version is not authentic, we deem it unnecessary to give the variations.

The heroine is supposed to have been the Elison Begbie —daughter of a farmer in the parish of Galston—to whom Burns made what was probably his first offer of marriage, in letters (1780-81), included in his published *Correspondence*. By some she is also supposed to have been the heroine of *And I'll Kiss Thee Yet* (Vol. iii. p. 34).

STANZA IX. LINE I. Scott Douglas substitutes '*Her bosom is*' for '*Her teeth are*,' on the supposition that the subject of the young lady's teeth being fully covered in Stanza XI. the Aldine Editor must have made an error in transcribing. But there is no authority for the emendation, if emendation it be.

STANZA XIV. See Prefatory Note to *It Is Na, Jean, Thy Bonie Face*, Vol. iii. p. 374.

THO' FICKLE FORTUNE

CROMEK (1808). Inscribed in the *First Common Place Book*, September 1785. 'The above was an extempore under the pressure of a heavy train of misfortunes, which, indeed, threatened to undo me altogether. It was just at the close of that dreadful period mentioned on page 8th (see Vol. i. p. 375, Prefatory Note to *A Prayer in the Prospect of Death*), and though the weather has brightened up a little with me, yet there has always been since, a "tempest brewing round me in the grim sky" of futurity, which I pretty plainly see will, some time or other, perhaps ere long, overwhelm me, and drive me into some doleful dell to pine in solitary, squalid wretchedness' (R. B.). He also states it to have been written 'in imitation of an old Scotch song well known among the country ingle sides,' and he sets down one stanza thereof, to mark the 'debt I owe to the author, as the repeating of that verse has lighted up my flame a thousand times':—

> 'When clouds in skies do come together
>   To hide the brightness of the sun,
> There will surely be some pleasant weather,
>   When a' the storms are past and gone.'

Slightly altered, Stanza I. stands for the final quatrain of *I Dream'd I Lay* (Vol. iii. p. 19).

RAGING FORTUNE

CROMEK (1808). Inscribed in the *First Common Place Book*, September 1785, next to *Tho' Fickle Fortune*. ' 'Twas at the same time I set about composing an air in the old Scotch style. I am not musical scholar enough to prick down my tune properly, so it can never see the light, and perhaps 'tis no great matter, but the following were the verses I composed to suit it. . . . The tune consisted of three parts, so that the above verses just went through the whole Air' (R. B.).

MY FATHER WAS A FARMER

CROMEK (1808). Tune, *The Weaver and his Shuttle, O*. Inscribed in the *First Common Place Book*, April 1784:— 'The following song is a wild rhapsody, miserably deficient in versification, but as the sentiments are the genuine feelings of my heart, for that reason I have a particular pleasure in conning it over' (R. B.). It faintly resembles a song in an old chap at Abbotsford, *My Father Was a Farmer, and a Farmer's Son Am I*.

O, LEAVE NOVÉLS

CURRIE (1801). Tune, *Donald Blue*. Included in Johnson's *Museum* (Vol. vi. 1803): 'By Burns.' We have omitted a refrain, 'Sing tal lal lay.'

THE MAUCHLINE LADY

CROMEK (1808). Inscribed in the *First Common Place Book*, August 1785. Made to the tune of *I Had a Horse, and I Had Nae Mair*, it is a kind of parody of that curious and very Scottish ballad :—

NOTES

  'I had a horse, I had nae mair :   THE
   I got him frae my daddy ;   MAUCHLINE
   My purse was light, and my heart was sair, LADY
   And my wit it was fu' ready.
   And sae I thought me on a time,
    Outwittens of my daddy,
   To fee myself to a lawland laird
    Wha had a bonny lady,' *etc.*

  LINE 1. 'Stewart Kyle': The northern half of the Kyle district of Ayrshire. Burns removed from Mount Oliphant (in King's Kyle) to Lochlie (in Kyle Stewart) in 1777 ; and in March 1784 he changed to Mossgiel (also in Kyle Stewart). 8. The 'Mauchline lady' was no doubt Jean Armour.

ONE NIGHT AS I DID WANDER

CROMEK (1808). Inscribed in the Glenriddell Abridgement of the *First Common Place Book.*

THERE WAS A LAD

CROMEK (1808). A different set is inscribed in the *Second Common Place Book,* Davie being substituted for Robin, and the chorus being that of the old song, *Daintie Davie* (see Vol. ii. p. 311) :—

   'Leeze me on thy curly pow,
   Bonie Davie, Dainty Davie !
   Leeze me on thy curly pow,
   Thou 'se ay my dainty Davy !'

The chorus finally adopted appears to trace back to the refrain of another old song, *The Roving Lad With the Tartan Plaid* :—' For he is a rantin, rovin lad,' *etc.*

  STANZA I. LINE 1. 'There was a *birkie* born in Kyle,' *Common Place Book* :—Kyle is an ancient division of Ayrshire.
  STANZA II. LINE 2. 'Was five-and-twenty days begun':— 'Jan. 25th, 1759, the date of my Bardship's vital existence' (R. B.). 4. 'Hansel'=the first gift. In Scotland, 'Hansel

THERE WAS A LAD

Monday' = the first Monday of the New Year, when children are accustomed to go in bands to beg 'hansel,' which may be given either in bread or money.

STANZA IV. LINE 3. 'He'll *gie his daddie's name a blaw,*' *Second Common Place Book.*

STANZA VI. is usually omitted by the Editorial Prude. LINES 1-2 in Cunningham read:—

'*Gude* faith,' quo scho 'I doubt you *gar*
The *bonie* lasses lie aspar.'

Cromek left a blank after lasses in Line 2. The reading we have adopted is that of the *Second Common Place Book.*

WILL YE GO TO THE INDIES, MY MARY

CURRIE (1800). Sent to Thomson in October 1792, as a substitute for *Will Ye Gang to the Ewe-bughts, Marion,* which Thomson, like the pedant he was, could not approve. 'In my very early years, when I was thinking of going to the West Indies, I took the following farewell of a dear girl. It is quite trifling, and has nothing of the merits of *Ewe-bughts,* but it will fill up this page.' Thomson replied that he did not mean to supplant *The Ewe-bughts,* and that what he wanted Burns to do was to try his 'hand on some of the inferior stanzas.' Burns took not the hint; nor did Thomson accept his song :—'This is a very poor song which I do not mean to include in my Collection.' For Mary Campbell, the supposed heroine (though this is at least doubtful), see Vol. iii. p. 308, Prefatory Note to *My Highland Lassie, O.*

HER FLOWING LOCKS

CROMEK (1808).

STANZA II. LINE 1. 'Her lips are roses wat wi' dew':— Cf. *The Blue-eyed Lassie,* Vol. iii. p. 83, Stanza I. Line 6; though the latter heroine's locks were, not 'the raven's wing,' but, 'golden ringlets bright.'

THE LASS O' BALLOCHMYLE

GRAY TRACTS, No. 2 (1799), *Polyhymnia*, No. 18 (1799), and Currie (1800). Sent to Miss Wilhelminia Alexander in a letter of 18th November 1786 :—' The enclosed song was the work of my return home, and perhaps but poorly answers what might have been expected from such a scene. I am going to print a second edition of my Poems, but cannot insert those verses without your permission.' The lady took no notice of the request; but a MS. Copy—MS. (A)—in the possession of Mr. Godfrey E. P. Arkwright of Adbury House, Newbury, sets forth this note :—' The above song cannot be published without the consent of the lady, which I have desired a common friend to ask.' In all probability this was the copy submitted to the 'jury of literati' in Edinburgh. It went unpublished—not because the writer could not get Miss Alexander's consent but—because it and a song on Miss Peggy Kennedy (*Young Peggy*, Vol. iii. p. 1) were 'found defamatory libels against the fastidious powers of Poesy and Taste.' In *Polyhymnia*, it is stated to 'have been composed by Robert Burns, from the emotions of gratitude and esteem which he felt for the worthy family, for the kindness and attention they had shewn him ' : a rather too Platonic theory of its origin.

Miss Wilhelminia Alexander was the sister of Claud Alexander, who succeeded the Whitefoords in Ballochmyle. She is referred to in one of the suppressed stanzas of *The Vision* :—

> 'While lovely Wilhelminia warms
> The coldest heart.'

Later in life she set a higher price than erst upon the compliment designed in Burns's verses. She died unmarried, as late as 1843.

A MS.—MS. (B)—is at Mossgiel; and the two last stanzas are included in a MS.—MS. (C)—in the possession of Mr. Adam Wood, Troon.

THE LASS O' BALLOCHMYLE

STANZA I. LINE 7. '*Unless* where green-wood echoes rang,' *Polyhymnia*.

STANZA II. LINES 7, 8. in MSS. (A and B), the Gray Tract, and *Polyhymnia* read:—

> '*The lily's hue and rose's dye
> Bespoke* the lass of Ballochmyle.'

STANZA III. LINES 1-4 in the Gray Tract read:—

> *Sweet* is *a* morn in flowery May,
> And *soft a* night in *harvest* mild,
> When *wandering in* the garden gay,
> Or *roaming thro'* the lonely wild.'

MS. (A) has *a* morn for 'the morn' and *an ev'n* for 'is night,' and *Polyhymnia* '*Harvest*,' for 'Autumn.' 7. '*And all* her other *charms* are foil'd,' MS. (B); and MS. (A) and *Polyhymnia* have the same reading with 'works' for '*charms.*'

STANZA IV. LINE 1. '*O if she were* a country maid,' MSS. (A and B); '*O gif she were*,' Gray Tract; '*O gin she were*,' *Polyhymnia*. 4. 'That ever rose on *Scotland's* plain,' Currie.

STANZA V. LINE 1. 'Then pride *may* climb the slippery steep,' *Polyhymnia*. 4. 'Or downward *dig* the Indian mine,' Gray Tract and *Polyhymnia*. 7. 'And every day *has* joys divine,' MSS. (A, B, and C); *brings* for '*has*,' *Polyhymnia*; '*bring*,' Gray Tract.

THE NIGHT WAS STILL

BLACKIE'S *Land of Burns* (1840). The MS. was given to one of the daughters of Dr. Lawrie of Newmilns; and commemorates a dance—when Burns for the first time heard the spinet—in the manse of Newmilns on the banks of Irvine. (See Vol. i. p. 405.)

MASONIC SONG

CUNNINGHAM (1834). Said to have been recited by Burns at his admission as an honorary member of the Kilwinning St. John's Lodge, Kilmarnock, 26th October 1786.

NOTES 89

'Willie' was Major William Parker, Grand Master (see MASONIC Vol. ii. p. 370, Prefatory Note to *To Hugh Parker*). SONG The MS. is in the possession of Sir Robert Jardine.

THE BONIE MOOR-HEN

CROMEK (1808). A MS. is in the possession of Mrs. Andrews, Newcastle.

A rather scandalous adaptation from *I Rede Ye Beware o' the Ripples, Young Man*, a song (attributed to Burns) in *The Merry Muses*. There is also a Jacobitish ditty (real or sham), *The Bonny Moorhen*:—

> 'My bony moorhen, my bony moorhen,
> Up in the gray hill, down in the glen:
> It's when ye gang butt the house, when ye gang ben,
> Ay drink a health to my bony moorhen,' *etc.*

Another *Muir Hen*, more in the manner of the Burns, was reprinted in the *Leslie Ballad Book*, 1827:—

> 'The bonie muir hen gaed doon the den
> To gather in her cattel;
> I bent my bow to fire at her,
> But I could never ettel,
> Sing Archie doodum diddledum dum, *etc.*
> And ay the nearer that I cam,
> It's ay she sang the louder:—
> "I loe the young men wondrous well,
> But they do want the powder,"' *etc.*

There is further '*The Bony Moor Hen*: A New Song' in *The Jolly Ploughman's Garland*, included in the Bell Collection of chaps at Abbotsford:—

> 'The bony moor Hen is gone over the main,
> And she will be back against summer again;
> I'll shoot her with an arrow, there no one shall ken
> That ever I ruffled the bony moor hen,' *etc.*

See also Vol. i., Prefatory Note to *Epistle to John Rankine*, p. 385.

THE BONIE MOOR-HEN

'Do not publish *The Moor-Hen*. Do not for your sake and mine' (Clarinda to Burns, January 30th, 1788).

STANZA I. LINE 2. 'Our lads gaed a-hunting, *one* day at the dawn,' MS.

STANZA III. LINE 4. '*But his* rays were outshone, and but mark'd where she lay,' MS.

HERE'S A BOTTLE

CROMEK (1808). A MS. was before the Aldine Editor (1839). Gilbert Burns expressed to Cromek his doubts of Robert's authorship; but he may have been influenced by a desire to disassociate his brother from the sentiment of the song. In any case it was possibly suggested by *The Bottle and Friend*, in the *Damon and Phillis Garland*, included in the Bell Collection at Abbotsford:—

> 'Bright glory is a trifle and so is ambition,
> I despise a false heart and a lofty condition,
> For pride is a folly, for it I'll not contend
> But I will enjoy my bottle and friend:
>   In a little close room
>   So neat and so trim,
>   O there I will enjoy
>   My bottle and friend,' etc.

THE BONIE LASS OF ALBANIE

CHAMBERS (1852). From a MS. then in the possession of B. Nightingale. For a copy of this MS.—MS. (B)—we are indebted to Mr. Davey, Great Russell Street, London. Suggested, it may be, by *The Bony Lass of Anglesey*, the song was also inscribed in the *Second Common Place Book*.

Charlotte Stuart, daughter of Charles Edward, the 'Young Pretender,' by Clementina Walkinshaw, was baptized 29th October 1753 (*Mémoire* in the Ministère des Affaires Étrangères, for an extract from which we are indebted to Mr. Andrew Lang). In the register of baptisms at Liège, the child is entered as the daughter of D. Johnson and the noble dame Charlotte Pitt; and there is other clear evidence that, though at this time Charles treated Miss Walkinshaw as his wife, she neither was married to him nor supposed herself to be his wife. After Charles's separation from his wife, the Countess of Albany, he sent for his illegitimate daughter Charlotte, who abode with him till his death, 30th January 1788. In 1784 he made out letters of legitimation, and these were confirmed by the Parlement of Paris, 6th December 1787, when she took the style of Duchess of Albany. But the legitimation did not imply (as was supposed at the time in England, and as, of course, was credited by Burns) that Miss Walkinshaw had been married to the Prince, but rather that Miss Walkinshaw had not. She died soon after her father.

THE BONIE LASS OF ALBANIE

STANZA II. LINE 1. 'The *lovely* maid's of Royal blood,' MS. (B). 4. '*They've* wranged the Lass of Albanie,' MS. (B).

STANZA III. LINE 3. 'And a town' :—Rothesay in the Isle of Bute. The eldest sons of the Scottish Kings were Dukes of Rothesay.

STANZA IV. LINE 1. 'But *there's* a youth,' erroneous reading. Both MSS. have '*There is*.'

STANZA VI. LINE 4. '*The time* may come,' MS. (B).

AMANG THE TREES

CROMEK (1808). Tune, *The King of France*. Written in honour of Niel Gow (1727-1807), the famous fiddler, whom Burns met during his Northern tour in 1787.

STANZA I. LINE 3. 'Drone':—The part of the bagpipe which produces the low bass note.

STANZA II. LINE 1. 'Capon craws'=castrate—(*i.e.* squeaky) —crowings. 5. 'But a royal ghaist':—James I. of Scotland, a great patron of musicians and artists.

THE CHEVALIER'S LAMENT

GRAY TRACTS (1799) and Currie (1800). Included also in Thomson (1799). 'Yesterday, my dear sir, as I was riding thro' a track of melancholy, joyless muirs, between Galloway and Ayrshire; it being Sunday, I turned my thoughts to psalms and hymns, and spiritual songs, and your favourite air, *Capt. O'Kean,* coming at length in my head, I tried these words to it. You will see that the first part of the tune must be repeated' (Burns to Cleghorn, 31st March 1788). Only stanza I. was sent to Cleghorn at that time. 'If I could hit on another stanza equal to *The Small Birds Rejoice,* I do myself honestly avow that I think it a very superior song' (R. B. to Thomson, 1st April 1793). He sent no more to Thomson either, and although that specialist included the song in his *Scottish Airs,* it was merely 'from a MS. by Burns.'

It is entered in the *Second Common Place Book*—MS. (A) —and there is a MS. at Lochryan—MS. (B)—with another in the possession of Lord Rosebery—MS. (C)—'composed at the desire of a friend who had equal enthusiasm for the air and the subject.'

STANZA I. LINE 3. 'The primroses *blush,*' MS. (B); 'The *hawthorntrees* blow,' Gray Tract. 4. 'Bedeck the green *vale,*' Gray Tract. 5. 'But what can *seem pleasant,*' Gray Tract.

STANZA II. LINE 2. 'To *set* on his throne,' Gray Tract. 4. '*But* I can find none,' MS. (A). 7. 'Your *deeds* proved so loyal,' MS. (A). 9. 'You no *sweeter* return,' MSS. (A and C) and Gray Tract.

YESTREEN I HAD A PINT O' WINE

OLIVER (1801), Cromek (1810), Clarke (1823), and *The Merry Muses.* The Anna of the song was Anne Park, niece of Mrs. Hyslop of the Globe Tavern, Dumfries.

NOTES

She bore a daughter to Burns, 31st March 1791, which was first sent to Mossgiel, and afterwards fostered by Mrs. Burns along with her baby, William Nicol, born ten days after it. According to Chambers it was Mrs. Burns's plain duty so to do: inasmuch as if she hadn't gone to visit relatives in Ayrshire, and thus provided her spouse with both an opportunity and an excuse, the child would never have been begotten. Be this as it may, nothing is known of the mother's after-life. Indeed, she is said by some to have died in childbed of this girl.

YESTREEN
I HAD A
PINT O'
WINE

The song was sent to Thomson in April 1793:— '*Shepherds, I Have Lost My Love* is to me a heavenly air— what would you think of a set of Scots verses to it? I have made one, a good while ago, which I think is the best love song I ever composed in my life, but in its original state is not quite a lady's song. I enclose the original, which please present with my best compliments to Mr. Erskine, and I also enclose an *altered* not *amended* copy for you, if you choose to set the tune to it, and let the Irish verses follow' (R. B.). Thomson did not choose to set the tune to it; but the copy—MS. (B)—is at Brechin Castle. It was also inscribed in the Glenriddell Book— MS. (A). Neither MS. has the Postscript. A set—with the Postscript—is included in Oliver (1801) and in Clarke's *Songs and Ballads of Robert Burns* (1823), and as *The Lovely Lass of Allan-Doon* was printed in a chapbook published by J. J. Niel, Airdrie.

STANZA I. LINE 4. 'The *raven* locks of Anna,' Oliver and chapbook.
STANZA II. LINE I. 'The *Israelite* in wilderness,' MS. (A).
STANZA III. LINE 4. 'The *lovely* form of Anna,' MS. (B).
STANZA IV. LINES 1, 2. in MS. (B) read:—

'While *rapt encircled* in her arms
I *speechless gaze on* Anna.'

POSTSCRIPT, STANZA I. 'The Kirk and State may *say so still*,' chapbook.

SWEET ARE THE BANKS

SCOTT DOUGLAS (1877). The first set of a song—of which the second is *Ye Flowery Banks* (p. 28), while the third —which, being the worst, is naturally the most popular —*The Banks o' Doon*, was published in Johnson's *Museum* (see Vol. iii. p. 124). It was sent in a letter to Alexander Cunningham, 11th March 1791 :—' My song is intended to sing to a Strathspey reel of which I am very fond, called in Cumming's Collection of Strathspeys, *Ballendaloch's Reel*; and in other collections that I have met with it is known by the name of *Camdelmore*. It takes three stanzas of four lines each to go through the whole tune' (R. B.).

YE FLOWERY BANKS

CROMEK (1808). The second set of *Sweet are the Banks* (see Prefatory Note, above). Sent in an undated letter— probably of March 1791—to John Ballantine of Ayr :— 'While here I sit, sad and solitary, by the side of a fire in a little country inn, and drying my wet clothes, in pops a poor fellow of a sodger, and tells me he is going to Ayr. By heavens! say I to myself, with a tide of good spirits which the magic of that sound "Auld Toon of Ayr" conjured up, I will send my last song to Mr. Ballantine' (R. B.).

CALEDONIA

CURRIE (1800). The MS. is in the Watson Collection. Sent to Johnson of the *Museum*, 23rd January 1789, with the following (hitherto) unpublished note :—'I shall be in Edinburgh, my dear sir, in about a month, when we shall overhaul the whole collection and report progress. The following I hope will suit the excellent tune it is designed for. Till we meet, adieu.' The tune was *Caledonian Hunt's Delight*; but Johnson did not publish the song.

NOTES

STANZA I. LINE I. 'There was *once a day*,' Currie.   CALEDONIA
STANZA III. LINE 5. 'And *terror* their cry,' Currie. 6.
'And *ruin'd* a world beside,' Currie.
STANZA IV. LINE I. 'Cameleon-Savage':—The Pict, who dyed and stained and parti-coloured his person with woad.
STANZA V. LINE 8. Haco the Norseman was defeated at Largs, according to the chroniclers, 2nd October 1263; and Kenneth III. of Scotland overthrew the Danes at Luncarty, Perthshire, in 970.

YOU'RE WELCOME, WILLIE STEWART

LOCKHART, *Life of Burns* (1829). Originally inscribed on a crystal tumbler, now at Abbotsford, the song is modelled on the same Jacobitism as *O Lovely Polly Stewart* (see Vol. iii. p. 429). See also Vol. ii. p. 379, Prefatory Note to *To William Stewart*. Stewart, who was factor at Closeburn, died in 1812.

STANZA I. LINE 3. 'The tappet hen':—A bottle shaped like a hen, and holding three quarts of claret. *Cf.* Allan Ramsay's *An Ode to the Ph——*:—

'That mutchkin stoup it hads but dribs,
Then let's get in the tappit hen':—

and the old song, *Andrew Wi' His Cutty Gun*:—

'For weel she lo'ed a Hawick gill,
And leugh to see a tappit hen.'

WHEN FIRST I SAW

CHAMBERS (1852), who states that it appeared in the *New York Mirror* for 1846, and that the heroine of it was Miss Jean Jeffrey, whom Burns celebrated in *The Blue-eyed Lassie* (see Vol. iii. p. 362, Prefatory Note to *The Blue-eyed Lassie*). But the song is so poor that, had not Alexander Smith (Edition 1868) collated the text 'with a copy in the poet's handwriting,' we should have classed it with the 'Improbables.'

NOTES

BEHOLD THE HOUR

FIRST SET

CLARINDA CORRESPONDENCE (1843). Sent to Clarinda, 27th December 1791. For the second and amended set, published in Thomson's *Scottish Airs*, see Vol. iii. p. 265. This first one differs little from the original in *The Charmer* (1782) and other books :—

> 'Behold the fatal hour arrive,
> Nicè, my Nicè, ah, farewell,
> Severed from thee, can I survive,
> From thee whom I have lov'd so well' :—

and one cannot choose but wonder that Burns, for all his habit of appropriation, should ever have palmed it off upon a sweetheart as his own.

HERE'S A HEALTH TO THEM THAT'S AWA

The Edinburgh Gazetteer (1792) and Cromek (1808), from a MS. now in the British Museum. Reprinted from the *Gazetteer* in the *Scots Magazine* for January 1818. Founded on a Jacobite song, of which Burns sent the following stanza (amended, or, it may be, perverted) to Johnson's *Museum* (No. 412, Vol. v. 1792) :—

> 'Here's a health to them that's awa,
> Here's a health to them that's awa;
> Here's a health to them that were here short syne,
> But canna be here the day.
> It's guid to be merry and wise,
> It's guid to be honest and true;
> It's guid to be aff wi' the auld love
> Before ye be on wi' the new.'

Stanza iv. and the last quatrain of Stanza v. are not in the British Museum MS. nor in Cromek. Hogg in his *Relics* gave a set from an old MS. collection of songs then in the possession of Hon. Mrs. Rollo. The main difference as regards the stanza quoted above consists in the substitu-

T. CRESWICK

THE BIRTHPLACE OF BURNS

"There wás a lad was born in Kyle,   I doubt it's hardly worth the while
But whatna day o' whatna style,   To be sae nice wi' Robin."
                                                       —*There was a Lad, Stanza i.*

NOTES

tion of 'him' for 'them,' 'durstna' for 'canna,' and HERE'S A 'King' for 'love.'   HEALTH

STANZA I. LINE 5. 'It's guid to be merry and wise.' *Cf.* the black-letter ballad (Roxburghe Collection), *The Good Fellow's Advice*, with the following refrain:—

> 'Good fellows, great and small,
> Pray let me you advise
> To have a care withal:
> 'Tis good to be merry and wise.'

This counsel also forms the refrains of other black-letter ballads, as *The Father's Wholesome Admonition* (Crawford, Pepys, and Roxburghe Collections); and a late derivative, *Be Merry and Wise*, included in a chap, of which we have seen a copy with the date 1794:—

> 'To be merry and wise is a proverb of old,
> But a maxim so good can't too often be told.
> Then attend to my song, nor my maxims despise,
> For I mean to be merry, but merry and wise.'

STANZA II. LINE 3. 'Charlie':—Charles James Fox.

STANZA III. LINE 3. 'Tammie, the Norland laddie':—The Hon. Thomas Erskine, afterwards Lord Erskine (1750-1823), who in 1792, being retained for Thomas Paine, resolved to obey the call to defend him, and was thereupon dismissed from his office as Attorney-General to the Prince of Wales.

STANZA IV. LINE 3. 'Maitland and Wycombe':—'Maitland' was James, eighth Earl of Lauderdale (1759-1839), who in July 1790 was elected a Scots representative peer, and during the debate in the House of Lords, 31st May 1792, on the King's Proclamation 'against seditious writings,' had come forward 'to vindicate himself, and those with whom he associated, from the gross calumnies levelled against them by the Proclamation,' which he 'stigmatised as a most malignant and impotent measure.' In August following he left for France along with Dr. John Moore. He became a strong sympathiser with the French Revolution, protested against the war with France, and on one occasion appeared in the House of Lords 'clothed in the rough garb of Jacobinism.' 'Wycombe' was John Henry

HERE'S A HEALTH Petty, second Marquis of Lansdowne (1765-1809): who, from 1784 until he succeeded his father in 1805, was styled Earl of Wycombe; at this time represented Chipping Wycombe; and in the House of Commons spoke against the Proclamation. His father, William Petty, first Marquis of Lansdowne (1739-1805), also in the House of Lords, supported Lauderdale.

STANZA V. LINE 3. 'Chieftain M'Leod':—Colonel Norman M'Leod of M'Leod (1754-1801), Member for Inverness.

AH, CHLORIS

ALDINE Edition (1839), from a MS. then in possession of the Editor. Tune, *Major Graham*. For Chloris see Vol. iii. p. 482, Prefatory Note to *Lassie Wi' the Lint-White Locks*.

The thing is strongly reminiscent of the delightful verses of Sir Charles Sedley (1639-1701), which Allan Ramsay swept into his *Tea-Table Miscellany*:—

> 'Ah Chloris, could I now but sit
> As unconcern'd as when
> Your infant beauty could beget
> Nor happiness, nor pain,' *etc.*

PRETTY PEG

Edinburgh Magazine (January 1808) with three additional stanzas, clearly not written by Burns. Again repeated in the *Edinburgh Magazine* for January 1818—without the additions, the correspondent affirming that he had copied from the Poet's MSS. As he also included a fragment, *Yon Wand'ring Rill*, undoubtedly by Burns, and part of a song sent to Thomson, the presumption is that he had genuine MSS. before him. The fragment appears in many Editions, but an alteration of a word is made to render it fit for print—and we have decided to draw the line at mutilation. *Pretty Peg* was published in the Aldine Edition (1839).

NOTES

MEG O' THE MILL
SECOND SET

CURRIE (1800). Sent to Thomson, April 1793—along with *There Was a Lass*. 'I know these songs are not to have the luck to please you, else you might be welcome to them' (R. B.). It was written for *Jackie Hume's Lament*. Thomson asked him to write another song to this air, but he replied :—' My song, *Ken Ye What Meg o' the Mill Has Gotten*, pleases me so much that I cannot try my hand at another song to the same air; so I shall not attempt it. I know you will laugh at this; but ilka man wears his belt his ain gait.' For the first set see Vol. iii. p. 200. The MS. is at Brechin Castle.

PHILLIS THE FAIR

CURRIE (1800). Sent to Thomson, August 1793. ' I likewise tried my hand on *Robin Adair*, and you will probably think with little success; but it is such a damned, crampt, out-of-the-way measure, that I despair of doing anything better to it. . . . So much for namby-pamby. I may, after all, try my hand on it in Scots verse. There I always find myself at home.' Thomson replied that he would be glad to see Burns ' give *Robin Adair* a Scottish dress,' but that ' Peter' was furnishing him with an English suit. The MS. is at Brechin Castle.

STANZA I. LINE 3. ' *Tasting* the breathing Spring,' Currie; but this was Thomson's suggestion. 7. ' Such thy *morn* ! did I cry,' Currie, from Thomson.

O, SAW YOU MY DEAR, MY PHILLY

CURRIE (1800). A degradation of *My Eppie M'Nab* (Vol. iii. p. 101). For the origin see also Vol. iii. p. 375, Prefatory Note to *My Eppie M'Nab*. Sent to Thomson, 19th October 1794 :—' To descend to business ; if you like my idea of *When She Cam Ben She Bobbit*, the following

O, SAW YOU MY DEAR, MY PHILLY stanzas of mine, altered a little from what they were formerly when set to another air, may perhaps do instead of worse stanzas' (R. B.). Thomson did not like them. There are two MS. copies at Brechin Castle. In the second '*Dear*' occurs throughout instead of 'Dearie' and 'Dearest.'

'TWAS NA HER BONIE BLUE E'E

CURRIE (1800). Sent to Thomson in April 1795, for the tune *Laddie Lie Near Me*. Thomson thought the song not equal to certain others sent at the same time, though 'very pleasing'; and Burns shortly afterwards wrote:— 'My verses to *Cauld Kail* I will suppress, and also those to *Laddie Lie Near Me*. They are neither worthy of my name nor of your book.' Thomson didn't publish the song. The MS. is at Brechin Castle.

WHY, WHY TELL THY LOVER

CURRIE (1800). Written for the tune, *Caledonian Hunt's Delight*: 'Such is the d—d peculiarity of the rhythm of this air that I find it impossible to make another stanza to suit it' (R. B. to Thomson, 3rd July 1795). Thomson replied:—'The fragment for *The Caledonian Hunt* is quite suited to the original measure of the air, and as it plagues you so, the fragment must content it.' But he inserted on the margin of the copy:—' Instead of this poor song I will take the one *Ye Banks and Braes o' Bonnie Doon*, for the air here mentioned; but I purpose attaching this to some other air, if I find one to suit it.' He didn't find one. The MS. is at Brechin Castle.

THE PRIMROSE

SENT to Thomson (who would none of it), 1793:—'For *Todlin Hame* take the following old English song, which I dare say is but little known' (R. B.). '*N.B.* I have altered it a little' (R. B.). 'This pretty little poem,' wrote Scott Douglas, 'is so much altered from the original . . . that it may almost be reckoned as Burns's own.' The criticism is fatuous, even for Scott Douglas; but a later than Scott Douglas has captured it bodily, and has equipped it with embellishments of his own. 'Not a little,' runs his commentary on Burns to Thomson: 'so much so (*sic*) that it is more Burns's than Ramsay's.' Thus the more modern Burnsite, and for once in a way he is found utterly at variance with the god of his idolatry; for if the song had been 'Ramsay's,' how could Burns have described it as 'English' and as 'little known'? As matter of fact there is nothing like it in Ramsay, the first set being Thomas Carew's (*Poems*, 1640), while the second is Robert Herrick's (*Hesperides*, 1648). Here is the Carew :— THE PRIMROSE

> 'Ask me why I send you here
> This firstling of the infant Year?
> Ask me why I send to you
> This Primrose, all bepearl'd with dew?
>   I straight whisper to your ears:—
>   "The sweets of Love are wash'd with tears."
>
> 'Ask me why this flower does show
> So yellow-green, and sickly too?
> Ask me why the stalk is weak,
> And bending, yet it does not break?
>   I must tell you:—"These discover
>   What doubts and fears are in a Lover."'

This set it is that was ravished for Thomson's book, and ravished so violently that in very deed it may 'almost be reckoned as'—neither Burns nor Carew. Here is the Herrick :—

> 'Ask me why I send you here
> This sweet Infanta of the Year?
> Ask me why I send to you
> This Primrose thus bepearl'd with dew?
>   I will whisper in your ears:—
>   "The sweets of Love are mix'd with tears.

THE PRIMROSE

'Ask me why this flower does show
So yellow-green, and sickly too?
Ask me why the stalk is weak
And bending (yet it doth not break)?
I will answer :—"These discover
What fainting hopes are in a lover."'

Now, it had not been wonderful if Scott Douglas had known nothing of either Carew or Herrick; for almost the sole concern of that loyal, illiterate soul was Burns. But for his successor, born to flourish in an age of literary handbooks and University Extension Lectures — his successor, who has seen a Ramsay, of which Burns knew nothing, and which does not (it appears) exist, but who has not discovered a pair of English classics which do—what is to be said of his successor? For Burns, his attitude is characteristic. He wanted a vamp for *Todlin Hame*; he recked nothing (and small blame to him) of either Herrick or Carew; and he laid hands, as was his wont, albeit more clumsily than was his wont, on the first 'old English song, which I dare say is but little known,' he came across—just as he would have laid hands on *Queen and Huntress* or on *Hear, Ye Ladies*, or *Bid Me to Live*, or anything not very much known which had served his turn. He did but ply his trade with a view to filling a page in Thomson's book; and as he claimed not the maker's honours, but was content with the vamper's, there is no more to be said about the matter in so far as *he* is concerned. But one can't help wishing that he'd lived to correct the enthusiasm of certain among his commentators.

O, WERT THOU IN THE CAULD BLAST

CURRIE (1800). Written during his last illness in honour of Jessie Lewars (see Vol. iii. p. 467, Prefatory Note to *Here's a Health to Her I Loe Dear*), after she had played *The Wren* to him on the piano.

NOTES

INTERPOLATIONS
YOUR FRIENDSHIP

INCLUDED in a poem to Clarinda, *Talk Not of Love,* which Burns altered for Johnson's *Museum* (No. 186, Vol. ii. 1788), where it appears as 'By a Lady,' and is signed M. The stanzas were substituted for this one of Clarinda's :—

> ' The hand of Friendship I accept,
> May Honour be your guard,
> Virtue our intercourse direct,
> Her smiles our dear reward !'

Clarinda's song was modelled on one found in *The Charmer* (1782) and other books :—

> ' Love never more shall give me pain,
> My fancy's fixt on thee,' *etc.*

FOR THEE IS LAUGHING NATURE

WRITTEN to complete a song by Clarinda, an additional quatrain being necessary to fill the tune, in Johnson's *Museum* (No. 190, Vol. ii. 1788). It was interpolated as the first quatrain of the second and last octave. The Clarinda, which is described as 'By a Lady,' and signed M., is entitled *To a Blackbird* :—

> ' Go on, sweet bird, and soothe my care !
> Thy cheerful notes will hush despair.
> Thy tuneful warblings, void of art,
> Thrill sweetly through my aching heart,' *etc.*

NO COLD APPROACH

INSERTED in the song, *The Tears I Shed,* by Miss Cranstoun, afterwards the second wife of Professor Dugald Stewart, to complete the last octave, and so fit it for the tune in Johnson's *Museum* (No. 340, Vol. iv. 1792). 'This song of genius was composed by a Miss Cranstoun. It wanted four lines to make all the stanzas suit the music, which I added, and are the first four of the last stanza' (R. B. in Interleaved Copy).

NOTES

ALTHO' HE HAS LEFT ME

INSERTED by Burns in a song from Herd's Collection, *As I Was a Walking*, the whole set of which he very slightly altered for Johnson's *Museum* (No. 348, Vol. iv. 1792), where it appears, *As I Was a Wand'ring*. This stanza was substituted for the last three in Herd.

LET LOOVE SPARKLE

INSERTED by Burns in *Jocky Fou and Jenny Fain* (in which he also made a few verbal changes) to complete an octave for the tune in Johnson's *Museum* (No. 381, Vol. iv. 1792).

AS DOWN THE BURN

CURRIE (1800). Sent to Thomson in September 1793, as a substitute for the final stanza of Robert Crawford's song, *Down the Burn, Davie*. 'I have this moment tried an alteration, leaving out the last half of the third stanza and the first half of the last stanza, thus' (R. B. to Thomson). Thomson at first accepted Burns's amendment, but in later editions substituted some rubbish of his own for Burns's vamp, in which, by the way, only Lines 2 and 4 and a word or two in Line 5 belong to that poet, the rest being absolute Crawford.

IMPROBABLES

ON ROUGH ROADS

SCOTT DOUGLAS (Kilmarnock Edition, 1876). According to him, 'it is very familiarly quoted in Ayrshire, as a stray impromptu of Burns's.' But he says not from whom he got it, and an impromptu which had lived for ninety years without getting written or printed—*ça donne furieusement à penser!*

Engraved by J. ROGERS   *From an Original Painting*

MRS. BURNS AND HER GRANDCHILD
(The Daughter of Mr. J. GLENCAIRN BURNS)

NOTES

ELEGY ON STELLA

INSCRIBED in the *Second Common Place Book* :—' This poem is the work of some hapless son of the Muses who deserved a better fate. There is a great deal of "the voice of Cona" in his solitary, mournful notes; and had the sentiments been clothed in Shenstone's language, they would have been no discredit to that elegant poet' (R. B.). He sent a copy to Mrs. Dunlop in a letter of 7th July 1789, in which he said that he had met the *Elegy* in MS., and marked the passages which struck him most. These are Stanzas I. IV. XIII. XIV. (last two lines) XVII. XVIII. and XIX.; and it is worth noting that he does not include with them Stanza XV., Stanza XVI., or Stanza XX.

The theory of Scott Douglas and others, that the verses were suggested by a visit to the West Highlands in June 1787, when Burns may have visited Mary Campbell's grave—(at Greenock: which, in defiance of geography, appears 'at the last limits of our isle')—is sheer sentiment. The truth is, there is no earthly reason, except the existence of that sentiment, for attributing the thing to Burns; and, as it is utterly unlike his work—especially his work in English, which is far less easy and less fluent —as, too, he suggests that another wrote it, we see not why it should ever have been printed as his. Scott Douglas unwarrantably inserted the first instead of the third person in Stanzas XV. and XVI.

POEM ON PASTORAL POETRY

CURRIE (1800), from a MS. in Burns's hand; but Gilbert Burns strongly doubted its authenticity, and internal evidence shows that it may have been written by some contemporary of Allan Ramsay. Thus in Stanza V. that maker is referred to as alive; while no mention is made of either Hamilton of Gilbertfield or Fergusson, one or other of whom may well have been the author. Burns,

ON PASTORAL POETRY again, knew nothing of Theocritus and nothing of Maro; and, had he written of pastoral verse, would certainly have quoted, not Pope but, his favourite Shenstone.

> STANZA VI. LINE 4. 'Tantallon':—A famous historic stronghold on the east coast of Scotland, near North Berwick.

ON THE DESTRUCTION OF DRUMLANRIG WOODS

HOGG AND MOTHERWELL (1835). First published in *The Scots Magazine* for July (1803), where it is stated that the verses had been found 'written on the window-shutter of a small inn on the banks of the Nith,' and that they were 'supposed to have been written by Burns.' This is a little vague. Cromek, who didn't print the verses, told Creech that they were written by Henry Mackenzie, but there is nothing beyond this statement to confirm the ascription : though one could credit Mackenzie with them far more easily than one could credit Burns.

THE JOYFUL WIDOWER

THIS very squalid performance, No. 98 in Johnson (Vol. i. 1787) is attributed by Stenhouse to Burns; but he never acknowledged it. It is included in a chap in the Motherwell Collection, — ' Three Excellent Songs, Entered According to Order '—one of the three being *The Duke of Hamilton and Mohun's Fight* (the duel took place in 1712); but the chap itself is undated. Again, it was published in *'The Pretty Maiden's Amusement*, being a Choice Collection of All the Favourite New Songs, Sung at Both the Theatres, Vauxhall, Renlagh, Marybone, Sadlers' Wells : Printed and sold in Alderney Churchyard, Bowlane' ; but this volume also is undated. There are many blackletter ballads — most of them unsavoury enough — on scolding wives.

WHY SHOULD WE IDLY WASTE OUR PRIME

Cunningham (1834). But Cunningham's authority is worthless.

THE TREE OF LIBERTY

Chambers (1838). In this particular case Chambers gave as his authority a ms. then in the possession of Mr. James Duncan, Morefield, Glasgow. *The Tree of Liberty* reads like a bad blend of *Scots Wha Hae* and *Is There For Honest Poverty*; and as the ms. has not been heard of since 1838, we may charitably conclude that Burns neither made the trash nor copied it.

TO A KISS

Chambers (1838). Published in a Liverpool paper called *The Kaleidoscope,* and there attributed to Burns. It, however, appeared originally (and anonymously) in *The Oracle,* January 29, 1796, long the favoured organ of the wretched Della Cruscan shoal; and it has the right Anna Matilda smack throughout. After all, too, that a thing is bad enough to have been written by Burns for Thomson is no proof that it is Burns's work.

DELIA: AN ODE

Stewart's Edition (1802) and *Lives of Scottish Poets,* by the Society of Ancient Scots (1822). This twaddle is said to have been sent to the London *Star* with the following note:—' Mr. Printer,—If the productions of a simple ploughman can merit a place in the same paper with Sylvester Otway and the other favourites of the Muses who illuminate *The Star* with the lustre of genius, your insertion of the enclosed trifle will be succeeded by future communications from yours, etc., R. Burns. Ellisland, near Dumfries, 18th May 1789.' The letter more resembles Burns's manner than the 'poem.' But we have found neither in *The Star*; and the fact that

DELIA: AN ODE   Burns was already in communication with Stuart, and had sent him poems for *The Star* (see Vol. ii. p. 280) is scarce in keeping with the letter-writer's air and tone.

TO THE OWL

CROMEK (1808). 'Found among the Poet's MSS. in his own handwriting, with occasional interlineations such as occur in all his primitive effusions'; but attributed by him to John M'Creddie, of whom nothing is known. To our mind, those who give the verses to Burns would give him anything.

THE VOWELS: A TALE

CROMEK (1808). Also found among the Poet's papers.

ON THE ILLNESS OF A FAVOURITE CHILD

CUNNINGHAM (1834). But it is hard to believe that Burns, though his taste in English was none of the finest, could even transcribe such immitigable rubbish.

ON THE DEATH OF A FAVOURITE CHILD

Edinburgh Magazine (July 1814). Burns's daughter, Elizabeth Riddell, died in the autumn of 1795. But this fact can scarce be regarded as proof of the authenticity of verses altogether in the manner of Mrs. Hemans.

ADDENDUM, ETC.

See *Mally's Meek* (Vol. iii. p. 207). The song is complete as it stands; but this additional stanza was accidentally omitted.

EARLY DRAFT OF "SCOTS, WHA HAE"
(From MS. in possession of Mrs. Lampson-Locker)

INDEX OF TITLES

	TEXT	NOTES
Ah, Chloris	37	98
Albanie, The Bonie Lass of	22	90
Altho' he has Left me	45	104
Amang the Trees	23	91
Approach, No Cold	44	103
A Ruined Farmer	1	81
As Down the Burn	45	104
Ballochmyle, The Lass o'	16	87
Banks, Sweet are the	27	94
Banks, Ye Flowery	28	94
Behold the Hour	34	96
Blast, O Wert Thou in the Cauld	43	102
Burn, As Down the	45	104
Caledonia	29	94
Cessnock Banks, The Lass of	3	82
Chevalier's Lament, The	24	92
Child, On the Death of a Favourite	68	108
Child, On the Illness of a Favourite	67	108
Chloris, Ah	37	98
Death of a Favourite Child, On the	68	108

INDEX OF TITLES

	TEXT	NOTES
Delia	63	107
Destruction of Drumlanrig Woods, On the	53	106
Drumlanrig Woods, On the Destruction of	53	106
E'e, 'Twas Na Her Bonie Blue	41	100
Elegy on Stella	46	105
Fair, Phillis the	39	99
Farmer, A Ruined	1	81
Farmer, My Father Was a	8	84
For Thee is Laughing Nature	44	103
Fortune, Raging	7	84
Fortune, Tho' Fickle	6	83
Friendship, Your	44	103
Health to Them That's Awa, Here's a	35	96
Here's a Bottle	21	90
Here's a Health to Them That's Awa	35	96
Her Flowing Locks	16	86
Hour, Behold the	34	96
Illness of a Favourite Child, On the	67	108
Indies, My Mary, Will Ye Go to the	15	86
Jeanie's Face, When First I Saw Fair	32	95
Joyful Widower, The	55	106
Kiss, To a	62	107
Lad, There was a	13	85
Lady, The Mauchline	12	84
Lament, The Chevalier's	24	92

INDEX OF TITLES

	TEXT	NOTES
Lass o' Ballochmyle, The	16	87
Lass of Albanie, The Bonie	22	90
Lass of Cessnock Banks, The	3	82
Left me, Altho' he has	45	104
Let Loove Sparkle	45	104
Liberty, The Tree of	58	107
Locks, Her Flowing	16	86
Loove Sparkle, Let	45	104
Lover, Why, Why Tell Thy	42	100
Mary, Will Ye Go to the Indies, My	15	86
Masonic Song	19	88
Mauchline Lady, The	12	84
Meg o' the Mill	38	99
Montgomerie's Peggy	3	82
Moor-Hen, The Bonie	20	89
My Father Was a Farmer	8	84
Nature, For Thee is Laughing	44	103
Night as I did Wander, One	12	85
Night was Still, The	18	88
No Cold Approach	44	103
Novéls, O, Leave	11	84
O, Leave Novéls	11	84
One Night as I did Wander	12	85
On Rough Roads	46	104
On the Death of a Favourite Child	68	108
On the Destruction of Drumlanrig Woods	53	106
On the Illness of a Favourite Child	67	108
O, Saw You my Dear, my Philly	40	99
O, Wert Thou in the Cauld Blast	43	102

INDEX OF TITLES

	TEXT	NOTES
Owl, To the	64	108
Pastoral Poetry, Poem on	50	105
Peggy, Montgomerie's	3	82
Peg, Pretty	37	98
Phillis the Fair	39	99
Philly, O, Saw You my Dear, my	40	99
Pint o' Wine, Yestreen I Had a	25	92
Poem on Pastoral Poetry	50	105
Pretty Peg	37	98
Prime, Why Should We Idly Waste Our	57	107
Primrose, The	42	100
Raging Fortune	7	84
Roads, On Rough	46	104
Song, Masonic	19	88
Stella, Elegy on	46	105
Stewart, You're Welcome, Willie	31	95
Sweet are the Banks	27	94
The Bonie Lass of Albanie	22	90
The Bonie Moor-Hen	20	89
The Chevalier's Lament	24	92
The Joyful Widower	55	106
The Lass o' Ballochmyle	16	87
The Lass of Cessnock Banks	3	82
The Mauchline Lady	12	84
The Night was Still	18	88
The Primrose	42	100
There was a Lad	13	85
The Tree of Liberty	58	107

INDEX OF TITLES

	TEXT	NOTES
The Vowels	66	108
Tho' Fickle Fortune	6	83
To a Kiss	62	107
To the Owl	64	108
Tree of Liberty, The	58	107
Trees, Amang the	23	91
'Twas Na Her Bonie Blue E'e . .	41	100
Vowels, The	66	108
Wander, One Night as I did . . .	12	85
When First I Saw Fair Jeanie's Face . .	32	95
Why Should We Idly Waste Our Prime .	57	107
Why, Why Tell Thy Lover . . .	42	100
Widower, The Joyful . . .	55	106
Will Ye Go to the Indies, My Mary . .	15	86
Wine, Yestreen I Had a Pint o' . .	25	92
Ye Flowery Banks	28	94
Yestreen I Had a Pint o' Wine . .	25	92
You're Welcome, Willie Stewart . .	31	95
Your Friendship	44	103

VOL. IV.   H

GLOSSARIAL INDEX

A', all.
A-back, (1) behind, i. 37. 3; (2) away, i. 16. 11.
Abiegh, aloof, off: 'stand abiegh,' i. 102. 11, and iii. 215. 7.
Ablins, v. *Aiblins*.
Aboon, (1) above [the usual sense]; also (2) up: 'a lift aboon,' i. 169. 6: 'temper-pins aboon,' ii. 100. 14; 'heart aboon,' iii. 193. 4; 'his heart will never get aboon' = his heart will never again rejoice, i. 58. 17.
Abread, abroad: 'beauties a' abread,' i. 154. 8.
Abreed, in breadth (R. B.): 'spread abreed thy weel-fill'd brisket,' i. 103. 15.
Ado, to do: 'mickle ado,' iii. 137. 10.
Adle, cow-lant, putrid water: 'deal brimstone like adle,' ii. 32. 5.
Ae, one.
Aff, off.
Aff-hand, at once: 'a carpet weaver aff-hand,' i. 213. 22; 'marriage aff-hand,' iii. 242. 12.
Aff-loof, off-hand, extempore: 'Just clean aff-loof,' i. 163. 16.

A-fiel, a-field.
Afore, before.
Aft, oft.
Aften, often.
Agley, askew: 'gang aft agley, i. 116. 20.
Ahin, behind: 'lan'-ahin,' ii. 40. 6; 'fur-ahin,' ii. 40. 16. See also Note, vol. ii. 337.
Aiblins, may be, perhaps.
Aik, oak.
Aiken, oaken.
Ain, own.
Air, early.
Airle, hansel, earnest money: 'airle-pennies three,' iii. 138. 14; 'an airle-penny,' iii. 90. 13.
Airles, hansel: 'the airles an the fee,' ii. 86. 19.
Airn, iron.
Airt, direction.
Airt, to direct: 'airt me to my treasure,' iii. 156. 16; 'airted till her a guid chiel,' ii. 126. 7.
Aith, oath.
Aits, oats.
Aiver, an old horse (R. B.): 'a noble aiver,' i. 72. 11.
Aizle, a cinder: 'an aizle brunt,' i. 93. 12.
A-jee, (1) ajar: 'the back-yett

be a-jee,' iii. 5. 10; (2) to one side: 'his bonnet he a thought a-jee,' iii. 104. 13.
Alake, alas.
Alane, alone.
Alang, along.
Amaist, almost.
Amang, among.
An, if.
An', and.
Ance, once.
Ane, one.
Aneath, beneath.
Anes, ones.
Anither, another.
Aqua-fontis, spring-water: 'aqua-fontis, what you please,' i. 197. 9.
Aqua-vitae, whisky.
Arle, v. *Airle*.
Ase, ashes.
Asklent, (1) askew [not according to Hoyle]: 'cam to the warl' asklent,' ii. 38. 9; (2) askance: 'look'd asklent,' iii. 215. 6.
Aspar, aspread: 'the lasses lie aspar,' iv. 14. 10.
Asteer, astir.
A' thegither, altogether.
Athort, athwart.
Atweel, in truth: 'eh! atweel na,' iii. 190. 6.
Atween, between.
Aught, eight.
Aught, possession: 'whase aught,'=who owns, ii. 149. 16.
Aughten, eighteen.
Aughtlins, at all, in any way: 'Aughtlins fawsont,' ii. 156. 5; v. *Oughtlins*.
Auld, old.

Auldfarran, auldfarrant (1) shrewd: 'a chap that's damn'd auldfarran,' i. 30. 5; (2) old-fashioned in the sense of sagacious: 'your auldfarrant frien'ly letter,' ii. 81. 6.
Auld-Light. See Note, vol. i. 384.
Auld Reekie, Edinburgh. See Note vol. ii. 346.
Auld-warld, old-world.
Aumous, alms: 'just like an aumous dish,' ii. 2. 8.
Ava, at all.
Awa, away.
Awald, backways and bent together: 'fell awald beside it,' iii. 201. 11.
Awauk, awake.
Awauken, awaken.
Awe, owe: 'devil a shilling I awe, man,' ii. 210. 16.
Awkart, awkward.
Awnie, bearded: 'aits set up their awnie horn,' i. 20. 8.
Ayont, beyond.

Ba', a ball.
Baby-clouts, babie-clouts, baby clothes: 'like baby-clouts a-dryin,' i. 212. 22; 'O wha my babie-clouts will buy,' iii. 70. 1.
Backet, bucket or box: 'auld saut-backets,' i. 291. 9.
Backit, backed: 'howe-backit now, an' knaggie,' i. 100. 3.
Backlins-comin, coming back, returning (R. B.), i. 173. 15.
Back-yett, gate at the back: 'the back-yett be a-jee,' iii. 5. 10.

GLOSSARIAL INDEX 117

Bade, endured: 'bade an unco bang,' i. 203. 16.
Bade, asked: 'and bade nae better,' ii. 129. 4.
Baggie, the belly, the stomach: 'a ripp to thy auld baggie,' i. 100. 2.
Baig'nets, bayonets.
Baillie, magistrate of a Scots burgh.
Bainie, bony, big-boned: the 'brawnie, bainie, ploughman chiel,' i. 22. 14.
Bairn, child.
Bairntime, brood, issue: 'thae bonie bairntime,' i. 71. 19; 'my pleugh is now thy bairntime a', i. 104. 13.
Baith, both.
Bakes, biscuits: 'bakes and gills,' i. 43. 8.
Ballats, ballads.
Balou, lullaby: 'The Highland Balou,' iii. 175.
Bamboozle, to trick by mystifying: 'wicked men bamboozle him,' ii. 56. 20.
Ban, swear [special Scottish meaning in addition to curse]: 'the devil-haet that I sud ban,' ii. 82. 15.
Ban', band [*i.e.* of the Presbyterian clergyman]: 'gown an' ban''=the clergyman, ii. 76. 14. See also Note, vol. ii. 357; 'and band upon his breastie,' ii. 91. 20.
Bane, bone.
Bang, an effort (R. B.), a blow, a large number. *Unco bang*, great or prolonged effort: 'he bade an unco bang,' i. 203. 16. See Note, vol. i. 395.

Bang, to thump: 'bang your hide,' iii. 146. 12; 'she bang'd me,' iii. 191. 2; 'bang'd the despot,' iv. 60. 36.
Banie, v. *Bainie*.
Bannet, bonnet.
Bannock, *bonnock*, a soft cake: 'twa mashlum bonnocks,' i. 32. 8; 'Saxpence an' a bannock,' ii. 126. 4. See also Note, vol. ii. 375; 'Bannocks o' Bear Meal, Bannocks o' Barley,' iii. 175; 'hauvermeal bannock,' iii. 2. 17. See also Note, vol. iii. 302.
Bardie, dim. of *bard*.
Barefit, barefooted.
Barket, barked.
Barley-brie or *-bree*, barley-brew =ale or whisky: 'barley-brie cement the quarrel,' i. 23. 7; 'taste the barley-bree,' iii. 80. 4.
Barm, yeast: 'that clarty barm should stain my laurels,' ii. 247. 13.
Barmie, yeasty: 'my barmie noddle,' i. 60. 8.
Barn-yard, stackyard, iii. 25. 5.
Bartie, the Devil: 'as fou as Bartie,' ii. 88. 16.
Bashing, abashing: 'bashing and dashing, ii. 105. 21.
Basin, *quarter-basin*, iii. 156. 4. See Note, vol. iii. 415.
Batch, a number, a company: 'batch o' wabster lads,' i. 39. 21.
Batts, the botts [applied to horses], the colic: 'a country laird had taen the batts,' i. 198. 19.
Bauckie-bird, the bat: 'waver-

ing like the bauckie-bird,' ii.
1. 2. See also Note, vol. ii.
307.
Baudrons, Baudrans, the cat:
'a winkin baudrons,' i. 214.
4; 'like baudrons by a rattan,' ii. 140. 2; 'auld baudrans by the ingle sits,' iii. 126.
5.
Bauk, cross-beam: 'grapit for the bauks,' i. 92. 16.
Bauk, v. *Bawk*.
Bauk-en', beam-end: 'or whether 'twas a bauk-en', i. 93. 2.
Bauld, bold.
Bauldest, boldest.
Bauldly, boldly.
Baumy, balmy.
Bawbee, a halfpenny [probably a babie penny].
Bawdrons, v. *Baudrons*.
Bawk, a field-path: 'a corn-inclosèd bawk,' iii. 33. 6.
Baws'nt, white-streaked: 'sonsie, baws'nt face,' i. 10. 13.
Bawtie, pet name for a dog: 'my auld teethless Bawtie,' ii. 59. 2.
Be, alone [*i.e.* as one is already]: 'an' let poor damnèd bodies be,' i. 47. 13; 'let a body be,' i. 253. 8.
Bear, barley.
Beas', beasts, vermin [*i.e.* lice]: 'grey wi' beas',' ii. 156. 9.
Beastie, dim. of *beast*.
Beck, a curtsy: 'she'll gie ye a beck,' ii. 207. 7.
Beet, feed, kindle, fan, add fuel to: 'beet his hymeneal flame,' i. 151. 6; 'it heats me, it beets me,' i. 121. 20; 'or noble Elgin beets,' i. 111.

10; 'it's plenty beets the lover's fire,' iii. 118. 12. Cf. Chaucer, 'Two fires on the autor [altar] gan she beete,' *Knight's Tale, Canterbury Tales*, 2292.
Befa', befall.
Behin', *behint*, behind.
Beild, v. *Biel*.
Belang, belong.
Beld, bald.
Bellum, assault: 'brawlie ward their bellum,' ii. 56. 5.
Bellys, bellows.
Belyve, by-and-by: 'belyve the elder bairns,' i. 107. 15; 'weel-swall'd kytes belyve are bent,' i. 238. 3.
Ben, a parlour. See Note, vol. i. 334.
Ben, into the spence or parlour (R. B.)
Benmost, inmost 'benmost bore,' ii. 4. 4; 'benmost neuk,' ii. 156. 18.
Be-north, to the northward of.
Be-south, to the southward of.
Bethankit, the grace after meat (R. B.), i. 238. 6.
Beuk, a book: 'devil's pictur'd beuks'=playing-cards, i. 18. 16.
Beyont, beyond.
Bicker, a wooden cup: 'in cog or bicker,' i. 22. 4. See also Note, vol. i. 323.
Bicker, a cupful, a glass: 'a hearty bicker,' ii. 72. 15.
Bicker, a short run: 'I took a bicker,' i. 192. 18.
Bicker, to flow swiftly and with a slight noise: 'bicker'd to the seas,' iv. 12. 14; 'bick-

GLOSSARIAL INDEX 119

erin dancin dazzle,' i. 98. 6.
Cf. also 'smoke and bickering flame,' Milton's *Paradise Lost*, vi. 766.
Bickerin, noisy and keen contention: 'there will be bickerin there,' ii. 193. 18.
Bickering, hurrying: 'bickering brattle,' i. 115. 4.
Bid, to ask, to wish, to offer: 'bid nae better,' ii. 154. 9; ne'er bid better,' ii. 101. 22. See also *Bade*.
Bide, abide. See also *Bade*.
Biel, bield, a shelter: 'hap him in a cozie biel,' i. 146. 14; 'the random bield o' clod or stane,' i. 137. 9; 'but buss and bield,' iii. 178. 11; 'thy bield should be my bosom,' iv. 43. 15.
Biel, bield, a sheltered spot: 'the sun blinks kindly in the biel,' iii. 114. 15; 'roses blaw in ilka bield,' iii. 117. 20.
Bien, prosperous, comfortable: 'bien and snug,' i. 117. 16; 'her house sae bien,' iii. 22. 1.
Bien, bienly, comfortably: 'that cleeds me bien,' iii. 114. 3; 'bienly clad,' ii. 38. 14.
Big, to build.
Biggin, building.
Biggin, a structure, a dwelling: 'the auld clay biggin,' i. 75. 8; 'houlet-haunted biggin,' i. 290. 7.
Bike, v. *Byke*.
Bill, the bull: 'as yell's the bill,' i. 50. 6.
Billie, fellow, comrade, brother [several examples of each of these meanings].
Billy, William.
Bings, heaps: 'potatoe-bings,' i. 201. 15.
Birdie, dim. of *bird*, also maidens: 'bonie birdies,' ii. 44. 6. See also *Burdie*.
Birk, the birch.
Birken, birchen.
Birkie, a fellow [usually implies conceit].
Birr, force, vigour: 'wi' a' my birr,' ii. 184. 7.
Birring, whirring: 'birring paitricks,' i. 222. 7.
Birses, bristles: 'tirl the hullions to the birses,' ii. 155. 26.
Birth, berth: 'a birth afore the mast,' i. 145. 21.
Bit, small [*e.g.* a bit beauty, bit brugh, bit lassie, etc.]
Bit, nick of time: 'just at the bit,' i. 50. 12.
Bitch-fou, completely drunk, ii. 49. 16.
Bizz, a flurry: 'that day when in a bizz,' i. 52. 1.
Bizz, to buzz.
Bizzard, the buzzard.
Bizzie, busy.
Black-bonnet, the elder: 'a greedy glowr black-bonnet throws,' i. 39. 8; 'an' douse black-bonnet,' ii. 76. 14. See also Note, vol. ii. 357.
Black-nebbit, black-beaked: 'black-nebbit Johnie,' ii. 194. 5.
Blae, blue, livid.
Blastet, blastit, blasted [used in contempt and =damn'd]: 'wee, blastit wonner,' i. 11. 19;

'creepin, blastit wonner,' i. 152. 19; 'onie blastit, moorland toop,' i. 55. 24.
Blastie, a blasted [*i.e.* damn'd] creature: 'the blastie's makin,' i. 154. 10; 'red-wud Kilbirnie blastie,' ii. 40. 19.
Blate, (1) modest: 'owre blate to seek,' i. 189. 3; (2) bashful, shy: 'nor blate nor scaur,' i. 48. 6; 'some unco blate,' i. 89. 12; 'but blate and laithfu',' i. 109. 11; 'young and blate,' ii. 104. 2; 'steer her up, an' be na blate,' iii. 188. 5.
Blather, bladder.
Blaud, a large quantity, a screed: 'a hearty blaud,' i. 162. 15; 'a blaud o' Johnie's morals,' ii. 89. 8.
Blaud, to slap: 'he's the boy will blaud her,' i. 211. 2.
Blaudin, driving, pelting: 'the bitter, blaudin show'r,' ii. 76. 8.
Blaw, to blow.
Blaw, to brag, to boast: 'blaw about mysel,' i. 159. 11; 'he brags and he blaws o' his siller,' iii. 84. 19.
Blawing, blowing.
Blawn, blown.
Bleer, to blear.
Bleer't, bleared.
Bleez'd, blazed.
Bleeze, a blaze.
Bleezin, blazing.
Blellum, (1) a babbler: 'drunken blellum,' i. 279. 14; (2) a railer: 'sour-mou'd, girnin blellum,' ii. 56. 1; (3) a blusterer: 'to cowe the blellums,' ii. 78. 6.

Blether, blethers, nonsense.
Blether, to talk nonsense.
Bletherin', talking nonsense.
Blin', blind.
Blin', to blind.
Blink, a glance, a moment, a short period [several examples of each of these meanings].
Blink, to glance, to shine.
Blinkers, (1) spies: 'seize the blinkers,' i. 25. 8; (2) oglers: 'delicious blinkers,' ii. 102. 9.
Blinkin, blinking, shining.
Blinkin, (1) smirking: 'Blinkin Bess of Annandale,' ii. 178. 1; (2) leering: 'are blinkin at the entry,' i. 39. 18.
Blin't, blinded: 'blin't his e'e,' iii. 35. 10.
Blitter, the snipe: 'blitter frae the boggie,' iii. 14. 10.
Blue-gown, the livery of the licensed beggar: 'the Blue-gown badge,' i. 177. 6. See also Note, vol. i. 385.
Bluid, blood.
Bluidy, bloody.
Blume, to bloom.
Bluntie, a stupid [*i.e.* one who isn't sharp]: 'gar me look like bluntie,' iii. 111. 14.
Blypes, shreds: 'till skin in blypes cam haurlin,' i. 97. 13.
Bobbed, curtsied: 'When She Cam Ben She Bobbed,' iii. 110.
Bocked, vomited: 'or thro' the mining outlet bocked,' i. 225. 17.
Boddle, a farthing [properly two pennies Scots, or one-third of an English penny]: 'he car'd na deils a boddle,'

GLOSSARIAL INDEX 121

i. 282. 26; 'I'll wad a boddle,' i. 204. 5.
Bodkin, tailor's needle: 'your bodkin's bauld,' ii. 96. 4.
Body, bodie, a person, a creature.
Boggie, dim. of *bog*: 'the blitter frae the boggie,' iii. 14. 10.
Bogle, a bogie, a hobgoblin: 'lest bogles catch him unawares,' i. 282. 2; 'nae nightly bogle make it eerie,' iii. 231. 10; 'Ghaist nor bogle,' iii. 269. 1; 'the silly bogles, Wealth and State,' iii. 222. 15.
Bole, a hole, or small recess in the wall: 'there sat a bottle in a bole,' iii. 108. 9.
Bonie, bonnie, pretty, beautiful.
Bonilie, prettily.
Bonnock, v. *Bannock*.
'Boon, above.
Boord, board, surface: 'the jinglin icy boord,' i. 50. 14.
Boord-en', board-end: 'sitting at yon boord-en',' iii. 36. 4.
Boortrees, 'the shrub - elder, planted much of old in hedges of barnyards' *etc.* (R. B.): 'thro' the boortrees comin,' i. 49. 3.
Boost, behove, must needs: 'I shortly boost to pasture,' i. 70. 17; 'like a blockhead, boost to ride,' ii. 40. 11.
Boot, payment to the bargain: 'the boot and better horse,' iii. 57. 10; 'the saul o' boot,' i. 186. 12; 'O' boot that night,' ii. 14. 22.
Bore, a chink, a small hole, an opening: 'thro' ilka bore the beams were glancing,' i. 282. 19; 'the benmost bore,' ii. 4. 4; 'to guard, or draw, or wick a bore,' i. 221. 18. See Note, vol. i. 403.
Botch, an angry tumour (R. B.): 'scabs and botches,' i. 52. 9.
Bouk, a human trunk [Eng. bulk: cf. 'to shatter all his bulk,' Shak. *Hamlet*, ii. 1. 95]: 'and monie a bouk did fa',' iii. 74. 4.
'Bout, about.
Bow-hough'd, bandy-thighed: 'she's bough-hough'd, she's hem-shin'd,' iii. 125. 17.
Bow-kail, cabbage: 'wandered thro' the bow-kail,' i. 89. 20; 'his bow-kail runt,' i. 91. 15.
Bow't, bent: 'like a sow-tail sae bow't,' i. 89. 23.
Brachens, ferns: 'amang the brachens,' i. 98. 10. See also *Breckan*.
Brae, a small hill, the slope of of a hill.
Braid, broad.
Braid-claith, broad-cloth.
Braik, a harrow: 'in pleugh or braik,' i. 161. 12.
Braing't, pulled rashly: 'thou never braing't, an' fetch't, an' fliskit,' i. 103. 13.
Brak, broke.
Brake, broke.
Brak's, broke his.
Branks, a wooden curb, a bridle: 'As cheeks o' branks,' i. 193. 10; 'goavin's he'd been led wi' branks,' ii. 50. 10; 'wi' braw new branks,' ii. 90. 7; 'if the beast and branks be spar'd,' ii. 75. 11.

122   GLOSSARIAL INDEX

Branky, spruce: 'whaur hae ye been sae brankie, O,' iii. 81. 14.
Bran'y, brandy.
Brash, short illness: 'monie a pain an' brash,' i. 23. 17.
Brats, small pieces, rags: 'brats o' claes,' i. 33. 12; 'brats o' duddies,' ii. 130. 2.
Brats, small children: 'our ragged brats and callets,' ii. 19. 3; 'wives and dirty brats,' ii. 156. 7.
Brattle, a spurt, a scamper: 'waur't thee for a brattle,' i. 103. 2; 'wi' bickering brattle,' i. 115. 4.
Brattle, noisy onset: 'brattle o' winter war,' i. 226. 3.
Braw, handsome, fine, gaily dressed [many examples of each of these meanings]. See also Note, vol. ii. 310.
Brawlie, finely, perfectly, heartily.
Braxies, sheep that have died of braxie [a disease]: 'guid fat braxies,' i. 172. 2.
Breastie, dim. of *breast*.
Breastit, sprang forward: 'thou never lap, an' sten't, an' breastit,' i. 104. 9.
Brechan, a horse collar: 'a braw new brechan,' ii. 90. 8.
Breckan, ferns: 'yon lone glen o' green breckan,' iii. 252. 15. See also *Brachens*.
Breedin, breeding, *i.e.* manners: 'has nae sic breedin,' ii. 59. 7.
Breeks, breeches.
Breer, briar.
Brent, brand: 'brent new frae France,' i. 283. 6. See also Note, vol. i. 440.
Brent, straight, steep [*i.e.* not sloping from baldness]: 'your bonie brow was brent,' iii. 63. 8.
Brief, writ: 'King David o' poetic brief,' ii. 96. 13.
Brier, briar.
Briery, briary.
Brig, bridge.
Brisket, breast: 'thy weel-fill'd brisket,' i. 103. 15.
Brither, brother.
Brock, a badger: 'a stinking brock,' i. 12. 22; 'wilcat, brock, an' tod,' ii. 22. 1.
Brogue, a trick: 'an' play'd on man a cursèd brogue,' i. 51. 19.
Broo, soup, broth: 'the flesh to him, the broo to me,' iii. 147. 7; 'suppin hen-broo,' iii. 189. 10; 'dogs like broo,' iii. 190. 10.
Broo, brew, liquid, water: 'the snaw-broo rowes,' i. 205. 10; 'I've borne aboon the broo,' i. 206. 24.
Brooses, wedding races from the church to the home of the bride: 'at brooses thou had ne'er a fellow,' i. 102. 15.
Brose, a thick mixture of meal and warm water, also a synonym for porridge: 'they maun hae brose,' ii. 130. 2; 'then cogs o' brose,' iii. 75. 15; 'ye butter'd my brose,' iii. 140. 9. See Note, vol. ii. 378, and also Note, vol. iii. 399.
Browst, malt liquor [and properly the whole liquor brewed

GLOSSARIAL INDEX 123

at one time]: 'the browst she brew'd,' iii. 15. 3.
Browster wives, ale wives: 'browster wives an' whisky-stills,' ii. 75. 3. See also Note, vol. ii. 357.
Brugh, a burgh, a borough.
Brulzie, brulyie, (1) a brawl: 'than mind sic brulzie,' i. 175. 22; (2) brangle: 'Hell mixed in the brulyie,' ii. 188. 12; 'wha in a brulyie,' iii. 176. 1.
Brunstane, brimstone.
Brunt, burned.
Brust, burst.
Buckie, dim. of *buck*, a smart younker: 'that daft buckie, Geordie Wales,' ii. 132. 21; 'envious buckies,' ii. 134. 5.
Buckle, a curl: 'his hair has a natural buckle,' iii. 61. 8.
Buckskin, Virginian: 'the buckskins claw,' i. 247. 22; 'the buckskin kye,' i. 179. 9. See also Note, vol. i. 385.
Budget, tinker's bag of tools: 'the budget and the apron,' ii. 13. 20; 'here's to budgets,' ii. 19. 1. See also Note, vol. ii. 311.
Buff, to bang, to thump: 'buff our beef,' ii. 24. 5.
Bughtin, folding [*i.e.* gathering sheep into the fold]: 'tells bughtin time is near, my jo,' iii. 284. 2.
Buirdly, (1) stout, stalwart: 'buirdly chiels,' i. 12. 15; (2) stately: 'a filly buirdly,' i. 100. 14.
Bum, the buttocks: 'many a tatter'd rag hanging over my bum,' ii. 3. 8.

Bum, to hum: 'ayont the dyke she's heard you bummin,' i. 49. 1; 'bum owre their treasure,' i. 171. 16.
Bum-clock, the beetle: 'the bum-clock humm'd wi' lazy drone,' i. 19. 1.
Bummle, a drone, a useless fellow: 'some drowsy bummle,' i. 145. 6.
Bunker, a seat: 'a wunnock-bunker in the east,' i. 283. 9.
Bunters, harlots: 'and kissing barefit bunters,' ii. 185. 22.
Burdies, dim. of *bird* or *burd* [a lady], maidens: 'ae blink o' the bonie burdies,' i. 284. 20. See also *Birdie*. Cf. *Burd Ellen*.
Bure, bore.
Burn, a rivulet.
Burnewin, the blacksmith [*i.e.* burn the wind]: 'then Burnewin comes on like death,' i. 22. 11.
Burnie, dim. of *burn* [a rivulet].
Burr-thistle, spear-thistle: 'the rough burr-thistle spreading wide,' ii. 105. 1.
Busk, (1) to dress, to garb: 'New Brig was buskit in a braw new coat,' i. 203. 17; 'they'll busk her like a fright,' ii. 54. 5; 'busking bowers,' ii. 175. 3; (2) to dress up: 'busks his skinklin patches,' iv. 51. 19; (3) to trim, to adorn: 'her bonie buskit nest,' ii. 53. 15; 'weel buskit up sae gaudy,' iii. 116. 2.
Busking, v. *Busk*.
Buskit, v. *Busk*.
Buss, a bush: 'like a rash-buss

stood in sight,' i. 49. 9; 'but buss or bield,' iii. 178. 11.
Bussle, bustle.
But, without.
But, butt, in the kitchen [*i.e.* the outer apartment], 'butt the house'=in the kitchen, ii. 125. 4. See also *Ben*.
By, past, aside.
By, beside.
By himsel, beside himself, off his wits: 'monie a day was by himsel,' i. 94. 16.
Bye attour [*i.e.* 'by and attour' =beside and at a distance], moreover: 'bye attour my gutcher has,' iii. 156. 5.
Byke, (1) a bees' nest, a hive: 'assail their byke,' i. 286. 2; (2) a swarm, a crowd: 'the glowrin byke,' ii. 15. 12; 'the hungry bike,' iv. 23. 15.
Byre, a cowhouse.

Ca', a call.
Ca', to call.
Ca', a knock.
Ca', to knock [*e.g.* a nail], to drive [*e.g.* cattle].
Ca'd, ca't, called.
Ca'd, ca't, knocked, driven.
Cadger, a hawker: 'a cadger pownie's death,' i. 157. 1; 'like onie cadger's whup,' ii. 2. 10.
Cadie, caddie, a varlet: 'e'en cowe the cadie,' i. 32. 4; 'Auld-Light caddies,' i. 174. 8.
Caff, chaff.
Caird, a tinker.
Calf-ward, grazing plot for calves [*i.e.* churchyard].
Callan, callant, a stripling.
Caller, cool, refreshing: 'the caller air,' i. 36. 4; 'little fishes' caller rest,' iii. 114. 14.
Callet, a trull: 'my bottle and my callet,' ii. 3. 9; 'our ragged brats and callets,' ii. 19. 3.
Cam, came.
Canie, cannie, (1) gentle: 'bonie wee thing, cannie wee thing,' iii. 103. 5; 'cannie young man,' iii. 44. 9; (2) tractable: 'tawie, quiet, an' cannie,' i. 101. 15; (3) quiet: 'a cannie errand,' i. 107. 18; 'a cannie hour at e'en,' i. 252. 5; 'then cannie,' i. 64. 11; 'kind and cannie,' ii. 134. 13; (4) prudent: 'wi' cannie care,' i. 90. 8; i. 177. 15; ii. 43. 20; and ii. 117. 1; (5) careful: 'cannie for hoarding o' money,' ii. 210. 13.
Cankrie, crabbed: 'O' cankrie Care,' ii. 100. 18.
Canna, cannot.
Cannie, (1) gently: 'straik her cannie,' i. 31. 18; (2) quietly: 'slade cannie to her bed,' i. 198. 17; (3) sensibly: 'and cannie wale,' iii. 118. 7; (4) carefully: 'I maun guide it cannie,' i. 250. 18; (5) expertly: 'nickin down fu' cannie,' ii. 73. 13.
Canniest, quietest: 'the canniest gate, the strife is sair,' iv. 118. 22.
Cannilie, cannily, quietly, prudently, cautiously: 'cannilie he hums them,' i. 43. 2; 'cannily keekit ben,' iii. 36. 2; 'cannily steal on a bonie moor-hen,' iv. 20. 4.

GLOSSARIAL INDEX 125

Cantie, cheerful, lively, jolly, merry [very many examples].
Cantraip, (1) magic: 'by cantraip wit,' i. 50. 10; 'cantraip sleight,' i. 283. 17; (2) witching: 'some cantraip hour,' ii. 103. 2.
Cants, (1) merry stories: 'monie cracks and cants,' i. 176. 7; (2) canters or sprees or merry doings: 'a' my cants,' ii. 97. 1.
Cape-stane, cope-stone.
Capon, castrate: 'their capon cries,' iv. 23. 13. See also Note, vol. iv. p. 91.
Car'd na by, cared not a jot, iii. 105. 3.
Care na by, (1) do not care, i. 251. 5; (2) care nothing, iii. 58. 15; (3) care not although you do, iii. 37. 8.
Carl, carle [from churl], a man, an old man.
Carl-hemp, male-hemp: 'thou stalk o' carl-hemp,' ii. 130. 14.
Carlie, a mannikin: 'a fusionless carlie,' iii. 140. 4.
Carlin, carline, a middle-aged, or old woman, a beldam, a witch.
Carmagnole, a violent Jacobin: 'that curst carmagnole Auld Satan,' ii. 140. 1. See also Note, vol. ii. 380.
Cartes, playing cards.
Cartie, dim. of *cart*: 'or hurl in a cartie,' ii. 89. 4.
Ca't, v. *Ca'd*.
Catch-the-plack, the hunt for coin, i. 160. 16.
Caudron, a caldron: 'fry them in his caudrons,' i. 214. 6; v. *cauldron*.

Cauf, a calf.
Cauf-leather, calf-leather.
Cauk, chalk: 'o' caulk and keel'=in chalk and ruddle, i. 290. 6.
Cauld, cold.
Cauld, the cold.
Cauldness, coldness.
Cauldron, caldron: 'clout the cauldron,' ii. 13. 16; v. *Caudron*.
Caup, a wooden drinking-vessel [*i.e.* cup]: 'the lugget caup,' i. 22. 10; 'yill-caup commentators,' i. 43. 7; 'in cogs an' caups,' i. 45. 10; 'that kiss'd his caup,' ii. 180. 17. See also Note, vol. i. 335.
Causey-cleaners, causeway-cleaners.
Cavie, a hen-coop: 'behint the chicken-cavie,' ii. 14. 17.
Chamer, chaumer, chamber.
Change-house, tavern.
Chanter, (1) bagpipes, the pipe of the bagpipes which produces the melody: 'your chanters tune,' i. 58. 14; 'chanters winna hain,' i. 168. 15; (2) syn. for *song*: 'quat my chanter,' ii. 76. 4. and ii. 126. 26. See also Notes, vol. i. 346 and 384.
Chap, a fellow, a young fellow.
Chap, to strike: 'ay chap the thicker,' ii. 72. 14.
Chapman, a pedlar.
Chaumer, v. *Chamer*.
Chaup (or *chap*), a stroke, a blow: 'at ev'ry chaup,' i. 22. 12.
Chear, cheer, to cheer.
Chearfu', cheerful.

Chearless, cheerless.
Cheary, cheery.
Cheek-for-chow, cheek-by-jowl [*i.e.* close beside]: 'cheek-for-chow, a chuffie vintner,' i. 28. 15; 'cheek-for-chow, shall jog thegither,' ii. 101. 21.
Cheep, peep, squeak: 'wi' tunefu' cheep,' i. 213. 1; 'cheeps like some bewildered chicken,' ii. 55. 18.
Chiel, chield [*i.e.* child], a fellow, a young fellow [indicates approval].
Chimla, chimney.
Chow, v. *Cheek-for-chow*.
Chows, chews.
Chuck, a hen, a dear: 'the martial chuck,' ii. 4. 7. Cf. 'pray chuck come thither,' Shak. *Othello*, iv. 2. 24.
Chuckie, dim. of *chuck*, but usually signifies mother-hen, an old dear: 'auld chuckie Reekie,'ii. 53. 13; 'a daintie[y] chuckie,' ii. 131. 7; iii. 22. 2.
Chuffie, fat-faced: 'a chuffie vintner,' i. 28. 15.
Chuse, to choose.
Cit, the civet: 'the cit and polecat stink,' i. 271. 18.
Cit, a citizen, a merchant.
Clachan, a small village about a church, a hamlet (R. B.): 'the clachan yill,' i. 192. 1; 'Jock Hornbook i' the clachan,' i. 195. 5; 'within the clachan,' ii. 45. 10.
Claeding, clothing.
Claes, claise, clothes.
Claith, cloth.
Claithing, clothing.

Claivers, v. *Clavers*.
Clankie, a severe knock: 'Clavers got a clankie, O,' iii. 82. 6.
Clap, the clapper of a mill: 'and still the clap plays clatter,' i. 218. 4.
Clark, clerkly, scholarly: 'learned and clark,' ii. 217. 11.
Clark, a clerk: 'like onie clark,' ii. 74. 12.
Clarkit, clerked, wrote: 'in a bank and clarkit,' i. 75. 19.
Clarty, dirty: 'clarty barm,' ii. 247. 13.
Clash, an idle tale, the story of a day (R. B.): 'the countra clash,' i. 60. 15.
Clash, to tattle, ii. 37. 16. See Note, vol. ii. 335.
Clatter, (1) noise: 'the clap plays clatter' [*i.e.* clapper], i. 218. 4; 'bade me mak nae clatter,' iii. 150. 6; (2) tattle, gossip: 'kintra clatter,' ii. 37. 14 and iii. 177. 16; (3) talk: 'sangs and clatter,' i. 280. 13; 'anither gies them clatter,' ii. 174. 14; (4) disputation: 'a' this clatter,' i. 175. 17; (5) babble: 'rhymin clatter,' ii. 81. 9.
Clatter, (1) to make a noise by striking: 'the pint-stowp clatters,' i. 43. 9; 'gar him clatter,' i. 160. 7; 'clatter on my stumps,' ii. 3. 6; (2) to babble: 'the gossips clatter bright,' i. 22. 20; (3) to prattle: 'clatters, "Tam Samson's dead,"' i. 223. 3.
Claught, clutched, seized: 'claught her by the rump,'

i. 286. 25; 'claught th' unfading garland,' ii. 227. 11.
Claughtin, clutching, grasping: 'claughtin't together,' ii. 210. 14.
Claut, (1) a clutch: 'our sinfu' saul to get a claut on,' ii. 140. 3; (2) a handful: 'a claut o' gear,' iii. 112. 1.
Claut, to scrape: 'ye claut my byre,' ii. 460. 13.
Clautet, scraped: 'the laggen they hae clautet,' i. 74. 8.
Claver, clover.
Clavers, (1) gossip: 'clavers and havers,' ii. 104. 13; (2) nonsense: 'heaps o' clavers,' iv. 51. 2.
Claw, a scratch, a blow.
Claw, to scratch, to strike.
Clay-cauld, clay-cold.
Claymore, a two-handed Highland sword: 'an' guid claymore,' ii. 9. 2; 'wi' dirk, claymore,' ii. 154. 4.
Cleckin, a brood: 'its minnie and the cleckin,' ii. 55. 19.
Cleed, to clothe.
Cleek, to snatch: 'cleek the sterlin,'=pinch the ready, ii. 8. 2. See also Note, vol. ii. 310.
Cleekit, took hold: 'they cross'd, they cleekit,' i. 284. 9.
Cleg, gadfly: 'the clegs o' feeling stang,' ii. 101. 9.
Clink, (1) a sharp stroke: 'her doup a clink,' ii. 46. 3; (2) jingle: 'o' rhymin clink,' ii. 82. 14.
Clink, (1) money, coin: 'o' needfu' clink,' ii. 126. 21; (2) wealth: 'the name o' clink,' iii. 37. 18.
Clink, to chink: 'he'll clink in the hand,' ii. 208. 3.
Clink, to rhyme: 'mak it clink,' i. 163. 9; 'gar them clink,' ii. 82. 6.
Clinkin, with a smart motion: 'clinkin' down beside him,' i. 40. 13.
Clinkum, *Clinkumbell*, the beadle, the bellman: 'auld Clinkum at the inner port,' ii. 97. 15; 'Clinkumbell, wi' rattlin tow,' i. 46. 10.
Clips, shears: 'ne'er cross'd the clips,' i. 58. 5.
Clish-ma-claver, (1) gossip, taletelling: 'for a' their clish-ma-claver,' i. 72. 13; (2) nonsense, idle talk: 'what farther clish-ma-claver might been said,' i. 208. 5.
Clockin-time, clucking-[=hatching-] time: 'the clockin-time is by,' i. 179. 5.
Cloot, the hoof in general, the half of the cloven hoof: 'upon her cloot she coost a hitch,' i. 53. 13; 'an' wear his cloots,' i. 55. 19.
Clootie, *Cloots*, Hoofie, Hoofs [a nickname of the Devil]: 'Auld Cloots,' i. 52. 19; 'Nick or Clootie,' i. 47. 7; 'auld Cloven-Clootie's haunts,' ii. 97. 3.
Clour, a bump or swelling after a blow (R. B.): 'clours an' nicks,' i. 174. 2.
Clout, (1) a cloth, a rag: 'wi' lies seam'd like a beggar's clout,' see vol. i. 440; (2) a

GLOSSARIAL INDEX

patch : 'perhaps a clout may fail in't,' iii. 196. 6. See also *Babie-clout*.

Clout, to patch : 'clout the cauldron,' ii. 13. 16; 'clout the bad girdin o't,' iii. 24. 8; 'reft and clouted,' i. 69. 20; 'cloutin a kettle,' iii. 66. 19.

Clud, a cloud.

Clunk, to make a hollow sound : 'made the bottle clunk,' ii. 14. 12. See also Note, vol. ii. 311.

Coatie, dim. of *coat*.

Coble, a broad and flat boat: 'wintle like a saumont-coble,' i. 102. 2.

Cock, the mark [in curling]: 'station at the cock,' i. 221. 15.

Cockie, dim. of *cock* [applied to an old man]: 'my guid auld cockie,' ii. 131. 9.

Cocks, fellows, good fellows : 'my hearty cocks,' i. 32. 3; 'the wale o' cocks,' i. 176. 2.

Cod, a pillow: 'a cod she laid below my head,' iii. 163. 9; 'the cradle wants a cod,' iii. 205. 2.

Coft, bought : 'coft for her wee Nannie,' i. 285. 12; 'I coft a stane o' haslock woo,' iii. 159. 5; 'that coft enjoyment,' iii. 209. 14.

Cog, (1) a wooden drinking-vessel ; 'in cogs an' caups,' i. 45. 10; 'in cog or bicker,' i. 22. 4; 'cog an' ye were ay fou,' iii. 26. 1; 'a cog o' guid swats,' iii. 234. 4; (2) a porridge-dish: 'their cogs o' brose,' iii. 75. 15; (3) a corn measure for horses: 'thy cog a wee bit heap,' i. 104. 3. See also Note, vol. i. 323.

Coggie, dim. of *cog*, a little dish.

Coil, *Coila*, Kyle [one of the ancient districts of Ayrshire]. See Note, vol. i. 320.

Collie, (1) a general, and sometimes a particular, name for country curs (R. B.) ; (2) a sheep-dog : 'a ploughman's collie,' i. 10. 5.

Collieshangie, a squabble : ' or how the collieshangie works,' ii. 131. 19.

Cood, cud.

Coof, v. *cuif*.

Cookin, cooking.

Cookit, hid: 'cookit underneath the braes,' i. 98. 7.

Coor, cover : 'coor their fuds,' ii. 17. 5.

Cooser, a courser, a stallion : 'a perfect kintra cooser,' ii. 132. 24.

Coost [*i.e.* cast], (1) looped: 'coost a hitch,' i. 53. 13 ; (2) threw off : 'coost their claes,' i. 249. 11; 'coost her duddies,' i. 284. 11; (3) toss'd : ' Maggie coost her head,' iii. 215. 5; (4) chucked : 'coost it in a corner,' ii. 257. 11.

Cootie, a small pail: 'the brunstane cootie,' i. 47. 10.

Cootie, leg-plumed: 'cootie moorcocks,' i. 222. 8.

Corbies, ravens, crows: 'corbies and clergy,' i. 207. 16.

Core, corps.

Corn mou, corn heap: 'commend me to the corn mou,' iii. 25. 6.

GLOSSARIAL INDEX

Corn't, fed with corn: 'thou was corn't,' i. 102. 13.
Corse, corpse: 'the pale corse on the plain,' iii. 211. 14.
Corss, cross: 'Mauchline Corss,' ii. 83. 14.
Cou'dna, couldna, couldn't.
Countra, country.
Coup, to capsize: 'coup the cran'=upset the pot, ii. 97. 9.
Couthie, couthy, (1) loving: 'couthie Fortune,' ii. 134. 13; (2) affable: 'fu' couthy and sweet,' ii. 243. 11.
Couthie, comfortably: 'kindle couthie, side by side,' i. 91. 1.
Cowe, to scare, to daunt: 'cowe the cadie,' i. 32. 4; 'cowe the louns,' i. 175. 5; 'cowe the blellums,' ii. 78. 6; 'cowe the lairds,' ii. 24. 16; 'cowe the rebel generation,' ii. 155. 15.
Cowe, to crop: 'cowe her measure shorter,' i. 215. 13.
Crack, (1) tale: 'tell your crack,' i. 28. 5; (2) a chat: 'a hearty crack,' ii. 265. 20; 'ca' the crack'=have a chat, i. 155. 8; (3) talk: 'hear your crack,' i. 157. 4 and 160. 18; 'for crack that day,' i. 46. 18.
Crack, to chat, to talk: 'the father cracks of horses,' i. 109. 9; 'wha will crack to me my lane,' iii. 70. 13.
Crackin, conversing: 'crackin crouse,' i. 14. 21.
Cracks, (1) stories: 'cracks and cants,' i. 176. 7; (2) conversation: 'gashing at their cracks,' i. 92. 12; 'an' friendly cracks,' i. 98. 6.

Craft, croft.
Craft-rig, croft-ridge.
Craig, the throat: 'that nicket Abel's craig,' i. 291. 19.
Craig, a crag.
Craigie, dim. of *craig*, the throat: 'weet my craigie,' ii. 14. 4; 'thy bonie craigie,' iii. 175. 5.
Craigy, craggy.
Craik, the corn-crake, the landrail: 'the craik amang the clover hay,' iii. 115. 1; 'mourn clam'ring craiks, at close o' day,' i. 264. 13.
Crambo-clink, rhyme: 'live by crambo-clink,' i. 144. 6.
Crambo-jingle, rhyming: 'I to the crambo-jingle fell,' i. 157. 7.
Cran, the support for a pot or kettle: 'coup the cran,' ii. 97. 9.
Crankous, fretful: 'in crankous mood,' i. 31. 5.
Cranks, creakings: 'what tuneless cranks,' i. 24. 15.
Cranreuch, hoar-frost, rime: 'cranreuch cauld,' i. 116. 16; 'hoary cranreuch drest,' ii. 1. 6.
Crap, crop.
Crap, to crop: 'that crap the heather bud,' i. 264. 2.
Craps, (1) crops: 'his craps and kye,' iii. 118. 15; (2) tops: 'craps o' heather'=heathertops, i. 35. 15.
Craw, crow.
Creel, an osier basket: 'my senses wad be in a creel'= I would be perplexed, i. 167. 13. See also Note, vol. i.

VOL. IV.

383; 'in Death's fish-creel,' i. 222. 5; 'nieves, like midden-creels,' iii. 126. 9. See vol. iii. 389.

Creepie-chair, stool of repentance: 'mount the creepie-chair,' iii. 70. 9. See also Note, vol. ii. 343 ('Cutty-stools').

Creeshie, greasy.

Crocks, old ewes: 'tent the waifs an' crocks,' ii. 20. 5.

Cronie, intimate friend.

Crooded, cooed: 'a cushat crooded o'er me,' iv. 12. 15.

Croods, coos: 'the cushat croods,' i. 170. 11.

Croon, (1) moan: 'wi' eldritch croon,' i. 48. 18; (2) a low: 'an outler quey gat up an' gae a croon,' i. 98. 13; (3) note: 'the melancholious croon,' i. 58. 15; 'melancholious, sairie croon,' ii. 100. 16.

Croon, to toll: 'jow an' croon,' i. 46. 11.

Croon'd, hummed: 'croon'd his gamut,' ii. 10. 16.

Crooning, humming: 'crooning to a body's sel,' i. 157. 9; 'crooning o'er some auld Scots sonnet,' i. 281. 26.

Croose, crouse, (1) cocksure: 'keen an' croose,' i. 50. 8; (2) set: 'when I grow crouse,' ii. 96. 7; (3) proud: 'crouse and canty,' iii. 216. 19.

Crouchie, hunchbacked; 'crouchie Merran Humphie,' i. 96. 6.

Crouse, cheerfully: 'crackin crouse,' i. 14. 21; v. *Croose*.

Crously, confidently: 'crousely craw,' i. 222. 8.

Crowdie, meal and cold water, meal and milk, porridge: 'wi' crowdie unto me,' iii. 75. 8; 'ance crowdie, twice crowdie,' etc., iii. 206. 1.

Crowdie-time, porridge-time [*i.e.* breakfast-time]; i. 38. 13.

Crowlin, crawling: 'ye crowlin ferlie,' i. 152. 13.

Crummie, a horned cow; 'auld Crummie's nicks,' ii. 85. 13.

Crummock, cummock, a cudgel, a crooked staff [cf. the Gaelic or Welsh *cam* or *cum* = the crook of a stick, and *camon* = Irish hockey]: 'louping and flinging on a crummock,' i. 284. 23; 'on a cummock driddle,' ii. 100. 11.

Crump, crisp: 'farls . . . fu' crump,' i. 39. 5.

Crunt, a blow: 'wi' hearty crunt,' i. 174. 4.

Cuddle, to fondle: 'bairns' bairns kindly cuddle,' ii. 81. 15; 'cuddle my kimmer,' iii. 67. 3.

Cuddl'd, fondled: 'cuddl'd me late and early,' iii. 140. 10.

Cuif, coof, (1) a dolt, a ninny, a weakling: 'fumbling cuifs,' i. 23. 1; 'blockhead, coof,' i. 76. 1; 'coofs on countless thousands rant,' i. 118. 5; 'cuifs o' later times,' i. 206. 10; 'a wealthy coof,' iii. 112. 5; 'a coof . . . wi' routh o' gear,' iii. 140. 17; 'he's but a cuif,' iii. 272. 12; 'will be nae coof,' iv. 13. 15; (2) a dastard: 'a cuif like him,' ii. 267. 3.

Cummock, v. *Crummock*.

Curch, a kerchief for the

GLOSSARIAL INDEX 131

head: 'her curch sae clean,' iii. 22. 1; 'I tint my curch,' iii. 23. 18.
Curchie, a curtsy: 'wi' a curchie low did stoop,' i. 37. 12.
Curler, one who plays at curling [a game on the ice]: 'the curlers quat their roaring play,' i. 74. 11; 'to the loughs the curlers flock,' i. 221. 13.
Curmurring, commotion: 'curmurring in his guts,' i. 198. 20.
Curpin, the crupper of a horse: 'haurls at his curpin,' i. 95. 9.
Curple, the crupper [*i.e.* buttocks]: 'hingin owre my curple,' ii. 106. 20.
Cushat, the wood pigeon.
Custock, the pith of the colewort: 'gif the custock's sweet or sour,' i. 90. 5.
Cutes, feet [properly of an animal], ankles: 'her bonie cutes sae sma',' ii. 61. 15.
Cutty, short: 'cutty sark,' i. 285. 7; 'Cutty-sark,' *ib.* 25; 'cutty sarks,' i. 287. 4.
Cutty-stools, stools of repentance: 'daft bargains, cutty-stools,' ii. 52. 18. See also Note, vol. ii. 343.

Dad, daddie, father.
Daez't, dazed.
Daffin, larking, fun: 'to spend an hour in daffin,' i. 38. 6; 'fits o' daffin,' i. 217. 16; 'towsing a lass i' my daffin,' ii. 7. 8.
Daft, mad, foolish.

Dails, planks: 'some carryin dails,' i. 39. 12.
Daimen icker, an odd ear of corn: 'a daimen icker in a thrave,' i. 115. 15.
Dam, pent up water, urine: 'ye tine your dam,' i. 35. 16.
Damie, dim. of *dame*.
Dang, dung [pret. of *ding*].
Danton, v. *Daunton*.
Darena, dare not.
Darg, labour, task, a day's labour: 'nought but his han' darg,' i. 12. 7; 'monie a sair darg,' i. 105. 1.
Darklins, in the dark: 'an' darklins grapit for the bauks,' i. 92. 16.
Daud, to pelt: 'set the bairns to daud her,' i. 211. 4; 'the bitter, daudin showers,' ii. 74. 8.
Daunton, to daunt.
Daur, dare.
Daurna, dare not.
Daur't, dared.
Daut, Dawte, to fondle, to pet: 'I kiss and daut thee,' ii. 38. 20; iii. 89. 2; 'kiss and dawte,' iii. 150. 10.
Dautet, Dawtit, petted; 'unco muckle dautet,' i. 74. 2; 'dawtit twal-pint hawkie,' i. 50. 5.
Daw, to dawn: 'the day may daw,' iii. 80. 3.
Dawds, lumps, large portions: 'an' dawds that day,' i. 45. 14.
Dawing, dawning.
Dawtingly, pettingly, caressingly: 'dawtingly did cheer me,' iii. 104. 10.

Dead-sweer, extremely reluctant, i. 150. 23.
Dearie, dim. of *dear*.
Deave, to deafen.
Deevil, v. *Deil*.
Deil, devil.
Deil-haet (1) nothing [Devil have it]: 'the deil-haet ails them,' i. 17. 20; (2) Devil have my soul; 'the devil-haet that I sud ban,' ii. 82. 15.
Deil-ma-care, no matter [the Devil may care, but not I], i. 178. 10; i. 195. 20; ii. 87. 5.
Deleeret, delirious, mad: 'an' liv'd an' died deleeret,' i. 93. 22.
Delvin, digging: 'dubs of your ain delvin,' i. 149. 25.
Dern'd, hid [from the Old Eng. *dearn* or *dern*: 'that dern time,' Craig's Oxford Shak. *King Lear*, iii. 1. 62]: 'dern'd in dens and hollows,' ii. 45. 11.
Descrive, to describe.
Deuk's, the duck has: 'The Deuk's Dang O'er My Daddie,' iii. 139.
Deuks, ducks: 'your deuks and geese,' ii. 156. 10.
Devel, a stunning blow: 'an unco devel,' i. 221. 9.
Diddle, to move quickly [of fiddling]: 'elbuck jink an' diddle,' ii. 81. 12, and ii. 100. 8.
Dight, to wipe.
Dight, winnowed, sifted: 'the cleanest corn that e'er was dight,' i. 217. 14.
Din, dun, muddy of complexion: 'dour and din,' ii. 206. 11, and iii. 125. 5.

Ding, to beat, to surpass.
Ding, be beaten or upset: 'facts are chiels that winna ding,' i. 69. 17.
Dink, trim: 'my lady's dink, my lady's drest,' iii. 199. 17.
Dinna, do not.
Dirl, to vibrate, to ring: 'played dirl'=went tinkle, i. 195. 21; 'roof and rafters a' did dirl,' i. 283. 14; 'she dirl'd them aff fu' clearly,' iv. 23. 10.
Diz'n, *dizzen*, dozen.
Dochter, daughter.
Doggie, dim. of *dog*.
Doited, (1) muddled: 'doited Lear,' i. 21. 5; 'a doited monkish race,' i. 206. 8; 'my very senses doited,' ii. 112. 4; (2) stupid, bewildered: 'doited stots,' ii. 62. 1; 'the doited beastie stammers,' ii. 90. 12; 'sae doited and blin',' iii. 157. 11.
Donsie, (1) vicious, bad-tempered: 'ye ne'er was donsie,' i. 101. 14; (2) restive: 'their donsie tricks,' i. 218. 11; (3) testy: 'ye wad na been sae donsie, O,' iii. 140. 8.
Dool, (1) woe: 'sing dool,' i. 189. 5; 'may dool and sorrow be his lot,' i. 268. 7; 'O, dool on the day,' iii. 94. 7; (2) sorrow: 'to sit in dool,' iii. 65. 19; 'bitter in dool,' iii. 67. 5; 'care and dool,' iii. 91. 14; 'dool and care,' iii. 154. 3; (3) 'dool to tell'=sad to tell,' ii. 21. 2.
Doolfu', doleful, woful: 'dool-

GLOSSARIAL INDEX 133

fu' clamour,' ii. 54. 20; 'the doolfu' tale,' iii. 114. 18.

Dorty, pettish : 'tho' a minister grow dorty,' i. 33. 7.

Douce, douse, sedate, sober, serious, prudent: 'douce honest woman,' i. 48. 20; 'O ye douce folk,' i. 66. 13; 'douce or merry tale,' i. 156. 14; 'douce conveners,' i. 206. 18; 'douce folk,' *ib.* 24; 'thrifty citizens an' douce,' i. 207. 7; 'douce Wisdom's door,' i. 218. 7; 'for ye sae douce,' i. 252. 9; 'sae cursèd douce,' ii. 125. 3.

Douce, doucely, dousely, (1) sedately : 'douce hingin owre my curple,' ii. 106. 20; (2) prudently: 'doucely manage our affairs,' i. 26. 3; 'doucely fill a throne,' i. 72. 12.

Doudl'd, dandled : 'doudl'd me up on his knee,' iii. 3. 2.

Dought [pret. of *dow*], could : 'as lang 's he dought,' i. 247. 21; 'do what I dought,' ii. 112. 5; 'dought na bear us,' ii. 244. 2.

Doukèd, ducked : 'in monie a well been doukèd,' ii. 8. 4.

Doup, the bottom.

Doup-skelper, bottom-smacker: 'vile doup-skelper, Emperor Joseph,' ii. 131. 17.

Dour, Doure, (1) stubborn, obstinate : 'teughly doure,' i. 203. 16; 'the tither's dour,' ii. 59. 7; 'and Sackville doure,' ii. 248. 3; 'dour and din,' ii. 206. 11, and iii. 125. 5; (2) cutting : 'fell and doure,' i. 225. 12.

Douse, v. *Douce.*

Douser, sedater : 'oughtlins douser,' ii. 132. 23.

Dow, dowe, am [is or are] able, can : 'the best they dow,' i. 46. 12; 'dow but hoyte and hobble,' i. 102. 1; 'as lang's I dow,' i. 164. 6; 'dow scarcely spread her wing,' i. 177. 18; 'hirples twa-fold as he dow,' iii. 31. 13; 'dow nocht but glow'r,' iii. 230. 15.

Dow, a dove, a pigeon : 'like frighted dows, man,' iii. 74. 20.

Dowf, dowff, dull : 'her dowff excuses,' i. 162. 13; 'dowff an' dowilie,' ii. 59. 20; 'dowf and weary,' iii. 284. 4.

Dowie, drooping, mournful: 'our Bardie, dowie,' i. 57. 1; 'dowie, stiff and crazy,' i. 100. 7; 'dowie she saunters,' ii. 116. 20; 'I wander dowie up the glen,' iii. 43. 6; 'some that are dowie,' iii. 44. 15.

Dowie, mournfully : 'his sad complaining dowie raves,' iii. 152. 16.

Dowilie, drooping : 'dowff an' dowilie they creep,' ii. 59. 20.

Downa, cannot.

Downa-do, cannot-do, iii. 140. 11.

Doylt, stupid, stupefied : 'doylt, drucken hash,' i. 23. 19; 'he's doylt and he's dozin,' iii. 93. 17.

Doytin, doddering: 'cam doytin by,' i. 53. 6.

Dozen'd, torpid : 'dearest member nearly dozen'd,' ii. 124. 12.

134   GLOSSARIAL INDEX

Dozin, torpid: 'he's doylt and he's dozin,' iii. 93. 17.
Draigl't, draggled.
Drants, prosings: 'to wait on their drants,' ii. 210. 11.
Drap, drop.
Drappie, dim. of *drop.*
Draunting, tedious: 'draunting drivel,' ii. 141. 6.
Dree, (1) endure: 'dree the kintra clatter,' iii. 177. 16; (2) suffer: 'the pangs I dree,' iii. 153. 6.
Dreigh, v. *Driegh.*
Dribble, drizzle: 'the winter's sleety dribble,' i. 116. 15.
Driddle, to toddle: 'us'd to trystes an' fairs to driddle,' ii. 10. 10; 'on a cummock driddle,' ii. 100. 11. See also Note, vol. ii. 310.
Driegh, tedious, dull: 'stablemeals ... were driegh,' i. 102. 8; 'the moor was dreigh,' iii. 19. 9.
Droddum, the breech: 'dress your droddum,' i. 153. 22.
Drone, part of the bagpipe: iv. 23. 7. See Note, vol. iv. p. 91.
Droop-rumpl't, short-rumped: 'droop-rumpl't cattle,' i. 103. 1.
Drouk, to wet, to drench: 'to drouk the stourie tow,' iii. 108. 12.
Droukit, wetted, soaked: 'my droukit sark-sleeve,' iii. 85. 14.
Drouth, thirst: 'Scotland's drouth,' i. 27. 13; 'their hydra drouth,' ii. 49. 20; 'holy drouth,' ii. 202. 8.
Drouthy, thirsty: 'drouthy neebors,' i. 278. 10; 'drouthy cronie,' i. 280. 10.
Druken, drucken, drunken.
Drumlie, (1) muddy: 'drumlie German-water,' i. 16. 1; 'the drumlie Dutch,' ii. 131. 16; (2) turbid: 'drumlie wave,' iii. 18. 16; 'waters never drumlie,' iii. 255. 9; (3) dull: 'drumlie winter,' iii. 262. 6.
Drummock, raw meal and cold water: 'a bellyfu' o' drummock,' i. 146. 2.
Drunt, the huff: 'took the drunt,' i. 91. 17.
Dry, thirsty: 'confoundedly dry,' ii. 7. 18; 'a' dry wi' drinken o't,' iii. 52. 5.
Dry, dryly: 'answer him fu' dry,' iii. 38. 8.
Dub, puddle, slush: 'thro' dub and mire,' i. 158. 15, and i. 281. 23; 'thro' dirt and dub,' ii. 42. 5.
Dub, a puddle: 'gumlie dubs,' i. 149. 25; 'the burning dub,' ii. 22. 17.
Duddie, ragged: 'tho' e'er sae duddie,' i. 10. 2; 'duddie weans,' i. 12. 6; 'duddie boy,' i. 154. 3; 'duddie, desperate beggar,' ii. 154. 3.
Duddies, dim. of *duds,* rags: 'coost her duddies,' i. 284. 11; 'their orra duddies,' ii. 1. 10; 'brats o' duddies,' ii. 130. 2.
Duds, rags, clothes: 'wi' reekit duds,' i. 52. 2; 'pawn'd their duds,' ii. 17. 4; 'flaffin wi' duds,' ii. 156. 9; 'tartan duds,' iii. 73. 17; 'shook his duds,' iii. 179. 9.
Dung, v. *Dang.*

GLOSSARIAL INDEX

Dunted, throbbed: 'wi' lifeblood dunted,' ii. 138. 3.
Dunts, blows, iii. 110. 4.
Durk, dirk.
Dusht, touch'd: 'eerie's I'd been dusht,' i. 76. 15.
Dwalling, dwelling.
Dwalt, dwelt.
Dyke, (1) a fence [of stone or turf], a wall: 'a sheugh or dyke,' i. 10. 12; 'biggin a dyke,' i. 12. 3; 'yont the dyke,' i. 49. 1; 'your lives a dyke,' i. 66. 18; 'sun oursels about the dyke,' ii. 11. 14; 'about the dykes,' ii. 20. 6; 'owre a dyke,' ii. 62. 6; 'lap o'er the dyke,' iii. 14. 15.
Dyke-back, the back of a fence, i. 157. 2.
Dyke-side, side of a fence: 'a lee dyke-side,' ii. 88. 3.
Dyvor, a bankrupt, 'rot the dyvors,' ii. 156. 2; 'dyvor, beggar loons,' iii. 149. 7.

Ear', early.
Eastlin, eastern.
E'e, eye.
E'ebrie, eyebrow.
Een, eyes.
E'en, even.
E'en, evening.
E'enin, evening.
E'er, ever.
Eerie, apprehensive, inspiring ghostly fear [many examples of both meanings]. See Note, vol. iii. 306.
Eild, eld.
Eke, also.
Elbuck, elbow.
Eldritch, (1) unearthly: 'eldritch squeel,' i. 41. 11; 'eldritch croon,' i. 48. 18; 'an eldritch, stoor "quaick, quaick,"' i. 49. 13; 'eldritch laugh,' i. 198. 1; 'eldritch skriech,'i. 286. 8; (2) haunted: 'eldritch tower,' i. 264. 20; (3) fearsome: 'eldritch part,' i. 290. 10.
Elekit, elected.
Ell [Scots], thirty-seven inches.
Eller, elder: 'me the Eller's dochter,' iii. 194. 12.
En', end.
Eneugh, enough.
Enfauld, infold.
Enow, enough.
Erse, Gaelic: 'a Lallan tongue or Erse,' i. 52. 17.
Ether-stane, adder-stone: 'and make his ether-stane,' ii. 176. 14. See Note, vol. ii. 395.
Ettle, aim: 'wi' furious ettle,' i. 286. 21.
Evermair, evermore.
Ev'n down, downright, positive: 'ev'n down want o' wark,' i. 17. 18.
Expeckit, expected.
Eydent, diligent: 'wi' an eydent hand,' i. 108. 12.

Fa', fall, to fall.
Fa', lot, portion.
Fa', (1) to have: 'best deserves to fa' that,' ii. 191. 14 and 18; (2) suit: 'weel does Selkirk fa' that,' ii. 192. 12; (3) claim: 'guid faith he mauna fa' that,' iii. 272. 20. See Note, vol. iii. 491; and, in addition, *cf.* Alexander Scott's *When His Wife Left*

136 GLOSSARIAL INDEX

Him: 'For fient a crumb of thee she fa's' [*i.e.* claims].
Faddom'd, fathomed.
Fae, foe.
Faem, foam.
Faiket, let off, excused: 'sic han's as you sud ne'er be faiket,' ii. 82. 3.
Fain, fond, glad. V. *Fidginfain*.
Fainness, fondness: 'wi' fainness grat,' iii. 104. 15.
Fair fa', good befall! welcome! 'fair fa' your honest sonsie face,' i. 237. 1; 'fair fa' my collier laddie,' iii. 116. 16. *Cf.* 'fair fall the bones that took the pains for me,' Shak. *King John*, i. 1. 78.
Fairin, a present from a fair: 'he gets his fairin,' i. 199. 22; 'thou'll get thy fairin,' i. 286. 9. See Note, vol. i. 393.
Fallow, fellow.
Fa'n, fallen.
Fand, found.
Far-aff, far-off.
Farls, small, thin oat-cakes: 'farls, bak'd wi' butter,' i. 39. 4.
Fash, annoyance: 'to gie ane fash,' ii. 37. 18; 'or fash o' fools,' ii. 52. 21.
Fash, (1) to trouble: 'fash your thumb'=care a rap, i. 27. 18; 'I never fash'=I never trouble about, i. 60. 17; 'fash your head,' i. 118. 7; (2) worry: 'fash me for't,' i. 178. 9; 'fash nae mair,' ii. 82. 22.
Fash'd, fash't, (1) bothered: 'they're fash't eneugh,' i. 12.

1; 'they seldom fash't him,' ii. 217. 1; (2) irked: 'fash'd wi' fleshly lust,' ii. 27. 6.
Fashious, troublesome: 'fin' them fashious,' ii. 126. 12.
Fasten-e'en, Fasten's Even [the evening before Lent], i. 155. 7.
Faught, a fight.
Fauld, the sheep-fold.
Fauld, folded: 'within his mouth was fauld,' ii. 461. 2.
Faulding, folding, sheep-folding: 'a-faulding let us gang,' iii. 268. 7. See also Note, vol. iii. 488; 'faulding slap'= fold gate; 'steeks his faulding slap,' i. 254. 5.
Faun, fallen.
Fause, false.
Fause-house, hole in a cornstack: 'kiutlin in the fause-house,' i. 90. 17; 'the fause-house in her min',' i. 92. 1. See also Note, vol. i. 358.
Faut, fault.
Fautor, transgressor: 'syne, say I was a fautor,' iii. 150. 12; 'tho' he be the fautor,' iii. 177. 10.
Fawsont, (1) seemly, well-doing: 'honest fawsont folk,' i. 15. 2; (2) good-looking: 'aughtlins fawsont,' ii. 156. 5.
Feat, spruce, i. 89. 6.
Fecht, a fight.
Fecht, to fight.
Feck, the bulk, the most part: 'the feck of a' the Ten Comman's,' i. 37. 21; 'the feck o' my life,' iii. 132. 5.
Feck, value, return: 'for little feck,' ii. 59. 14.

GLOSSARIAL INDEX 137

Fecket, (1) sleeve-waistcoat [used by farm-servants as both vest and jacket]: 'got me by the fecket,' ii. 138. 13; (2) waistcoat [without sleeves]; 'his fecket is white,' iii. 61. 10.

Feckless, weak, pithless, feeble: 'as feckless as a wither'd rash,' i. 238. 14; 'an auld wife's tongue's a feckless matter,' ii. 37. 17.

Feckly, partly, or mostly: 'carts ... are feckly new,' ii. 40. 25.

Feg, a fig.

Fegs, faith! 'but fegs! the Session,' ii. 97. 7.

Feide, feud: 'wi' deadly feide,' i. 223. 8.

Feint, v. *Fient*.

Feirrie, lusty: 'the feirrie auld wife,' iii. 139. 15.

Fell, (1) keen, cruel, dreadful, deadly [many examples of each shade of meaning]; (2) pungent: 'her weel-hain'd kebbuck fell,' i. 110. 15.

Fell, the cuticle under the skin: 'the skin an' fell,' i. 215. 1. *Cf.* 'flesh and fell,' Shak. *King Lear*, v. 3. 24.

Felly, relentless: 'felly spite,' iii. 88. 2.

Fen', a shift: 'might mak a fen,' iii. 84. 14.

Fen', fend, (1) to look after, to care for: 'fend themsel,' i. 55. 2; (2) keep off: 'fend the show'rs,' i. 39. 15; (3) defend, 'feeht and fen''=shift for themselves, iii. 91. 10; 'how do ye fen'?'=how are you getting on? iii. 129. 7.

Fenceless, defenceless.

Ferlie, ferly, (1) a wonder [implying also disgust]: 'ye crowlin ferlie,' i. 152. 13; (2) 'nae ferlie[y]'=no wonder, no marvel, i. 67. 8, and iii. 141. 3.

Ferlie, to marvel: 'an' ferlie at the folk in Lon'on,' i. 14. 8.

Fetches, catches, gurgles: 'fetches at the thrapple,' ii. 71. 19.

Fetch't, stopped suddenly: 'braing't, an' fetch't, an' fliskit,' i. 103. 13.

Fey, fated to death: 'fey men died,' iii. 74. 10.

Fidge, (1) to fidget, to wriggle, 'fidge your back,' i. 28. 3; 'fidge an' claw,' i. 210. 1; (2) 'fidge fu' fain'=tingle with delight, i. 168. 13; (3) 'fidg'd fu' fain'=fidgeted with fondness, i. 285. 21.

Fidgin-fain, (1) tingling-wild: 'fidgin-fain to hear't,' i. 156. 7; (2) tingling with fondness, iii. 70. 14. See Note, vol. iii. 355.

Fiel, well: 'haps me fiel and warm,' iii. 114. 4.

Fient, fiend, a petty oath (R. B.)

Fient a, not a: 'the fient a'= nothing of a.

Fient haet, nothing [fiend have it].

Fient haet o', not one of.

Fient-ma-care, the fiend may care [I don't!]

Fier, fiere, companion, my trusty fier[e],' ii. 129. 11, and iii. 148. 17.

GLOSSARIAL INDEX

Fier, sound: 'hale and fier,' i. 118. 10.
Fin', to find.
Fish-creel, v. *Creel*.
Fissle, tingle, fidget with delight | it is also used of the agitation caused by frying]: 'gar me fissle,' i. 161. 7.
Fit, foot.
Fittie-lan', the near horse of the hindmost pair in the plough: 'a noble fittie-lan',' i. 103. 7. See Note, vol. i. 361.
Flae, a flea.
Flaffin, flapping: 'flaffin wi' duds,' ii. 156. 9.
Flainin, flannen, flannel.
Flang, flung.
Flee, to fly.
Fleech'd, wheedled: 'Duncan fleech'd, and Duncan pray'd,' iii. 215. 9.
Fleechin, wheedling: 'a fleechin, fleth'rin Dedication,' i. 147. 6.
Fleesh, fleece: 'a bonier fleesh ne'er cross'd the clips,' i. 58. 5.
Fleg, (1) either a scare [as the word is used by Ramsay], or a blow: 'jirt an' fleg,' i. 164. 1; (2) action, movement: 'uncouth countra fleg,' ii. 183. 12.
Fleth'rin, flattering: 'fleth'rin dedication,' i. 147. 6.
Flewit, a sharp lash: 'a hearty flewit,' ii. 98. 20.
Fley, to scare: 'Want and Hunger fley me,' iii. 206. 9.
Fley'd, scared: 'fley'd an' eerie,' i. 95. 18; 'but be na fley'd,' i. 193. 18; 'fley'd awa,' iii. 279. 20.

Flichterin, fluttering: as young nestlings when their dam approaches (R. B.); 'flichterin noise and glee,' i. 107. 9.
Flinders, shreds, broken pieces (R. B.), i. 145. 14.
Flinging, kicking out in dancing, capering: 'louping and flinging on a crummock,' i. 284. 23.
Flingin-tree, a piece of timber hung by way of partition between two horses in a stable, a flail (R. B.): 'the thresher's weary flingin-tree,' i. 74. 16.
Fliskit, fretted, capered: 'fetch't an' fliskit,' i. 103. 13.
Flit, to shift.
Flittering, fluttering.
Flyte, scold: 'e'en let her flyte her fill,' iii. 188. 4.
Fock, focks, folk.
Fodgel, dumpy: 'a fine, fat, fodgel wight,' i. 290. 2.
Foor, fared [*i.e.* went]: 'o'er the moor they lightly foor,' iii. 19. 13.
Foorsday, Thursday.
Forbears, forebears, forefathers.
Forby, forbye, besides.
Forfairn, (1) worn out: 'wi' crazy eild I'm sair forfairn,' i. 204. 19; (2) forlorn: 'Fenwick, sair forfairn,' i. 213. 8.
Forfoughten, exhausted [*i.e.* by labour or conflict]: 'tho' forfoughten, sair eneugh,' ii. 104. 5.
Forgather, to meet with, to fall in with.
Forgie, to forgive.

GLOSSARIAL INDEX 139

Forjesket, jaded with fatigue (R. B.): 'forjesket sair, with weary legs,' i. 162. 1.
Forrit, forward.
Fother, fodder.
Fou, fow, full [*i.e.* drunk].
Foughten, troubled [*i.e.* by conflict with difficulties]: 'sae foughten an' harass'd,' i. 16. 9. See *Forfoughten*.
Foursome, a quartette: 'foursome reels,' iii. 142. 1.
Fouth, fulness, abundance: 'fouth o' auld nick-nackets,' i. 291. 5.
Fow, v. *Fou*.
Fow, a bushel.
Frae, from.
Freath, to froth.
Fremit, estranged, hostile: 'is now a fremit knight,' ii. 180. 18.
Fu', full. V. also *Fou*.
Fu'-han't, full-handed [having abundance]: 'ay fu'-han't is fechtin best,' iii. 118. 23.
Fud, a short tail [of a rabbit or hare]: 'cock your fud fu' braw,' i. 222. 9; 'to coor their fuds,' ii. 17. 5.
Fufft, puffed: 'she fufft her pipe wi' sic a lunt,' i. 93. 10.
Fur, furr, a furrow.
Fur-ahin, the hindmost plough-horse in the furrow: 'my fur-ahin's a wordy beast,' ii. 40. 16. See Note, vol. ii. 337.
Furder, success.
Furder, to succeed.
Furm, a wooden form.
Fusionless, pithless, sapless, tasteless: 'he is but a fusionless carlie,' iii. 140. 4.
Fyke, fret: 'as bees bizz out wi' angry fyke,' i. 286. 1.
Fyke, (1) to fuss: 'fyke an' fumble,' i. 145. 7; (2) to fidget [*i.e.* from annoyance or pain]: 'until ye fyke,' ii. 82. 2.
Fyle, to defile, to foul: 'her face wad fyle the Logan Water,' iii. 126. 11.
Fyled, soiled: 'that fyl'd his shins,' i. 40. 3.

Gab, the mouth, the jaw: 'his gab did gape,' i. 283. 24; 'steek your gab for ever,' i. 123. 15; 'she held up her greedy gab,' ii. 2. 7; 'his teethless gab,' iii. 31. 14; 'set a' their gabs a-steerin,' i. 99. 11.
Gab, to talk, to speak: 'gab like Boswell,' i. 29. 8.
Gabs, talk: 'some wi' gabs,' i. 89. 12.
Gae, gave.
Gae, to go.
Gaed, went.
Gaen, gone.
Gaets, ways, manners: 'learn the gaets,' i. 55. 5.
Gairs, slashes: 'my lady's gown, there's gairs upon 't,' iii. 198. 13.
Gane, gone.
Gang, to go.
Gangrel, vagrant: 'o' randie, gangrel bodies,' ii. 1. 8.
Gar, to cause, to make, to compel.
Gar't, made, compelled.
Garten, garter.

Garten'd, gartered.

Gash, (1) wise: 'a gash an' faithfu' tyke,' i. 10. 11; (2) self-complacent [implying prudence and prosperity]: 'here farmers gash,' i. 38. 19; (3) talkative and self-complacent: 'a gawsie, gash guidwife,' i. 45. 15.

Gashing, talking, gabbing: 'gashing at their cracks,' i. 92. 12.

Gat, got.

Gate, way, road, manner.

Gatty, enervated: 'auld an' gatty,' ii. 75. 19.

Gaucie, v. *Gawsie*.

Gaud, a goad, iii. 76. 3. See Note, vol. iii. 358.

Gaudsman, goadsman, driver of the plough-team: 'a gaudsman ane, a thrasher t' other,' ii. 41. 3. See Note, vol. ii. 337.

Gau'n, Gavin.

Gaun, going.

Gaunted, gaped, yawned: 'I've grain'd and gaunted,' ii. 131. 14.

Gawky, a foolish woman or lad [the female of *gowk*, *q.v.*]: 'gawkies, tawpies, gowks, and fools,' ii. 54. 13. See Note, vol. ii. 346.

Gawky, cuckooing, foolish: 'the senseless, gawky million,' ii. 87. 6. Cf. *A Dream*, i. 68, Stanza ii. Lines 3-4:—

'*God save the King*'s a cuckoo song That's unco easy said ay.'

Gawsie, (1) buxom: 'her strappin limb an' gawsie middle,' ii. 10. 11; (2) buxom and jolly: 'a gawsie, gash guidwife,' i. 45. 15; (3) big and joyous: 'his gawsie tail,' i. 10. 17.

Gaylies, gaily: 'but they do gaylies,' ii. 155. 24.

Gear, (1) money, wealth; (2) goods; (3) stuff: 'taste sic gear as Johnie brews,' ii. 84. 2.

Geck, (1) to sport: 'may Freedom geck,' i. 71. 6; (2) to toss the head: 'ye geck at me because I'm poor,' iii. 37. 11.

Ged, a pike: 'and geds for greed,' i. 222. 4; 'Johnie Ged's Hole'=the grave, i. 197. 17. See Note, vol. i. 393.

Gentles, gentry.

Genty, trim and elegant: 'genty waist,' iii. 46. 7; 'her genty limbs,' iii. 199. 13.

Genty, trimly: 'sae genty sma',' iii. 76. 6.

Geordie, dim. of *George*, a guinea.

Get, issue, offspring, breed: 'nae get o' moorlan tips,' i. 58. 1; 'a true, guid fallow's get,' i. 70. 21.

Ghaist, ghost.

Gie, to give.

Gied, gave.

Gien, given.

Gif, if.

Giftie, dim. of *gift*.

Giglets, giggling youngsters or maids: 'the giglets keckle,' ii. 52. 7. *Cf.* 'a giglet wench' =a light woman, Shak. 1 *Henry VI.*, iv. 7. 41.

Gillie, dim. of *gill* [glass of whisky].

Gilpey, young girl: 'I was a gilpey then,' i. 94. 3.

GLOSSARIAL INDEX 141

Gimmer, a young ewe.
Gin, (1) if, should, whether; (2) by : 'their hearts o' stane, gin nicht, are gane,' i. 46. 21.
Girdle, plate of metal for firing cakes, bannocks, etc.; 'the vera girdle rang,' ii. 1. 14. See Note, vol. ii. 308.
Girn, (1) to grin, to twist the face [but from pain or rage, not joy]; 'it makes good fellows girn an' gape,' i. 58. 9; (2) gapes: 'that girns for the fishes and loaves,' ii. 196. 20; (3) snarls: 'girns and looks back,' ii. 71. 2.
Girnin, grinning, snarling [see under *Girn*]: 'wi' girnin spite,' i. 175. 2; ii. 102. 12; 'thy girnin laugh,' ii. 141. 1; 'every sour-mou'd girnin blellum,' ii. 56. 1.
Gizz, wig: 'an' reestit gizz,' i. 52. 2. See also *Jiz*.
Glaikit, foolish, thoughtless, giddy: 'glaikit Folly's portals,' i. 218. 8; 'I'm red ye're glaikit,' ii. 81. 17; 'ye glaikit, gleesome, dainty damies,' ii. 129. 17; 'glaikit Charlie,' i. 132. 14.
Glaizie, glossy, shiny: 'sleek an' glaizie,' i. 100. 9.
Glaum'd, grasped [Coll. a 'glaum' or 'glam'=a 'grab']: 'glaum'd at kingdoms three, man,' iii. 73. 18.
Gled, a hawk, a kite [Anglo-Sax. 'Gleida'=the glider]: 'a bizzard gled,' ii. 202. 18; 'or I had fed an Athole gled,' iii. 82. 7.
Gleede, a glowing coal, a blaze [Anglo-Sax. 'Glēd'; *cf.* 'the cruel ire reed [red] as any gleede,' Chaucer, *Knight's Tale*, *Canterbury Tales*, 1997]: 'cheery blinks the ingle-gleede,' iii. 22. 3.
Gleg, (1) nimble: 'gleg as onie wumble,' i. 145. 9; (2) sharp, quick, keen: 'Death's gleg gullie,' i. 225. 5; 'as gleg's a whittle,' ii. 73. 10; (3) keen-witted: 'he's gleg enough,' ii. 86. 1; 'wee Davoc's grown sae gleg,' ii. 41. 9; 'gleg as light are lover's een,' iii. 249. 3.
Gleg, smartly: 'he'll shape you aff fu' gleg,' i. 291. 17.
Gleib, a portion: 'a gleib o' lan',' iii. 112. 1. See vol. iii. 382.
Glib-gabbet, smooth-tongued, i. 30. 3.
Glinted, sparkled: 'thou glinted forth,' i. 137. 3; 'glinted by,' iii. 28. 3.
Glintin: 'wi' glorious light was glintin,' i. 36. 6; v. *Glinted*.
Gloamin, (1) gloaming, twilight, dusk [gleaming of light after the sun has set]: 'an' darker gloamin brought the night,' i. 18. 22; 'when ance life's day draws near the gloamin,' i. 63. 5; 'the hour o' gloamin grey,' iii. 285. 1; 'beside me gin the gloaming,' iii. 104. 8; 'now it was the gloamin,' iii. 179. 13; (2) 'gloamin-shot' =sunset, iii. 151. 1.
Glow'r, a stare.
Glow'r, to stare.
Glowrin, staring.

Glunch, a frown, a growl: 'twists his gruntle wi' a glunch,' i. 24. 9.
Glunch, to frown, to growl, i. 27. 17.
Goavin, (1) looking dazedly: 'goavin's he'd been led wi' branks,' ii. 50. 10; (2) mooning: 'idly goavin, whyles we saunter,' ii. 100. 1.
Gorcock, the moorcock: 'the gorcock springs on whirring wings,' i. 181. 21; 'where gorcocks thro' the heather pass,' iii. 199. 10.
Gotten, got.
Gowan, the wild, or mountain daisy.
Gowany, covered with wild daisies.
Gowd, gold.
Gowdie, the head: 'heels o'er gowdie'=topsy turvy, ii. 140. 19.
Gowff'd, struck as in the game of golf: 'gowff'd Willie like a ba', man,' i. 249. 10.
Gowk, the cuckoo, a dolt: 'conceited gowk,' i. 204. 17; 'Andro' Gowk,' ii. 34. 9; 'gowks and fools,' ii. 54. 13. See vol. ii. 346.
Gowling, lamenting [as a dog in grief]: 'Misfortunes gowling bark,' i. 151. 1.
Graff, (1) a grave: 'cauld in his graff,' i. 186. 9; 'your green graff,' iii. 156. 15; (2) a vault: 'your marble graffs,' ii. 237. 7.
Grain'd, groaned.
Graip, a dung-fork.
Graith, (1) implements, gear: 'ploughmen gather wi' their graith,' i. 22. 8; (2) instruments: 'her spinnin-graith,' iii. 19. 19; (3) furniture of all kinds: 'a' my graith,' ii. 39. 19. (4) attire, garb: 'farmers gash in ridin graith,' i. 38. 19; 'in shootin graith adorned,' i. 222. 14; 'in heav'nly graith,' i. 249. 5.
Graithing, gearing, vestments: 'Episcopal graithing,' ii. 94. 6.
Grane, a groan.
Grane, to groan.
Grannie, Graunie, grandmother.
Grape, grope.
Graped, grapet, groped.
Grat, wept.
Graunie, v. *Grannie*.
Gree, (1) the prize [degree]: 'bear'st the gree'=tak'st the prize, ii. 52. 22; 'carry the gree'=bear the bell, ii. 207. 16; 'bear the gree'=have the first place, iii. 273. 4; 'bure the gree'=bore off the prize [*i.e.* won the victory], i. 169. 21; 'wan the gree'=gained the prize, iv. 22. 18.
Gree, to agree.
Gree't, agreed.
Greet, to weep.
Greetin, weeping.
Groanin maut, groaning malt, iii. 70. 6. See Note, vol. iii. 354.
Grozet, a gooseberry: 'plump an' grey as onie grozet,' i. 153. 18.
Grumphie, the pig: 'wha was it but grumphie,' i. 96. 8.

GLOSSARIAL INDEX

Grun', the ground.
Gruntle, the face, the phiz: 'twists his gruntle,' i. 24. 9.
Gruntle, dim. of *grunt*: 'a grane an' gruntle, i. 95. 20.
Grunzie, the snout: 'she dights her grunzie wi' a hushion,' iii. 126. 8.
Grushie, growing: 'grushie weans an' faithfu' wives,' i. 13. 20.
Grutten, wept.
Gude, God.
Guid [also *Gude*], good.
Guid-een also *Gudeen*], good evening.
Guid-father, father-in-law.
Guid-man [also *Gude-man*], the husband.
Guid-wife [also *Gude-wife*], the mistress of the house, the landlady.
Guid-Willie [also *Gude-Willie*], hearty, full of goodwill: 'a right guid-willie waught,' iii. 148. 19. See Note, vol. iii. 410.
Gullie, gully, a large knife: 'see, there's a gully,' i. 193. 22; 'Death's gleg gullie,' i. 225. 5; 'lang-kail gullie,' i. 291. 22. See Note, vol. i. 447.
Gumlie, muddy: 'gumlie dubs of your ain delvin,' i. 149. 25; 'gumlie jaups up to the pouring skies,' i. 205. 16.
Gumption, wisdom, skill [sometimes of the nostrum variety]: 'her quacks wi' a' their gumption,' ii. 71. 13.
Gusty, tasty: 'an' gusty sucker,' i. 22. 6.
Gutcher, goodsire, grandfather:

'Bye attour, my gutcher has,' iii. 156. 5.

Ha', hall.
Ha' folk, the servants: 'the ha' folk fill their pechan,' i. 11. 16.
Haddin, holding, inheritance: 'Hell for his haddin,' ii. 194. 7.
Hae, have.
Haet, v. *Devil-haet* and *fient-haet*.
Haffet, hauffet, the temple, the side of the head: 'in some beggar's hauffet,' i. 153. 5; 'her haffet locks as brown's a berry,' iii. 20. 18.
Haffets, side-locks: 'his lyart haffets,' i. 111. 2.
Hafflins, half, partly: 'hafflins is afraid to speak,' i. 109. 4; 'like hafflins-wise o'ercomes him' = nearly half o'ercomes him, i. 43. 4.
Hag, a moss, a broken bog: 'owre monie a weary hag,' i. 223. 5; 'sendin the stuff o'er muirs an' haggs,' ii. 74. 3.
Haggis, a special Scots pudding, made of sheep's entrails, onions, and oatmeal boiled in a sheep's stomach [the *pièce de résistance* at Burns Club Dinners, and an esteemed antidote to whisky].
Hain, to spare, to save.
Hairst, har'st, harvest.
Haith, faith [an oath].
Haivers, v. *Havers*.
Hal', hald, holding, possession: 'house an' hal'[d]' = house and possession, i. 52. 8; 116. 14; and 119. 7.
Hale, hail, the whole.

Hale, hail, whole, healthy.
Halesome, wholesome.
Half, half.
Hallan, a partition wall, a porch: 'yont the hallan,' i. 110. 13; 'ne'er at your hallan ca',' ii. 106. 26; 'glowrin by the hallan en',' iii. 206. 10; 'jouk behint the hallan,' iii. 52. 9; 'to his ain hallan-door,' iii. 130. 9.
Halloween, All Saints' Eve (31st October).
Hallowmas, All Saints' Day (1st November).
Haly, holy.
Hame, home.
Han', haun, hand.
Han-darg [or *daurk*]. See *Darg.*
Hand-wal'd, hand-picked [*i.e.* choicest]: 'my hand-wal'd curse,' ii. 101. 11.
Hangie, hangman [nickname of the Devil]: 'hear me, Auld Hangie, for a wee,' ii. 47. 11.
Hansel, the first gift: 'blew hansel in on Robin,' iv. 13. 12.
Hap, a wrap, a covering against cold: 'mair vauntie o' my hap,' ii. 106. 19; 'the stacks get on their winter hap,' i. 201. 13.
Hap, to shelter: 'hap him in a cozie biel,' i. 146. 14; 'and haps me fiel,' iii. 114. 4.
Hap, to hop: 'while tears hap o'er her auld brown nose,' ii. 116. 22.
Happer, hopper [of a mill].
Happing, hopping [as a bird].
Hap-step-an'-lowp, hop-step-and-jump [an important item in Scots athletic gatherings, but here used, of course, metaphorically]: i. 37. 10.
Harkit, hearkened: 'to guid advice but harkit,' i. 75. 17.
Harn, coarse cloth [cloth spun of 'hards,' *i.e.* coarse flax]: 'her cutty sark, o' Paisley harn,' i. 285. 7.
Harst, v. *Hairst.*
Hash (1) an oaf : 'doylt, drucken hash,' i. 23. 19; (2) a dunderhead: 'conceited hashes,' i. 158. 7.
Haslock woo, the wool on the neck [*i.e.* throat] of a sheep, iii. 159. 5. See Note, vol. iii. 417.
Haud, to hold, to keep.
Hauf, half.
Haughs, low-lying rich lands, valleys (R. B.): 'let husky wheat the haughs adorn,' i. 20. 7; 'haughs an' woods,' i. 170. 7; 'holms and haughs,' iv. 53. 13.
Haun, v. *Han'.*
Haurl, to trail: 'and haurls at his curpin,' i. 95. 9; 'till skin in blypes cam haurlin,' i. 97. 13; 'haurl thee hame to his black smiddie,' i. 262. 3.
Hause, cuddle: 'hause in ither's arms,' iii. 89. 7.
Haveril, hav'rel, one who talks nonsense, a half-witted person: 'poor hav'rel Will,' i. 89. 18; 'hav'rel Jean,' ii. 46. 7.
Havers, nonsense.
Havins, manners, conduct: 'pit some havins in his breast,' i. 55. 16; 'havins,

GLOSSARIAL INDEX

sense, an' grace,' i. 160. 14; 'to havins and sense,' ii. 34. 21.

Hawkie, a white-faced cow, a cow.

Heal, v. *Hale*.

Healsome, v. *Halesome*.

Hecht, (1) to promise: 'they hecht him some fine braw ane,' i. 97. 7; 'hecht them courtly gifts,' ii. 179. 9; 'hecht an honest heart,' ii. 179. 11; (2) to menace: 'some mortal heart is hechtin,' ii. 89. 16.

Heckle, a flax-comb.

Heels-o'er-gowdie. See *Gowdie*.

Heeze, to hoist: 'higher may they heeze ye,' i. 71. 20; 'heeze thee up a constellation,' ii. 117. 6.

Heich, *heigh*, high.

Helicon, a mountain in Greece, ii. 16. 4; iii. 59. 2. See Note, vol. ii. 313.

Hem-shin'd, crooked-shin'd, iii. 125. 17. See Note, vol. iii. 389.

Here awa, here about.

Herry, to harry.

Herryment, spoliation: 'the herryment and ruin of the country,' i. 207. 10.

Hersel, herself.

Het, hot.

Heugh, (1) a hollow or pit: 'yon lowin heugh,' i. 48. 3; (2) a crag, a steep bank: 'the water rins owre the heugh,' iii. 45. 7.

Heuk, a hook, a reaping-hook.

Hilch, to hobble, to halt: 'hilchin Jean M'Craw,' i. 96. 5; 'hilch, an' stilt, an' jimp,' i. 123. 9.

Hillock, dim. of *hill*, a mound.

Hiltie-skiltie, helter-skelter, ii. 82. 21.

Himsel, himself.

Hiney, *hinny*, honey.

Hing, to hang.

Hirple, to move unevenly, to hop, to limp: 'the hares were hirplin down the furs,' i. 36. 7; 'hirplin owre the field,' i. 63. 3; 'he hirpl'd up, an' lap like daft,' ii. 14. 20; 'November hirples o'er the lea,' i. 303. 5; 'he hirples twa-fauld as he dow,' iii. 31. 13; 'he hoasts and he hirples,' i. 93. 15.

Hissels, so many cattle as one person can attend (R. B.): 'the herds an' hissels were alarm'd,' i. 173. 18.

Histie, bare: 'histie stibble-field,' i. 137. 11.

Hizzie, a hussy, a wench.

Hoast, a cough: 'an' barkin hoast,' i. 25. 1; 'hoast-provoking smeek,' i. 75. 7.

Hoast, to cough: 'hoast up some palaver,' ii. 92. 4; 'he hoasts and he hirples,' iii. 93. 15.

Hoddin, the motion of a sage countryman riding on a cart horse (R. B.): 'gaed hoddin by their cotters,' i. 38. 20.

Hoddin-grey, clownish-grey, coarse grey woollen [and retaining the natural colour of the wool]: 'wear hoddin grey, an' a' that,' iii. 272. 2.

Hoggie, dim. of *hog*, a lamb: 'My Hoggie,' iii. 14.

Hog-score, a term in curling: 'Death's hog-score,' i. 221. 21. See Note, vol. i. 403.

Hog-shouther, a kind of horseplay by justling with the shoulder, to justle (R. B.), i. 171. 12.

Hoodie-craw, the hooded crow, the carrion-crow, ii. 55. 20.

Hoodock, grasping, vulturish: 'the harpy, hoodock, purseproud race,' ii. 101. 12.

Hookèd, caught: 'monie a pursie she had hookèd,' ii. 8. 3. See Note, vol. ii. 310.

Hool, the outer case, the sheath: 'poor Leezie's heart maist lap the hool,' i. 98. 14.

Hoolie, softly: 'something cries "Hoolie,"' i. 61. 8.

Hoord, hoard.

Hoordet, hoarded.

Horn, (1) a horn spoon: 'horn for horn they stretch an' strive,' i. 238. 1; (2) a toothed comb of horn: 'whare horn nor bane ne'er daur unsettle,' i. 153. 9.

Hornie, the Devil.

Host, v. *Hoast*.

Hotch'd, jerked [the action of a bagpiper's arm]: 'hotch'd and blew wi' might and main,' i. 285. 22.

Houghmagandie, fornication (R. B.), i. 47. 4.

Houlet, v. *Howlet*.

Houpe, hope.

Howdie, howdy, a midwife: 'nae howdie gets a social night,' i. 23. 3; 'afore the howdy,' ii. 97. 12.

Howe, a hollow, a dell.

Howe, hollow.

Howk, (1) to dig: 'mice an' moudieworts they howkit,' i. 10. 22; 'howkin in a sheugh,' i. 12. 2; (2) 'howkit dead' = disburied dead, i. 49. 22. See Note, vol. i. 342.

Howlet, the owl.

Hoyse, a hoist: 'they'll gie her on the rape a hoyse,' i. 215. 12.

Hoy't, urged (R. B.): 'they hoy't out Will, wi' sair advice,' i. 97. 6.

Hoyte, to amble crazily (R. B.). See also Note, vol. i. 361. 'Now ye dow but hoyte and hobble,' i. 102. 1.

Hughoc, dim. of *Hugh*.

Hullions, slovens: 'tirl the hullions to the birses,' ii. 155. 26.

Hunder, a hundred.

Hunkers, hams: 'upon his hunkers bended,' ii. 13. 2.

Hurcheon, the hedgehog: 'o'er hurcheon hides,' i. 262. 4.

Hurchin, urchin.

Hurdies, the loins, the crupper (R. B.) [*i.e.* the buttocks]: 'hung owre his hurdies wi' a swirl,' i. 10. 18; 'row't his hurdies in a hammock,' i. 146. 5; 'meekly gie your hurdies to the smiters,' i. 206. 22; 'your hurdies like a distant hill,' i. 237. 8; 'I wad hae gi'en them off my hurdies,' i. 284. 19; 'their ample hurdies,' ii. 44. 8.

Hurl, to trundle: 'or hurl in a cartie,' ii. 89. 4.

Hushion, a footless stocking:

GLOSSARIAL INDEX

'she dights her grunzie wi' a hushion,' iii. 126. 8.
Hyte, furious, ii. 102. 10.

I', in.
Icker, an ear of corn: 'a daimen icker in a thrave,' i. 115. 15.
Ier-oe, a great-grandchild: 'wee curlie John's ier-oe,' i. 151. 15.
Ilk, ilka, each, every.
Ill o't, bad at it: 'wretched ill o't,' i. 150. 23.
Ill-taen, ill-taken.
Ill-Thief, the Devil: 'the Ill-Thief blaw the Heron south,' ii. 128. 15.
Ill-willie, ill-natured, malicious, niggardly (R. B.): 'your native soil was right ill-willie,' i. 146. 20.
Indentin, indenturing: 'his saul indentin,' i. 15. 8.
Ingine, (1) genius, ingenuity (R. B.): 'he had ingine,' i. 156. 10; (2) wit: 'wi' right ingine,' ii. 84. 10.
Ingle, the fire, the fireside [very frequent].
Ingle-cheek, fireside [properly the *jam* of the fireplace]: 'lanely by the ingle-cheek,' i. 75. 5.
Ingle-gleede, v. *Gleede*.
Ingle-lowe, ingle low, the flame or light of the fire: 'by my ingle-lowe I saw,' i. 76. 9; 'beyont the ingle low'=at the back of the fire-place, iii. 108. 10.
I'se, I shall, or will.
Ither, other, another.
Itsel', itself.

Jad, a jade.
Janwar, January.
Jauk, (1) to trifle, to dally: 'she made nae jaukin,' i. 92. 20; 'to jauk and play,' i. 108. 13.
Jauner, gabber: 'haud your tongue and jauner,' iii. 156. 10.
Jauntie, dim. of *jaunt*: 'your wee bit jauntie,' ii. 128. 11.
Jaup, to splash: 'that jaups in luggies,' i. 239. 8.
Jaups, splashes: 'gumlie jaups up to the pouring skies,' i. 205. 16.
Jaw, talk, impudence: 'deil-ma-care about their jaw,' ii. 87. 5.
Jaw, to throw, to dash: 'and in the sea did jaw, man,' i. 246. 14.
Jeeg, to jog: 'and jeeg the cradle wi' my tae,' iii. 23. 11.
Jillet, a jilt: 'a jillet brak his heart at last,' i. 145. 19.
Jimp, small, slender: 'thy waist sae jimp,' iii. 59. 14.
Jimply, neatly: 'sae jimply lac'd,' iii. 46. 7.
Jimps, stays: 'but Jenny's jimps,' iii. 198. 15.
Jink, the slip: 'our billie's gien us a' a jink,' i. 144. 9.
Jink (1) to frisk: 'thro' wimplin worms thou jink,' i. 20. 2; (2) to sport: 'and jinkin hares, in amorous whids,' i. 170. 9; (3) 'jink an' diddle'=dance and shake, ii. 81. 12, and ii. 100. 8; (4) to dodge: 'he'll turn a corner jinkin,' i. 53. 3; 'Rab slips out, an' jinks about,' i. 90. 12; 'jink there

148 GLOSSARIAL INDEX

or here,' ii. 45. 2; (5) 'the swallow jinkin'=the swallow darting, iii. 115. 3; (6) move out and in: 'and drawers jink,' ii. 43. 10.

Jinker, (1) 'a jinker noble'=a noble goer, i. 102. 3; (2) dodger, gamester [*i.e.* coquette], ii. 102. 8.

Jirkinet, bodice: 'Jenny's jimps and jirkinet,' iii. 198. 15.

Jirt, a jerk: 'monie a jirt an' fleg,' i. 164. 1.

Jiz, a wig, ii. 44. 16.

Jo, a sweetheart: 'John Anderson, My Jo,' iii. 63, etc.

Jocteleg, a clasp-knive, i. 90. 6; i. 291. 21 (*q.v.*); and ii. 74. 11.

Jouk, to duck, to cower, to dodge: 'jouk beneath Misfortune's blows,' i. 66. 9; 'to Nobles jouk,' ii. 192. 17; 'jouk behint the hallan,' iv. 52. 9.

Jow, to jow, a verb which includes both the swinging motion and pealing sound of a large bell (R. B.): 'to jow an' croon,' i. 46. 11.

Jumpet, jumpit, jumped.

Jundie, to justle (R. B.), i. 171. 12.

Jurr, a servant wench: 'Geordie's jurr,' ii. 45. 6.

Kae, a jackdaw: 'thievish kaes,' i. 33. 13.

Kail, kale, (1) the colewort [also cabbage, but see *Bow-Kail*]; (2) Scots broth.

Kail-blade, the leaf of the colewort, i. 196. 15.

Kail-gullie, a cabbage-knife; v. *Gullie*.

Kail-runt, the stem of the colewort, i. 196. 6.

Kail-whittle, a cabbage knife, ii. 45. 3.

Kail-yard, a kitchen garden.

Kain, kane, rents in kind: 'his kain, an' a' his stents,' i. 11. 6; 'to Death she's dearly pay'd the kain,' i. 221. 3.

Kame, a comb: 'clawed her wi' the ripplin-kame,' iii. 150. 17.

Kebars, rafters: 'he ended; and the kebars sheuk,' ii. 4. 1.

Kebbuck, a cheese: 'syne draws her kebbuck an' her knife,' i. 45. 17; 'her weel-hain'd kebbuck, fell,' i. 110. 15; 'a kebbuck-heel'=the last crust of a cheese, i. 46. 7.

Keckle, to cackle, to giggle loudly [as a girl]: 'the giglets keckle,' ii. 52. 7.

Keek, (1) a look, a glance: 'he by his shouther gae a keek,' i. 95. 21; (2) a stolen glance: 'at ev'ry kindling keek,' ii. 105. 20.

Keek, (1) to look, to peep, to glance: 'now the sinn keeks in the wast,' ii. 76. 2; 'I cannily keekit ben,' iii. 36. 2; 'the gossip keekit in his loof,' iv. 13. 13; (2) to pry: 'but keek thro' ev'ry other man,' i. 142. 3.

Keekin-glass, the looking-glass, ii. 249.

Keel, v. *Cauk*.

Keepit, kept.

GLOSSARIAL INDEX 149

Kelpies, river-demons [usually shaped as horses]: 'water-kelpies haunt the foord,' i. 50. 15; 'fays, spunkies, kelpies,' i. 203. 11.
Ken, to know.
Kend, kent, known.
Kenna, know not.
Kennin, a very little [merely as much as can be perceived]: 'a kennin wrang,' i. 219. 23. See also vol. i. 402.
Kent, v. *Kend*.
Kep, to catch [a thing thrown or falling]: 'shall kep a tear,' i. 265. 12.
Ket, the fleece on a sheep's body: 'tawted ket, an' hairy hips,' i. 58. 2.
Key, quay.
Key-stane, key-stone.
Kiaugh, cark: 'his weary kiaugh and care beguile,' i. 107. 13.
Kilt, to tuck up: 'her tartan petticoat she'll kilt,' i. 31. 12; 'she kiltit up her kirtle weel,' ii. 61. 14.
Kimmer (1) a wench, a gossip: 'despite the kittle kimmer' [Dame Fortune], i. 164. 11; 'ye weel ken, kimmers a',' ii. 180. 14; 'loosome kimmers'= lovable girls, ii. 88. 8; 'guid e'en to you, kimmer,' iii. 189. 13; (2) a wife or bed-fellow: 'the kimmers o' Largo,' iii. 137. 15; 'I buddle my kimmer,' iii. 67. 3.
Kin', kind.
King's-hood, the second stomach in a ruminant [equivocal for the scrotum]: 'Deil mak his king's-hood in a spleuchan,' i. 195. 6. See vol. i. 393.
Kintra, country.
Kirk, church.
Kirn, a churn: 'plunge an' plunge the kirn in vain,' i. 50. 2.
Kirn, harvest-home: 'the jovial, ranting kirns,' i. 14. 10; 'an' ay a rantin kirn we gat,' i. 94. 7; 'at kirns an' weddins we'se be there,' ii. 11. 9.
Kirsen, to christen: 'and kirsen him wi' reekin water,' i. 160. 8.
Kist, (1) a chest; (2) a counter [humorous]: 'behint a kist to lie an' sklent,' i. 164. 14.
Kitchen, to relish [to add relish to]: 'thou kitchens fine,' i. 21. 16.
Kittle, (1) difficult: 'kittle to be misleared,' i. 194. 3-4 [see Note, vol. i. 392]; (2) ticklish: 'are a shot right kittle,' i. 207. 16; (3) delicate: 'to paint an angel's kittle wark,' ii. 241. 13; (4) fickle: 'despite the kittle kimmer,' i. 164. 11.
Kittle, to tickle: 'to kittle up our notion,' i. 43. 22; 'kittle up your moorland harp,' i. 163. 19; 'I kittle up my rustic reed,' i. 168. 11; 'while I kittle hair on thairms,' ii. 12. 2.
Kittlin, a kitten: 'as cantie as a kittlin,' i. 97. 16.
Kiutlin, cuddling: 'kiutlin in the fause-house,' i. 90. 17.
Knaggie, knobby: 'tho' thou's howe-backit now, an' knaggie,' i. 100. 3.
Knappin-hammers, hammers

150 GLOSSARIAL INDEX

for breaking stones [from *knap*, to strike], i. 158. 6.
Knowe, a knoll, a hillock.
Kye, cows, kine.
Kyles, v. *Nine-pin kyles*.
Kytes, bellies: 'weel-swalled kytes,' i. 238. 3.
Kythe, to show: 'fu' sweetly kythe hearts leal,' i. 89. 8. See Note, vol. i. 358.

Laddie, dim. of *lad*.
Lade, a load.
Lag, backward: 'thou's neither lag nor lame,' i. 48. 5.
Laggen, the bottom of a wooden dish: 'the laggen they hae clautet,' i. 74. 8.
Laigh, low.
Lair, lore, learning.
Laird, landowner [the lord of houses or lands].
Lairing, sticking or sinking in moss or mud: 'deep-lairing, sprattle,' i. 226. 5.
Laith, loath.
Laithfu', loathful, sheepish: 'but blate and laithfu', scarce can weel behave,' i. 109. 11.
Lallan, Lalland, lowland: 'wad ding a Lallan tongue, or Erse,' i. 52. 17; 'the lalland laws he held in scorn,' ii. 8. 10; 'a lalland face he fearèd none,' ii. 9. 7.
Lallans, Scots Lowland vernacular: 'in plain, braid Lallans,' i. 172. 17.
Lammie, dim. of *lamb*.
Lan', land.
Lan'-afore, the foremost horse on the unploughed land side, ii. 40. 4. See Note, vol. ii. 337.
Lan'-ahin, the hindmost horse on the unploughed land side, ii. 40. 6. See Note, vol. ii. 337.
Lane, lone.
Lang, long.
Lang syne, long since.
Lap, leapt.
Lassie, dim. of *lass*.
Lave, the rest, the remainder, the others.
Laverock, *Lav'rock*, the lark.
Lawin, the reckoning, 'landlady count the lawin,' iii. 25; 'guidwife, count the lawin,' iii. 91.
Lea, grass, untilled land [also used in an equivocal sense].
Lear, lore, learning.
Leddy, lady.
Lee-lang, live-long.
Leesome, lawful [allowable]: 'the tender heart o' leesome loove,' iii. 119. 7.
Leeze me on [from Leis me = dear is to me], blessings on, commend me to: 'leeze me on thee, John Barleycorn,' i. 20. 11; 'leeze me on drink,' i. 43. 15; 'leeze me on rhyme,' ii. 83. 1; 'leeze me on the calling,' etc., iii. 18. 3; 'O leeze me on my spinninwheel,' iii. 114; 'leeze me on thy bonie craigie,' iii. 175. 5.
Leister, a fish-spear: 'a three-tae'd leister on the ither,' i. 193. 3.
Len', to lend.
Leugh, laugh'd: 'how graceless

GLOSSARIAL INDEX 151

Ham leugh at his dad,' i. 211. 17.
Leuk, look.
Ley-crap, lea-crop [used equivocally]; 'waly fa' the leycrap,' iii. 205. 15.
Libbet, castrate: 'how libbet Italy was singing,' ii. 132. 6.
Licket, lickit, licked, beaten, whipt: 'ye sud be lickit,' ii. 82. 1; 'how I've been licket,' ii. 138. 11.
Licks, a beating, punishment: 'monie a fallow gat his licks,' ii. 174. 3.
Lien, lain.
Lieve, lief.
Lift, the sky.
Lift, a load: 'gie me o' wit an' sense a lift,' i. 165. 6.
Lightly, (1) to disparage: 'whyles ye may lightly my beauty a wee,' iii. 6. 2; (2) to scorn: 'for lack o' gear ye lightly me,' iii. 37. 7.
Lilt, to sing: 'lilt wi' holy clangor,' i. 211. 7.
Limmer, (1) a jade: 'still persecuted by the limmer,' i. 164. 9; 'ye little skelpie-limmer's-face,' i. 93. 15; (2) a mistress: 'or speakin lightly o' their limmer,' i. 16. 18.
Limpet, limpit, limped.
Lin, v. *Linn*.
Link, (1) to trip or dance with the utmost possible activity: 'and linket at it in her sark,' i. 284. 12; (2) to hurry: 'will send him linkin,' i. 53. 1.
Linn, a waterfall.
Lint, flax: 'sin' lint was i' the bell,' i. 110. 18; 'I bought my wife a stane o' lint,' iii. 108. 5.
Lint-white, flax-coloured [a pale yellow]: 'Lassie wi' the lintwhite locks,' iii. 259.
Lintwhite, the linnet: 'the lintwhites chant amang the buds,' i. 170. 8; 'the mavis and the lintwhite sing,' i. 253. 12; 'the blackbird strong, the lintwhite clear,' i. 297. 13; 'the lintwhites in the hazel braes,' iii. 114. 19; 'the little lintwhite's nest,' iii. 281. 15.
Lippen'd, trusted: 'I lippen'd to the chiel,' ii. 129. 3.
Lippie, dim. of *lip*.
Loan, a lane, a field-path, the private road to a farm or house: 'the kye stood rowtin i' the loan,' i. 19. 2; 'and up the loan she shaw'd me,' iii. 149. 16.
Loanin, the private road to a farm, a road: 'wi' double plenty o'er the loanin,' ii. 138. 7.
Lo'ed, loved.
Lon'on, London.
Loof [*pl.* looves], the palm of the hand: 'an 's loof upon her bosom,' i. 40. 17; 'an' heav'd on high my waukit loof,' i. 76. 2; 'hear'st thou, laddie—there's my loof,' iii. 112. 7; 'an' wi' her loof her face a-washin,' iii. 126. 6; 'O lay thy loof in mine, lass,' iii. 202. 13; 'the gossip keekit in his loof,' iv. 13. 13; 'wi' well-spread looves, an' lang wry faces,' i. 149. 19.

152 GLOSSARIAL INDEX

Loon, lown, lown, a fellow, a varlet [very frequent].
Loosome, lovable: 'loosome kimmers,' ii. 88. 8.
Loot, let: 'loot a winze,' i. 97. 12; 'I never loot on that I kenn'd it,' iii. 242. 13.
Loove, love.
Looves, v. Loof.
Losh, a minced oath [a mild form of Lord]: 'Losh, man, hae mercy wi' your natch,' ii. 96. 3.
Lough, a pond, a lake: 'ayont the lough,' i. 49. 8 ; 'when to the loughs the curlers flock,' i. 221. 13.
Loup, lowp, to leap.
Low, lowe, a flame: 'the sacred lowe o' weel-plac'd love,' i. 142. 5. See also Ingle-lowe.
Lowin, lowing, (1) flaming: 'lowin brunstane,' i. 44. 20; 'tho' yon lowin heugh's thy hame,' i. 48. 3; (2) burning: 'to quench their lowin drouth,' ii. 17. 6.
Lown, v. loon.
Lowp, v. Loup.
Lowse, louse, (1) to untie: 'lowse his pack,' ii. 17. 9 ; (2) let loose: 'lows'd his ill-tongued wicked scaul,' i. 52. 11; 'lows'd his tinkler jaw,' i. 248. 8; 'louse Hell upon me,' ii. 77. 10.
Luc ,(1) a grandmother, an old woman: 'honest Lucky,' ii. 103. 7, and ii. 131. 6; (2) an ale-wife: 'Lady Onlie, Honest Lucky,' iii. 21. See Note, vol. ii. 364.
Lug, the ear.

Lugget, having ears, 'lugget caup'=twy-eared cup, i. 22. 10.
Luggie, a porringer: 'the luggies three are ranged,' i. 98. 20 ; 'that jaups in luggies,' i. 239. 8.
Lum, the chimney.
Lume, a loom: 'wark-lume'=a tool, i. 50. 9.
Lunardi, a balloon-bonnet [named after Lunardi, a famous balloonist]: 'Miss's fine Lunardi,' i. 154. 5.
Lunches, full portions: 'dealt about in lunches,' i. 45. 13.
Lunt, a column of smoke or steam: 'she fuff't her pipe wi' sic a lunt,' i. 93. 10 ; 'butter'd sow'ns, wi' fragrant lunt,' i. 99. 10.
Luntin, smoking: 'the luntin pipe,' i. 14. 19.
Luve, love.
Lyart, (1) grey in general: 'but ane wi' lyart lining,' i. 37. 2 ; (2) discoloured by decay or old age: 'lyart haffets wearing thin and bare,' i. 111. 2 ; 'lyart pow,' i. 164. 4; 'lyart gray,' iii. 159. 9; 'lyart leaves,' ii. 1. 1. See Note, vol. iii. 417.
Lynin, lining.

Mae, more.
Mailen, mailin, a farm: 'than stocket mailins,' ii. 39. 10 ; 'there's Meg wi' a mailen,' iii. 62. 1 ; 'a mailen plenish'd fairly,' iii. 214. 10 ; 'a weel-stocket mailen,' iii. 242. 11.
Mailie, Molly.

GLOSSARIAL INDEX 153

Mair, more.
Maist, most.
Maist, almost.
Mak, make.
Mak o', *make o'*, to pet, to fondle: 'I will mak o' my guidman,' iii. 89. 3; 'makin of's the best thing,' iii. 139. 7. See Note, vol. iii. 398.
Mall, *Mally*, Moll, Molly, [Mary].
Manlie, iii. 166. 6. See Note, iii. 423.
Manteele, a mantle, i. 37. 1.
Mark, or *merk*, an old Scots coin [13½d. sterling].
Mashlum, of mixed meal: 'mashlum bonnocks,' i. 32. 7.
Maskin-pat, the teapot, i. 246. 13.
Maukin, a hare: 'hunger'd maukin taen her way,' i. 74. 12; 'ye maukins, cock your fud fu' braw,' i. 222. 9; 'ye maukins, whiddin through the glade,' i. 263. 21; 'the coward maukin sleep secure,' i. 297. 19; 'skip't like a maukin owre a dyke,' ii. 62. 6; 'are hunted like a maukin,' iii. 64. 20.
Maun, must.
Maunna, mustn't.
Maut, malt.
Mavis, the thrush.
Mawin, mowing.
Mawn, mown.
Mawn, a large basket: 'and cover him under a mawn, O,' iii. 157. 4. *Cf.* 'A thousand favours from a maund she drew,' Shakespeare, *Lover's Complaint*, 1. 36.

Mear, a mare.
Meikle, *mickle*, *muckle*, much, great.
Melder, the quantity of corn sent to be ground: 'ilka melder wi' the miller,' i. 279. 17.
Mell, to meddle; 'wi' bitter deathfu' wines to mell,' i. 24. 5; 'to moop an' mell,' i. 55. 25.
Melvie, to meal-dust: 'melvie his braw claithing,' i. 46. 4.
Men', to mend.
Mense, tact, discretion: 'could behave hersel wi' mense,' i. 57. 12; 'ye but show your little mense,' i. 204. 7.
Menseless, unmannerly: 'like other menseless, graceless brutes,' i. 55. 20.
Merle, the blackbird: 'the merle, in his noontide bower,' i. 269. 3.
Merran, Marian, i. 92. 10, and i. 96. 6.
Mess John, Mass John [the parish priest, the minister; in Chaucer and Shakespeare 'Sir John' is the name for the priest], ii. 98. 3, and iii. 24. 7. See Note, vol. ii. 363.
Messin, a cur, a mongrel: 'a tinkler-gipsy's messin,' i. 1. 18.
Midden, a dunghill: 'better stuff ne'er claw'd a midden,' ii. 59. 8.
Midden-creels, manure-baskets: 'her walie nieves like midden-creels,' iii. 126. 9. See Note, vol. iii. 389.
Midden dub, midden puddle, ii. 62. 2. See Note, vol. ii. 351.

154 GLOSSARIAL INDEX

Midden-hole, a gutter at the bottom of the dunghill (R. B.): 'an' ran thro' midden-hole an' a', i. 97. 3.
Milking shiel, the milking shed, iii. 118. 1, and iii. 171. 7.
Mim, prim, affectedly meek (R. B.): 'an' meek an' mim has view'd it,' i. 42. 15.
Mim - mou'd, prim - lipped: 'some mim-mou'd, pouther'd priestie,' ii. 91. 18; 'mim-mou'd Meg o' Nith,' ii. 179. 17.
Min', mind, remembrance.
Mind, to remember, to bear in mind.
Minnie, mother.
Mirk, dark, gloomily dark.
Misca', to miscall, to abuse: 'an' Russell sair misca'd her,' i. 210. 13; 'they sair misca' thee,' i. 292. 10; 'misca'd waur than a beast,' ii. 77. 17.
Mishanter, mishap: 'mishanter fa' me,' ii. 37. 7; 'till some mishanter,' ii. 100. 3.
Mislear'd, mischievous, unmannerly (R. B.); i. 194. 4. See Note, vol. i. 392.
Miss't, mist, missed.
Mistak, mistake.
Mistcuk, mistook.
Mither, mother.
Monie, many.
Mools, crumbling earth, dust: 'worthy frien's laid i' the mools,' ii. 52. 19; 'he wha could brush them down to mools,' ii. 54. 17.
Moop, (1) to nibble: 'to moop an' mell,' i. 55. 25; (2) to keep close company, to meddle: 'gars me moop wi' the servant hizzie,' iii. 193. 10.
Mottie, dusty: 'mottie, misty clime,' i. 75. 11.
Mou', the mouth.
Moudieworts [Old Engl. *moldwarp*, *i.e.* the warper of the mold or earth], moles: 'whyles mice an' moudieworts they howkit,' i. 10. 22.
Muckle, v. *Meikle*.
Muslin-kail, beefless broth: 'water brose or muslin-kail,' i. 66. 3.
Mutchkin, an English pint: 'her mutchkin stowp as toom's a whistle,' i. 28. 8; 'come, bring the tither mutchkin in,' i. 215. 15; 'ae hauf-mutchkin does me prime,' ii. 73. 7.
Mysel, myself.

Na, *nae*, no, not.
Naething, *naithing*, nothing.
Naig, a nag.
Naigie, dim. of *naig*.
Nane, none.
Nappy, ale, liquor: 'twalpennie worth o' nappy,' i. 14. 1; 'the nappy reeks wi' mantling ream,' *ib.* 17; 'while we sit bousing at the nappy,' i. 278. 13; 'drown'd himsel amang the nappy,' i. 280. 22; 'there's naething like the honest nappy,' ii. 72. 19.
Natch, a notching implement: 'hae mercy wi' your natch,' ii. 96. 3.
Neebor, *neibor*, neighbour.
Needna, needn't.
Negleckit, neglected.
Neive, v. *Nieve*.

GLOSSARIAL INDEX 155

Neuk, newk, a nook, a corner.
New-ca'd, newly - driven [not newly calved]: 'while new-ca'd kye rowte at the stake' [Burns's kye did not make it a habit to calve, all, or the most of them, at a particular hour of the same evening, and that the 21st of April], i. 161. 11.
New-Light. See Note, vol. i. 384.
Nick [*Auld*], *Nickie-ben,* a name of the Devil.
Nick, (1) to sever: 'to nick the thread,' i. 194. 15; 'nickin down fu' cannie, the staff o' bread,' ii. 73. 13-14; (2) to slit: 'that nicket Abel's craig,' i. 291. 19; (3) to nail, to seize away: 'by fell Death was nearly nicket,' ii. 138. 12.
Nickie-ben, v. *Nick.*
Nick-nackets, curiosities, i. 291. 5.
Nicks, (1) cuts: 'clours an' nicks,' i. 174. 2; (2) the rings on a cow's horns: 'auld Crummie's nicks,' ii. 85. 13.
Niest, next.
Nieve, the fist.
Nieve-fu', fistful: 'their worthless nieve-fu' of a soul,' i. 166. 8.
Niffer, exchange: 'and shudder at the niffer,' i. 218. 14.
Nit, a nut.
No, not.
Nocht, nothing.
Norland, Northern [Northland].
Nowt, nowte [Engl. *Neat*], cattle.

O', of.

O'erword, (1) the refrain: 'the o'erword o' the spring,' iv. 18. 19; (2) catchword: 'prudence is her o'erword ay,' iii. 222. 7.
Onie, any.
Or, ere, before.
Orra, extra: 'their orra duddies,' ii. 1. 10.
O't, of it.
Ought, aught.
Oughtlins, aughtlins, aught in the least, at all: 'oughtlins douser,' ii. 132. 23; v. *Aughtlins.*
Ourie, shivering, drooping (R. B.): 'the ourie cattle,' i. 226. 2.
Oursel, oursels, ourselves.
Outler, unhoused, in the open fields: 'an outler quey,' i. 98. 12.
Owre, over, too.
Owsen, oxen.
Oxter'd, held up under the arms: 'the priest he was oxter'd,' iii. 201. 7.

Pack an' thick, confidential: 'unco pack an' thick the-gither,' i. 10. 20.
Paidle, (1) to paddle, to wade: 'thro' dirt and dub for life I'll paidle,' ii. 42. 5; 'we twa hae paidl'd in the burn,' iii. 148. 13; (2) to walk with a weak action: 'he was but a paidlin body, O,' iii. 139. 16.
Painch, the paunch.
Paitrick (1) a partridge; (2) used equivocally, [the bird was once esteemed salacious]: 'I brocht a paitrick to the

156 GLOSSARIAL INDEX

grun,' i. 178. 3. See Note, vol. i. 385.
Pang, to cram: 'it pangs us fu' o' knowledge,' i. 43. 18.
Parishen, the parish [*i.e.* the persons of the parish]: 'the pride of a' the parishen,' iii. 159. 12.
Parritch, porridge.
Parritch-pats, porridge-pots.
Pat, pot.
Pat, put.
Pattle, pettle, a plough-staff: 'my new pleugh-pettle,' i. 31. 1; 'wi' murdering pattle,' i. 115. 6; 'as ever drew before a pettle,' ii. 40. 3.
Paughty, haughty; 'yon paughty dog,' i. 73. 1; 'the paughty feudal throne,' i. 164. 19.
Paukie, pauky, pawkie, artful: 'the slee'st, pawkie thief,' i. 59. 1; 'her paukie een,' ii. 105. 17; 'a thief sae pawkie is my Jean,' iii. 249. 1.
Pechan, the stomach: 'the ha' folk fill their pechan,' i. 11. 16.
Pechin, panting, blowing: 'up Parnassus pechin,' ii. 90. 10.
Penny-wheep, small beer: 'be't whisky-gill or penny-wheep,' i. 43. 19.
Pettle, v. *Pattle*.
Philibeg, the Highlander's kilt: 'Adam's philibeg,' i. 291. 18; 'with his philibeg an' tartan plaid,' ii. 9. 1; 'the philibegs and skyrin tartan trews,' iii. 74. 11-12.
Phraisin, flattering, wheedling: 'phraisin terms,' i. 167. 11.

Phrase, to flatter, to wheedle; 'to phrase you an' praise you,' ii. 86. 25.
Pickle, (1) a few, a little: 'a pickle nits,' i. 96. 14; (2) a 'pickle siller,' ii. 126. 8.
Pint [Scots], two English quarts.
Pit, put.
Plack, four pennies Scots [but only the third of an English penny].
Plackless, penniless: 'poor, plackless devils like mysel,' i. 24. 3.
Plaiden, coarse woollen cloth: 'to warp a plaiden wab,' iii. 4. 2; 'a wab o' plaiden,' iii. 194. 6. See Note, vol. iii. 304.
Plaister, plaster.
Plenish'd, stocked: 'a mailen plenished fairly,' iii. 214. 10.
Pleugh-pettle, v. *Pattle*.
Pleugh, plew, a plough.
Pliskie, a trick: 'play'd her that pliskie,' i. 31. 8.
Pliver, a plover.
Pock, a poke, a small bag, a wallet: 'the auld guidman raught down the pock,' i. 95. 1; 'they toom'd their pocks,' ii. 17. 4.
Poind, to seize [originally in war, or as prey], to distrain, to impound: 'poind their gear,' i. 13. 6.
Poind, distrained: 'poind and herriet,' ii. 155. 27.
Poortith, poverty.
Poosie-Nansie's. See Note, vol. i. 308.
Pou, to pull.

GLOSSARIAL INDEX 157

Pouch, pocket.
Pouk, to poke: 'and pouk my hips,' i. 195. 10.
Poupit, pulpit.
Pouse, a push: 'a random pouse,' ii. 96. 8. See Note, vol. ii. 308.
Poussie, a hare [also a cat]: 'poussie whiddin seen,' i. 155. 3; v. *Pussie*.
Pouther, powther, powder.
Pouts, chicks: 'an' the wee pouts begin to cry,' i. 179. 6.
Pow, the poll, the head.
Pownie, a pony.
Pow't, pulled: 'an' pow't, for want o' better shift,' i. 89. 21.
Pree'd, pried [proved], tasted: 'for ay he pree'd the lassie's mou',' iii. 179. 3; 'Rob, stownlins, pried her bonie mou',' i. 92. 7.
Preen, a pin: 'my memory's no worth a preen,' i. 172. 7.
Prent, print.
Prief, proof: 'for ne'er a bosom yet was prief,' i. 59. 5; 'stuff o' prief,' ii. 133. 11.
Priggin, haggling: 'priggin owre hops an' raisins,' i. 207. 26.
Primsie, dim. of *prim*, precise: 'primsie Mallie,' i. 91. 16.
Proveses, provosts [chief magistrate of a Scots burgh]: 'ye worthy proveses,' i. 206. 16.
Pu', to pull.
Puddock - stools, toad-stools, mushrooms: 'like simmer puddock-stools,' ii. 54. 15.
Puir, poor.
Pun', pund, pound.

Pursie, dim. of *purse*.
Pussie, a hare: 'as open pussie's mortal foes,' i. 286. 3; v. *Poussie*.
Pyet, a magpie: 'cast my een up like a pyet,' ii. 125. 10.
Pyke, to pick: 'sae merrily the banes we'll pyke,' ii. 11. 13.
Pyles, grains: 'may hae some pyles o' caff in,' i. 217. 14.

Quat, quit, quitted.
Quean, a young woman, a lass: 'now Tam, O Tam! had thae been queans,' i. 284. 13; 'the sonsie quean,' ii. 105. 15; 'wha follows onie saucie quean,' iii. 38. 3.
Quey, a young cow [that has not calved].
Quire, choir.
Quo', quod, quoth.

Rab, Rob [dim. of *Robert*].
Rade, rode.
Raep, a rope.
Ragweed, ragwort, benweed [*Senecio Jacobea*, Linn.]: 'on ragweed nags,' i. 49. 18.
Raibles, recites by rote: 'an' Orthodoxy raibles,' i. 42. 20.
Rair, to roar.
Rairin, roaring.
Rair't, roared.
Raise, rase, rose.
Raize, to excite: 'that daur't to raize thee,' i. 100. 11.
Ramfeezl'd, exhausted: 'the tapetless, ramfeezl'd hizzie,' i. 162. 7.
Ramgunshoch, surly: 'our ramgunshoch, glum guidman,' iii. 150. 7.

158 GLOSSARIAL INDEX

Ram-stam, headlong: 'harum-scarum, ram-stam boys,' i. 67. 9.

Randie, lawless, obstreperous: 'a merrie core o' randie, gangrel bodies,' ii. 1. 8.

Randie, randy, (1) a scoundrel: 'bann'd the cruel randy,' iii. 150. 22; (2) a rascal: 'reif randies, I disown thee,' iii. 149. 12.

Rant, (1) to rollick; (2) to roister [frequent examples of both meanings].

Rants, (1) merry meetings, sprees: 'our fairs and rants,' i. 21. 18; 'drucken [drunken] rants,' i. 176. 8, and ii. 97. 2; (2) rows: 'an' bloody rants,' i. 96. 16.

Rape, v. *Raep.*

Raploch, homespun; 'tho' rough an' raploch be her measure,' ii. 83. 5.

Rash, a rush: 'as feckless as a wither'd rash,' i. 238. 14; 'green grow the rashes,' ii. 251.

Rash-buss, a clump of rushes: 'ye, like a rash-buss, stood in sight,' i. 49. 9.

Rashy, rushy: 'aboon the plain sae rashy, O,' iii. 10. 14.

Rattan, ratton, a rat: 'an' heard the restless rattons squeak,' i. 75. 9; 'a ratton rattl'd up the wa',' i. 97. 1; 'while frighted rattons backward leuk,' ii. 4. 3; 'like baudrons by a ratton,' ii. 140. 2; v. *Rottan.*

Ratton-key, the Rat-Quay: i.

205. 13. See Note, vol. i. p. 396.

Raucle, (1) strong, bitter: 'a raucle tongue,' i. 32. 19; (2) sturdy: 'a raucle carlin,' i. 8. 1.

Raught, reached: 'the auld guidman raught down the pock,' i. 95. 1.

Raw, a row.

Rax, to stretch, to extend: 'and may ye rax Corruption's neck,' i. 71. 8; 'rax your leather'=fill your stomach, i. 105. 17; 'ye wha leather rax,' i. 210. 3; 'raxin conscience'=elastic conscience, ii. 77. 14; 'how cesses, stents, and fees were rax'd,' ii. 132. 17.

Ream, cream, foam: 'the nappie reeks wi' mantling ream, i. 14. 17.

Ream, to cream, to foam: 'ream owre the brink,' i. 20. 3; 'thou reams the horn in,' i. 22. 2; 'wi' reaming swats, that drank divinely,' i. 280. 8; 'the swats sae ream'd in Tammie's noddle,' i. 282. 25; 'but there it streams, an' richly reams,' ii. 16. 3.

Reave, to rob: 'reave an' steal,' i. 55. 7.

Rebute, rebuff: 'ne'er break your heart for ae rebute,' iii. 188. 9.

Red, advised, afraid: 'I'm red ye're glaikit,' ii. 81. 17.

Red, rede, to advise, to counsel.

Rede, counsel: 'and may ye better reck the rede,' i. 144. 3. Cf. 'Recks not his own

GLOSSARIAL INDEX 159

rede,' Shakespeare, *Hamlet*, i. 3. 51.

Red-wat-shod, red-wet-shod : 'still pressing onward, red-wat-shod,' i. 170. 5.

Red-wud, stark mad : 'an' now she's like to rin red-wud,' i. 31. 9.

Reek, smoke.

Reek, to smoke.

Reekie, reeky, smoky.

Reestit, scorched : 'wi' reekit duds an' reestit gizz,' i. 52. 2.

Reestit, refused to go: 'in cart or car thou never reestit,' i. 104. 7.

Reif, thieving: 'reif randies,' iii. 149. 12 ; v. *Rief*.

Remead, remedy.

Rickles, ricklets [small stacks of corn in the fields]: 'nor kick your rickles aff their legs,' ii. 74. 2.

Rief, plunder: 'that e'er attempted stealth or rief,' i. 59. 2 ; v. *Reif*.

Rig, a ridge [of land].

Riggin, (1) the roof-tree : 'rattons squeak about the riggin,' i. 75. 9-10 ; (2) the roof : 'or kirk deserted by its riggin,' i. 290. 8.

Rigwoodie, ancient, lean : 'rigwoodie hags wad spean a foal,' i. 284. 22. See Note, vol. i. 441.

Rin, to run.

Ripp, a handful of corn from the sheaf : 'teats o' hay an' ripps o' corn,' i. 55. 4 ; 'there's a ripp to thy auld baggie,' i. 100. 2.

Ripplin-kame, the wool- or flax-comb: 'he claw'd her wi' the ripplin-kame,' iii. 150. 17.

Riskit, cracked : 'wad rair't, an' riskit,' i. 103. 17.

Rive, (1) to split : 'he rives his father's auld entails,' i. 15. 20 ; 'they'll rive it wi' the plew,' i. 197. 21 ; (2) to tear : 'are riven out baith root an' branch,' i. 15. 3 ; 'rives't aff their back,' i. 177. 4 ; 'rivin the words to gar them clink,' ii. 82. 6 ; (3) to tug : 'till him rives Horatian fame,' iv. 51. 14 ; (4) to burst : 'maist like to rive,' i. 238. 5.

Rock, a distaff.

Rockin, a social meeting, i. 155. 7. See vol. i. 381.

Roon, round, shred : 'wore by degrees, till her last roon,' i. 173. 1.

Roose, to praise, to flatter.

Roose, reputation : 'ye hae made but toom roose,' ii. 33. 18.

Roosty, rusty.

Rottan, a rat : 'the tail o' a rottan,' iii. 200. 15 ; v. *Rattan*.

Roun', round.

Roupet, exhausted in voice : 'my roupet muse is haerse,' i. 26. 7 ; 'till ye are haerse an' roupet,' ii. 59. 10. See Note, vol. i. 324.

Routh, v. *Rowth*.

Routhie, well-stocked : 'a routhie butt, a routhie ben,' iii. 118. 8.

Row, rowe, (1) to roll : 'if bowls row right,' ii. 149. 3 ; (2) to flow, as a river [very frequent]; (3) to wrap [also very frequent].

Rowte, to low, to bellow: 'while new-ca'd kye rowte at the stake,' i. 161. 11; 'rowte outowre the dale,' i. 212. 12; 'to hear you roar and rowte,' i. 217. 2: 'the kye stood rowtin,' i. 19. 2.

Rowth, plenty, a store: 'ay, a rowth,' ii. 139. 11; 'rowth o' rhyme[s],' i. 25. 13, and i. 65. 10; 'routh o' gear,' iii. 140. 17.

Rozet, rozin: 'mercurial rozet,' i. 153. 19.

Run-deils, downright devils, i. 18. 12, and ii. 41. 2.

Rung, a cudgel: 'she's just a devil wi' a rung,' i. 32. 20; 'a meikle hazel-rung,' iii. 78. 3; 'round about the fire wi' a rung she ran,' iii. 146. 9; 'wi' a rung decide it,' iii. 195. 16.

Runkl'd, wrinkled: 'yon runkl'd pair,' i. 38. 7.

Runt, a cabbage- or colewortstalk: 'a runt, was like a sow-tail,' i. 89. 22; 'his bowkail runt,' i. 91. 15; 'runts o' grace,' i. 212. 16.

Ryke, to reach, ii. 11. 1.

Sab, to sob.
Sae, so.
Saft, soft.
Sair, sore, hard, severe, strong.
Sair, to serve: 'what sairs your grammars'=what avails your grammars, i. 158. 4; 'some less maun sair,' ii. 81. 10; 'your clerkship he should sair,' ii. 85. 16; 'I'd better gaen an' sair't the king,' i. 177. 21; 'your billie Satan sair us,' ii. 244. 4; 'he'll sair them as he sair't his King,' ii. 398.

Sair, sairly, sorely, etc.
Sairie, (1) sorrowful: 'the melancholious, sairie croon,' ii. 100. 17; (2) sorry: 'some sairie comfort at the last,' iii. 191. 9.

Sall, shall.
Sandy, Sannock, dim. of *Alexander*.
Sark, a shirt.
Saugh, the willow: 'o' saugh or hazle,' i. 103. 6; 'saugh woodies'=willow twigs, ii. 130. 5.

Saul, soul.
Saumont, sawmont, the salmon.
Saunt, saint.
Saut, salt.
Saut-backets, v. *Backets*.
Saw, to sow.
Sawney, v. *Sandy*.
Sax, six.
Scar, to scare.
Scathe, scaith, damage; v. *Skaith*.
Scaud, to scald.
Scaul, scold: 'his ill-tongu'd wicked scaul,' i. 52. 11.
Scauld, to scold.
Scaur, afraid, apt to be scared: 'nor blate nor scaur,' i. 48. 6.

Scaur, a jutting cliff or bank of earth: 'whyles round a rocky scaur it strays,' i. 98. 3; 'beneath a scaur,' i. 226. 6.

Scho, she.
Scone, a soft cake: 'souple

GLOSSARIAL INDEX

scones,' i. 20. 14; 'hale breeks, a scone, and whisky gill,' i. 25. 12; 'an' barley-scone shall cheer me,' ii. 88. 4. See Note, vol. i. 323.

Sconner, disgust, i. 238. 10.

Sconner, sicken [with disgust]: 'until they sconner,' i. 65. 16.

Scraichin, calling hoarsely: 'and paitricks scraichin loud at e'en,' i. 155. 2.

Screed, a rip, a rent: 'a screed some day,' i. 37. 23; 'or lasses gie my heart a screed,' i. 168. 8.

Screed, to repeat rapidly, to rattle: 'he'll screed you aff "Effectual Calling,"' ii. 41. 11.

Scriechin, screeching: 'and scriechin out prosaic verse,' i. 27. 3; v. *Skriech*.

Scriegh, *skriegh*: 'thou wad prance, an' snore, an' skriegh,' i. 102. 9; v. *Skriegh*.

Scrievin, careering: 'gae downhill, scrievin,' i. 21. 3; 'owre the hill gaed scrievin,' i. 97. 20; 'then hiltie-skeltie, we gae scrievin,' ii. 82. 21.

Scroggie, *scroggy*, scrubby; 'amang the braes sae scroggie,' iii. 14. 8; 'down yon scroggy glen,' iii. 155. 14.

Sculdudd'ry, bawdry: 'sculdudd'ry an' he will be there,' i. 197. 2.

See'd, saw [pret. of *see*].

Seisins, freehold possessions: 'in bonds and seisins,' i. 207. 26.

Sel, *sel'*, *sell*, self.

Sell'd, *sell't*, sold.

VOL. IV.

Semple, simple: 'semple folk'= humble folk, iii. 91. 10.

Sen', send.

Set, to set off, to start: 'for Hornbook sets,' i. 199. 1; 'while for the barn she sets,' i. 96. 16.

Set, sat.

Sets, becomes: 'it sets you ill,' i. 24. 4; 'nane sets the lawn-sleeve sweeter,' i. 72. 20.

Shachl'd, shapeless: 'how her new shoon fit her auld, shachl'd feet,' iii. 243. 13.

Shaird, shred, shard: 'the hindmost shaird,' i. 175. 13.

Shangan, a cleft stick: 'he'll clap a shangan on her tail,' i. 211. 3.

Shanna, shall not.

Shaul, shallow: 'an' Peebles shaul,' ii. 23. 6.

Shaver, a funny fellow: 'he was an unco shaver,' i. 72. 17.

Shaw, a wood.

Shaw, to show.

Shearer, a reaper [with a hook originally, but now reapers in general].

Sheep-shank, a sheep's trotter: 'nae sheep-shank bane'=a person of no small importance, i. 165. 1, and i. 204. 1.

Sheerly, wholly: 'priests wyte them sheerly,' ii. 102. 3.

Sheers, scissors.

Sherra-moor, Sheriffmuir.

Sheugh, a small cutting to allow water to run away, a ditch, a furrow: 'as ever lap a sheugh or dyke,' i. 10. 12; 'a cottar howkin in a sheugh,' i. 12. 2; 'they'll a' be trench'd

L

162   GLOSSARIAL INDEX

wi' monie a sheugh,' i. 198. 5; 'and reekin-red ran monie a sheugh,' iii. 73. 14.

Sheuk, shook.

Shiel, a shed, cottage: 'the swallow jinkin round my shiel,' iii. 115. 3. See also *Milking-shiel*.

Shill, shrill.

Shog, a shake: 'an' gied the infant warld a shog,' i. 51. 21. Cf. 'His gang garis all your chalmeris schog,' Dunbar, *On James Dog*.

Shool, a shovel.

Shoon, shoes.

Shore, (1) to offer: 'even as I was he shor'd me,' i. 296. 14; 'and shor'd them "Dainty Davie,"' ii. 14. 21; 'I doubt na Fortune may you shore,' ii. 91. 17; (2) to menace, to threaten: 'had shor'd them with a glimmer of his lamp,' i. 208. 2; 'has shor'd the Kirk's undoin,' i. 213. 7; 'an' shore him weel wi' "Hell,"' ii. 86. 8; 'if e'er Detraction shore to smit you,' ii. 90. 3; 'like good mothers, shore before ye strike,' ii. 149. 20; 'first shore her wi' a gentle kiss,' iii. 188. 1.

Short syne, a little ago: 'as short syne broken-hearted,' iii. 104. 20.

Shouldna, should not.

Shouther, showther, shoulder.

Shure, shore [did shear]: 'Robin shure in hairst,' iii. 194.

Sic, such.

Siccan, such very.

Sicker, (1) steady: 'to keep me sicker,' i. 192. 16; (2) 'sicker score'=strict conditions, ii. 36. 12; (3) certain: 'thy sicker treasure,' ii. 140. 18.

Sidelins, sideways: 'sidelins sklented,' i. 167. 9.

Siller, silver, money in general, wealth.

Simmer, summer.

Sin, son: 'his sin gat Eppie Sim wi' wean,' i. 94. 12.

Sin', since.

Sindry, sundry.

Singet, singed, shrivelled: 'singet Sawnie,' ii. 32. 17.

Sinn, the sun: 'the sinn keeks,' ii. 76. 2.

Sinny, sunny: 'in the pride o' sinny noon,' iii. 120. 10.

Skaith, damage.

Skaith, to harm, to injure: 'the Deil he couldna skaith thee,' iii. 224. 13; 'think, wicked sinner, wha ye're skaithing,' i. 177. 5.

Skellum, a good-for-nothing, a scullion: 'thou was a skellum,' i. 279. 13; 'ilk self-conceited critic-skellum,' ii. 56. 3; 'by worthless skellums,' ii. 78. 4.

Skeigh, skiegh, skittish: 'when thou an' I were young and skiegh,' i. 102. 7; 'and Meg was skeigh,' iii. 19. 5; 'look'd asklent and unco skeigh,' iii. 215. 6.

Skelp, a slap, a smack: 'I gie them a skelp as they're creeping along,' iii. 234. 3; 'skelp — a shot'=crack — a shot, i. 34. 15.

Skelp, (1) to spank [*i.e.* to trounce,

GLOSSARIAL INDEX 163

to slap]: 'to skelp and scaud poor dogs like me,' i. 47. 16; 'or else I fear, some ill ane skelp him,' i. 148. 2; 'wi' your priest-skelping turns,' ii. 36. 2; (2) 'skelpin at it'= driving at it, ii. 74. 7; (3) to spank [*i.e.* to hasten, to move quickly]: 'cam skelpin up the way,' i. 36. 13; 'skelpin barefit,' i. 39. 1; 'the words come skelpin rank an' file,' i. 123. 2; 'Tam skelpit on thro' dub and mire,' i. 281. 23; 'and barefit skelp,' ii. 92. 7; (4) 'skelpin jig an' reel'= dancing jig and reel, ii. 137. 13; (5) 'a skelpin kiss'=a sounding kiss, ii. 2. 6.

Skelpie-limmer's-face, a technical term in female scolding [R. B.]: 'ye little skelpie-limmer's-face,' i. 93. 15.

Skelvy, shelvy: 'foaming down the skelvy rocks,' i. 296. 17.

Skiegh, v. *Skeigh*.

Skinking, watery: 'nae skinking ware,' i. 239. 7.

Skinklin, small: 'skinklin patches,' iv. 51. 19.

Skirl, to cry or sound shrilly: 'skirlin weanies'=squalling babies, i. 22. 19; 'loud skirl'd a' the lasses,' i. 90. 15; 'an' skirl up the *Bangor*,' i. 211. 9; 'he screw'd his pipes, and gart them skirl,' i. 283. 13; 'he skirl'd out *encore*,' ii. 4. 6.

Sklent, a slant, a turn: 'my notion's taen a sklent,' i. 61. 5.

Sklent, (1) to slant, to squint: 'wi' sklentin light,' i. 49. 6; 'an' sklented on the man of Uzz,' i. 52. 5; 'ironic satire, sidelins sklented,' i. 167. 9; 'an' sklent on poverty their joke,' ii. 84. 15; (2) to cheat: 'to lie an' sklent,' i. 164. 14.

Skouth, play [freedom]: 'to gie their malice skouth,' ii. 79. 7.

Skriech, a scream: 'wi' monie an eldritch skriech and hollo,' i. 286. 8.

Skriegh, to scream, to whinny: 'prance an' snore an' skriegh,' i. 102. 9.

Skyrin, flaring: 'skyrin tartan trews, man,' iii. 74. 12.

Skyte, squirt, lash [the primary meaning of *to skyte* is to eject forcibly=to stool]: 'when hailstanes drive wi' bitter skyte,' ii. 1. 4.

Slade, slid.

Slae, the sloe.

Slap, (1) a breach in a fence, an opening: 'to slink thro' slaps,' i. 55. 7; 'at slaps the billies halt a blink,' i. 46. 14; 'the mosses, waters, slaps, and styles,' i. 279. 2; (2) a gate: 'the sheep-herd steeks his faulding slap,' i. 254. 5.

Slaw, slow.

Slee, sly, ingenious.

Sleekit, (1) sleek: 'wee, sleekit, cow'rin, tim'rous beastie,' i. 115. 1; (2) crafty: 'sleekit Chatham Will,' ii. 132. 13.

Slidd'ry, slippery: 'Fortune's slidd'ry ba',' i. 184. 14.

Sloken, to slake: 'their hydra drouth did sloken,' i. 49. 20.

Slypet, slipped: 'an' slypet owre'=fallen smoothly over, i. 103. 18.

GLOSSARIAL INDEX

Sma', small.
Smeddum, a powder: 'or fell, red smeddum,' i. 153. 20.
Smeek, smoke.
Smiddy, smithy.
Smoor'd, smothered.
Smoutie, smutty.
Smytrie, a small collection, a litter: 'a smytrie o' wee duddie weans,' i. 12. 6.
Snakin, sneering: 'wi' hingin lip an' snakin,' ii. 29. 16.
Snapper, to stumble: 'Blind Chance let her snapper and stoyte on her way,' iii. 234. 13.
Snash, abuse: 'how they maun thole a factor's snash,' i. 13. 4.
Snaw, snow.
Snaw-broo, snow-brew [melted snow]: 'the snaw-broo rowes,' i. 205. 10. Cf. 'A man whose blood is very snow-broth,' Shak., *Measure for Measure*, i. 4. 58.
Sned, (1) to crop: 'an' legs, an' arms, an' heads will sned,' i. 239. 3; (2) to prune: 'I'll sned besoms,' ii. 130. 5.
Sneeshin mill, a snuff-box: 'the luntin pipe, the sneeshin mill,' i. 14. 19.
Snell, bitter, biting: 'snell and keen,' i. 116. 4; 'the snellest blast at mirkest hours,' iii. 276. 5.
Snick, a latch: 'when click! the string the snick did draw,' i. 76. 7; snick-drawing=scheming: 'ye auld, snick-drawing dog,' i. 51. 17; 'he weel a snick can draw'=he is good at cheating, ii. 86. 21. See Note, vol. ii. 359. Cf. Engl. a draw-latch.
Snirtle, to snigger: 'he feign'd to snirtle in his sleeve,' ii. 13. 7.
Snoods, fillets: 'and silken snoods he gae me twa,' iii. 95. 10.
Snool, (1) to cringe: 'owre proud to snool,' i. 189. 3; (2) to snub: 'they snool me sair,' iii. 111. 13.
Snoove, to go slowly: (1) 'thou snoov't awa'=thou jogged along, i. 104. 12; (2) 'snoov'd awa'=toddled off, ii. 97. 20.
Snowkit, pried with the nose [expressive of the sound made by the dog's nose]: 'snuff'd and snowkit,' i. 10. 21.
Sodger, *soger*, a soldier.
Sonsie, *sonsy*, pleasant, good-natured, jolly: 'his honest, sonsie, bawsn't face,' i. 10. 13; 'an unco sonsie,' i. 101. 16; 'fair fa' your honest, sonsie face,' i. 237. 1; 'sonsie, smirking, dear-bought Bess,' ii. 41. 21; 'women sonsie, saft, and sappy,' ii. 73. 1; 'the sonsie quean,' ii. 105. 15; 'sae sonsy and sweet,' ii. 209. 3.
Soom, to swim.
Soor, sour.
Sough, v. *Sugh*.
Souk, suck: 'and ay she took the tither souk,' iii. 108. 11.
Soupe, sup, liquid: 'the soupe their only hawkie does afford' =the milk, i. 110. 12; v. *Sowp*.
Souple, supple: 'souple scones,' i. 20. 14. See Note, vol. i. 323; 'souple tail,' i. 222. 3; 'souple jad,' i. 285. 18.

GLOSSARIAL INDEX 165

Souter, cobbler: 'Souter Hood,' i. 187. 1; 'Souter Johnie,' i. 280. 9.
Sowps, sups: 'wi' sowps o' kail,' i. 33. 12; 'sowps o' drink,' i. 144. 5.
Sowth, to hum or whistle in a low tone: 'we'll sit an' sowth a tune,' i. 119. 16.
Sowther, to solder: 'sowther a' in deep debauches,' i. 18. 6; 'a night o' guid fellowship sowthers it a',' iii. 234. 10.
Spae, to foretell: 'to spae your fortune,' i. 93. 18.
Spails, chips: 'a' to spails,' ii. 156. 1.
Spairge, (1) to splash: 'spairges about the brunstane cootie,' i. 47. 10; (2) to spatter: 'a name not envy spairges,' i. 70. 22.
Spak, spoke.
Spates, floods: 'bombast spates,' iv. 53. 6. See also *Speat*.
Spavie, the spavin.
Spavit, spavined.
Spean, to wean: 'wad spean a foal' [by disgust], i. 284. 22.
Speat, a flood: 'the roaring speat,' i. 205. 11.
Speel, to climb: 'Moodie speels the holy door,' i. 40. 21; 'ance that five-an'-forty's speel'd,' i. 62. 20; 'to speel . . . the braes o' fame,' i. 167. 14-16; 'if on a beastie I can speel,' ii. 89. 3; 'now sma' heart hae I to speel the steep Parnassus,' ii. 139. 3-4.
Speer, *spier*, to ask.
Speet, to spit: 'to speet him like a pliver,' ii. 12. 14.

Spence, the parlour: 'keeps the spence,' i. 57. 15; 'ben i' the spence,' i. 75. 3.
Spier, v. *Speer*.
Spleuchan, (1) tobacco-pouch made of some sort of peltry: 'Deil mak his king's-hood in a spleuchan,' i. 195. 6; (2) [equivocally], 'hurt her spleuchan,' ii. 45. 8.
Splore, (1) a frolic: 'a random-splore,' i. 144. 12; (2) a carousal: 'in Poosie-Nansie's held the splore,' ii. 1. 9; (3) a row: 'he bred sic a splore,' ii. 28. 20.
Spontoon, ii. 5. 7. See Note, vol. ii. 309.
Sprachl'd, clambered: 'I sprachl'd up the brae,' i. 49. 14.
Sprattle, scramble: 'sprawl and sprattle,' i. 153. 6; 'deep-lairing, sprattle,' i. 226. 5.
Spreckled, speckled.
Spring, a quick tune, a dance: 'I've play'd mysel a bonie spring,' i. 177. 19; 'he play'd a spring, and danc'd it round,' iii. 9. 7; 'Charlie gat the spring to pay,' iii. 21. 3; 'the o'erword o' the spring,' iv. 18. 7.
Sprittie, full of roots of sprits [a kind of rush]: 'sprittie knowes,' i. 103. 17.
Sprush, spruce.
Spunk, (1) a match: 'we'll light a spunk,' i. 215. 21; (2) a spark: 'a spunk o' Allan's glee,' i. 158. 19; (3) fire, spirit: 'a man o' spunk,' ii. 14. 10; 'life and spunk,' ii. 116. 15.

GLOSSARIAL INDEX

Spunkie, sprightful, full of spirit: 'a spunkie Norland billie,' i. 30. 7.

Spunkie, liquor, spirits: 'and spunkie ance to mak us mellow,' ii. 84. 11.

Spunkies, jack-o'-lanthorns: 'moss-traversing spunkies,' i. 50. 19; 'fays, spunkies, kelpies,' i. 203. 11.

Spurtle-blade, the pot-stick [=sword], i. 291. 1.

Squattle, to squat, to settle: 'in some beggar's hauffet squattle,' i. 153. 5.

Stacher, (1) to totter: 'th' expectant wee-things, toddlin, stacher through,' i. 107. 8; (2) to stagger: 'I stacher'd whyles,' i. 192. 3; 'except when drunk he stacher't thro' it,' ii. 116. 6.

Staggie, dim. of *staig* [a young horse].

Staig, a young horse.

Stan', stand.

Stane, stone.

Stan't, stood.

Stang, sting.

Stank, (1) a moat: 'out-owre a stank,' i. 101. 3; (2) a pond: 'the Muses' stank,' ii. 16. 1; 'soor Arminian stank,' ii. 21. 19.

Stap, to stop.

Stapple, a stopper: 'for every hole to get a stapple,' ii. 71. 18.

Stark, strong: 'an' thou was stark,' i. 101. 10; 'baith wight and stark,' ii. 217. 8.

Starnies, dim. of *starn* or *star*: 'ye twinkling starnies bright,' i. 266. 3.

Starns, stars: 'ye hills, near neebors o' the starns,' i. 262. 13.

Startle, to course: 'or down Italian vista startles,' i. 15. 23.

Staumrel, half-witted: 'staumrel, corky-headed, graceless gentry,' i. 207. 9.

Staw, a stall: 'your horns shall tie you to the staw,' iii. 146. 11.

Staw, to surfeit, to sicken: 'olio that would staw a sow,' ii. 138. 8.

Staw, stole: 'auld hermit Ayr staw thro' his woods,' i. 78. 9; 'the lasses staw frae 'mang them a',' i. 90. 10; 'staw my rose', iii. 124. 13, iv. 27. 19, and iv. 29. 3; 'staw the linin o't,' iii. 159. 4; 'staw a branch,' iv. 59. 19.

Stechin, cramming: 'the gentry first are stechin,' i. 11. 15.

Steek, a stitch: 'thro' the steeks,' i. 11. 11; 'ne'er a wrang steek in them a', man,' ii. 210. 4.

Steek, to shut, to close: 'their solemn een may steek,' i. 35. 7; 'steek their een,' i. 89. 17; 'steek your gab for ever,' i. 213. 16; 'the sheep-herd steeks his faulding slap,' i. 254. 5; 'and bonie bosoms steekit' [*i.e.* closed in], ii. 43. 16.

Steer, (1) to stir: 'steer about the toddy,' i. 44. 4; 'set a' their gabs a-steerin' [*i.e.* moving], i. 99. 11; (2) rouse; 'O steer her up,' iii. 187; (3) to touch, meddle with: 'the Deil, he daurna steer,' ii. 63.

GLOSSARIAL INDEX 167

11, and ii. 134. 18; 'nae cauld nor hunger e'er can steer them,' i. 16. 23; 'thy servant true wad never steer her,' ii. 27. 22; 'misfortune sha'na steer thee,' iii. 225. 2.

Steeve, compact: 'a filly, buirdly, steeve, an' swank,' i. 100. 14.

Stell, a still.

Sten, a leap, a spring: 'foaming, strang, wi' hasty stens,' i. 263. 9; 'my heart to my mou gied a sten,' iii. 85. 10.

Sten't, sprang: 'thou never lap an' sten't an' breastit,' i. 104. 9.

Stented, erected, set on high: 'my watchman stented,' i. 30. 13. See Note, vol. i. 327.

Stents, assessments, dues: 'an' a' his stents,' i. 11. 6; 'how cesses, stents, and fees were rax'd,' ii. 132. 17.

Steyest, steepest: 'the steyest brae thou wad hae fac't it,' i. 104. 8.

Stibble, stubble.

Stibble-rig, chief harvester [with the hook], i. 94. 10.

Stick-an-stowe, completely: 'ruin'd stick-an'-stowe,' i. 174. 14.

Stilt, limp [with the aid of stilts]: 'hilch an' stilt, an' jump,' i. 123. 9.

Stimpart, a quarter peck, i. 105. 11.

Stirk, a young bullock or heifer [after one year old].

Stock, a plant of cabbage or colewort.

Stoited, stumbled: 'down George's Street I stoited,' ii. 112. 2.

Stoiter'd, staggered: 'stoiter'd up'=struggled up, ii. 6. 6.

Stoor, (1) harsh [in sound]: 'an eldritch, stoor "quaick, quaick,"' i. 49. 13; (2) stern: 'a carlin stoor and grim,' ii. 181. 2.

Stoun', stound.

Stoure, dust [literal and figurative].

Stourie, dusty.

Stown, stolen.

Stownlins, by stealth: 'Rob, stownlins, prie'd her bonie mou,' i. 92. 7; 'an' stow'n-lins we sall meet again,' iii. 166. 16.

Stoyte, to stagger: 'let her snapper and stoyte on her way,' iii. 234. 13.

Strae death, death in bed [*i.e.* on straw], i. 198. 7.

Straik, to stroke.

Strak, struck.

Strang, strong.

Straught, straight.

Straught, to stretch: 'will straught on a board,' ii. 208. 19.

Streekit, stretched: 'ance ye were streekit owre frae bank to bank,' i. 204. 2; 'streekit out to bleach,' ii. 56. 15.

Striddle, to straddle: 'striddle owre a rig,' i. 164. 2.

Stron't, lanted: i. 10. 4.

Strunt, liquor: 'a social glass o' strunt,' i. 99. 12; 'a dram o' guid strunt,' iii. 201. 3.

168 GLOSSARIAL INDEX

Strunt, to swagger: 'ye strunt rarely,' i. 152. 15.

Studdie, an anvil: 'till block an' studdie ring an' reel,' i. 22. 17; 'come o'er his studdie,' i. 262. 5.

Stumpie, dim. of *stump*; a worn quill: 'doun gaed stumpie in the ink,' i. 163. 6.

Sturt, worry, trouble: 'sturt and strife,' ii. 241. 5, and iii. 10. 1.

Sturt, to fret, to vex: 'ay the less they hae to sturt them,' i. 17. 11.

Sturtin, frighted, staggered: 'tho' he was something sturtin,' i. 95. 6.

Styme, the faintest outline: 'or see a styme,' ii. 73. 6.

Sucker, sugar: 'gusty sucker,' i. 22. 6.

Sud, should.

Sugh, sough, (1) sigh: 'sough for sough,' iii. 73. 15; (2) moan: 'wi' waving sugh,' i. 49. 10; (3) wail: 'wi' angry sugh,' i. 106. 10; (4) swish: 'the clanging sugh of whistling wings,' i. 203. 2.

Sumph, a churl: 'ye surly sumphs,' ii. 106. 5.

Sune, soon.

Suthron, Southern [*i.e.* English].

Swaird, the sward.

Swall'd, swelled.

Swank, limber: 'steeve, an' swank,' i. 100. 14.

Swankies, strapping fellows: 'swankies young,' i. 38. 21.

Swap, exchange: 'a swap o' rhymin-ware,' i. 160. 5; 'the swap we yet will do 't,' i. 186. 10.

Swapped, swopped, exchanged: 'we swappèd for the worse,' iii. 57. 9.

Swarf, to swoon: 'amaist did swarf, man,' iii. 75. 6.

Swat, sweated.

Swatch, a sample: 'a chosen swatch,' i. 40. 5; 'a swatch o' Hornbook's way,' i. 199. 11; 'a swatch o' Manson's barrels,' ii. 89. 9.

Swats, new ale: 'reaming swats, that drank divinely,' i. 280. 8; 'the swats sae ream'd in Tammie's noddle,' i. 282. 25.

Sweer, v. *Dead-sweer*.

Swirl, a curl: 'hung owre his hurdies wi' a swirl,' i. 10. 18.

Swirlie, twisted, knaggy: 'a swirlie, auld moss-oak,' i. 97. 10.

Swith, (1) haste, off and away: 'then swith! an' get a wife to hug,' i. 73. 3; 'swith! in some beggar's hauffet squattle,' i. 153. 5; 'swith to the Laigh Kirk,' i. 210. 5; 'swith awa,' iii. 149. 11.

Swither, doubt, hesitation: 'a hank'ring swither,' i. 34. 13; 'an eerie swither,' i. 192. 20; 'I've little swither,' ii. 101. 19.

Swoom, swim.

Swoor, swore.

Sybow, a young onion: a sybow-tail,' ii. 88. 3.

Syne, since, then.

Tack, possession, lease: 'stand as tightly by your tack,' i.

GLOSSARIAL INDEX 169

28. 2; 'or Poland, wha had now the tack o't,' ii. 132. 4; 'a tack o' seven times seven,' ii. 134. 3.

Tacket, shoe nail: 'wad haud the Lothians three in tackets,' i. 291. 7.

Tae, to.

Tae, toe.

Tae'd, toed: 'a three-tae'd leister,' i. 193. 3.

Taed, toad; 'sprawlin like a taed,' ii. 202. 20.

Taen, taken.

Tairge, to target [with importunities]: 'I on the *Questions* tairge them tightly,' ii. 41. 8. See Note, vol. ii. 337.

Tak, to take.

Tald, told.

Tane, one in contrast to other: 'the tane is game,' ii. 59. 5; 'the heat o' the tane,' iii. 192. 13.

Tangs, tongs.

Tap, top.

Tapetless, pithless: 'the tapetless, ramfeezl'd hizzie,' i. 162. 7.

Tapmost, topmost.

Tappet-hen, a crested hen-shaped bottle holding three quarts of claret: 'the tappet hen, gae bring her ben,' iv. 31. 7. See Note, vol. iv. p. 95.

Tap-pickle, the grain at the top of the stalk: 'her tap-pickle maist was lost,' i. 90. 16. See Note, vol. i. 358.

Tapsalteerie, topsy-turvy: i. 252. 8, and iv. 23. 12.

Tarrow, to tarry [the original sense in Henryson and the older writers, a secondary sense being to haggle], to be reluctant, to murmur: 'that yet hae tarrow't at it,' i. 74. 6; (2) to weary: 'if you on your station tarrow,' ii. 156. 21.

Tassie, a goblet: 'the silver tassie,' iii. 53. 14.

Tauk, talk.

Tauld, told.

Tawie, tractable: 'hamely, tawie, quiet, an' cannie,' i. 101. 15.

Tawpie, a foolish woman: 'gawkies, tawpies, gowks, and fools,' ii. 54. 13. See vol. ii. 346.

Tawted, matted [*i.e.* hanging with matted tawts or teats]: 'nae tawted tyke,' i. 10. 2; 'wi' tawted ket,' i. 58. 2.

Teats, small quantities: 'wi' teats o' hay,' i. 55. 4.

Teen, vexation: [common in Shakespeare, *e.g.* 'of sorrow and of teen,' *Love's Labour's Lost*, iv. 3. 164]; 'spite and teen,' i. 296. 9.

Tell'd, told.

Temper-pin, (1) a fiddle-peg: 'screw your temper-pins,' ii. 100. 15; (2) the regulating pin of the spinning-wheel: 'and ay she shook the temper-pin,' iii. 19. 12.

Tent, heed: 'tak [or took] tent' = take [or took] care, i. 61. 9; i. 192. 3; ii. 196. 6.

Tent, to tend, to heed, to observe [very frequent].

170 GLOSSARIAL INDEX

Tentie, (1) watchful: 'wi' tentie e'e,' i. 91. 6; 'wi' tentie care,' i. 105. 15; (2) careful: 'wi' joy the tentie seedsman stalks,' i. 253. 14; (3) heedful: 'some tentie rin,' i. 107. 17.

Tentier, more watchful: 'a tentier way,' ii. 138. 20.

Tentless, careless: 'tentless heed,' i. 62. 1, and i. 180. 5.

Tester [Old Fr. *Test*, a head], an old Scots silver coin about sixpence in value: 'till she has scarce a tester,' i. 70. 13. Cf. 'Hold, here's a tester for thee,' Shak., 2 *Henry IV.*, iii. 2. 296.

Teugh, tough.

Teuk, took.

Thack, thatch: 'thack and rape'=the covering of a house, and therefore used as a simile for home necessities, i. 12. 8; 'thack and rape' [of a corn-stack], i. 201. 14.

Thae, those.

Thairm, (1) small guts: 'painch, tripe, or thairm,' i. 237. 4; (2) catgut [a fiddle-string]: 'thairm-inspiring,' i. 208. 15, and ii. 99. 13; 'o'er the thairms be tryin,' i. 213. 2; 'kittle hair on thairms,' ii. 12. 2.

Theckit, thatched; 'an' theckit right,' ii. 75. 14.

Thegither, together.

Themsel, themsels, themselves.

Thick, v. *Pack an' thick*.

Thieveless, forbidding, spiteful: 'thieveless sneer,' i. 203. 25.

Thiggin, begging: 'come thiggin at your doors an' yetts,' ii. 156. 8.

Thir, these.

Thirl'd, thrilled: 'it thirl'd the heart-strings,' i. 155. 17.

Thole, to endure, to suffer: 'thole a factor's snash,' i. 13. 4; 'thole the winter's sleety dribble,' i. 116. 15; 'thole their blethers,' i. 179. 16; 'thole their mither's ban,' ii. 97. 11; 'the scathe and banter We're forced to thole,' ii. 100. 5-6.

Thou'se, thou shalt.

Thowe, thaw.

Thowless, lazy, useless: '"Conscience," says I, "ye thowless jad,"' i. 162. 14.

Thrang, (1) busy: 'that were na thrang at hame,' i. 1. 5; 'aiblins thrang a parliamentin,' i. 15. 7; 'thrang winkin on the lasses,' i. 40. 8; (2) thronging in crowds, 'the lasses, skelpin barefit, thrang, i. 39. 1; 'thick an' thrang,' i. 43. 10; (3) busily: 'complimented thrang,' i. 68. 10; (4) at work: 'are whistling thrang,' i. 61. 20.

Thrang, (1) a throng, a crowd: 'aff the godly pour in thrangs,' i. 41. 21; (2) a company: 'the jovial thrang,' ii. 17. 7.

Thrapple, the windpipe: 'see now she fetches at the thrapple,' ii. 71. 19; 'as murder at his thrapple shor'd,' ii. 188. 11.

Thrave, twenty-four sheaves of corn: 'a daimen icker in a thrave,' i. 115. 15.

Thraw, a twist: 'she turns the key wi' cannie thraw,' i. 96. 19.

GLOSSARIAL INDEX

Thraw, (1) to twist, to turn: 'for thrawin'=against twisting or bending, i. 97. 9; 'great Mackinlay thrawn his heel,' i. 220. 14; 'thraw saugh woodies,' ii. 130. 5; 'did our hellim thraw,' i. 246. 10; (2) to thwart: 'the German chief to thraw, man,' i. 248. 4; 'did his measures thraw,' *ib.* 14; 'a mortal sin to thraw that,' ii. 16. 8.

Thraws, throes: 'ease the thraws,' iii. 230. 17.

Threap, maintain [with asseverations]: 'wad threap auld folk the thing misteuk,' i. 173. 12.

Threesome, v. *Foursome.*

Thretteen, thirteen.

Thretty, thirty.

Thrissle, thistle.

Thristed, thirsted.

Through: 'mak to through'= make good, i. 207. 14.

Throw'ther, [through other] pell-mell: 'cry a' throu-'ther,' i. 90. 2.

Thummart, polecat, ii. 22. 1.

Thy lane, alone: 'no thy lane, In proving foresight may be vain,' i. 116. 17-18.

Tight, girt, prepared: 'he should been tight that daur't to raize thee,' i. 100. 11.

Till, to.

Till 't, to it.

Timmer, (1) timber [common]; (2) material [as also timber in English], 'the timmer is scant, when ye're taen for a saunt' =the saintly material is scant when you are taken for one, ii. 35. 20. [Some wiseacres affirm the meaning to be *the wood* (for the gallows) *is scant*: but (1) if this were the meaning the article 'the' would be superfluous; (2) it is absurd to suppose that there was then not wood enough to erect a gallows; (3) wood was less essential than a rope, and (4) 'material' is quite a common meaning of 'timmer.']

Tine, to lose, to be lost [frequent].

Tinkler, a tinker.

Tint, lost [very frequent]: 'tint as win'=lost as soon as won, iii. 145. 12.

Tippence, twopence.

Tippenny, two-penny ale: 'wi' tippenny we fear nae evil,' i. 282. 23.

Tirl, to strip: 'tirlin the kirks,' i. 48. 10; 'tirl the hullions to the birses,' ii. 155. 26.

Tirl, to knock for entrance: 'tirl'd at your door,' ii. 244. 1; 'tirl'd at the pin,' iii. 155. 6. See Note, vol. iii. 414.

Tither, the other [very frequent].

Tittlin, whispering: 'a raw o' tittlin jads,' i. 39. 19.

Tocher, dowry.

Tocher, to give a dowry.

Tod, the fox.

To-fa', the fall: 'to-fa' o' the night,' ii. 197. 20.

Toom, empty.

Toop, a tup.

Toss, the toast: 'the toss of Ecclefechan,' iii. 156. 8.

Tousie, shaggy: 'his tousie

172 GLOSSARIAL INDEX

back,' i. 10. 15; 'a tousie tyke,' i. 283. 11.

Tow, flax, a rope.

Towmond, towmont, a twelvemonth.

Towsing, rumpling [equivocal]: 'towsing a lass i' my daffin,' ii. 7. 8. Cf. 'Damn me if he sha't have the tousling of her,' Fielding, *Tom Jones*.

Toyte, to totter: 'toyte about wi' ane anither,' i. 105. 14.

Tozie, flushed with drink: 'the tozie drab,' ii. 2. 5.

Trams, shafts [of a barrow or cart]: 'baith the trams are broken,' ii. 40. 27.

Trashtrie, small trash: 'sauce, ragouts, an' sic like trashtrie,' i. 11. 17.

Trews, trousers: 'skyrin tartan trews,' iii. 74. 12; v. *Trouse*.

Trig, neat, trim: 'the lads sae trig,' i. 89. 10; 'and trig an' braw,' ii. 54. 4; 'he sae trig lap o'er the rig,' iii. 104. 9; 'Willie's wife is nae sae trig,' iii. 126. 7.

Trin'le, the wheel of a barrow, ii. 40. 29.

Troggin, wares: 'buy braw troggin,' ii. 201. 1.

Troke, to barter: 'wi' you nae friendship I will troke,' ii. 84. 17.

Trouse, trousers: 'will be him trouse and doublet,' iii. 189. 15.

Trowth, In truth.

Tryste, a fair, a cattle-market: 'to trystes an' fairs to driddle,' ii. 10. 10; 'the tryste o' Dalgarnock,' iii. 243.

2: 'he gaed wi' Jeanie to the tryste,' iii. 282. 5.

Trysted, appointed, agreed upon: 'the trysted hour,' iii. 286. 6.

Trysting, meeting: 'trystin time,' iii. 167. 2; 'trysting thorn,' iii. 212. 19.

Tulyie, Tulzie, a squabble, a tussle: 'The Holy Tulyie,' ii. 20; 'in logic tulzie,' i. 175. 20; 'amid this mighty tulyie,' ii. 188. 9; 'the tulyie's teugh 'tween Pitt and Fox,' ii. 59. 3.

Twa, two.

Twafauld, two-fold, double: 'he hirples twa-fauld,' iii. 31. 13.

Twal, twelve; the twal=twelve at night, i. 200. 3.

Twalpennie worth = a penny worth [sterling], i. 14. 1. See Note, vol. i. 321.

Twang, a twinge, ii. 52. 1.

Twa-three, two or three.

Tway, two: 'ne'er a ane but tway,' ii. 178. 16.

Twin, also *Twine*, to rob: 'twins ... o' half his days,' i. 23. 19-20; 'may twin auld Scotland o' a life,' ii. 154. 5; 'has twined ye o' your stately trees,' iv. 55. 2.

Twistle, a twist, a sprain: 'the Lord's cause gat na sic a twistle,' ii. 21. 9.

Tyke, a dog.

Tyne, to tine.

Tysday, Tuesday.

Ulzie, oil: 'wi' pouther and wi' ulzie,' ii. 44. 17.

Unchancy, dangerous: 'an' mair

GLOSSARIAL INDEX

unchancy,' ii. 83. 18. See *Wanchancie*.

Unco, (1) remarkably, uncommonly: 'unco pack an' thick,' i. 10. 20; 'unco happy,' i. 14. 2; 'unco weel,' i. 17. 16, etc.; (2) excessively, mightily [sarcastic]: 'Address to the Unco Guid,' i. 217, etc.

Unco, (1) remarkable, uncommon: 'an unco calf,' i. 216. 4, etc. ; (2) terrible [sarcastic]: 'an unco loun,' iii. 23. 19 ; (3) strange: 'unco folk,' iii. 6. 15.

Uncos, news, strange things, wonders: 'each tells the uncos that he sees or hears,' i. 108. 4.

Unkend, unknown.

Unsicker, uncertain: 'feeble, and unsicker,' ii. 139. 15.

Unskaithed, unhurt.

Usquabae, usquebae, whisky.

Vauntie, proud: 'and she was vauntie,' i. 285. 10; 'vauntie o' my hap,' ii. 106. 19 ; 'your letter made me vauntie,' ii. 128. 9.

Vera, very.

Virls, rings: 'virls and whirlygigums,' i. 203. 20.

Vittle [victual], (1) grain: 'a' the vittel in the yard,' ii. 75. 13; (2) food: 'a' my winter vittle,' iii. 194. 14.

Vogie, vain: 'and vow but I was vogie,' iii. 14. 4.

Wa', waw, a wall.
Wab, a web.
Wabster, a weaver.

Wad, to wager: 'I'll wad my new pleugh-pettle,' i. 31. 1 ; 'I'll wad a groat,' i. 199. 21; 'wad a boddle,' i. 204. 5.

Wad, to wed: 'and or I wad another jad,' iii. 109. 3.

Wad, would, would have.

Wad 'a, would have.

Wadna, would not.

Wadset, a mortgage: 'here's a little wadset,' ii. 202. 5.

Wae, woful, sorrowful [also sarcastic].

Wae, woe : ' wae's me'=woe is to me. Cf. 'I am woe for it, sir,' Shakespeare, *Tempest*, v. 1. 139.

Waesucks, alas ! ' waesucks ! for him that gets nae lass,' i. 46. 1.

Wae worth, woe befall.

Wair, v. *Ware*.

Wale, to choose.

Wale, choice.

Walie, wawlie, choice, ample, large: 'walie nieve,' i. 239. 1 ; 'walie nieves,' iii. 126. 9 ; 'this walie boy,' iv. 13. 15; 'ae winsome wench and wawlie,' i. 284. 26.

Wallop, (1) to kick, to dangle: 'may Envy wallop in a tether,' i. 171. 21 ; 'wallop in a tow,' iii. 109. 4 ; (2) to gallop, to dance: 'wallopèd about the reel,' ii. 61. 16. See Note, vol. ii. 351.

Waly fa'=ill befall, iii. 205. 15.

Wame, the belly.

Wamefou, bellyful.

Wan, won.

Wanchancie, dangerous: 'that

174 GLOSSARIAL INDEX

vile wanchancie thing—a rape,' i. 58. 8. See *Unchancie*.
Wanrestfu', restless: 'wanrestfu' pets,' i. 55. 6.
Ware, wair, to spend, bestow: 'and ken na how to ware't,' i. 118. 6; 'to ware his theologic care on,' ii. 129. 7; 'tho' wair'd on Willie Chalmers,' ii. 91. 8.
Ware, worn: 'gratefully be ware,' ii. 106. 17.
Wark, work.
Wark-lume, v. *Lume*.
Warl', warld, world.
Warlock, a wizard.
Warl'y, warldly, worldly.
Warran, warrant.
Warse, worse.
Warsle, warstle, wrestle.
Was na, was not.
Wast, west.
Wastrie, waste, i. 11. 18.
Wat, wet.
Wat, wot, know.
Water-fit, water-foot [the river's mouth], i. 42. 12.
Water-kelpies, v. *Kelpies*.
Wauble, to wobble: 'ran them a' till they did wauble,' i. 102. 5.
Waught, a draught: 'a right guid-willie waught,' iii. 148. 19. See Note, vol. iii. 410.
Wauk, to awake.
Wauken, to waken.
Waukin, awake.
Waukit [with toil], horny: 'my waukit loof,' i. 76. 2.
Waukrife, wakeful: 'till waukrife morn,' i. 265. 4; 'waukrife winkers,' ii. 102. 11.
Waur, worse.

Waur, to worst: 'and faith, he'll waur me,' i. 195. 4; 'waur them a',' ii. 182. 1.
Waur't, worsted, beat [in running]: 'might aiblins waur't thee for a brattle,' i. 103. 2.
Wean [wee one], a child.
Weanies, babies: 'when skirlin weanies see the light,' i. 22. 19.
Weason, weasand.
Wecht, a measure for corn: 'three wechts o' naething,' i. 96. 11. See Note, vol. i. 359.
Wee, a little; *a wee*, a short space, or time.
Wee things, children, i. 90. 3, and i. 107. 8.
Weel, well.
Weel-faured, well-favoured.
Weel-gaun, well-going.
Weel-hain'd, well-saved: 'her weel-hain'd kebbuck,' i. 110. 15; 'weel-hain'd gear,' i. 207. 12.
Weepers, mournings [on the sleeve, or hat]: 'auld cantie Kyle may weepers wear,' i. 145. 11.
Werena, were not.
We'se, we shall.
Westlin, western.
Wha, who.
Whaizle, wheeze: 'and gar't them whaizle,' i. 103. 4.
Whalpet, whelped.
Wham, whom.
Whan, when.
Whang, a shive, a large slice: 'in monie a whang,' i. 39. 3.
Whang, flog: 'and gloriously she'll whang her,' i. 211. 13.
Whar, whare, where.

GLOSSARIAL INDEX

Wha's, whose.
Wha's, who is.
Whase, whose.
What for, whatfore, wherefore: 'What for no?'=Why not? ii. 98. 11 and 15.
Whatna, what [partly in contempt]: 'whatna day o' whatna style,' iv. 13. 6.
What reck, what matter, nevertheless: 'but yet, what reck, he at Quebec,' i. 247. 5; 'when I, whatreck, did least expeck,' iii. 104. 11.
Whatt, whittled, ii. 74. 11. See Note, vol. ii. 357.
Whaup, the curlew, ii. 70. 12. See Note, vol. ii. 355.
Whaur, where.
Wheep, v. *Penny-wheep*.
Wheep, jerk: 'to see our elbucks wheep,' i. 213. 3.
Whid, a fib: 'a rousing whid at times to vend,' i. 191. 5.
Whiddin, scudding: 'an' morning poussie whiddin seen,' i. 155. 3; 'ye maukins whiddin through the glade,' i. 263. 21.
Whids, gambols: 'jinkin hares, in amorous whids,' i. 170. 9.
Whigmeleeries, crotchets: 'whigmeleeries in your noddle,' i. 204. 6.
Whingin, whining: 'if onie whiggish, whingin sot,' i. 268. 5.
Whins, furze: 'thro' the whins an' [and] by the cairn,' i. 97. 19, and i. 282. 9.
Whirlygigums, flourishes, i. 203. 20.

Whisht, silence: 'held my whisht'=kept silence, i. 76. 13.
Whissle, whistle.
Whitter, a draught: 'tak our whitter,' i. 160. 9.
Whittle, a knife.
Wi', with.
Wick: 'wick a bore,' i. 221. 18. See Note, vol. i. 403.
Wi's, with his.
Wi't, with it.
Widdifu', gallows-worthy: 'a widdifu', bleerit knurl', iv. 38. 15.
Widdle, wriggle: 'the weary widdle,' ii. 81. 13, and ii. 100. 9.
Wiel, eddy: 'whyles in a wiel it dimpl't,' i. 98. 4.
Wight, strong, stout: 'wight an' wilfu',' ii. 40. 5; 'wight and stark,' ii. 217. 8.
Wighter, more influential, ii. 178. 7.
Willcat, wild cat.
Willyart, disordered: 'willyart glow'r,' ii. 50. 8.
Wimple, to meander.
Win, won: 'like fortune's favours, tint as win'=lost as soon as won, iii. 145. 12.
Winn, to winnow: 'to winn three wechts o' naething,' i. 96. 11.
Winna, will not.
Winnin, winding: 'the warpin o't, the winnin o't,' iii. 159. 2.
Winnock, window.
Winnock-bunker, v. *Bunker*.
Win't, did wind: 'an' ay she win't,' i. 92. 19.

Wintle, a somersault: 'tumbled wi' a wintle,' i. 95. 22.
Wintle, (1) to stagger: 'wintle like a saumont-cobble,' i. 102. 2; (2) to swing, to wriggle: 'wintle in a woodie,' ii. 46. 17; 'that wintles in a halter,' ii. 265. 4.
Winze, a curse: 'loot a winze,' i. 97. 12.
Wiss, wish.
Won, to dwell: 'there was a wife wonn'd in Cockpen,' iii. 192. 1; 'there wons auld Colin's bonie lass,' iii. 199. 11; 'Auld Rob Morris that wons in yon glen,' iii. 210. 1. Cf. 'The wild beast, where he wons,' Milton, *Paradise Lost*, vii. 457.
Wonner, a wonder, a marvel: 'blastit wonner,' i. 11. 19, and i. 152. 19.
Woo', wool.
Woodie, woody, a rope [originally of withes]: (1) 'the meikle Devil wi' a woodie,' i. 262. 2; (2) a gallows rope: 'wintle in a woodie,' ii. 46. 17; (3) the gallows: 'the waefu' woodie,' ii. 8. 6; 'learning in a woody dance,' ii. 24. 20.
Woodies, twigs, withes: 'saugh woodies,' ii. 130. 5.
Wooer-babs: love-knots, i. 89. 10.
Wordy, worthy: 'wordy of a grace,' i. 237. 5; 'a wordy beast,' ii. 40. 16.
Worset, worsted: 'her braw, new worset apron,' i. 93. 13.
Worth, v. *Wae Worth.*
Wrang, wrong.
Wud, wild, mad: 'as wud as wud can be,' i. 23. 6; 'like onie wud bear,' iii. 131. 1. See also *Red-wud*.
Wumble, wimble: 'gleg as onie wumble,' i. 145. 9.
Wyliecoat, undervest, i. 154. 4.
Wyte [weight], blame: 'Had I the wyte?' iii. 149.
Wyte, to blame, to reproach, i. 23. 12; ii. 102. 3.

Yard, a garden, a stackyard.
Yaud, an old mare: 'the auld grey yaud,' ii. 198. 19.
Yealings, coevals, i. 206. 14.
Yell, dry [milkless]: 'as yell's the bill,' i. 50. 6.
Yerd, earth: 'their green beds in the yerd,' iii. 92. 14. See *Yird*.
Yerkit, jerked: 'yerkit up sublime,' i. 60. 9.
Yerl, Earl.
Ye'se, ye shall.
Yestreen, last night.
Yett, a gate.
Yeuk, to itch: 'If Warren Hastings' neck was yeukin,' ii. 132. 16; 'yeuks wi' joy,' ii. 140. 15.
Yill, ale.
Yill-caup, ale-stoup. See *Caup*.
Yird, yearth, earth; v. *Yerd*.
Yokin, yoking; (1) a spell, a day's work: 'a yokin at the pleugh,' ii. 104. 4; (2) a set to: 'a hearty yokin at "sang about,"' i. 155. 11-12.
Yon, yonder.
'Yont, beyond.
Yowe, ewe.
Yowie, dim. of *ewe*; a pet ewe.
Yule, Christmas.

GENERAL INDEX OF TITLES AND FIRST LINES[1]

	TEXT	NOTES
A Bard's Epitaph	i. 189	391
Aberfeldie, The Birks of	iii. 7	306
Adair, Eppie	iii. 72	356
Adam Armour's Prayer	ii. 44	339
Additional Lines at Stirling	ii. 244	435
Additional Stanzas on Fergusson	ii. 269	452
Address of Beelzebub	ii. 154	388
—— Spoken by Miss Fontenelle	ii. 152	387
—— to a Haggis	i. 237	407
—— to Edinburgh	i. 239	408
—— to the Deil	i. 47	335
—— to the Shade of Thomson	i. 288	444
—— to the Toothache	ii. 51	342
—— to the Unco Guid	i. 217	402
A Dedication to Gavin Hamilton, Esq.	i. 147	378
Adieu! a Heart-warm, Fond Adieu	i. 184	388
Admiring Nature in her Wildest Grace	i. 301	451
Adown winding Nith I did wander	iii. 227	460
A Dream	i. 68	348
Ae day, as Death, that Gruesome Carl	ii. 264	450
Ae fond Kiss, and then we Sever	iii. 105	379
Afar the Illustrious Exile Roams	ii. 157	388
A Fragment: When Guilford Good	i. 246	411
Afton, Sweet	iii. 134	394
Again Rejoicing Nature Sees	i. 253	416
Against the Earl of Galloway	ii. 252	440

[1] Includes index of the proper names in the titles.

VOL. IV. M

GENERAL INDEX OF

	TEXT	NOTES
Again the Silent Wheels of Time	i. 236	407
A Guid New-Year I wish thee, Maggie	i. 100	360
Ah, Chloris, since it may not be	iv. 37	98
A Head, Pure, Sinless quite of Brain and Soul	ii. 246	436
A Highland Welcome	ii. 245	436
Ah, Woe is Me, my Mother Dear	ii. 212	410
Aiken, Esq., For Robert	i. 188	390
Ainslie in Church, On Miss	ii. 243	433
A Lass wi' a Tocher	iii. 229	461
Albanie, The Bonie Lass of	iv. 22	90
A Little Upright, Pert, Tart, Tripping Wight	ii. 235	425
Allan Stream, By	iii. 231	462
All Hail, Inexorable Lord	i. 139	376
All Villain as I am—a Damnèd Wretch	ii. 233	423
Altho' he has Left me for Greed o' the Siller	iv. 45	104
Altho' my Back be at the Wa'	iii. 177	431
Altho' my Bed were in yon Muir	iv. 3	82
Altho' Thou maun never be Mine	iii. 237	467
Amang the Trees, where Humming Bees	iv. 23	91
A Mauchline Wedding	ii. 42	338
Among the Heathy Hills and Ragged Woods	i. 302	451
A Mother's Lament	iii. 67	352
Ance Mair I Hail Thee, Thou Gloomy December	iii. 185	437
Anderson My Jo, John, John	iii. 63	349
And I'll Kiss Thee Yet	iii. 34	330
A New Psalm for the Chapel of Kilmarnock	ii. 162	391
An Honest Man Here Lies at Rest	ii. 264	450
Anna, Thy Charms My Bosom Fire	i. 293	447
Ann, Beware o' Bonie	iii. 46	338
An Somebodie Were Come Again	iii. 57	346
A Poet's Grace	ii. 262	449
A Poet's Welcome to his Love-Begotten Daughter	ii. 37	334

TITLES AND FIRST LINES 179

	TEXT	NOTES
Apology to John Syme	ii. 259	447
Apostrophe to Fergusson	ii. 211	408
A Prayer in the Prospect of Death	i. 135	375
A Red, Red Rose	iii. 143	402
Armour's Prayer, Adam	ii. 44	339
A Rose-Bud, by My Early Walk	iii. 33	329
A Ruined Farmer	iv. 1	81
As Cauld a Wind as Ever Blew	ii. 249	439
As doun the Burn they took their Way	iv. 45	104
As Father Adam First was Fool'd	i. 186	389
As I Came O'er the Cairney Mount	iii. 171	427
As I Gaed Down the Water-Side	iii. 65	350
As I Gaed Up by Yon Gate-End	iv. 37	98
As I Stood by Yon Roofless Tower	iii. 144	406
As I was Walking up the Street	iii. 207	446
Ask why God Made the Gem so Small	ii. 248	437
A Slave to Love's Unbounded Sway	iii. 203	444
As Mailie, an' her Lambs Thegither	i. 53	343
A Sonnet upon Sonnets	ii. 232	422
As on the Banks of Winding Nith	iv. 53	106
As Tam the Chapman on a Day	ii. 265	450
At Brownhill we Always Get Dainty Good Cheer	ii. 249	438
At Carron Ironworks	ii. 243	434
At Friars Carse Hermitage	ii. 259	447
At Inveraray	ii. 243	433
At Roslin Inn	ii. 241	430
At the Globe Tavern	ii. 263	449
At the Globe Tavern, Dumfries	ii. 250	439
At Whigham's Inn, Sanquhar	ii. 245	436
August, Composed in	i. 181	387
Auld Chuckie Reekie's Sair Distrest	ii. 53	344
Auld Comrade Dear and Brither Sinner	ii. 124	375
Auld Lang Syne	iii. 147	407
Auld Neebor, I'm Three Times Doubly o'er Your Debtor	ii. 81	358
Auld Rob Morris	iii. 210	449

GENERAL INDEX OF

	TEXT	NOTES
A' the Lads o' Thorniebank	iii. 21	320
A Waukrife Minnie	iii. 77	358
Awa, Whigs, Awa	iii. 64	350
Awa wi' Your Witchcraft o' Beauty's Alarms	iii. 229	461
A Winter Night	i. 225	404
A' Ye Wha Live by Sowps o' Drink	i. 144	378
Ayr, The Brigs of	i. 200	393
Ay Waukin, O	iii. 45	337
Babington's Looks, On Dr.	ii. 257	445
Ballads on Mr. Heron's Election, 1795:		
First	ii. 191	401
Second: The Election	ii. 193	402
Third: John Bushby's Lamentation	ii. 197	405
Fourth: The Trogger	ii. 201	406
Ballochmyle, The Braes o'	iii. 69	353
Ballochmyle, The Lass o'	iv. 16	87
Bannocks o' Bear Meal	iii. 175	430
Barleycorn, John	i. 243	409
Beauteous Rosebud, Young and Gay	i. 292	447
Beelzebub, Address of	ii. 154	388
Behind Yon Hills Where Lugar Flows	i. 249	412
Behold the Hour, the Boat Arrive	{ iii. 265 { iv. 34	487 96
Bell, Bonie	iii. 135	396
Below Thir Stanes Lie Jamie's Banes	i. 187	390
Beware o' Bonie Ann	iii. 46	338
Birthday Ode for 31st December 1787	ii. 157	388
Blacklock, To Dr.	ii. 128	377
Blair, Elegy on the Death of Sir James Hunter	ii. 218	413
Bless Jesus Christ, O Cardoness	ii. 273	456
Blest be M'Murdo to his Latest Day	ii. 229	419
Blythe Hae I Been on Yon Hill	iii. 230	461
Blythe Was She	iii. 29	326
Boghead, Here lies	ii. 264	449
Bonie Bell	iii. 135	396

TITLES AND FIRST LINES 181

	TEXT	NOTES
Bonie Dundee	iii. 2	301
Bonie Wee Thing	iii. 103	378
Braw, Braw Lads on Yarrow Braes . .	iii. 209	448
Braw Lads o' Galla Water . . .	iii. 209	448
Bright ran thy Line, O Galloway . .	ii. 252	440
Brownhill Inn, At	ii. 249	438
Bruar Water, The Humble Petition of .	i. 295	449
Burnet of Monboddo, Elegy on the late Miss	ii. 224	417
Burns, Under the Portrait of Miss . .	ii. 242	432
Bushby of Tinwald Downs, On John .	ii. 274	457
Bushby's Lamentation, John . . .	ii. 197	405
But Lately Seen in Gladsome Green . .	iii. 178	431
But Warily Tent when Ye Come to Court Me	iii. 5	304
By Allan Stream I Chanc'd to Rove .	iii. 231	462
By Love and by Beauty	iii. 72	356
By Oughtertyre Grows the Aik . .	iii. 29	326
By Yon Castle Wa' at the Close of the Day	iii. 92	367
Caledonia	iv. 29	94
Can I Cease to Care	iii. 261	484
Canst Thou Leave Me	iii. 232	463
Carl, an the King Come	iii. 57	346
Carron Ironworks, At	ii. 243	434
Castle Gordon	ii. 60	349
Ca' the Yowes to the Knowes (First Set) .	iii. 65	350
(Second Set)	iii. 268	488
Cauld blaws the Wind frae East to West .	iii. 16	315
Cauld is the E'enin' Blast . . .	iii. 203	444
Cease, ye Prudes, your Envious Railing .	ii. 242	432
Cessnock Banks, The Lass of . . .	iv. 3	82
Chalmers' Sweetheart, To Willie . .	ii. 90	361
Charlie He's My Darling	iii. 154	414
—— O'er the Water to	iii. 32	328
Chloris, Ah	iv. 37	98
—— Inscription to	ii. 142	381
—— Mark, My	iii. 256	481

GENERAL INDEX OF

	TEXT	NOTES
Chloris, On	ii. 256	444
Clarinda, Mistress of My Soul	iii. 39	334
—— Sylvander to	ii. 112	368
—— with a Pair of Wine Glasses, To	ii. 115	370
Cock Up Your Beaver	iii. 89	366
Come Boat Me O'er, Come Row Me O'er	iii. 32	328
Come, Bumpers High! Express your Joy	iv. 31	95
Come, Let Me Take Thee to My Breast	iii. 233	463
Comin' Thro' the Rye, Poor Bodie	iii. 151	411
Composed in August	i. 181	387
Composed in Spring	i. 253	416
Contented wi' Little and Cantie wi' Mair	iii. 234	464
Corn Rigs	i. 180	385
Craigdarroch, Fam'd for Speaking Art	ii. 236	427
Craigieburn, Sweet Fa's the Eve on	iii. 225	459
—— Wood	iii. 86	363
Creech, Lament for the Absence of William	ii. 53	344
—— On William	ii. 235	425
Crookieden, I Hae Been at	iii. 99	374
Cruickshank, A. M., For William	ii. 270	453
—— To Miss	i. 292	447
Cuddy, The Cooper o'	iii. 157	416
Cunningham, To Alexander	ii. 118	371
Curs'd be the Man, the Poorest Wretch in Life	ii. 248	438
Curse on Ungrateful Man, that can be Pleas'd	ii. 211	408
Daer, Lines on Meeting with Lord	ii. 49	340
Daughter of Chaos' Doting Years	ii. 159	389
Davie, a Brother Poet, Epistle to	i. 117	365
—— Second Epistle to	ii. 81	358
Davies, Lovely	iii. 106	380
—— On Miss	ii. 248	437
Davison, Duncan	iii. 19	319
Dear ——, I'll Gie ye Some Advice	ii. 241	431
Dear Peter, dear Peter	ii. 133	378

TITLES AND FIRST LINES

	TEXT	NOTES
Dear Sir, at onie Time or Tide	ii. 124	375
Dear Smith, the Slee'st, Pawkie Thief	i. 59	347
Death and Doctor Hornbook	i. 191	391
Delia	iv. 63	107
Deluded Swain, the Pleasure	iii. 217	454
De Peyster, To Colonel	ii. 139	380
Despondency	i. 127	372
Devon Banks, Fairest Maid on	iii. 258	481
—— The Banks of the	iii. 22	320
Dire was the Hate at Old Harlaw	ii. 204	406
Does Haughty Gaul Invasion Threat	iii. 195	441
Doon, Sweet are the Banks o'	iv. 27	94
—— The Banks o'	iii. 124	388
—— Ye Flowery Banks o' Bonie	iv. 28	94
Dost Ask Me Why I send Thee Here	iv. 42	100
Dost Thou not Rise, Indignant Shade	ii. 227	418
Dove, On John	ii. 267	451
Drumlanrig Woods, On the Destruction of	iv. 53	106
Dumfries, Prologue Spoken at the Theatre of	ii. 146	383
Dumourier's Desertion	ii. 228	419
Dunbar, Sweet Tibbie	iii. 42	335
Duncan Davison	iii. 19	319
Duncan Gray (First Set)	iii. 23	321
—— —— (Second Set)	iii. 215	452
Dundas, On the Death of Lord President	ii. 221	414
Dundee, Bonie	iii. 2	301
Dweller in Yon Dungeon Dark	i. 260	420
Ecclefechan, The Lass o'	iii. 156	415
Edina! Scotia's Darling Seat	i. 239	408
Edinburgh, Address to	i. 239	408
Election Ballad Addressed to Robert Graham, Esq. of Fintry	ii. 183	399
Election Ballad for Westerha'	ii. 182	397
Election, Ballads on Mr. Heron's, 1795	ii. 191	401
Elegy on Captain Matthew Henderson	i. 262	423

GENERAL INDEX OF

	TEXT	NOTES
Elegy on Stella	iv. 46	105
Elegy on the Death of Sir James Hunter Blair	ii. 218	413
—— on the Death of Robert Ruisseaux	ii. 216	412
—— on the Departed Year 1788	ii. 58	348
—— on the Late Miss Burnet of Monboddo	ii. 224	417
—— on Willie Nicol's Mare	ii. 223	416
Eliza, From Thee	i. 183	388
Elphinstone's Translation of Martial, On	ii. 242	431
Envy, if thy Jaundiced Eye	ii. 245	436
Epistle to a Young Friend	i. 140	376
—— to Davie, a Brother Poet	i. 117	365
—— —— Second	ii. 81	358
—— to James Smith	i. 59	347
—— to J. Lapraik	i. 155	380
—— —— Second	i. 161	382
—— —— Third	ii. 73	357
—— to John Rankine	i. 176	384
Eppie Adair	iii. 72	356
Esopus to Maria, From	ii. 66	353
Expect na, Sir, in this Narration	i. 147	378
Extempore in the Court of Session	ii. 240	430
Extempore to Gavin Hamilton	ii. 93	362
Fair Eliza	iii. 119	385
Fair Empress of the Poet's Soul	ii. 115	370
Fairest Maid on Devon Banks	iii. 258	481
Fair Fa' Your Honest, Sonsie Face	i. 237	407
Fair Maid, You Need not Take the Hint	ii. 243	433
Fair the Face of Orient Day	iv. 63	107
Farewell, Dear Friend! May Guid Luck Hit You	ii. 90	360
Farewell, Old Scotia's Bleak Domains	ii. 215	411
Farewell, Thou Fair Day, Thou Green Earth, and Ye Skies	iii. 133	394
Farewell, Thou Stream that Winding Flows	iii. 235	465
Farewell to a' our Scottish Fame	iii. 127	391
Farewell to the Brethren of St. James's Lodge, Tarbolton	i. 184	389

TITLES AND FIRST LINES

	TEXT	NOTES
Farewell to the Highlands, Farewell to the North	iii. 62	348
Farewell, ye Dungeons Dark and Strong	iii. 9	307
Fate Gave the Word—the Arrow Sped	iii. 67	352
Fergusson, Additional Stanzas on	ii. 269	452
—— Apostrophe to	ii. 211	408
—— Lines on	ii. 224	416
—— On Robert	ii. 268	451
Ferrier, To Miss	ii. 111	367
Fill Me with the Rosy Wine	ii. 260	448
Fintry, My Stay in Worldly Strife	ii. 183	399
—— see Graham.		
First, When Maggie was My Care	iii. 58	346
Flow Gently, Sweet Afton, Among Thy Green Braes	iii. 134	394
Fontenelle, Address Spoken by Miss	ii. 152	387
—— On Miss	ii. 254	441
For an Altar of Independence	ii. 259	448
For Gabriel Richardson	ii. 275	461
For Gavin Hamilton, Esq.	i. 188	390
For Lords or Kings I Dinna Mourn	ii. 58	348
Forlorn My Love, no Comfort Near	iii. 266	487
For Mr. Walter Riddell	ii. 272	455
For Mr. William Michie	ii. 269	453
For Robert Aiken, Esq.	i. 188	390
For Shame! Let Folly and Knavery	ii. 242	432
For the Author's Father	i. 188	390
For Thee is Laughing Nature Gay	iv. 44	103
For the Sake o' Somebody	iii. 158	416
Forth, Out over the	iii. 153	413
For William Cruickshank, A.M.	ii. 270	453
For William Nicol	ii. 269	452
Fourteen, a Sonneteer Thy Praises Sings	ii. 232	422
Fox, Inscribed to The Right Hon. C. J.	ii. 165	392
Frae the Friends and Land I Love	iii. 88	363
Friars Carse Hermitage, At	ii. 259	447
—— —— —— Verses in	ii. 57	347

GENERAL INDEX OF

	TEXT	NOTES
Friars Carse Hermitage, Written in	i. 258	418
Friday First's the Day Appointed	ii. 89	360
Friend of the Poet, Tried and Leal	ii. 137	380
From Esopus to Maria	ii. 66	353
From Thee, Eliza, I Must Go	i. 183	388
From the White-blossom'd Sloe My Dear Chloris Requested	ii. 256	444
From those Drear Solitudes and Frowsy Cells	ii. 66	353
Full Well Thou Know'st I Love Thee Dear——	iii. 258	481
Fyers, Lines on the Fall of	i. 302	451
Fy, Let Us A' to Kirkcudbright	ii. 193	402
Galla Water, Braw Lads o'	iii. 209	448
Galloway, Against the Earl of	ii. 252	440
—— Laird, On a	ii. 273	456
Gane is the Day, and Mirk's the Night	iii. 91	366
Gat Ye Me, O, Gat Ye Me	iii. 156	415
Gaul Invasion Threat, Does Haughty	iii. 195	441
Glen, Tam	iii. 84	363
Glencairn, Lament for James, Earl of	i. 274	431
Glenriddell's Fox Breaking his Chain, On	ii. 168	392
Globe Tavern, Dumfries, At the	{ ii. 250 { ii. 263	439 449
Go, Fetch to Me a Pint o' Wine	iii. 53	343
Goldie's Brains, On Commissary	ii. 251	440
Goldie, To John	ii. 70	355
Gordon Castle	ii. 60	349
Gordon's Reel Dancing, On the Duchess of	ii. 61	350
Gracie, Thou Art a Man of Worth	ii. 259	447
Graham, Esq. of Fintry, Election Ballad Addressed to Robert	ii. 183	399
—— Esq. of Fintry, Sonnet to Robert	ii. 127	376
—— —— To Robert	{ i. 271 { ii. 119	427 371
—— of Fintry, Inscription to Miss	ii. 136	379

TITLES AND FIRST LINES 187

	TEXT	NOTES
Graham of Mossknowe, On William .	ii. 274	457
Grant Me, Indulgent Heaven, that I may Live	ii. 252	440
Gray, Duncan (First Set)	iii. 23	321
—— —— (Second Set)	iii. 215	452
—— To Symon	ii. 110	367
—— Wee Willie	iii. 188	438
Green Grow the Rashes, O . . .	i. 251	414
Gregory, Lord	iii. 220	455
Grieve, Laird of Boghead, Tarbolton, On James	ii. 264	449
Grizzel Grimme, On	ii. 275	458
Grose, On Captain Francis . . .	{ ii. 62	352
	ii. 247	437
Grose's Peregrinations Thro' Scotland, On the Late Captain	i. 289	445
Gude Pity Me, Because I'm Little . .	ii. 44	339
Guid E'en to You, Kimmer . . .	iii. 189	438
Guid-mornin' to Your Majesty . . .	i. 68	348
Guid Speed and Furder to You, Johnie .	ii. 73	357
Guidwife, Count the Lawin . . .	iii. 91	366
—— I Mind it Weel, in Early Date .	ii. 104	364
Guilford Good, When	i. 246	411
Had I a Cave	iii. 236	467
Had I the Wyte? Had I the Wyte . .	iii. 149	410
Hail, Poesie! thou Nymph reserv'd . .	iv. 50	105
Hail, Thairm-inspirin', Rattlin' Willie .	ii. 99	363
Halloween	i. 88	356
Hamilton, Esq., A Dedication to Gavin .	i. 147	378
—— —— Extempore to Gavin . .	ii. 93	362
—— —— For Gavin	i. 188	390
—— —— To Gavin	ii. 85	359
Hampden, On Johnson's Opinion of .	ii. 242	432
Hark, the Mavis' E'ening Sang . .	iii. 268	488
Harry, Highland	iii. 42	335
Has Auld Kilmarnock Seen the Deil .	i. 220	402

	TEXT	NOTES
Ha! Whare Ye Gaun, Ye Crowlin' Ferlie.	i. 152	379
Health to the Maxwells' Vet'ran Chief	ii. 133	378
Hear, Land o' Cakes, and Brither Scots	i. 289	445
Heard ye o' the Tree o' France	iv. 58	107
He Clench'd His Pamphlets in His Fist	ii. 240	430
Hee Balou, My Sweet Wee Donald	iii. 175	429
He Looked Just as Your Sign-post Lions Do	ii. 246	436
Henderson, Elegy on Captain Matthew	i. 262	423
Her Daddie Forbad, Her Minnie Forbad	iii. 15	315
Here Awa', There Awa', Wandering Willie	iii. 208	446
Here Brewer Gabriel's Fire's Extinct	ii. 275	458
Here Cursing, Swearing Burton Lies	ii. 274	458
Here Holy Willie's Sair Worn Clay.	ii. 266	451
Here is the Glen, and Here the Bower	iii. 218	454
Here Lies a Mock Marquis, Whose Titles were Shamm'd	ii. 275	458
Here Lies Boghead Amang the Dead	ii. 264	449
Here Lies in Earth a Root of Hell	ii. 274	457
Here Lies John Bushby—Honest Man	ii. 274	457
Here Lies Johnie Pigeon	ii. 267	451
Here Lie Willie Michie's Banes	ii. 269	453
Here Lyes with Dethe Auld Grizzel Grimme	ii. 275	458
Here's a Bottle	iv. 21	90
Here's a Health	iii. 237	467
Here's a Health to Them That's Awa	iv. 35	96
Here's his Health in Water	iii. 177	431
Here Souter Hood in Death Does Sleep	i. 187	389
Here Stewarts Once in Glory Reigned	ii. 244	434
Here's to Thy Health, My Bonie Lass	iii. 181	433
Here, Where the Scottish Muse Immortal Lives	ii. 136	379
Her Flowing Locks, the Raven's Wing	iv. 16	86
Heron's Election, 1795, Ballads on	ii. 191	407
He Who of Rankine Sang, Lies Stiff and Deid	ii. 275	461
Hey, Ca' Thro'	iii. 137	397

TITLES AND FIRST LINES 189

	TEXT	NOTES
Hey the Dusty Miller	iii. 17	318
Highland Harry	iii. 42	335
—— Laddie	iii. 172	428
—— Mary	iii. 255	430
His Face with Smile Eternal Drest	ii. 246	436
Holy Willie's Prayer	ii. 25	320
Hood, Here Souter	i. 187	389
Hornbook, Death and Dr.	i. 191	391
How Can My Poor Heart be Glad	iii. 269	488
How Cold is that Bosom that Folly Once Fired	ii. 271	455
How Cruel are the Parents	iii. 238	468
How Daur Ye Ca' Me Howlet-Face	ii. 249	439
How Lang and Dreary is the Night	iii. 27	324
How, 'Liberty!' Girl, Can it be by Thee Nam'd	ii. 256	444
How Pleasant the Banks of the Clear Winding Devon	iii. 22	320
How Wisdom and Folly Meet, Mix, and Unite	ii. 165	392
Humid Seal of Soft Affections	iv. 62	107
Husband, Husband, Cease Your Strife	iii. 239	469
I Am a Keeper of the Law	ii. 70	355
I Am My Mammie's ae Bairn	iii. 6	305
I Bought My Wife a Stane o' Lint	iii. 108	380
I Call no Goddess to Inspire My Strains	ii. 127	376
I Coft a Stane o' Haslock Woo	iii. 159	417
I Do Confess Thou Art Sae Fair	iii. 96	371
I Dream'd I Lay Where Flowers Were Springing	iii. 18	318
I Fee'd a Man at Martinmas	iii. 138	397
If Thou Should Ask My Love	iii. 53	342
If Ye Gae Up to Yon Hill-Top	ii. 206	407
If You Rattle Along Like Your Mistress's Tongue	ii. 255	442
I Gaed a Waefu' Gate Yestreen	iii. 82	362

	TEXT	NOTES
I Gaed Up to Dunse.	iii. 194	440
I Gat Your Letter, Winsome Willie.	i. 167	383
I Had Sax Owsen in a Pleugh.	iii. 193	440
I Hae a Wife o' My Ain.	iii. 109	381
I Hae Been at Crookieden	iii. 99	374
I Hold It, Sir, My Bounden Duty.	ii. 85	359
I Lang Hae Thought, My Youthfu' Friend	i. 140	376
I'll Ay Ca' in by Yon Town.	iii. 166	423
Ill-fated Genius! Heaven-taught Fergusson	ii. 224	416
I'll Go and be a Sodger.	ii. 211	408
I Love My Love in Secret	iii. 41	335
I Married with a Scolding Wife	iv. 55	106
I'm now Arrived—Thanks to the Gods!	iv. 46	104
I'm O'er Young to Marry Yet.	iii. 6	305
Impromptu on Mrs. Riddell's Birthday	ii. 230	420
—— to Captain Riddell.	ii. 123	374
I Murder Hate by Field or Flood	ii. 250	439
In a Lady's Pocket-Book.	ii. 252	440
In Comin' by the Brig o' Dye.	iii. 20	320
I Never Saw a Fairer	iii. 285	498
In Honest Bacon's Ingle-Neuk.	ii. 135	379
Inhuman Man, Curse on Thy Barbarous Art	i. 287	441
In Lamington Kirk.	ii. 249	439
In Mauchline There Dwells Six Proper Young Belles.	ii. 212	410
Inscribed on a Work of Hannah More's.	ii. 213	411
Inscribed to the Right Hon. C. J. Fox	ii. 165	392
Inscription to Chloris	ii. 142	381
Inscription to Miss Graham of Fintry	ii. 136	379
In Se'enteen Hunder 'n Forty-Nine.	ii. 257	446
In Simmer, When the Hay was Mawn	iii. 117	384
Instead of a Song, Boys, I'll Give You a Toast	ii. 170	392
In Tarbolton, Ye Ken, There are Proper Young Men	ii. 207	408
In this Strange Land, this Uncouth Clime	ii. 116	370

TITLES AND FIRST LINES 191

	TEXT	NOTES
In Vain would Prudence with Decorous Sneer	ii. 239	429
Inveraray, At	ii. 243	433
Inverness, The Lovely Lass of	iii. 142	401
In Wood and Wild, Ye Warbling Throng	ii. 270	454
I Rue the Day I Sought Her, O	iii. 51	341
I See a Form, I See a Face	iii. 248	473
I Sing of a Whistle, a Whistle of Worth	i. 304	452
Is there a Whim-inspirèd Fool	i. 189	391
Is there for Honest Poverty	iii. 271	489
Is this thy Plighted, Fond Regard	iii. 232	463
It is na, Jean, thy Bonie Face	iii. 100	374
It was a' for our Rightfu' King	iii. 182	433
It was in Sweet Senegal	iii. 132	392
It was the Charming Month of May	iii. 241	469
It was upon a Lammas Night	i. 180	385
Jamie comes Hame, There'll never be Peace till	iii. 92	367
Jamie, Come Try Me	iii. 52	342
Jamie, Thou Hast Left Me Ever	iii. 254	480
Jeanie's Face, When First I Saw Fair	iv. 32	95
Jean, thy Bonie Face, It is na,	iii. 100	374
Jessie, Young	iii. 226	459
Jockie's Ta'en the Parting Kiss	iii. 201	444
Jockie was the Blythest Lad, Young	iii. 76	358
John Anderson My Jo, John	iii. 63	349
John Barleycorn	i. 243	409
John, Come Kiss Me Now, O,	iii. 88	365
Johnie, On Wee	i. 187	390
John, Jumpin	iii. 14	315
J——n, To the Beautiful Miss Eliza	ii. 256	444
Johnson's Opinion of Hampden, On	ii. 242	432
Jumpin John	iii. 14	315
Kellyburn Braes	iii. 129	391
Kemble in Yarico, On Seeing Mrs.	ii. 257	445
Kemble, Thou Cur'st my Unbelief	ii. 257	445

192   GENERAL INDEX OF

	TEXT	NOTES
Kenmure's On and Awa, Willie, O	iii. 112	382
Kennedy, To John	ii. 83	358
—— —— A Farewell	ii. 90	360
Ken Ye Ought o' Captain Grose	ii. 62	352
Killiecrankie	iii. 81	361
Kilmarnock Wabsters Fidge an' Claw	i. 210	397
Kind Sir, I've Read Your Paper Through	ii. 131	378
Kirk and State Excisemen	ii. 254	442
Know Thou, O Stranger to the Fame	i. 188	390
Kyle, There was a Lad was Born in	iv. 13	85
Laddie, Lie Near Me	iii. 47	338
Lady Mary Ann	iii. 126	388
Lady Onlie, Honest Lucky	iii. 21	320
Laggan, On the Laird of	ii. 253	441
Lament for James, Earl of Glencairn	i. 274	431
Lament for the Absence of William Creech	ii. 53	344
Lament Him, Mauchline Husbands a'	ii. 268	451
Lament in Rhyme, Lament in Prose	i. 56	344
Lament of Mary Queen of Scots	i. 268	425
Lamington Kirk, In	ii. 249	439
Landlady, Count the Lawin	iii. 25	323
Lang hae we Pairted Been	iii. 47	338
Lapraik, Epistle to { First	i. 155	380
Second	161	382
Third	ii. 73	357
Lascelles, On Captain	ii. 273	456
Lassie wi' the Lint-White Locks	iii. 259	482
Last May a Braw Wooer Cam Down the Lang Glen	iii. 242	470
Late Crippl'd of an Arm and now a Leg	i. 271	427
Lesley, O Saw Ye Bonie	iii. 224	458
Let Loove Sparkle in her E'e	iv. 45	104
Let not Women e'er Complain	iii. 219	455
Let Other Heroes Boast Their Scars	ii. 47	340
Let Other Poets Raise a Frácas	i. 19	322
Lewars, To Miss Jessie	ii. 141	380

TITLES AND FIRST LINES 193

	TEXT	NOTES
Lewars, Versicles to Jessie	ii. 260	448
Life Ne'er Exulted in so Rich a Prize	ii. 224	417
Light Lay the Earth on Billie's Breast	ii. 273	456
Lines on Fergusson	ii. 224	416
—— on Meeting With Lord Daer	ii. 49	340
—— on the Fall of Fyers	i. 302	451
—— to Sir John Whitefoord, Bart.	i. 278	433
—— Written on a Bank Note	ii. 214	411
Logan, To Major	ii. 99	363
——, To Miss	i. 236	407
—— Water	iii. 262	484
Lone on the Bleaky Hills, the Straying Flocks	ii. 221	414
Long Life, My Lord, an' Health be Yours	ii. 154	388
Long, Long the Night	iii. 260	484
Lord Gregory	iii. 220	455
Lord, Thee We Thank, and Thee Alone	ii. 263	449
Lord, to Account Who does Thee Call	ii. 251	440
Loud Blaw the Frosty Breezes	iii. 16	318
Louis, What Reck I by Thee	iii. 149	410
Lovely Davies	iii. 106	380
Lovely Polly Stewart	iii. 174	429
Lugar Flows, Behind Yon Hills Where	i. 249	412
M'Adam of Cragen-Gillan, To Mr.	ii. 87	359
Mackenzie, To Dr.	ii. 89	360
M'Leod, Esq., On the Death of John	i. 294	448
——, To Miss Isabella	ii. 109	367
M'Math, To the Rev. John	ii. 76	357
M'Murdo, On John	ii. 229	419
Macnab, My Eppie	iii. 101	375
M'Pherson's Farewell	iii. 9	307
Maggie, The Auld Farmer's New-Year Morning Salutation to His Auld Mare	i. 100	360
Mailie, The Death and Dying Words of Poor	i. 53	343
Mailie's Elegy, Poor	i. 56	344

GENERAL INDEX OF

	TEXT	NOTES
Mally's Meek, Mally's Sweet	iii. 207	446
	iv. 69	108
Man was Made to Mourn	i. 130	373
Maria, From Esopus to	ii. 66	353
Mark Yonder Pomp of Costly Fashion	iii. 273	492
Mary Ann, Lady	iii. 126	388
Mary, Highland	iii. 255	480
Mary Morison	iii. 286	499
Mary Queen of Scots, Lament of	i. 268	425
Mary, Will ye Go to the Indies, My	iv. 15	86
Masonic Song	iv. 19	88
Mauchline Belles, O Leave Novéls	iv. 11	84
Mauchline Lady, The	iv. 12	84
Mauchline, The Belles of	ii. 212	410
Maule of Panmure, To the Hon. Wm. R.	ii. 256	444
Maxwell, Esq. of Terraughtie, To John	ii. 133	378
—— If Merit Here You Crave	ii. 255	443
——, To Dr.	ii. 255	443
Meg o' the Mill	iii. 200	444
	iv. 38	99
Menzies' Bonnie Mary, Theniel	iii. 20	320
Michie, For Mr. William	ii. 269	453
Mild Zephyrs Waft Thee to Life's Farthest Shore	ii. 237	427
Mitchell, To Collector	ii. 137	380
Monody on a Lady Famed for Her Caprice	ii. 271	455
Montgomerie's Peggy	iv. 3	82
More's, Inscribed on a Book of Hannah	ii. 213	411
Morison, Mary	iii. 286	499
Morris, Auld Rob	iii. 210	449
Muir in Tarbolton Mill, On Wm.	ii. 264	450
—— On Robert	ii. 270	454
Musing on the Roaring Ocean	iii. 28	325
My Blessings on Ye, Honest Wife	ii. 241	430
My Chloris, Mark how Green the Groves	iii. 256	481
My Collier Laddie	iii. 115	383

TITLES AND FIRST LINES

	TEXT	NOTES
My Curse upon Your Venom'd Stang	ii. 51	342
My Eppie Macnab	iii. 101	375
My Father was a Farmer upon the Carrick Border, O	iv. 8	84
My Godlike Friend—Nay, do not Stare	ii. 118	371
My Harry was a Gallant Gay	iii. 43	335
My Heart is a-Breaking, Dear Tittie	iii. 34	363
My Heart is Sair—I Dare na Tell	iii. 158	416
My Heart is Wae, and Unco Wae	iv. 22	90
My Heart's in the Highlands	iii. 62	348
My Heart was Ance as Blythe and Free	iii. 3	303
My Highland Lassie, O	iii. 10	308
My Hoggie	iii. 14	313
My Honor'd Colonel, Deep I Feel	ii. 139	380
My Lord a-Hunting He is Gane	iii. 198	443
My Lord, I Know, Your Noble Ear	i. 295	449
My Lov'd, My Honor'd, Much Respected Friend	i. 106	361
My Love, She's but a Lassie Yet	iii. 51	341
My Love was Born in Aberdeen	iii. 68	353
My Nanie, O	i. 249	412
My Nanie's Awa	iii. 244	472
My Peggy's Face, My Peggy's Form	iii. 186	437
Myra, the Captive Ribband's Mine	iii. 60	348
My Sandy Gied to Me a Ring	iii. 41	335
My Tocher's the Jewel	iii. 90	366
My Wife's a Winsome Wee Thing	iii. 285	498
Nae Gentle Dames, Tho' Ne'er Sae Fair	iii. 10	308
Nae Heathen Name shall I Prefix	ii. 111	367
Nanie O, My	i. 249	412
Nanie's Awa, My	iii. 244	472
Nature's Law	ii. 47	340
New Year's Day, 1791	ii. 64	352
Nicol, For William	ii. 269	452
Nicol's Mare, Elegy on	ii. 223	416
Ninetieth Psalm Versified	i. 234	407

GENERAL INDEX OF

	TEXT	NOTES
Nithsdale's Welcome Hame	iii. 116	384
Nith, The Banks o'	iii. 83	362
No Churchman am I for to Rail and to Write	i. 256	417
No Cold Approach, no Altered Mien	iv. 44	103
No More of Your Guests, be They Titled or Not	ii. 259	447
No More, Ye Warblers of the Wood, No More	ii. 231	422
No Sculptur'd Marble Here, nor Pompous Lay	ii. 268	451
No Song nor Dance I Bring from Yon Great City	ii. 146	383
No Spartan Tube, No Attic Shell	ii. 171	393
No Stewart Art Thou, Galloway	ii. 252	440
Now Haply Down Yon Gay Green Shaw	iii. 167	424
Now Health Forsakes that Angel Face	iv. 67	108
Now Honest William's Gaen to Heaven	ii. 270	453
Now in Her Green Mantle Blythe Nature Arrays	iii. 244	472
Now Kennedy, if Foot or Horse	ii. 83	358
Now Nature Cleeds the Flowery Lea	iii. 259	482
Now Nature Hangs Her Mantle Green	i. 268	425
Now Robin Lies in His Last Lair	ii. 216	412
Now Rosy May Comes in wi' Flowers	iii. 245	473
Now Simmer Blinks on Flow'ry Braes	iii. 8	306
Now Spring has Clad the Grove in Green	iii. 246	473
Now Westlin' Winds and Slaught'ring Guns	i. 181	387
O, an Ye were Dead, Guidman	iii. 146	407
O a' ye Pious Godly Flocks	ii. 20	314
O, Ay My Wife She Dang Me	iii. 191	439
O, Bonie was Yon Rosy Brier	iii. 263	486
O, Cam' Ye Here the Fight to Shun	iii. 73	356
O, Can Ye Labour Lea	iii. 138	397
O, Could I Give Thee India's Wealth	ii. 127	375
O Death, Had'st Thou but Spar'd His Life	i. 186	389

TITLES AND FIRST LINES 197

	TEXT	NOTES
O Death! Thou Tyrant Fell and Bloody	i. 262	423
Ode for General Washington's Birthday	ii. 171	393
Ode Sacred to the Memory of Mrs. Oswald	i. 260	420
Ode to the Departed Regency Bill	ii. 159	389
O'er the Water to Charlie	iii. 32	328
Of all the Numerous Ills that Hurt our Peace	ii. 234	424
Of a' the Airts the Wind Can Blaw	iii. 56	345
Of Lordly Acquaintance You Boast	ii. 249	439
O for Ane-and-Twenty, Tam	iii. 111	382
O Goudie, Terror o' the Whigs	ii. 70	355
O, Guid Ale Comes	iii. 193	440
O, Had each Scot of Ancient Times	ii. 247	437
O Had the Malt thy Strength of Mind	ii. 258	446
O, How Can I be Blythe and Glad	iii. 94	369
O, How Shall I, Unskilfu', Try	iii. 106	380
O, I am Come to the Low Countrie	iii. 184	436
O John, Come Kiss Me Now	iii. 88	365
O, Kenmure's On and Awa, Willie	iii. 112	382
O, Ken Ye What Meg o' the Mill has Gotten	iii. 200 / iv. 38	444 / 99
O, Lady Mary Ann Looks o'er the Castle Wa'	iii. 126	388
O Lassie, Are Ye Sleepin' Yet	iii. 275	492
O, Lay Thy Loof in Mine, Lass	iii. 202	444
Old Winter, with His Frosty Beard	ii. 230	420
O, Leave Novéls, Ye Mauchline Belles	iv. 11	84
O, Leeze Me on My Spinnin-wheel	iii. 114	383
O, Let Me in this Ae Night	iii. 274	492
O Logan, Sweetly Did'st Thou Glide	iii. 262	484
O Lord, When Hunger Pinches Sore	ii. 263	449
O, Luve Will Venture in Where it Daur na Weel be Seen	iii. 122	386
O Mary, at Thy Window Be	iii. 286	499
O May, Thy Morn was Ne'er sae Sweet	iii. 170	427
O, Meikle Thinks my Luve o' my Beauty	iii. 90	366
O, Merry Hae I Been Teethin a Heckle	iii. 66	351

198 GENERAL INDEX OF

	TEXT	NOTES
O, Mirk, Mirk is This Midnight Hour	iii. 220	455
O, My Luve is Like a Red, Red Rose	iii. 143	402
On a Bank of Flowers in a Summer Day	iii. 49	339
On a Beautiful Country Seat	ii. 248	438
On a Celebrated Ruling Elder	i. 187	389
On a Galloway Laird	ii. 273	456
On a Goblet	ii. 258	447
On a Henpecked Squire, Epigram	i. 186	389
—— —— ——, Epitaph	i. 186	389
On a Lap-Dog	ii. 270	454
On Andrew Turner	ii. 257	446
On an Innkeeper Nicknamed 'The Marquis'	ii. 275	458
On a Noisy Polemic	i. 187	390
On a Noted Coxcomb	ii. 273	456
On a Scotch Bard	i. 144	378
On a Suicide	ii. 274	457
On a Swearing Coxcomb	ii. 274	458
On a Wag in Mauchline	ii. 268	451
On a Work of Hannah More's, Inscribed	ii. 213	411
On Being Appointed to an Excise Division	ii. 247	437
On Captain Francis Grose	ii. 247	437
On Captain Grose	ii. 62	352
On Captain Lascelles	ii. 273	456
Once Fondly Lov'd and Still Remember'd Dear	ii. 92	361
On Cessnock Banks a Lassie Dwells	iv. 3	82
On Chloris	ii. 256	444
On Commissary Goldie's Brains	ii. 251	440
On Dr. Babington's Looks	ii. 257	445
On Elphinstone's Translation of Martial	ii. 242	431
One Night as I Did Wander	iv. 12	85
One Queen Artemisa, as Old Stories Tell	i. 186	389
On General Dumourier's Desertion	ii. 228	419
On Glenriddell's Fox Breaking his Chain	ii. 168	392
On Grizzel Grimme	ii. 275	458
On Hearing a Thrush Sing in a Morning Walk in January	ii. 229	419

TITLES AND FIRST LINES

	TEXT	NOTES
On Holy Willie	ii. 266	451
On James Grieve, Laird of Boghead, Tarbolton	ii. 264	449
On John Bushby of Tinwald Downs	ii. 274	457
On John Dove	ii. 267	451
On John M'Murdo	ii. 229	419
On John Rankine	ii. 264	450
On Johnson's Opinion of Hampden	ii. 242	432
Onlie, Honest Lucky, Lady	iii. 21	320
On Maria Riddell	ii. 253	441
On Marriage	ii. 261	448
On Miss Ainslie in Church	ii. 243	433
On Miss Davies	ii. 248	437
On Miss Fontenelle	ii. 254	441
On Miss Jean Scott	ii. 247	437
On Mr. James Gracie	ii. 259	447
On Peace an' Rest my Mind was Bent	iii. 191	439
On Robert Fergusson	{ ii. 224 / ii. 268	416 / 451
On Robert Muir	ii. 270	454
On Rough Roads	iv. 46	104
On Scaring some Water-Fowl in Loch Turit	i. 299	450
On Seeing a Wounded Hare	i. 287	441
On Seeing Mrs. Kemble in Yarico	ii. 257	445
On Seeing the Royal Palace at Stirling in Ruins	ii. 244	434
On some Commemorations of Thomson	ii. 227	418
On Tam the Chapman	ii. 265	450
On Thanksgiving for a National Victory	ii. 255	442
On the Author	ii. 275	461
On the Birth of a Posthumous Child	i. 303	452
On the Commemoration of Rodney's Victory	ii. 170	392
On the Death of a Favourite Child	iv. 68	108
On the Death of John M'Leod, Esq.	i. 294	448
On the Death of Lord President Dundas	ii. 221	414

GENERAL INDEX OF

                                                    TEXT   NOTES

On the Death of Robert Riddell of Glenriddell, Sonnet	ii. 231	422
On the Destruction of Drumlanrig Woods	iv. 53	106
On the Duchess of Gordon's Reel Dancing	ii. 61	350
On the Earl of Galloway, on the Author being Threatened with Vengeance	ii. 253	440
On the Illness of a Favourite Child	iv. 67	108
On the Laird of Laggan	ii. 253	441
On the late Captain Grose's Peregrinations thro' Scotland	i. 289	445
On the Same [*i.e.* the Earl of Galloway]	ii. 252	440
On Wee Johnie	i. 187	390
On William Creech	ii. 235	425
On Wm. Graham of Mossknowe	ii. 274	457
On Wm. Muir in Tarbolton Mill	ii. 264	450
On William Smellie	ii. 236	425
O, Once I Lov'd a Bonie Lass	iii. 197	442
O, Open the Door some Pity to Shew	iii. 211	450
O Philly, Happy be that Day	iii. 277	493
O Poortith Cauld and Restless Love	iii. 221	456
Oppress'd with Grief, Oppress'd with Care	i. 127	372
O, Raging Fortune's Withering Blast	iv. 7	84
O, Rattlin, Roarin Willie	iii. 35	330
O Rough, Rude, Ready-Witted Rankine	i. 176	384
Orthodox! Orthodox	ii. 30	324
O, Sad and Heavy should I part	iii. 165	422
O, Saw Ye Bonie Lesley	iii. 224	458
O, Saw Ye my Dearie, my Eppie Macnab	iii. 101	375
O, Saw Ye my Dear, my Philly	iv. 40	99
O' Shanter, Tam	i. 278	433
O, Sing a New Song to the Lord	ii. 162	391
O, Some will Court and Compliment	iii. 89	365
O, Stay, Sweet Warbling Wood-Lark	iii. 223	457
O, Steer Her up, an' Haud Her Gaun	iii. 187	438
Oswald, Ode Sacred to the Memory of Mrs.	i. 260	420
O, Sweet be thy Sleep in the Land of the Grave	iv. 68	108

TITLES AND FIRST LINES

	TEXT	NOTES
O, That I Had ne'er been Married	iii. 206	446
O, This is no My Ain Lassie	iii. 248	473
O Thou Dread Power, Who Reign'st Above	i. 231	405
O Thou Great Being! What Thou Art	i. 233	406
O Thou, in Whom We Live and Move	ii. 262	449
O Thou Pale Orb that Silent Shines	i. 123	370
O Thou that in the Heavens does Dwell	ii. 25	320
O Thou the First, the Greatest Friend	i. 234	407
O Thou Unknown, Almighty Cause	i. 135	375
O Thou! Whatever Title Suit Thee	i. 47	335
O Thou, Who Kindly dost Provide	ii. 262	449
O Thou Whom Poesy Abhors	ii. 242	431
O Tibbie, I hae Seen the Day	iii. 37	333
Our Thrissles Flourish'd Fresh and Fair	iii. 64	350
Out over the Forth, I Look to the North	iii. 153	413
O, Wat Ye Wha's in Yon Town	iii. 167	424
O, Wat Ye Wha that Lo'es Me	iii. 249	474
O, Were I on Parnassus Hill	iii. 59	347
O, Were my Love yon Lilac Fair	iii. 279	493
O, Wert Thou in the Cauld Blast	iv. 43	102
O, Wha my Babie-clouts will Buy	iii. 70	354
O, Whare Live Ye, my Bonie Lass	iii. 115	383
O Whar Gat Ye that Hauver-Meal Bannock	iii. 2	301
O, Wha Will to Saint Stephen's House	ii. 174	394
O, When She cam Ben, She Bobbed fu' Low	iii. 110	381
O, Why the Deuce should I Repine	ii. 211	408
O, Willie Brewed a Peck o' Maut	iii. 80	359
O, Wilt Thou Go wi' Me, Sweet Tibbie Dunbar	iii. 42	335
O Ye, Wha are sae Guid Yoursel	i. 217	402
O Ye Whose Cheek the Tear of Pity Stains	i. 188	390
Paraphrase of the First Psalm	i. 232	406
Parker, To Hugh	ii. 116	370

	TEXT	NOTES
Parnassus Hill, O, Were I on . . .	iii. 59	346
Passion's Cry	ii. 237	427
Pegasus at Wanlockhead. . . .	ii. 226	418
Peggy, Montgomerie's	iv. 3	82
Peggy's Face, My Peggy's Form, My .	iii. 186	437
Peg Nicholson was a good Bay Mare .	ii. 223	416
Peg, Pretty	iv. 37	98
Phillis the Fair	iv. 38	99
—— Wherefore Sighing art Thou . .	iii. 169	426
Philly, Happy be that Day, O . . .	iii. 277	493
—— O Saw Ye my Dear, my . . .	iv. 40	99
Pinned to Mrs. Walter Riddell's Carriage	ii. 255	442
Poem on Pastoral Poetry	iv. 50	105
Poor Mailie's Elegy	i. 56	344
'Praise Woman Still,' His Lordship Roars	ii. 253	441
Prayer under the Pressure of Violent Anguish	i. 233	406
Pretty Peg	iv. 37	98
Primrose, The	iv. 42	100
Prologue Spoken at the Theatre of Dumfries	ii. 146	383
—— Spoken by Mr. Woods . . .	ii. 144	381
Raging Fortune	iv. 7	84
Rankine, Epistle to John . . .	i. 176 ii. 70	384 355
—— On John	ii. 264	450
Rash Mortal, and Slanderous Poet, thy Name	ii. 244	435
Rattlin, Roarin Willie	iii. 35	330
Raving Winds around Her Blowing .	iii. 26	323
Remorse	ii. 234	424
Remorseful Apology	ii. 137	380
Renton of Lamerton	ii. 109	367
Reply to an Invitation	ii. 88	359
—— to a Note from Captain Riddell .	ii. 124	375

TITLES AND FIRST LINES 203

	TEXT	NOTES
Reply to a Trimming Epistle from a Tailor	ii. 96	362
—— to the Threat of a Censorious Critic	ii. 245	435
Reverèd Defender of Beauteous Stuart	ii. 107	365
Richardson, For Gabriel	ii. 275	461
Riddell, For Mr. Walter	ii. 272	455
——, Impromptu on Captain	ii. 123	374
—— of Glenriddell, Sonnet on the Death of	ii. 231	422
——, On Maria	ii. 253	441
——, Reply to a Note from	ii. 124	375
Riddell's Birthday, Impromptu on Mr.	ii. 230	420
—— Carriage, Pinned to Mrs. Walter	ii. 255	442
Right, Sir! Your Text I'll Prove It True	i. 216	401
Robin Shure in Hairst	iii. 194	440
Roddick of Corbiston, On Captain Wm.	ii. 273	456
Rodney's Victory, On the Commemoration of	ii. 170	392
Ronalds of the Bennals, The	ii. 207	408
Roslin Inn, At	ii. 241	430
Ruisseaux, Elegy on the Death of Robert	ii. 216	412
Rusticity's Ungainly Form	ii. 235	425
Sad Bird of Night, what Sorrow Calls thee forth	iv. 64	108
Sad thy Tale, thou Idle Page	i. 294	448
Sae Far Awa	iii. 165	422
Sae Flaxen were her Ringlets	iii. 160	418
Samson's Elegy, Tam	i. 220	402
Sandy Gied to Me a Ring, My	iii. 41	335
Saw Ye Bonie Lesley	iii. 224	458
Say, Sages, What's the Charm on Earth	ii. 261	448
Scotch Drink	i. 19	322
Scots Prologue for Mrs. Sutherland	ii. 147	384
Scots Wha hae wi' Wallace Bled	iii. 251	474

	TEXT	NOTES
Scott, On Miss Jean	ii. 247	437
Scroggam	iii. 192	440
Searching Auld Wives' Barrels	ii. 247	437
Sensibility how Charming	iii. 96	372
She Kiltit up her Kirtle Weel	ii. 61	350
She Mourns, Sweet Tuneful Youth, thy Hapless Fate	ii. 262	459
Sherramuir, The Battle of	iii. 73	356
She's Fair and Fause that Causes my Smart	iii. 140	399
Should Auld Acquaintance be Forgot	iii. 148	407
Simmer's a Pleasant Time	iii. 45	337
Simpson of Ochiltree, To William	i. 167	383
Sing on, Sweet Thrush, upon the Leafless Bough	ii. 229	419
Sir, as your Mandate did Request	ii. 39	336
Sir, o'er a Gill I Gat your Card	ii. 87	359
Sir, Yours this Moment I Unseal	ii. 88	359
Sketch for an Elegy	ii. 236	427
Sleep'st Thou or Wauk'st Thou, Fairest Creature	iii. 280	494
Smellie, On William	ii. 236	425
Smith, Epistle to James	i. 59	347
So Heavy, Passive to the Tempest's Shocks	ii. 246	436
Some Books are Lies frae End to End	i. 191	391
Sonnet on the Death of Robert Riddell of Glenriddell	ii. 231	422
—— to Robert Graham, Esq. of Fintry	ii. 127	376
So Vile was Poor Wat, such a Miscreant Slave	ii. 272	455
Spare me thy Vengeance, Galloway	ii. 253	440
Stanzas in Prospect of Death	i. 229	404
Stay, my Charmer, can you Leave me	iii. 12	312
Stella, Elegy on	iv. 46	105
Stewart, Lovely Polly	iii. 174	429
—— To William	ii. 135	379
—— You're Welcome Willie	iv. 31	95

TITLES AND FIRST LINES

	TEXT	NOTES
Still Anxious to Secure your Partial Favour	ii. 152	387
Stirling, Additional Lines at	ii. 244	435
—— in Ruins, On Seeing the Royal Palace at	ii. 244	434
St. James' Lodge, Tarbolton, Farewell to the Brethren of	i. 184	388
'Stop Thief!' Dame Nature Call'd to Death	ii. 274	457
Strait is the Spot, and Green the Sod	iv. 46	105
Strathallan's Lament	iii. 13	312
Streams that Glide in Orient Plains	ii. 60	349
Stuart, To Peter	ii. 133	378
Stumpie, The Reel o'	iii. 166	422
Such a Parcel of Rogues in a Nation	iii. 127	391
Sutherland, Scots Prologue for Mrs.	ii. 147	384
Sweet Afton	iii. 134	394
Sweet are the Banks	iv. 27	94
Sweet Closes the Ev'ning on Craigieburn Wood	iii. 86	363
Sweetest May, Let Love Inspire Thee	iii. 200	444
Sweet Fa's the Eve on Craigieburn	iii. 225	459
Sweet Flow'ret, Pledge o' Meikle Love	i. 303	452
Sweet Naïveté of Feature	ii. 254	441
Sweet Tibbie Dunbar	iii. 42	335
Sylvander to Clarinda	ii. 112	367
Syme, Apology to John	ii. 259	446
Syme of Ryedale, To John	ii. 258	446
Symon Gray, You're Dull To-day	ii. 110	367
Talk not to Me of Savages	ii. 260	448
Tam Glen	iii. 84	363
Tam o' Shanter	i. 278	433
Tam Samson's Elegy	i. 220	402
Tam the Chapman, On	ii. 265	450
Tarbolton Lasses	ii. 206	407
Tennant of Glenconner, To James	ii. 124	375
That Hackney'd Judge of Human Life	ii. 261	448

GENERAL INDEX OF

	TEXT	NOTES
That there is a Falsehood in his Looks	ii. 257	445
The Auld Farmer's New-Year Morning Salutation to his Auld Mare, Maggie	i. 100	360
The Author's Earnest Cry and Prayer	i. 26	324
The Bairns Gat out wi' an Unco Shout	iii. 139	398
The Banks o' Doon	iii. 124	388
The Banks of Nith	iii. 83	362
The Banks of the Devon	iii. 22	320
The Battle of Sherramuir	iii. 73	356
The Belles of Mauchline	ii. 212	410
The Birks of Aberfeldie	iii. 7	306
The Blude-Red Rose at Yule may Blaw	iii. 30	327
The Blue-Eyed Lassie	iii. 82	362
The Bonie Lad that's far Awa	iii. 94	369
The Bonie Lass of Albanie	iv. 22	90
The Bonie Moor-Hen	iv. 20	89
The Bonniest Lad that e'er I Saw	iii. 172	428
The Book-Worms	ii. 241	431
The Braes o' Ballochmyle	iii. 69	353
The Brigs of Ayr	i. 200	393
The Calf	i. 216	401
The Captain's Lady	iii. 55	344
The Captive Ribband	iii. 60	348
The Cardin o't	iii. 159	417
The Cares o' Love are Sweeter far	ii. 239	430
The Catrine Woods were Yellow Seen	iii. 69	353
The Chevalier's Lament	iv. 24	92
The Cooper o' Cuddy Came Here Awa	iii. 157	416
The Cotter's Saturday Night	i. 106	361
The Crimson Blossom Charms the Bee	ii. 109	367
The Day Returns, my Bosom Burns	iii. 50	340
The Dean of the Faculty	ii. 204	406
The Death and Dying Words of Poor Mailie	i. 53	343
The Deil cam Fiddlin' thro' the Town	iii. 141	399
The Deil's Awa wi' th' Exciseman	iii. 141	399
The Deuk's Dang o'er my Daddie	iii. 139	398

TITLES AND FIRST LINES

	TEXT	NOTES
The Devil got Notice that Grose was a-Dying	ii. 247	437
The Dusty Miller	iii. 17	318
The Farewell	ii. 215	411
The Fête Champetre	ii. 174	394
The Five Carlins	ii. 177	395
The Flower it Blaws, it Fades, it Fa's	iii. 174	429
The Friend whom, Wild from Wisdom's Way	ii. 137	380
The Gallant Weaver	iii. 136	396
The Gard'ner wi' his Paidle	iii. 48	339
The Gloomy Night is Gath'ring Fast	i. 255	416
The Greybeard, Old Wisdom, may Boast of his Treasures	ii. 250	439
The Heather was Blooming, the Meadows were Mawn	iv. 20	89
The Highland Balou	iii. 175	429
The Highland Widow's Lament	iii. 184	436
The Holy Fair	i. 36	328
The Holy Tulyie	ii. 20	314
The Humble Petition of Bruar Water	i. 295	449
The Inventory	ii. 39	336
Their Groves o' Sweet Myrtle let Foreign Lands Reckon	iii. 252	478
The Jolly Beggars, a Cantata	ii. 1	291
The Joyful Widower	iv. 55	106
The Keekin Glass	ii. 249	439
The Kirk's Alarm	ii. 30	324
The Laddies by the Banks o' Nith	ii. 182	397
The Lament	i. 123	370
The Lamp of Day with Ill-Presaging Glare	ii. 218	413
The Lass o' Ballochmyle	iv. 16	87
The Lass o' Ecclefechan	iii. 156	415
The Lass of Cessnock Banks	iv. 3	82
The Lass that Made the Bed	iii. 162	419
The Lazy Mist Hangs from the Brow of the Hill	iii. 54	344

GENERAL INDEX OF

	TEXT	NOTES
The Lea-Rig	iii. 284	497
The Lovely Lass of Inverness	iii. 142	401
The Man, in Life Wherever Plac'd	i. 232	406
The Mauchline Lady	iv. 12	84
Theniel Menzies' Bonie Mary	iii. 20	320
The Night was Still	iv. 18	88
The Noble Maxwells and their Powers	iii. 117	384
The Old Cock'd Hat, the Brown Surtout the Same	ii. 236	425
The Ordination	i. 210	397
The Ploughman, He's a Bonie Lad	iii. 24	322
The Poor Man Weeps—Here Gavin Sleeps	i. 188	390
The Posie	iii. 122	386
The Rantin Dog, the Daddie o't	iii. 70	354
The Reel o' Stumpie	iii. 166	422
There Grows a Bonie Brier-Bush in our Kail-Yard	iii. 180	432
There Lived a Carl in Kellyburn Braes	iii. 129	391
There'll never be Peace till Jamie comes Hame	iii. 92	367
There's Auld Rob Morris that Wons in yon Glen	iii. 210	449
There's a Youth in this City, it were a Great Pity	iii. 61	348
There's Death in the Cup, so Beware	ii. 258	447
There's Nane shall Ken, there's Nane can Guess	iii. 166	423
There's News, Lasses, News	iii. 205	445
There's Nought but Care on ev'ry Han'	i. 251	414
There's Three True Guid Fellows	iii. 160	418
There was a Bonie Lass, and a Bonie, Bonie Lass	iii. 204	445
There was a Lad was Born in Kyle	iv. 13	85
There was a Lass, and She was Fair	iii. 281	495
There was a Lass, They Ca'd her Meg	iii. 19	319
There was a Wife Wonn'd in Cockpen	iii. 192	440
There was Five Carlins in the South	ii. 177	395

TITLES AND FIRST LINES

	TEXT	NOTES
There was on a Time, but Old Time was then Young	iv. 29	94
There was Three Kings into the East	i. 243	409
The Rights of Woman	ii. 150	386
The Ronalds of the Bennals	ii. 207	408
The Silver Tassie	iii. 53	343
The Simple Bard, Rough at the Rustic Plough	i. 200	393
The Slave's Lament	iii. 132	392
The Small Birds Rejoice in the Green Leaves Returning	iv. 24	92
The Smiling Spring comes in Rejoicing	iii. 135	396
The Solemn League and Covenant	ii. 258	446
The Song of Death	iii. 133	394
The Sun had Clos'd the Winter Day	i. 74	350
The Sun he is Sunk in the West	iv. 1	81
The Tailor Fell thro' the Bed, Thimble an' a'	iii. 44	336
The Tailor he Cam here to Sew	iii. 179	432
The Tarbolton Lasses	ii. 206	407
The Thames Flows Proudly to the Sea	iii. 83	362
The Tither Morn, when I Forlorn	iii. 104	379
The Toadeater	ii. 249	439
The Tree of Liberty	iv. 58	107
The Twa Dogs	i. 9	318
The Twa Herds	ii. 20	314
The Tyrant Wife	ii. 248	438
The Vision	i. 74	350
The Vowels	iv. 66	108
The Weary Pund o' Tow	iii. 108	380
The Whistle	i. 304	452
The White Cockade	iii. 68	353
The Wind Blew Hollow frae the Hills	i. 274	431
The Winter it is Past, and the Simmer comes at Last	iii. 40	334
The Winter of Life	iii. 178	431
The Wintry West Extends his Blast	i. 134	374

GENERAL INDEX OF

	TEXT	NOTES
The Young Highland Rover	iii. 16	318
They Snool me Sair, and Haud me Down	iii. 111	382
Thickest Night, Surround my Dwelling	iii. 13	312
Thine am I, my Faithful Fair	iii. 253	479
Thine be the Volumes, Jessie Fair	ii. 141	380
This Day Time Winds th' Exhausted Chain	ii. 64	352
This Wot ye All whom it Concerns	ii. 49	340
Tho' Cruel Fate should Bid Us Part	iii. 12	312
Tho' Fickle Fortune has Deceived Me	iv. 6	83
Thomson, On some Commemorations of	ii. 227	418
Thou Flatt'ring Mark of Friendship Kind	ii. 213	411
Thou Fool, in thy Phaeton Towering	ii. 256	444
Thou Gloomy December	iii. 185	437
Thou hast Left Me ever, Jamie	iii. 254	480
Thou, Liberty, thou Art my Theme	ii. 168	392
Thou Ling'ring Star, with Less'ning Ray	iii. 71	355
Thou of an Independent Mind	ii. 259	448
Thou's Welcome, Wean! Mishanter Fa' Me	ii. 37	334
Thou whom Chance may Hither Lead	i. 258 / ii. 57	418 / 347
Thou, who thy Honour as thy God Rever'st	i. 278	433
Tho' Women's Minds, like Winter Winds	iii. 78	359
Through and Through th' Inspirèd Leaves	ii. 241	431
Tibbie, I hae Seen the Day, O	iii. 37	333
'Tis Friendship's Pledge, my Young, Fair Friend	ii. 142	381
To a Gentleman who had Sent a Newspaper	ii. 131	378
To a Haggis, Address	i. 237	407
To a Kiss	iv. 62	107
To Alex. Cunningham	ii. 118	371
To a Louse	i. 152	379
To a Mountain Daisy	i. 136	375
To a Mouse	i. 115	365
To an Artist	ii. 241	431

TITLES AND FIRST LINES

	TEXT	NOTES
To an Old Sweetheart	ii. 92	361
To a Young Friend, Epistle	i. 140	376
To Clarinda with a Pair of Wine-Glasses	ii. 115	370
To Collector Mitchell	ii. 137	380
To Colonel De Peyster	ii. 139	380
To Daunton Me	iii. 30	327
To Davie, a Brother Poet, Epistle	i. 117	365
—— —— Second Epistle	ii. 81	358
To Dr. Blacklock	ii. 128	377
To Dr. Mackenzie	ii. 89	360
To Dr. Maxwell	ii. 255	443
To Edinburgh, Address	i. 239	408
To Gavin Hamilton, Esq.	ii. 85	359
—— —— A Dedication	i. 147	378
—— —— Extempore	ii. 93	362
To Hugh Parker	ii. 116	371
To James Smith, Epistle	i. 59	347
To James Tennant of Glenconner	ii. 124	375
To J. Lapraik, Epistle	i. 155	380
—— ——, Second Epistle	i. 161	382
—— ——, Third Epistle	ii. 73	357
To John Goldie	ii. 70	355
To John Kennedy	ii. 83	358
—— —— A Farewell	ii. 90	360
To John Maxwell, Esq., of Terraughtie	ii. 133	378
To John M'Murdo	ii. 127	375
To John Rankine	ii. 70	355
—— —— Epistle	i. 176	384
To John Syme of Ryedale	ii. 258	446
—— ——, Apology	ii. 259	447
To Major Logan	ii. 99	363
To Miss Cruickshank	i. 292	447
To Miss Ferrier	ii. 111	367
To Miss Graham of Fintry	ii. 136	379
To Miss Isabella Macleod	ii. 109	367
To Miss Jessie Lewars	ii. 141	380
To Miss Logan	i. 236	407

	TEXT	NOTES
To Mr. M'Adam of Craigen-Gillan	ii. 87	359
To Mr. Renton of Lamerton	ii. 109	367
To Peter Stuart	ii. 133	378
To Riddell, Much-Lamented Man	ii. 259	447
To Robert Graham of Fintry, Esq.	{ i. 271 ii. 119	427 371
—— —— —— —— Sonnet	ii. 127	376
To Ruin	i. 139	376
To Symon Gray	ii. 110	367
To the Beautiful Miss Eliza J——n	ii. 256	444
To the Deil, Address	i. 47	335
To the Guidwife of Wauchope House	ii. 104	364
To the Hon. Wm. R. Maule of Panmure	ii. 256	444
To the Owl	iv. 64	108
To the Right Hon. C. J. Fox, Inscribed	ii. 165	392
To the Rev. John M'Math	ii. 76	357
To the Shade of Thomson, Address	i. 288	444
To the Toothache, Address	ii. 51	342
To the Unco Guid, Address	i. 217	402
To the Weaver's gin ye Go	iii. 3	303
To William Simpson of Ochiltree	i. 167	383
To William Stewart	ii. 135	379
To Willie Chalmers' Sweetheart	ii. 90	361
To Wm. Tytler, Esq. of Woodhouselee	ii. 107	365
To You, Sir, this Summons I've Sent	ii. 93	362
Tragic Fragment	ii. 233	423
Trogger, The	ii. 201	406
True-hearted was He, the Sad Swain o' the Yarrow	iii. 226	459
Turn again, Thou Fair Eliza	iii. 119	385
Turner, On Andrew	ii. 257	446
'Twas Even: the Dewy Fields were Green	iv. 16	87
'Twas in that Place o' Scotland's Isle	i. 9	318
'Twas in the Seventeen Hunder Year	ii. 197	405
'Twas na her Bonie Blue E'e	iv. 41	100
'Twas on a Monday Morning	iii. 154	414
Tytler, Esq. of Woodhouselee, To Wm.	ii. 107	365

TITLES AND FIRST LINES

	TEXT	NOTES
'Twas Where the Birch and Sounding Thong are Ply'd	iv. 66	108
Under the Portrait of Miss Burns	ii. 242	432
Up in the Morning Early	iii. 15	315
Upon a Simmer Sunday Morn	i. 36	328
Upon that Night, when Fairies Light	i. 88	356
Up wi' the Carls of Dysart	iii. 137	397
Verses in Friars Carse Hermitage	ii. 57	347
Verses Intended to be Written below a Noble Earl's Picture	ii. 217	412
Verses Written with a Pencil at Taymouth	i. 301	451
Versicles on Sign-posts	ii. 246	436
Versicles to Jessie Lewars	ii. 260	448
Wae is my Heart and the Tear's in my E'e	iii. 176	430
Wae Worth thy Power, thou Cursed Leaf	ii. 214	411
Wandering Willie	iii. 208	446
Wantonness for Evermair	iii. 154	414
Wap and Rowe, Wap and Rowe	iii.* 166	422
Washington's Birthday, Ode for General	ii. 171	393
Wastle, Willie	iii. 125	388
Wauchope House, To the Guidwife of	ii. 104	364
Weary Fa' You, Duncan Gray	iii. 23	321
We Cam na Here to View your Warks	ii. 243	434
Wee, Modest, Crimson-tippèd Flow'r	i. 136	375
Wee, Sleekit, Cowrin, Tim'rous Beastie	i. 115	365
Wee Willie Gray an' his Leather Wallet	iii. 188	438
We Grant they're Thine, those Beauties all	ii. 248	438
We're a' Noddin	iii. 189	438
Westerha', Election Ballad for	ii. 182	397
Wha in a Brulyie	iii. 175	430
Wha is That at my Bower Door	iii. 102	375
Wham will we Send to London Town	ii. 191	401
Whare are you Gaun, my Bonie Lass	iii. 77	358

	TEXT	NOTES
Whare ha'e ye Been sae Braw, Lad	iii. 81	361
What Ails ye now, ye Lousie Bitch	ii. 96	362
What can a Young Lassie	iii. 93	368
What dost Thou in that Mansion Fair	ii. 252	440
What Man could Esteem, or what Woman could Love	ii. 270	454
What Needs this Din about the Town o' Lon'on	ii. 147	384
What will I Do gin my Hoggie Die	iii. 14	313
Wha will Buy my Troggin	ii. 201	406
When Biting Boreas, Fell and Doure	i. 225	404
When by a Generous Public's Kind Acclaim	ii. 144	381
When Chapman Billies Leave the Street	i. 278	433
When Chill November's Surly Blast	i. 130	372
When Dear Clarinda, Matchless Fair	ii. 112	368
When Death's Dark Stream I Ferry o'er	ii. 245	436
When Eighty-Five was Seven Months Auld	ii. 42	338
When First I Came to Stewart Kyle	iv. 12	84
When First I Saw Fair Jeanie's Face	iv. 32	95
When First my Brave Johnie Lad Came to the Town	iii. 89	366
When Guilford Good our Pilot Stood	i. 246	411
When in my Arms, wi' a' thy Charms	iii. 34	330
When Januar' Wind was Blawin' Cauld	iii. 162	419
When Lascelles Thought fit from this World to Depart	ii. 273	456
When Lyart Leaves Bestrow the Yird	ii. 1	291
When Morine, Decras'd, to the Devil went down	ii. 253	441
When Nature her Great Masterpiece Design'd	ii. 119	371
When o'er the Hill the Eastern Star	iii. 284	497
When Rosy May comes in wi' Flowers	iii. 48	339
When she Cam Ben, she Bobbed	iii. 110	381
When the Drums do Beat	iii. 55	344

TITLES AND FIRST LINES

	TEXT	NOTES
When Wild War's Deadly Blast was Blawn	iii. 212	451
Where are the Joys I hae Met in the Morning	iii. 264	486
Where, Braving Angry Winter's Storms	iii. 36	332
Where Cart Rins Rowin to the Sea	iii. 136	396
Wherefore Sighing art Thou, Phillis	iii. 169	426
Whigham's Inn, Sanquhar, At	ii. 245	436
While at the Stook the Shearers Cow'r	ii. 76	357
While Briers an' Woodbines Budding Green	i. 155	380
While Europe's Eye is Fix'd on Mighty Things	ii. 150	386
While Larks with Little Wing	iv. 39	99
While New-ca'd Kye Rowte at the Stake	i. 161	382
While Virgin Spring by Eden's Flood	i. 288	444
While Winds frae aff Ben Lomond Blaw	i. 117	365
Whistle an' I'll Come to You, my Lad	iii. 5	304
Whistle o'er the Lave o't	iii. 58	346
Whiteford, Bart., Lines to Sir John	i. 278	433
Whoe'er be He that Sojourns Here	ii. 243	433
Whoe'er Thou art, O Reader, Know	i. 187	390
Whose is that Noble, Dauntless Brow	ii. 217	412
Why am I Loth to Leave this Earthly Scene	i. 229	404
Why should We idly Waste our Prime	iv. 57	107
Why, why Tell thy Lover	iv. 42	100
Why, ye Tenants of the Lake	i. 299	450
Wi' Braw New Branks, in Mickle Pride	ii. 90	361
Willie Brew'd a Peck o' Maut	iii. 80	359
Willie, On Holy	ii. 266	451
Willie, Rattlin, Roarin	iii. 35	330
Willie, Wandering	iii. 208	446
Willie Wastle Dwalt on Tweed	iii. 125	388
Will ye Go to the Indies, my Mary	iv. 15	86
Wilt Thou be my Dearie	iii. 173	428
Winter	i. 134	374

GENERAL INDEX

	TEXT	NOTES
Wishfully I Look and Languish	iii. 103	378
With Æsop's Lion, Burns Says:—'Sore I Feel	ii. 245	435
With Pegasus upon a Day	ii. 226	418
Woods, Prologue Spoken by Mr.	ii. 144	381
Wow, but your Letter Made me Vauntie	ii. 128	377
Written in Friars Carse Hermitage	i. 258	418
Ye Banks and Braes and Streams around	iii. 255	480
Ye Banks and Braes o' Bonie Doon	iii. 124	388
Ye Flowery Banks o' Bonie Doon	iv. 28	94
Ye Gallants Bright, I Rede you Right	iii. 46	338
Ye Hypocrites! are these your Pranks?	ii. 255	442
Ye Irish Lords, ye Knights and Squires	i. 26	324
Ye Jacobites by name	iii. 120	386
Ye Maggots, feed on Nicol's Brain	ii. 269	452
Ye Men of Wit and Wealth, why all this Sneering	ii. 254	442
Ye Sons of Old Killie, assembled by Willie	iv. 19	88
Yestreen I had a Pint o' Wine	iv. 25	92
Yestreen I met you on the Moor	iii. 37	333
Ye True Loyal Natives	ii. 251	440
Yon Rosy Brier	iii. 263	486
Yon Wild Mossy Mountains sae Lofty and Wide	iii. 97	373
Young Jamie	iii. 152	413
Young Jessie	iii. 226	459
Young Jockie was the Blythest Lad	iii. 76	358
Young Peggy	iii. 1	299
Your Billet, Sir, I grant Receipt	ii. 109	367
Your Friendship much can make me blest	iv. 44	103
You're Welcome to Despots, Dumourier	ii. 228	419
You're Welcome, Willie Stewart	iv. 31	95
Your News and Review, Sir	ii. 123	374

INDEX OF PERSONS AND PLACES

ABERCROMBIE, Colonel and Mrs., ii. 349.
Aberfeldie, Birks of, iii. 306.
Adair, Dr., iii. 321.
Afton, iii. 395.
Aiken, Andrew Hunter, i. 376.
—— Miss Grace, i. 263.
—— Peter Freeland, i. 376.
—— Robert, Ayr, i. 363, 390, 394; ii. 321, 323, 330, 336, 338, 411, 412, 413.
Ailsa Craig, iii. 454.
Ainslie, Miss, ii. 433.
—— Robert, i. 439; ii. 433; iii. 371, 438, 441.
Alexander, Miss Wilhelmina, iv. 87; i. 352
Allan Water, iii. 462.
Alloway Kirk, i. 433, 437-9.
Andrew, Hugh, i. 320.
Annan, ii. 396.
Argyll, Duke of, iii. 430.
Armour, Adam, ii. 339.
—— Jean, i. 319, 328, 353, 363, 369, 370, 376, 387, 416; 11. 318, 340, 358, 410, 450; iii. 303, 305, 310, 345, 354, 371, 381, 424; iv. 85, 93.
Atholl, Duke of, i. 427, 449.
Auchinleck, i. 351.
Auld, Rev. William, Mauchline, ii. 317; i. 379; ii. 320, 323, 331, 363.
Ayton, Sir Robert, iii. 371.

BABINGTON, Dr., ii. 445.
Bacon (Honest), ii. 379.
Baillie, Miss Leslie, of Mayfield, iii. 458, 462.
Ballantine, John, i. 393, 363, 404; ii. 330; iv. 94.
Ballochmyle, i. 352.
Barskimming, Sir Thomas Miller, Lord, i. 354.
Beattie, Dr. James, i. 400.
Begbie, Elison, iii. 330, 499; iv. 82.
Begg, Mrs. (sister of Burns), i. 387, 413; iii. 333, 433.
Ben Ledi, iii. 462.

217

218 INDEX OF PERSONS AND PLACES

Ben Lomond, i. 369.
Birtwhistle, Alexander, Provost of Kirkcudbright, ii. 399, 405.
Bishop, John, Polkemmet, ii. 334.
Black, Elizabeth, ii. 308.
Blacklock, Dr. Thomas, ii. 377; i. 406, 416; iii. 344.
Blackstock, Miss Jane, iii. 456.
Blair, Dr. Hugh, ii. 342, 446.
—— Major, of Dunskey, ii. 405.
—— Provost, Dumfries, ii. 376.
—— Sir James Hunter, ii. 413.
Boconnock, i. 327.
Boswell, James, of Auchinleck, i. 325; ii. 395, 427.
Boyd, Rev. William, of Fenwick, i. 400.
Brown, Dr. John, iii. 337.
Brownhill Inn, ii. 438.
Bruar Falls, i. 449.
Bruce, King Robert, i. 357; iii. 477.
Buchan, Dr. William, i. 393.
—— Earl of, i. 444; ii. 418, 441; iii. 301, 476.
Burness, William, i. 318, 346, 390; ii. 325, 360; iv. 81.

Burnet, Miss Elizabeth, of Monboddo, ii. 417; i. 409.
Burns, Alexander Cunningham, ii. 371.
—— Elizabeth Riddell, iv 106.
—— Gilbert, i. 318, 335, 343, 361, 365, 369, 370, 374, 381, 391, 405, 413, 438; ii. 280, 383, 395, 408; iii. 456, 476, 499; iv. 90.
—— James Glencairn, i. 432.
—— Miss, ii. 432.
—— William, junr., i. 401.
Bushby, John, ii. 403, 405, 457.
—— Maitland, ii. 355, 404.
—— William, ii. 404.

CAMPBELL, Lord FREDERICK, i. 326.
—— Sir Islay, i. 326; ii. 430.
—— Mary, iii. 309, 330, 355, 373, 395, 426, 480; iv. 75, 86, 103.
—— of Netherplace, i. 389.
Campbells of Loudoun, i. 356.
Candlish, James, ii. 410; iii. 292.
—— Rev. Dr., ii. 410.
Caprington, i. 353.
Carron, ii. 434.

INDEX OF PERSONS AND PLACES

Carmichael, or Hay, Miss Rebekah, ii. 409.
Cassilis, i. 357.
Catrine, i. 354; ii. 340.
Cessnock Banks, ii. 333; iv. 82.
Chalmers, Margaret, iii. 332; ii. 372; iii. 341, 437, 481.
—— William, ii. 361; i. 408; ii. 417.
Charles I., ii. 400.
—— II., iii. 419.
—— Edward, Prince, iii. 318, 328, 414, 427; iv. 90, 92.
Chloris. *See* Lorimer, Jean.
Clarinda. *See* Maclehose, Mrs. Agnes.
Claverhouse, ii. 401; iii. 361.
Cleghorn, Robert, Saughton, i. 423; iii. 301; iv. 92.
Clunie, Rev. John, iii. 351.
Cochrane, Charlie, iii. 390.
Cockburn, Mrs. Alison, ii. 417.
Cockpen, iii. 381, 440.
Coil, iii. 452; *v.* Coila.
——, Auld King, i. 354, 320.
Coila, i. 384; ii. 353; iii. 464; *v.* Coil.
Colean, Cove and House, i. 357.
Colzean Castle, i. 357.

Constable, Lady Winifred Maxwell, i. 425; ii. 366; iii. 384.
Copeland of Collieston, ii. 404.
Corsancone, Corsincon, iii. 348, 441.
Covington, iii. 373.
Craigieburn, iii. 364, 459.
Cranstoun, Miss (Mrs. Dugald Stewart), iv. 101.
Cree, The, iii. 454.
Creech, William, ii. 344, 425, 432.
Criffel, iii. 441.
Crochallan Fencibles, ii. 426.
Cromek, ii. 305.
Cruickshank, Miss Jane, i. 447; ii. 454; iii. 329.
—— William, ii. 453; i. 447.
Cumnock, i. 352.
Cunningham (Ayrshire), ii. 309.
Cunningham, Alexander, i. 442, 443, 447; ii. 279, 305, 371, 415, 417, 419, 428, 447; iii. 360, 367, 399, 413, 458, 467, 468; iv. 94.
—— Lady Elizabeth, i. 431; ii. 326, 385.
—— James, 14th Earl of Glencairn. *See* Glencairn.

220 INDEX OF PERSONS AND PLACES

Cunningham, Mrs., of Lainshaw, ii. 411.
—— William, of Annbank, ii. 394.
Cunynghame, Sir W. Augustus, 4th Bart. of Livingstone, i. 326.
Curtis, Sir Roger, ii. 309.

DAER, BASIL - WILLIAM DOUGLAS HAMILTON, Lord, ii. 340.
Dalgarnock, iii. 471.
Dalnacardoch, ii. 436.
Dalrymple, James, of Orangefield, i. 431.
—— Rev. William, Ayr, ii. 318; i. 396; ii. 324, 330.
Dalswinton, ii. 439.
Dalziel, Alexander, i. 431.
Davidson, John, Shoemaker, Glenfoot of Ardlochan, i. 437.
Davies, Miss Debora, iii. 378; ii. 438; iii. 380.
Dempster, George, of Dunnichen, i. 325, 348, 356.
De Peyster, Colonel, ii. 376, 380.
Derbyshire, Dr., iii. 338.
Devon, The, iii. 320, 481.
Dewar, Mr. Forest, ii. 371.
Don, Lady, i. 432, 442; ii. 307, 336, 337, 361, 390.
Douglas, David, Tavernkeeper, ii. 426.

Douglas, James, ii. 404.
—— Sir William, ii. 404.
Dove, John, Whitefoord Arms, ii. 451; *v.* Dow.
Dow, John, Innkeeper, ii. 358, 359; *v.* Dove.
Drumlanrig, iv. 104.
Drummond, James, iii. 313.
Dumfries, ii. 396; iii. 400.
Dumouriez, Charles François, ii. 419.
Dunbar, Tibbie, iii. 335.
—— William, i. 418; ii 427; iii. 330.
Duncan, Rev. Robert, Dundonald, ii. 317.
Dundas, Henry, i. 326; iv. 79.
—— Lord President, ii. 414.
—— Robert, of Arniston, ii. 407, 415.
Dundee. *See* Claverhouse.
Dunlop, Mrs., ii. 352; i. 349, 350, 354, 365, 372, 420, 423, 425, 428, 430, 438, 439, 441, 443, 448, 452; ii. 325, 327, 330, 338, 370, 384, 385, 391, 392, 393, 395, 397, 417, 425, 428, 438, 443, 444, 445, 455, 456; iii. 309, 324, 334, 343, 353, 355, 362, 372, 394, 407, 446, 458; iv. 103.

ECCLEFECHAN, iii. 415, 424.

INDEX OF PERSONS AND PLACES

Edinburgh, i. 408; ii. 346.
Eglinton, Archibald Montgomerie, 11th Earl of, i. 325.
Elliot, George Augustus, Lord Heathfield, ii. 309.
Elphinstone, James, ii. 431.
Erskine, Hon. Andrew, iii. 447.
—— Henry, i. 326, 411; ii. 407, 430; iv. 93.
—— Thomas, Lord Erskine, i. 326; iv. 97.

FALSTAFF, Sir JOHN, i. 349.
Fergusson, Sir Adam, Bart., of Kilkerran, i. 325, 405.
—— Alexander, of Craigdarroch, i. 453; ii. 400, 427.
—— James, of Craigdarroch, iii. 352.
—— Robert, ii. 408, 416, 451.
Ferintosh, i. 323.
Ferrier, Jane, ii. 367.
Findlay, James, ii. 410; iii. 377.
Fisher, William (Holy Willie), ii. 320, 451.
Fleming, Agnes, Tarbolton, i. 413.
Fontenelle, Miss, ii. 386, 387, 441.
Forbes, Duncan, of Culloden, i. 323.

Fox, Hon. Charles J., ii. 389, 392; iv. 97.
Fraser (oboist), iii. 461, 480.
Friars Carse, i. 418; ii. 347, 374, 447.
Fullarton, Colonel William, i. 355, 353, 356.
—— Dr., i. 353.
Fyers, Fall of, i. 451.

GALLOWAY, JAMES STEWART, 7th Earl of, ii. 440, 405, 406.
Garlies, Lord, ii. 404.
Garpal Water, i. 396.
Geddes, Bishop, ii. 415, 417.
George III., ii. 389.
—— IV., i. 349.
Gibson, George, ii. 339.
—— Mrs. Agnes (Poosie Nansie), ii. 308; i. 331; ii. 291, 339.
—— Janet (Racer Jess), i. 331, 339.
Gillespie, Mr., iii. 364, 482.
Glenbuck, i. 396.
Glencairn, James Cuningham, 14th Earl of, i. 431, 411; ii. 344, 412.
—— Lady, ii. 326.
Globe Tavern, ii. 439, 449; iii. 367, 419.
Goldie, Colonel, of Goldielea, ii. 405.
—— Commissary, ii. 440.

222 INDEX OF PERSONS AND PLACES

Gordon, Duke and Duchess of, i. 448 ; ii. 349, 350; iv. 77.
—— (or Goudie), John, Galston, ii. 355.
—— John, of Kenmure (or Kenmore), ii. 404.
—— Mrs., ii. 454.
—— Thomas, of Balmaghie, ii. 401, 403.
Gow, Niel, iv. 91.
Gracie, James, ii. 447.
Graham, Douglas, farmer, Shanter, i. 437.
—— James, Marquis of Graham, i. 325.
—— of Fintry, i. 427 ; ii. 326, 371, 376, 395, 399, 418.
—— Miss, of Fintry, ii. 379; iii. 447, 451.
—— Mrs., of Fintry, i. 425 ; ii. 386.
—— William, of Mossknowe, ii. 457.
Grant, Rev. David, of Ochiltree, ii. 332.
Gray, Mr. Farquhar, i. 352.
—— Symon, ii. 367.
Greenfield, Rev. William, Edinburgh, ii. 347.
Gregory, Dr. James, ii. 347; i. 442.
Grieve, James, ii. 449.
Grizzel Grimme, ii. 458.
Grose, Captain Francis, i. 445, 434, 438; ii. 352, 437.

Haco, iv. 95.
Haliburton of Pitcur, iii. 361.
Hamilton, Charlotte, iii 321, 332, 481.
—— Gavin, i. 378, 363, 390, 401 ; ii. 320, 323, 324, 326, 331, 357, 359, 360, 362, 412, 428, 449, 450 ; iii. 299, 321.
—— of Gilbertfield, i. 383 ; iii. 411.
—— Rev. Mr., Gladsmuir, ii. 435.
Hampden, John, ii. 432.
Hay, Charles, Advocate, ii. 415.
—— Mrs. Lewis, iii. 332 ; v. Chalmers, Margaret.
Helicon, ii. 313; iii. 347.
Henderson, Captain Matthew, i. 423 ; ii. 427.
Henri, Mons. and Mrs., i. 452 ; ii. 352 ; iii. 372.
Henry v., i. 349.
Herd, David, iii. 296.
Heron, Colonel, ii. 405.
—— of Kerroughtie, ii. 401, 405, 406, 448.
—— Lady Elizabeth, of Heron, iii. 454.
—— Major, ii. 405.
—— Robert, ii. 377.
Hill, Peter, i. 430 ; ii.

INDEX OF PERSONS AND PLACES 223

281, 385, 425, 433, 445, 455.
Hislop, William, Taverner; v. Hyslop.
Holyrood House, ii. 414.
Home, ii. 383.
Hood, William, senr., Tarbolton, i. 389.
Hopetoun, Earl of, ii. 400.
Howe, Admiral, ii. 442.
Hoy, Mr., ii. 349; iii. 291.
Hume, ii. 383.
Humphry, James, Mauchline, i. 390.
Hutchieson, David, ii. 337.
Hyslop, Mrs., Globe Tavern, iv. 92.
—— William, Tavernkeeper, ii. 449.

INVERARAY, ii. 433.

JEFFREY, Miss JEAN, iii. 362; iv. 95.
Johnson of Clackleith, ii. 334.
—— James (Edinburgh), iii. 291, 423, 437; iv. 94.
—— Dr. Samuel, ii. 432.
Johnston, Lucy, iii. 425.
Johnstone, Captain, ii. 418.
—— Sir James, of Westerhall, ii. 395, 397, 400.
J——n, Miss Eliza, ii. 444.

KELLYBURN, iii. 391.

Kemble, Mrs. Stephen, ii. 445.
Kenmure, Viscount, iii. 382.
Kennedy, Jean, Kirkoswald, i. 439.
—— John, ii. 358; i. 375; ii. 334, 360.
—— Margaret, iii. 299; ii. 425; iii. 388; iv. 87.
—— Thomas, ii. 450.
Kenneth III., iv. 95.
Kilbaigie, ii. 311.
Kilkerran, i. 325.
Killie (Kilmarnock), i. 404.
Killiecrankie, iii. 361.
Kilmarnock, i. 397-9; ii. 391; v. Killie.
Kirkcudbright, ii. 396.
Kyle, i. 320, 356, 378; iv. 85.
Kyle, King's, i. 320; iv. 85.
Kyle-Stewart, i. 320, 361; iv. 85.

LAGGAN, Laird of, ii. 441.
Lamington, ii. 439.
Landsdowne, Marquis of, iv. 97.
Lapraik, J., i. 380, 382, 384; ii. 357.
Lascelles, Captain, ii. 456.
Lauderdale, Earl of, iv. 97.
Lawrie, Rev. Dr., i. 405, 416; iv. 88.
—— Mrs., of Newmilns, ii. 425.

Lawrie, Walter Sloan, of Redcastle, ii. 404.
Lawson, Wine Merchant, ii. 400.
Lewars, Jessie, ii. 380, 448, 468; iv. 100.
Lincluden Abbey, ii. 458; iii. 406.
Lindsay, Rev. William, Kilmarnock, i. 399.
Lochlie, iv. 85.
Lochmaben, ii. 396.
Logan, John, of Knockshinnoch and Afton, ii. 326, 334.
—— Miss, i. 407; ii. 364.
—— Major William, ii. 363.
Logan Water, iii. 484.
Lonsdale, Earl of, ii. 354.
Lorimer, Jean (Chloris), iii. 482; ii. 381, 444; iii. 305, 364, 419, 424, 456, 479, 481, 486, 487, 492; iv. 98.
Lowries of Maxwelton, i. 453; ii. 400.

MAITLAND, JAMES, 8th Earl of Lauderdale, iv. 97.
Manson, Tavern-keeper, ii. 360.
Markland, Miss, ii. 410.
Martial, ii. 431.
Masterton, Allan, iii. 312, 353, 359.
—— Ann, iii. 338.

Mauchline, i. 328, 352; ii. 291.
Maule, The Hon. William R., of Panmure, ii. 444.
Maxwell, David, of Cardoness, ii. 456, 404, 438.
—— James, ii. 435.
—— John, of Terraughtie, ii. 378, 405.
—— of Buittle, ii. 404.
—— Dr. William, ii. 443; iii. 490.
Mayne, John, ii. 281.
Melville, Viscount, i. 326.
Menzies, Theniel, iii. 320.
Michie, William, ii. 453.
Miller, Rev. Alexander, of Kilmaurs, i. 333.
—— Eliza, Elizabeth, or Betty, i. 388; ii. 338, 410.
—— Miss, of Dalswinton, ii. 439; iii. 428.
—— Mrs., iii. 324.
—— Nell, ii. 338, 410.
—— Captain Patrick, i. 283; ii. 395, 400, 443.
—— Patrick, of Dalswinton, ii. 400.
—— Sir Thomas, Lord Barskimming, i. 354.
—— Sir William, of Barskimming, ii. 405.
Mitchell, Rev. Andrew, of Monkton and Prestwick, ii. 332.
—— Collector, ii. 380.

INDEX OF PERSONS AND PLACES 225

Mitchell, Rev. Thomas, of Lamington, ii. 439.
Moness, Falls of, iii. 306.
Mons Meg, ii. 400.
Montgomerie, Captain, ii. 427.
—— Captain James, i. 351, 389.
—— Colonel Hugh, of Coilsfield, i. 326, 320, 325.
Montgomeries, i. 325, 397.
Montrose, Duke of, ii. 401.
—— 3rd Duke of, i. 325.
Moodie, Rev. Alexander, Riccarton, i. 331; ii. 314, 316, 331.
Moore, Dr., i. 374, 386, 391, 416, 420, 424, 425; ii. 314, 361; iii. 442.
More, Hannah, ii. 411.
Morine, ii. 441.
Morison, Mary, iii. 499.
Morton, Miss, ii. 410.
Mossgiel, iv. 85.
Mount Oliphant, iv. 85.
Muir, Robert, Kilmarnock, ii. 454; i. 322, 401, 403; ii. 340, 370.
—— William, Tarbolton Mill, ii. 450; i. 392.
Muirhead, Rev. —, of Urr, ii. 404.
Multrie, Rev. John, Kilmarnock, i. 400.
Murray of Broughton, ii. 403, 406.

Murray, Miss Euphemia, of Lintrose, iii. 326.
—— Sir William, Oughtertyre, i. 450; iii. 326.

M'ADAM OF CRAIGEN-GILLAN, ii. 306, 359, 404.
M'Doual, Colonel, of Logan, ii. 354, 405; iii. 300.
MacGill, Dr. William, ii. 324; i. 333, 396; ii. 326, 330, 332.
M'Kay, General, iii. 361.
Mackenzie, Dr., i. 333, 401; ii. 341, 360.
—— Henry, ii. 347; iv. 104.
M'Kenzie, Colonel, of Cassencarry, ii. 405.
Mackinlay, Rev. James, of Kilmarnock, i. 397, 399, 403; ii. 331.
M'Lachlan, Mrs., iii. 326.
Maclehose, Mrs. Agnes (Clarinda), ii. 369; i. 426; ii. 370, 428, 429, 431, 435, 442, 455; iii. 334, 373, 379, 427, 437, 446, 472, 479, 487; iv. 96, 101.
M'Leod, Miss Isabella, i. 448; ii. 367; iii. 324.
—— John, of Rasay, i. 448.
—— Colonel Norman, of M'Leod, iv. 98.
M'Laughlin, i. 397.
M'Math, Rev. John, Tarbolton, ii. 319, 357.
M'Murdo, John, of Drum-

VOL. IV.   P

lanrig, i. 424; ii. 334, 375, 380, 400, 419.
M'Murdo, Jean, iii. 495.
—— Phyllis, iii. 460.
Macnab, Eppie, iii. 375; iv. 99.
M'Pherson, James, iii. 307.
M'Quhae, Rev. William, ii. 319.

NANSIE, POOSIE. *See* Gibson, Mrs. Agnes.
Nasmyth, Alexander, ii. 430.
Nicholson, Margaret, ii. 416.
Nicol, William, i. 449; ii. 383, 416, 452; iii. 359.
Niven, William, of Kirkoswald, i. 377.
North Berwick, iii. 343.

OLIPHANT, Rev. JAMES, Kilmarnock, i. 399.
Onlie, Lady, iii. 320.
Orangefield, i. 353.
Orr, Thomas, i. 387.
Osnaburg, Bishop of, i. 349.
Oswald, Richard, of Auchencruive, ii. 404.
—— Mrs. Richard, iii. 425, 355.
—— Mrs., of Auchencruive, i. 420, 422.
Oughtertyre, i. 450; iii. 326.

PAINE, THOMAS, IV. 97.

Park, Anne, iv. 92.
Parker, Hugh, ii. 370.
—— Major William, ii. 370; iv. 89.
Paton, Elizabeth, i. 385; ii. 334, 338, 355, 412; iii. 354.
Paul, Rev. Hamilton, i. 377, 413.
Peebles, Rev. William, i. 332; ii. 317, 324, 332, 412.
Peggy, Montgomerie's, i. 387; iv. 82.
Perry, Editor, *Morning Chronicle*, ii. 282, 395; iii. 474.
Phyllis, Philly, iii. 426, 493.
Pindar, Peter, iii. 455.
Pitt, William, i. 327; ii. 389; iv. 79.

QUEENSBERRY, WILLIAM DOUGLAS, 4th Duke of ('Old Q'), ii. 397, 398, 400.

RACER JESS. *See* Janet Gibson.
Ramsay, Allan, i. 383.
—— Editor, *Edinburgh Evening Courant*, ii. 280.
Ramsay of Ochtertyre, ii. 319.
Rankine, John, i. 384; ii. 355, 388, 450, 461.

INDEX OF PERSONS AND PLACES 227

Reid, Hugh, of the Langlands, i. 392.
Renton, Mr., of Lamerton, ii. 367.
Richardson, Gabriel, ii. 461.
Richmond, John, i. 318, 322, 335, 360, 363, 397; ii. 291, 304, 306, 340.
Riddell, John, of Glengarnock, iii. 352.
―― Captain Robert, of Glenriddell, ii. 374; i. 418, 438, 453; ii. 282, 375, 392, 400, 422; iii. 340, 360, 362.
―― Mrs. Walter, of Woodley Park, ii. 420, 353, 380, 419, 441, 442, 455, 456; iii. 446, 463, 465.
―― Walter, i. 453; ii. 420, 455.
Robertson, Rev. John, Kilmarnock, i. 400, 403.
Robina, iii. 385.
Roddick, Captain W., ii. 273.
Rodney, Admiral, ii. 392.
Ronalds of the Bennals, ii. 408.
Russell, Rev. John, of Kilmarnock, i. 334, 332, 398; ii. 314, 316, 330, 356.

St. Anthony's Chapel, ii. 414.
―― Well, ii. 414.

St. James's Lodge, Tarbolton, i. 388.
Samson, Tam, Kilmarnock, i. 402.
Sanquhar, ii. 396.
Scott, Miss Jean, ii. 437.
―― Mrs., of Wauchope House, ii. 364.
―― Sir Walter, i. 439; ii. 305, 447; iii. 331, 384, 434.
Selkirk, Earl of, ii. 404.
Shaw, Rev. Andrew, ii. 319.
―― Rev. David, ii. 319.
Shepherd, Rev. John, of Muirkirk, ii. 333.
Sheriffmuir, iii. 356.
Sillar, David, i. 365; ii. 358; iii. 329.
Simpson, William, of Ochiltree, i. 383; ii. 316, 362.
Skinner, Rev. John, iii. 291.
Sloan, John, ii. 418.
Smellie, William, ii. 425, 421, 427.
Smith, Adam, ii. 424.
―― Rev. George, of Galston, i. 332; ii. 320, 333.
―― James, i. 347, 388; ii. 291, 410, 412, 451.
―― Miss, ii. 410.
Smythe, Mr., of Methven, iii. 326.
Souter Johnie, i. 437.
Staig, Provost, Dumfries, ii. 385, 400.

228 INDEX OF PERSONS AND PLACES

Staig, Miss Jessie, ii. 443, 460.
Stair. Earl of, i. 351.
Steven, Rev. James, Kilwinning, i. 401.
Stevenson, Isabella, iii. 333.
Stewart, Dugald (Professor), i. 355, 397; ii. 340, 347, 360, 383; iii. 354; iv. 101.
—— Dugald, Mrs.; v. Cranstoun.
—— of Hillside, ii. 401.
—— Dr. Matthew, i. 354.
—— Hon. Montgomery, ii. 406
—— The Hon. Mrs., ii. 438.
—— Mrs., of Afton, iii. 353.
—— Miss Anne (Mrs. Dewar), ii. 371.
—— Mrs., of Stair, i. 397, 442.
—— Polly or Mary, iii. 429.
—— William, Factor, Closeburn, ii. 379; iv. 95.
Stinchar, i. 413.
Stirling, ii. 434, 435.
Strathallan, James Drummond of, iii. 313.
Stuart, Charlotte, Duchess of Albany, iv. 90.
—— Daniel, ii. 280.
—— Peter, Editor of *The Star*, i. 421, 447; ii. 280, 378; iv. 77, 105.
Succoth, Lord, i. 326.

Sundrum, i. 351.
Sutherland, Mr., Actor, ii. 383.
—— Mrs., ii. 384.
Syme, John, ii. 446, 279, 405, 419, 440, 447, 457; iii. 424, 475.

Tam o' Shanter, i. 437.
Tam the Chapman, ii. 450.
Tantallon, iv. 104.
Taylor, Dr., of Norwich, i. 401; ii. 357.
—— John, ii. 418.
Taymouth, i. 451.
Tennant, John, of Glenconner, ii. 375.
Thomson, George, i. 386, 413, 415; ii. 305, 443; iii. 293, 305, 324, 351, 386, 395, 407, 408, 415, 418, 424, 447, 449, 450, 451, 454, 455, 456, 459, 460, 461, 462, 463, 464, 465, 466, 467, 469, 471, 473, 474, 475, 478, 479, 480, 481, 482, 484, 486, 487, 488, 489, 492, 493, 497, 498, 499; iv. 86, 92, 93, 99, 100, 102.
—— James, i. 444.
—— Peggy, i. 387, 413; ii. 361.
Tinnock, Nanse, i. 327, 328; ii. 359.
Tootie, Master, ii. 359.
Trot, John, ii. 339.

INDEX OF PERSONS AND PLACES

Turnbull, C., ii. 354.
Turner, Andrew, ii. 446.
Tytler, A. F., of Woodhouselee, i. 430, 433; ii. 347.
—— William, of Woodhouselee, ii. 335, 365; iii. 292.

WALKER, Professor JOSIAH, i. 416, 449; ii. 360; iii. 313.
—— Rev. Dr., Moffat, iii. 313.
—— Thomas, Tailor, ii. 362.
Walkinshaw, Clementina, iv. 90.
Wallace of Craigie and Riccarton, i. 354.
—— Sir William, i. 354, 365; iii. 477.
Wanlockhead, ii. 418.
Wanton Willie, iii. 411.
Warton, Thomas, i. 349.
Washington, General, ii. 393.
Wastle, Willie, iii. 388.
Welsh, Sheriff of Dumfriesshire, ii. 400.
Whigham, Innkeeper, ii. 436.

Whitefoord, Sir John, i. 433; ii. 360, 395; iii. 354.
—— Mary Anne, iii. 354.
William Henry, Prince, afterwards William IV., i. 349.
Williamson, James, ii. 353.
—— Mass David, ii. 312.
Willie, Holy. *See* Fisher, William.
Wilson, Agnes, ii. 339.
—— John, Schoolmaster, Tarbolton, i. 391.
—— John, i. 390.
Wodrow, Rev. Patrick, Tarbolton, ii. 319.
Wolfe, General, ii. 309.
Wood, Alexander, Surgeon, ii. 415.
Woodburn, David, ii. 306.
Woods, William, Actor, ii. 381.
Wycombe, Earl of, iv. 98.

YORK AND ALBANY, FREDERICK AUGUSTUS, Duke of, i. 349.
Young, Mrs. Grizzel, ii. 458.
—— Rev. James, of Cumnock, ii. 332.
—— Rev. Stephen, of Barr, ii. 333.

LIFE, GENIUS
ACHIEVEMENT
BY W. E. HENLEY

TO

T. F. HENDERSON

IN MEMORY OF

MUCH DIFFICULT YET SATISFYING

WORK

HIS FELLOW IN BURNS

W. E. H

MUSWELL HILL,
    8th July 1897.

W. H. BARTLETT

INTERIOR OF THE BIRTHPLACE OF BURNS

"Our monarch's hindmost year but ane
Was five and twenty days begun,
'Twas then a blast o' Januar win'
Blew hansel in on Robin."—*There was a Lad.*

ROBERT BURNS

(1759-1796)

IN 1759 the Kirk of Scotland, though a less potent and offensive tyranny than it had been in the good old times, was still a tyranny, and was still offensive and still potent enough to make life miserable, to warp the characters of men and women, and to turn the tempers and affections of many from the kindly, natural way. True it is that Hutcheson (1694-1746) had for some years taught, and taught with such authority as an University chair can give, a set of doctrines in absolute antagonism with the principles on which the Kirk of Scotland's rule was based, and with the ambitions which the majority in the Kirk of Scotland held in view. But these doctrines, sane and invigorating as they were, had not reached the general; and in all departments of life among the general the Kirk of Scotland was a paramount influence, and, despite the intrusion of some generous intelligences, was largely occupied with the work of narrowing the minds, perverting the instincts, and constraining the spiritual and social liberties of its subjects. In 1759, however, there was secreted the certainty of a revulsion against its ascendency; for that year saw the birth of the most popular poet, and the most anti-clerical withal, that Scotland ever bred. He came of the people on both sides; he had a high courage, a proud heart, a daring mind, a matchless gift of speech, an abundance of humour and wit and fire; he was a poet in whom were quintessentialised the elements of the Vernacular Genius, in whose work the effects and the traditions of the Vernacular School, which had struggled back into being in the Kirk's despite, were repeated with surpassing brilliancy; and in the matter of the Kirk he did for the people a piece of service equal and similar to that which was done on other lines and in other spheres by Hutcheson and Hume and Adam Smith. He was apostle and avenger as well as maker. He did more than give Scotland songs to sing and rhymes to read: he showed that laughter and the joy of life need be no crimes, and that freedom of thought and sentiment and action is within the reach of him that will stretch forth his hand to take it. He pushed his demonstration to extremes; often his teaching has been grossly misread and misapprehended; no doubt, too, he died of his effort—and himself. But most men do as they must —not as they will. It was Burns's destiny, as it was Byron's in his turn, to be 'the passionate and dauntless soldier of a forlorn hope'; and if he fell in mid-assault, he found, despite the circumstances of his passing, the best death man can find. He had faults and failings not a few. But he was ever a leader among men; and if the manner of his leading were not seldom reckless, and he did some mischief, and gave the Fool a great deal of what passes for good Scripture for his folly, it will be found in the long-run that he led for truth—

the truth which 'maketh free'; so that the Scotland he loved so well, and took such pride in honouring, could scarce have been the Scotland she is, had he not been.

I

His father, William Burness (or Burnes), and his mother, Agnes Brown, came both of yeoman stock: native the one to Kincardineshire, the other to Ayrshire. William Burness began life as a gardener, and was plying his trade in the service of one Fergusson, the then Provost of Ayr, when, with a view to setting up for himself, he took a lease of seven acres in the parish of Alloway, with his own hands built a two-roomed clay cottage—(still standing, but in use as a Burns Museum),—and in the December of 1757 married Agnes Brown, his junior by eleven years. She was red-haired, dark-eyed, square-browed, well-made, and quick-tempered. He was swarthy and thin; a man of strong sense, a very serious mind, the most vigilant affections,[1] and a piety not even the Calvinism in which he had been reared could ever make brooding and inhumane. And in the clay cottage to which he had taken his new-married wife, Robert, the first of seven children, was born to them on the 25th January 1759.

---

[1] In times of storm, he would seek out and stay with his daughter, where she was herding in the fields, because he knew that she was afraid of lightning; or, when it was fair, to teach her the names of plants and flowers. He wrote a little theological treatise for his children's guidance, too, and was, it is plain, an exemplary father, and so complete a husband that there is record of but a single unpleasantness between him and Agnes his wife.

The Scots peasant lived hard, toiled incessantly, and fed so cheaply that even on high days and holidays his diet (as set forth in *The Blithesome Bridal*) consisted largely in preparations of meal and vegetables and what is technically known as 'offal.' But the Scots peasant was a creature of the Kirk; the noblest ambition of Knox[1] was an active influence in the Kirk; and the Parish Schools enabled the Kirk to provide its creatures with such teaching as it deemed desirable. William Burness was 'a very poor man' (R. B.). But he had the right tradition; he was a thinker and an observer; he read whatever he could get to read; he wrote English formally but with clarity;[2] and he did the very best he could for his children in the matter of education. Robert went to school at

---

[1] The Reformer had a vast deal more in common with Burns than with the 'sour John Knox' of Browning's ridiculous verses. He was the man of a crisis, and a desperate one; and he played his part in it like the stark and fearless opposite that he was. But he was a humourist, he loved his glass of wine, he abounded in humanity and intelligence, he married two wives, he was as well beloved as he was extremely hated and feared. He could not foresee what the collective stupidity of posterity would make of his teaching and example, nor how the theocracy at whose establishment he aimed would presently assert itself as largely a system of parochial inquisitions. The minister's man who had looked through *his* keyhole would have got short shrift from *him*; and in the Eighteenth Century he had as certainly stood with Burns against the Kirk of Scotland, as represented by Auld and Russell and the like, as in the Sixteenth he stood with Moray and the nobles against the Church of Rome, as figured in David Beaton and the 'twa infernal monstris, Pride and Avarice.'

[2] See the aforesaid treatise :—'*A Manual of Religious Belief, in a Dialogue between Father and Son,* compiled by William Burnes, farmer at Mount Oliphant, and transcribed, with grammatical corrections, by John Murdoch, teacher.'

six;[1] and in the May of the same year (1765) a lad of eighteen, one John Murdoch, was 'engaged by Mr. Burness and four of his neighbours to teach, and accordingly began to teach, the little school at Alloway': his 'five employers' undertaking to board him 'by turns, and to make up a certain salary at the end of the year,' in the event of his 'quarterly payments' not amounting to a specified sum. He was an intelligent pedagogue—(he had William Burness behind him)—especially in the matter of grammar and rhetoric; he trained his scholars to a full sense of the meaning and the value of words; he even made them 'turn verse into its natural prose order,' and 'substitute synonymous expressions for poetical words and . . . supply all the ellipses.'[2] One of his school-books was the Bible, another Masson's *Collection of Prose and Verse*, excerpted from Addison[3] and Steele and Dryden,

---

[1] 'I was a good deal noted at these years,' says the *Letter to Moore*, 'for a retentive memory, a stubborn, sturdy *something* in my disposition, and an enthusiastic *idiot*-piety. . . . In my infant and boyish days, too, I owed much to an old maid of my mother's, remarkable for her ignorance, credulity, and superstition,' who had, 'I suppose, the largest collection in the county of tales and songs concerning devils, ghosts, fairies, brownies, witches, warlocks, spunkies, kelpies, elf-candles, death-lights, wraiths, apparitions, cantraips, enchanted towers, giants, dragons, and other trumpery. This cultivated the latent seeds of Poesy,' *etc.*

[2] As Robert Louis Stevenson has remarked (*Some Aspects of Robert Burns*):—' We are surprised at the prose style of Robert; that of Gilbert need surprise us no less.'

[3] 'The earliest thing of composition I recollect taking pleasure in, was *The Vision of Mirza*, and a hymn of Addison's beginning, "How are thy servants blessed, O Lord"' (R. B., *Letter to Moore*). 'The first two books,' he adds, 'I ever read in private, and which gave me more pleasure than any two books I ever read again, were the *Life of Hannibal* and the *History of Sir William*

from Thomson and Shenstone, Mallet and Henry Mackenzie, with Gray's *Elegy*, scraps from Hume and Robertson, and scenes from *Romeo and Juliet*, *Othello*, and *Hamlet*. And one effect of his method was that Robert, according to himself, 'was absolutely a critic in substantives, verbs, and participles,' and, according to Gilbert, 'soon became remarkable for the fluency and correctness of his expression, and read the few books that came in his way with much pleasure and improvement.' It is very characteristic of Murdoch that when, his school being broken up, he came to take leave of William Burness at Mount Oliphant, 'he brought us,' Gilbert says, a present and memorial of him, a small English grammar and the tragedy of *Titus Andronicus*,' and that 'by way of passing the evening' he 'began to read the play aloud.' Not less characteristic of all concerned was the effect of his reading. His hearers melted into tears at the tale of Lavinia's woes, and, 'in an agony of distress,' implored him to read no more. Ever sensible and practical, William Burness remarked that, as nobody wanted to hear the play, Murdoch need not leave it. Robert, ever a sentimentalist and ever an indifferent Shakespearean,[1]

Wallace. Hannibal gave my young ideas such a turn that I used to strut in raptures up and down after the recruiting-drum and bag-pipe, and wish myself tall enough that I might be a soldier; while the story of Wallace poured a Scottish prejudice in my veins which will boil along there (*sic*) till the floodgates of life shut in eternal rest.'

[1] If we may judge him from his extant work. *Cf.* the absurd line :—

'Here *Douglas* forms wild Shakespeare into plan.'

He cribs but once from Shakespeare, and the happiest among his

—' Robert replied that, if it was left, he would burn it.' And Murdoch, ever the literary guide, philosopher, and friend, was so much affected by his pupil's 'sensibility,' that 'he left *The School for Love* (translated, I think, from the French)' in Shakespeare's place.[1]

At this time Burns had but some two and a half years of Murdoch. William Burness liked and believed in the young fellow; for when, still urged by the desire to better his children's chance, he turned from gardening to cultivation on a larger scale, and took, at a £40 rental, the farm of Mount Oliphant, his two sons went on with Murdoch at Alloway, some two miles off. The school once broken up, however, Robert and his brother fell

---

few quotations is prefixed to one of the most felicitous—and therefore the least publishable—of his tributes to the Light-heeled Muse. 'Sing me a bawdy song,' he says with Sir John Falstaff, 'to make us merry.' And he adds this note, in which he is Shakespearean once again:—'There is—there must be some truth in original sin. My violent propensity to b—dy convinces me of it. Lack a day! If that species of composition be the special sin never-to-be-forgotten in this world nor in that which is to come, then I am the most offending soul alive. Mair for token,' etc. (R. B. to Cleghorn, 25th October 1793).

[1] There is no trace of any *School for Love*. It is therefore probable that what Gilbert meant was *The School for Lovers*: 'A Comedy. As it is acted at the Theatre Royal in Drury Lane. By William Whitehead, Esq.; Poet Laureat. London: Printed for R. and J. Dodsley in Pall-Mall; and Sold by J. Hinxman, in Pater-noster-row. MDCCLXII.' The first sentence of the author's *Advertisement* runs thus:—'The following Comedy is formed on a plan of Monsieur de Fontenelle's, never intended for the stage, and printed in the eighth volume of his works, under the title of *Le Testament*.' The names of the chief 'persons represented' are Sir John Dorilant, Modely, Belmour, Lady Beverley, Cælia, and Araminta: an unlikely lot, one would say, for an Ayrshire farmstead, even though it sheltered the youthful Burns.

into their father's hands, and, for divers reasons, Gilbert says, 'we rarely saw any body but the members of our own family,' so that 'my father was for some time the only companion we had.' It will scarce be argued now that this sole companionship was wholly good for a couple of lively boys; but it is beyond question that it was rather good than bad. For, 'he conversed on all subjects with us familiarly, as if we had been men,' and, further, 'was at great pains, as we accompanied him in the labours of the farm, to lead the conversation to such subjects as might tend to increase our knowledge or confirm our virtuous habits.' Also, he got his charges books — a *Geographical Grammar*, a *Physico and Astro-Theology,* Stackhouse's *History of the Bible,* Ray's *Wisdom of God in the Creation*; and these books Robert read 'with an avidity and industry scarcely to be equalled.'[1] None, says Gilbert, 'was so voluminous as to slacken his industry or so antiquated as to damp his research': with the result that he wasn't very far on in his

---

[1] Robert's list (*Letter to Moore*) includes Guthrie and Salmon's *Geographical Grammar*; *The Spectator*; Pope; 'some plays of Shakespear' (acting editions? or odd volumes?); 'Tull and Dickson on Agriculture'; *The Pantheon*; Locke *On the Human Understanding*; Stackhouse; with 'Justice's *British Gardener,* Boyle's *Lectures,* Allan Ramsay's *Works,* Dr. Taylor's *Scripture Doctrine of Original Sin, A Select Collection of English Songs,* and Harvey's *Meditations.*' Later he knew Thomson, Shenstone, Beattie, Goldsmith, Gray, Fergusson, Spenser even: with *The Tea-Table Miscellany* and many another song-book, Adam Smith's *Theory of the Moral Sentiments,* Reid's *Inquiry into the Human Mind,* Bunyan, Boston (*The Fourfold State*), Shakespeare, John Brown's *Self-Interpreting Bible,* and *The Wealth of Nations,* which last he is found reading (at Ellisland) with a sense of wonder that so much wit should be contained between

'teens ere he had 'a competent knowledge of ancient history,' with 'something of geography, astronomy and natural history.' Then, owing to the mistake of an uncle, who went to Ayr to buy a *Ready Reckoner or Tradesman's Sure Guide*, together with a *Complete Letter-Writer*, but came back with 'a collection of letters by the most eminent writers,' he was moved by 'a strong desire to excel in letter-writing.' At thirteen or fourteen he was sent ('week about' with Gilbert) to Dalrymple Parish School to better his handwriting; 'about this time' he fell in with *Pamela*, Fielding, Hume, Robertson, and the best of Smollett; and 'about this time' Murdoch set up as a schoolmaster in Ayr, and 'sent us Pope's *Works* and some other poetry, the first that we had an opportunity of reading, excepting what is contained in the *English Collection* and in the volume of the *Edinburgh Magazine* for 1772.'[1] The summer after

---

the boards of a single book. One favourite novel was *Tristram Shandy*; another, the once renowned, now utterly forgotten *Man of Feeling*. At Ellisland, again, he is found ordering the works of divers dramatists—as Jonson, Wycherley, Molière—with a view to reading and writing for the stage. But you find no trace of them in his work; nor is there any evidence to show that he could ever have written a decent play, though there is plenty of proof that he could *not*. No doubt, *The Jolly Beggars* will be quoted against me here. But the essential interests of that masterpiece are character and description. Now, there go many more things to the making of a play than character, while, as for description, the less a play contains of that the better for the play.

[1] The *English Collection* I take to be Masson's aforesaid. At all events I can find no other. So far as verse is concerned, another exception was found in 'those *Excellent new Songs* that are hawked about the country in baskets or spread on stalls in the streets' (G. B.). They were probably as interesting to Robert as Pope's *Works* or the poetry in *The Edinburgh Magazine*. At

the writing-lessons at Dalrymple, Robert spent three weeks with Murdoch at Ayr, one over the English Grammar, the others over the rudiments of French. The latter language he was presently able to read,[1] for the reason that Murdoch would go over to Mount Oliphant on half-holidays, partly for Robert's sake and partly for the pleasure of talking with Robert's father. Thus was Robert schooled; and 'tis plain that in one, and that an essential particular, he and his brother were exceptionally fortunate in their father and in the means he took to train them.[2]

In another respect—one of eminent importance—their luck was nothing like so good. Mount Oliphant was made up of 'the poorest land in Ayrshire'; William Burness had started it on a borrowed hundred; he was soon in straits; only by unremitting diligence and the strictest economy could he hope to make ends meet; and the burden of hard work lay heavy on the whole family—heavier, as I think, on the growing lads than on

---

any rate, his first essays in song were imitated from them, and he had the trick of them, when he listed, all his life long.

[1] Currie saw his Molière at Dumfries. There is no question but he would have got on excellent well with Argan and Jourdain and Pourceaugnac; but could he have found much to interest him in Arnolphe and Agnès, in Philinte and Alceste and Célimène? I doubt it. On the other hand, he would certainly have loved the *flon-flons* which Collé wrote for the Regent's private theatre; and I have always regretted that he read (1789) to no better purpose the La Fontaine of the *Contes*: a Scots parallel to which he was exactly fitted to achieve.

[2] Robert mastered, besides, the first six books of Euclid, and even dabbled a little in Latin now and then: reverting to his 'Rudiments' (says Gilbert) when he was crossed in love, or had tiffed with his sweetheart.

the made man and woman. 'For several years,' says Gilbert, 'butcher's meat was a stranger to the house.' Robert was his father's chief hand at fifteen —'for we kept no hired servant'—and could afterwards describe his life at this time as a combination of 'the cheerless gloom of a hermit with the unceasing toil of a galley-slave.' The mental wear was not less than the physical strain: for William Burness grew old and broken, and his family was seven strong, and of money there was as little as there seemed of hope. The wonder is, not that Robert afterwards broke *out* but, that Robert did not then break *down*: that he escaped with a lifelong tendency to vapours and melancholia, and at the time of trial itself with that 'dull headache' of an evening, which 'at a future period . . . was exchanged,' says Gilbert, 'for a palpitation of the heart and a threatening of fainting and suffocation in his bed in the night-time.' William Burness is indeed a pathetic figure; but to me the Robert of Mount Oliphant is a figure more pathetic still. Acquired or not, stoicism was habitual with the father. With the son it was not so much as acquired; for in that son was latent a world of appetites and forces and potentialities the reverse of stoical. And, even had this not been: if Robert hadn't proved a man of genius, with the temperament which genius sometimes entails: he must still have been the worse for the experience. He lived in circumstances of unwonted harshness and bitterness for a lad of his degree; with a long misery of anticipation, he must endure a quite unnatural strain on forming muscle and on nerves and a brain yet immature; he had perforce to face the necessity of diverting an absolute example of the artistic temperament to laborious and squalid ends, and to assist in the repression of all those natural instincts—of sport and reverie and companionship —the fostering of which is for most boys, have they genius or have they not, an essential process of development; and the experience left him with stooping shoulders and a heavy gait, an ineradicable streak of sentimentalism, what he himself calls 'the horrors of a diseased nervous system,' and that very practical exultation in the *joie de vivre*, once it was known, which, while it is brilliantly expressed in much published and unpublished verse and prose, is nowhere, perhaps, so naïvely signified as in a pleasant parenthesis addressed, years after Mount Oliphant, to the highly respectable Thomson :— ' Nothing (*since a Highland wench in the Cowgate once bore me three bastards at a birth*) has surprised me more than,' *etc.* The rest is not to my purpose: which is to argue that, given Robert Burns and the apprenticeship at Mount Oliphant, a violent reaction was inevitable, and that one's admiration for him is largely increased by the reflection that it came no sooner than it did. William Burness knew that it must come; for, as he lay dying, he confessed that it troubled him to think of Robert's future. This, to be sure, was not at Mount Oliphant: when Robert had done no worse than insist on going to a dancing-school : but years after, at Lochlie, when Robert had begun to assert himself. True it is that at Kirkoswald—a smuggling village, whither he went, at seventeen, to study mensuration, 'dialling,' and the like—he had learned, he says, to look unconcernedly on a large tavern bill and mix without fear in a drunken squabble.' True it is, too, that at Lochlie the visible reaction had set in. But, so far as is known, that reaction was merely formal; and one may safely conjecture that, as boys are not in the habit of telling their fathers everything, William Burness knew little or nothing of those gallant hours at Kirkoswald. For all this, though, he seems to have discerned, however dimly and vaguely, some features of the prodigious creature he had helped into the world; and that he should not have discerned them till thus late is of itself enough to show how stern and how effectual a discipline Mount Oliphant had proved.

II

The Mount Oliphant period lasted some twelve years, and was at its hardest for some time ere it reached its term. 'About 1775 my father's generous master died,'[1] says Robert; and 'to clench the curse we fell into the hands of a factor, who sat for the picture[2] I have drawn of one in my tale of "Twa Dogs." ... My father's spirit was soon irritated, but not easily broken. There was a free-

---

[1] This was that Fergusson (of Ayr) in whose service William Burness had been at the time of his marriage with Agnes Brown, and (apparently) for some years after it—in fact, till he took on Mount Oliphant. This he did on a hundred pounds borrowed from his old employer; and one may conjecture that the legal proceedings which Robert thus resented were entailed upon Fergusson's agents by the work of winding up the estate.

[2] 'Sat for the picture I have drawn of one' is precise and definite enough. But surely the Factor verses in *The Twa Dogs*

dom in his lease in two years more, and to weather these *we retrenched expenses*'—to the purpose and with the effect denoted! Then came easier times. In 1777 William Burness removed his family to Lochlie, a hundred-and-thirty-acre farm, in Tarbolton Parish. 'The nature of the bargain,' Robert wrote to Moore, ' was such as to throw a little ready money in his hand in the commencement,' or 'the affair would have been impracticable.' At this place, he adds, 'for four years we lived comfortably'; and at this place his gay and adventurous spirit began to free itself, his admirable talent for talk to find fit opportunities for exercise and display. The reaction set in, as I have said, and he took life as gallantly as his innocency might, wore the only tied hair in the parish, was recognisable from afar by his fillemot plaid, was made a ' Free and Accepted Mason,'[1] founded a Bachelors' Club,[2] and

---

are less a picture than a record of proceedings, a note on the *genus* Factor :—

> 'He'll stamp and threaten, curse and swear,
> He'll apprehend them, poind their gear,
> While they must stand, wi' aspect humble,
> An' hear it a', and fear and tremble.'

The statement is accurate enough, no doubt, but where is the 'picture'? Compare the effect of any one of Chaucer's Pilgrims, or the sketches of Cæsar and Luath themselves, and the Factor as individual is found utterly wanting.

[1] Burns was always an enthusiastic Mason. The Masonic idea —whatever that be—went home to him; and in honour of the Craft he wrote some of his poorest verses. One set, the 'Adieu, Adieu,' *etc.*, of the Kilmarnock Volume, was popular outside Scotland. At all events, I have seen a parody in a Belfast chap which is set to the tune of *Burn's Farewell*.

[2] It was, in fact, part drinking-club and part debating-society. But Rule X. of its constitution insisted that every member must

took to sweethearting with all his heart and soul and strength. He had begun with a little harvester at fifteen; and at Kirkoswald he had been enamoured of Peggy Thomson to the point of sleepless nights. Now, says his brother Gilbert, 'he was constantly the victim of some fair enslaver'—sometimes of two or three at a time; and 'the symptoms of his passion were often such as nearly to equal those of the celebrated Sappho,' so that 'the agitation of his mind and body exceeded anything I know in real life.' Such, too, was the quality of what he himself was pleased to call 'un penchant à (*sic*) l'adorable moitié du genre humain,' in combination with that 'particular jealousy' he had ' of people that were richer than himself, or who had more consequence in life,' that a plain face was quite as good as a pretty one: especially and particularly if it belonged to a maid of a lower degree than his own. To condescend upon one's women— to some men that is an ideal. It was certainly the ideal of Robert Burns. 'His love,' says Gilbert, 'rarely settled upon persons of this description'— that is, persons 'who were richer than himself, or who had more consequence in life.' He must still be Jove—still stoop from Olympus to the plain. Apparently he held it was an honour to be admired by him; and when, a short while hence (1786), he ventured to celebrate, in rather too realistic a strain,

---

have at least one love-affair on hand; and if potations were generally thin, and debates were often serious, there can be no question that the talk ran on all manner of themes, and especially on that one theme which men have ever found fruitful above all others. The club was so great a success that an offshoot was founded, by desire, on Robert's removal to Mossgiel.

the Lass of Ballochmyle, and was rebuffed for his impertinence—(it was so felt in those unregenerate days!)—he was, 'tis said, extremely mortified. In the meanwhile, his loves, whether pretty or plain, were goddesses all; and the Sun was 'entering Virgo, a month which is always a carnival in my imagination' the whole year round; and the wonder is that he got off so little of it all in verse which he thought too good for the fire. Rhyme he did (of course), and copiously: as at this stage every coming male must rhyme, who has instinct enough to 'couple but *love* and *dove.*' But it was not till the end of the Lochlie years that he began rhyming to any purpose. Indeed, the poverty of the Lochlie years is scarce less 'wonderful past all whooping' than the fecundity of certain memorable months at Mauchline: especially if it be true, as Gilbert and himself aver, that the Lochlie love-affairs were 'governed by the strictest rules of modesty and virtue, from which he never deviated till his twenty-third year.'[1] For desire makes verses, and verses

---

[1] Saunders Tait, the Tarbolton poetaster, insists that, long before Mossgiel, Burns and Sillar—'Davie, a Brother Poet'—were the most incontinent youngsters in Tarbolton Parish; and, after asseverating, in terms as solemn as he can make them, that in all Scotland

'There's none like you and Burns can tout
The bawdy horn,'

goes on to particularise, and declares that, what with 'Moll and Meg,

Jean, Sue, and Lizzey, a' decoy't,
There's sax wi' egg.'

Worse than all, he indites a 'poem,' a certain *B—ns in his Infancy*, which begins thus:—

W. H. BARTLETT

ALLOWAY KIRK WITH BURNS MONUMENT

"By Alloway's auld, haunted kirk."—*Tam o' Shanter.*

rather good than bad, as surely as fruition leaves verses, whether bad or good, unmade.

It was natural and honourable in a young man of this lusty and amatorious habit to look round for a wife and to cast about him for a better means of keeping one than farm-service would afford. In respect of the first he found a possibility in Ellison Begbie, a Galston farmer's daughter, at this time a domestic servant, on whom he wrote (they say) his 'Song of Similes,' and to whom he addressed some rather stately, not to say pedantic, documents in the form of love-letters. For the new line in life, he determined that it might, perhaps, be flax-dressing; so, at the midsummer of 1781 (having just before been sent about his business by, as he might himself have said, 'le doux objet de son attachement') he removed to Irvine, a little port on the Firth of Clyde, which was also a centre of the industry in which he hoped to excel. Here he established himself, on what terms is not known, with one Peacock, whom he afterwards took occa-

> 'Now I must trace his pedigree,
> *Because he made a song on me,*
> And let the world look and see,
>   Just wi' my tongue,
> How he and Clootie did agree
>   When he was young':—

and of which I shall quote no more. But Robert and his brother are both explicit on this point; and, despite the easy morals of the class in which the Bard sought now and ever 'to crown his flame,' it must be held, I think, as proven that he was *déniaisé* by Richard Brown at Irvine and by Betty Paton at Lochlie.

This is the place to say that I owe my quotations from Saunders Tait to Dr. Grosart, who told me of the copy (pro-

sion to describe as 'a scoundrel of the first water, who made money by the mystery of Thieving';[1] here he saw something more of life and character and the world than he had seen at Mount Oliphant and Lochlie; here, at the year's end, he had a terrible attack of vapours (it lasted for months, he says, so that he shuddered to recall the time); here, above all, he formed a friendship with a certain Richard Brown. According to him, Brown being the son of a mechanic, had taken the eye of 'a great man in the neighbourhood,' and had received

---

bably unique) of that worthy's Poems and Songs: 'Printed for and Sold by the Author Only, 1796': in the Mitchell Library, Glasgow, and at the same time communicated transcripts which he had made from such numbers in it as referred to Burns. As my collaborator, Mr. T. F. Henderson, was then in Scotland, I asked him to look up Tait's volume. It was found at last, after a prolonged search; was duly sent to the Burns Exhibition; and in a while was pronounced 'a discovery.' Tait, who was pedlar, tailor, soldier in turn, had a ribald and scurrilous tongue, a certain rough cleverness, and a good enough command of the vernacular; so that his tirades against Burns—(he was one of the very few who dared to attack that satirist)—are still readable, apart from the interest which attaches to their theme. It is a pity that some Burns Club or Burns Society has not reprinted them in full, coarse as they are.

[1] Nobody knows what this may mean. It seems to be only Robert's lofty way of saying that Peacock swindled him. What follows is explicit (*Letter to Moore*):—'To finish the whole, while we were giving a welcome carousal to the New Year, our shop, by the drunken carelessness of my partner's wife, took fire, and burned to ashes, and I was left, like a true poet, not worth sixpence.' How much is here of fact, how much of resentment, who shall say? What is worth noting in it all is that Burns, despite his 'penchant à l'adorable,' *etc.*, is first and last a peasant so far as 'l'adorable moitié' is concerned, and, for all his sentimentalism, can face facts about it with all the peasant's shrewdness and with all the peasant's cynicism.

'a genteel education, with a view to bettering his situation in life.' His patron had died, however, and he had had perforce to go for a sailor (he was afterwards captain of a West-Indiaman). He had known good luck and bad, he had seen the world, he had the morals of his calling, at the same time that 'his mind was fraught with courage, independance, and magnanimity, and every noble, manly virtue'; and Burns, who 'loved him,' and 'admired him,' not only 'strove to imitate him' but also 'in some measure succeeded.' 'I had,' the pupil owns, 'the pride before'; but Brown 'taught it to flow in proper channels.' Withal, Brown 'was the only man I ever saw who was a greater fool than myself when Woman was the presiding star.' Brown, however, was a practical amorist; and he 'spoke of a certain fashionable failing with levity, which hitherto I had regarded with horror.' In fact, he was Mephisto to Burns's Faust;[1] and 'here,' says the Bard, 'his friendship did me a mischief, and the consequence was, that soon after I assumed the plough, I wrote the enclosed *Welcome.*' This enclosure (to Moore) was that half-humorous, half-defiant, and wholly delightful *Welcome to His Love-Begotten Daughter*,[2] through which the spirit of the

---

[1] Brown denied it. 'Illicit love!' quoth he. 'Levity of a sailor! When I first knew Burns he had nothing to learn in that respect.' It is a case of word against word; and I own that I prefer the Bard's.

[2] 'The same cheap self-satisfaction finds a yet uglier vent when he plumes himself on the scandal at the birth of his first bastard child.' Thus Stevenson. But Stevenson, as hath been said, had in him 'something of the Shorter Catechist'; and either he did not see, or he would not recognise, that Burns's

true Burns—the Burns of the good years: proud, generous, whole-hearted, essentially natural and humane—thrills from the first line to the last. And we have to recall the all-important fact, that Burns was first and last a peasant,[1] and first and last a peasant in revolt against the Kirk, a peasant resolute to be a buck, to forgive the really scandalous contrast presented in those versions of the affair—(versions done in the true buckish style: the leer and the grin and the slang in full blast)—which he has given in *The Fornicator*, the *Epistle to John Rankine*, and—apparently—the *Reply to a Trimming Epistle from a Tailor*. At the same time we must clearly understand that we recall all this for the sake of our precious selves, and not in any way, nor on any account, for the sake of Burns. He was absolutely of his station and his time; the poor-living, lewd, grimy, free-spoken, ribald, old Scots peasant-world[2] came to a full, brilliant, even majestic close in his work; and, if we would appreciate aright the environment in which he wrote, and the audience to which such writings were addressed, we must transliterate into the Vernacular Brantôme and the *Dames Galantes* and Tallemant and the *Historiettes*. As for reading

---

rejoicings in the fact of paternity were absolutely sincere throughout his life.

[1] Here and elsewhere the word is used, not opprobriously but, literally. Burns was specifically a peasant, as Byron was specifically a peer, and as Shakespeare was specifically a man of the burgess class.

[2] I do not, of course, forget its many solid and admirable virtues; but its elements were mixed, and it was to the grosser that the Burns of these and other rhymes appealed.

them in Victorian terms—Early-Victorian terms, or Late—that way madness lies: madness, and a Burns that by no process known to gods or men could ever have existed save in the lubber-land of some Pious Editor's dream.

At Lochlie, whither he seems to have returned in the March of 1782, the studious years[1] and the old comparative prosperity had come, or were coming, to a close. There had been a quarrel between William Burness and his landlord, one M'Clure, a merchant in Ayr; and this quarrel, being about money, duly passed into the Courts. Its circumstances are obscure; but it is history that arbitration went against the tenant of Lochlie, that he was ordered to 'quite possession,' that he was strongly suspected of 'preparing himself accordingly by dispossessing of his stock and crops,' and that a certain 'application at present craving' resulted, on shrieval authority, in the 'sequestration' of all the Lochlie stock and plenishing and gear. Whatever the rights and wrongs of the affair, an end came to it with the end of William Burness. By this time his health was broken—he was far gone in what Robert calls 'a phthisical consumption'; and he died in the February of the next year (1784), when, as the same Robert romantically puts it in his fine, magniloquent fashion, 'his all went among the rapacious hell-hounds that growl in the Kennel of Justice.'[2] The fact that Robert and

---

[1] It was parish gossip that, if you called on William Burness at meal-time, you found the whole family with a book in one hand and a horn spoon in the other.

[2] M'Clure's 'answers' and 'counter-answers,' together with the sheriff's officer's account of the seizure at Lochlie, were published

Gilbert were able (Martinmas 1783), when their father's affairs were 'drawing to a crisis,' to secure another farm—Mossgiel—in Mauchline Parish, some two or three miles off Lochlie, is enough to show that neither errors nor crosses, neither sequestrations nor lampoons, had impaired the family credit.

III

William Burness had paid his children wages during his tenancy of Lochlie; and the elder four, by presenting themselves as his creditors for wages due, were enabled to secure a certain amount of 'plenishing

---

in *The Glasgow Herald* early in the present year (1897). I need scarce say that Saunders Tait produced a *Burns at Lochly*, in which he fell on his enemy tooth and claw. His statements are as specific as M'Clure's, and are substantially in agreement with some of them, besides:—

> 'To Lochly ye came like a clerk,
> And on your back was scarce a sark,
> The dogs did at your buttocks bark,
>   But now ye 're bra',
> *Ye pouch't the rent, ye was sae stark,*
>   *Made payment sma'.*'

In another stanza, 'M'Clure,' he says—

> 'Ye scarcely left a mite
>   To fill his horn.
> You and the Lawyers gied him a skyte,
>   Sold a' his corn.'

In a third he appears to record the particulars of a single combat between Robert and his father's landlord :—

> 'His ain gun at him he did cock,
>   An' never spared,
> Wi't owre his heid came a clean knock
>   Maist killed the laird.'

And in the last of all, after bitterly reproaching Robert and the whole Burns race with ingratitude :—

and gear' wherewith to make a start at Mossgiel. It was a family venture, in whose success the Burnesses were interested all and severally, and to which each one looked for food and clothes and hire (the brothers got a yearly fee of £7 apiece); and, as all were well and thoroughly trained in farming work, and had never lived other than sparely, it was reasonable in them to believe that the enterprise would prosper. That it did not begin by prospering was no fault of Robert's. He made excellent resolutions, and, what was more to the purpose, he kept them—for a time. He 'read farming books' (thus he displays himself), he 'calculated crops,' he 'attended markets'; he worked hard in the fields,

> 'M'Clure he put you in a farm,
> And coft you coals your a—— to warm
>   And meal and maut. . . .
> He likewise did the mailin stock,
>   And built you barns':—

he sets forth explicitly this charge:—

> 'M'Clure's estate has ta'en the fever,
> And heal again it will be never,
> The vagabonds, they ca' you clever,
>   Ye're sic a sprite,
> To rive fra' him baith ga' and liver,
>   And baith the feet.'

The fact of the Laird's generosity is reaffirmed with emphasis in *A Compliment*:—

> 'The horse, corn, pets, kail, kye, and ewes,
> Cheese, pease, beans, rye, wool, house and flours,
> Pots, pans, crans, tongs, bran-spits, and skewrs,
>   The milk and barm,
> Each thing they had was a' M'Clure's,
>   He stock'd the farm.' . . .

And with the remark that '*Five hundred pounds they were behind*,' the undaunted Saunders brings his libel to a close.

he kept his body at least in temperance and soberness, and, as for thrift, there is Gilbert's word for it, that his expenses never exceeded his income of £7 a year. It availed him nothing. Gilbert is said to have been rather a theorist than a sound practician; and Robert, though a skilled farmer, cared nothing for business, and left him a free hand in the conduct of affairs. Luck, too, was against them from the first; and very soon the elder's genius was revealed to him, and he had other than farmer's work to do. 'In spite of the Devil,' he writes, 'the world, and the flesh, I believe I should have been a wise man; but the first year, from unfortunately buying in bad seed, the second, from a late harvest, we lost half of both our crops.' Naturally, 'this' (and some other things) 'overset all my wisdom, and I returned, "like the dog to his vomit"—(be it remembered, it is Robert Burns who speaks: not I)—"and the sow that was washed, to her wallowing in the mire."' That the confession, with its rather swaggering allusion to the Armour business, was true, is plain. But we do not need Burns's assurance to know that, though he could do his work, and prided himself on the straightness of his furrows, he was scarce cut out for a successful farmer—except, it may be, in certain special conditions. Endurance, patience, diligence, a devout attention to one's own interest and the land's, an indomitable constancy in labour to certain ends and in thought on certain lines—these are some of the qualities which make the husbandman; and, this being so, how should Mossgiel have prospered under Rab the Ranter? His head was full of other things than crops and cattle. He was bursting with intelligence, ideas, the consciousness of capacity, the desire to take his place among men; and in Mauchline he found livelier friends [1] and greater opportunities than he had found elsewhere. Being a Scot, he was instinctively a theologian; being himself, he was inevitably liberal-minded; born a peasant of genius, and therefore a natural rebel, he could not choose but quarrel with the Kirk—especially as her hand was heavy on his friends and himself,—and it was as a Mauchline man that the best of his anti-clerical work was done.[2]

[1] As his landlord, the lawyer Gavin Hamilton, to whom he dedicated the Kilmarnock Volume, and the story of whose wrangle with the Mauchline Kirk-Session (see Vol. i. pp. 147-152, 188, 378-9, etc.) is to some extent that of Burns's assault upon the Kirk (see Vol. ii. *Holy Willie's Prayer*, pp. 25-30, and Notes, pp. 320-324). Another was Robert Aiken, also a lawyer, by whom he was 'read into fame,' to whom he dedicated *The Cotter's Saturday Night*, and whom he celebrated in an Epitaph (Vol. i. p. 188). Yet another was Richmond, the lawyer's clerk, whose room he was afterwards to share in Edinburgh, and who appears to be partly responsible for the preservation of *The Jolly Beggars*. Again, there was the Bachelors' Club, on the model of that he had founded at Tarbolton, for whose edification, and in explanation of whose function, he appears to have written *The Fornicator* and *The Court of Equity*. This last is Burns's idea of what the proceedings of the Kirk-Session ought, in certain cases, to have been. It is capital fun, but something too frank and too particular for latter-day print.

[2] He was ever a theological liberal and a theological disputant—a champion of Heterodoxy, in however mild a form, whose disputations made him notorious, so that his name was as a stumbling-block and an offence to the Orthodox. For the series of attacks which he delivered against the Kirk—*The Holy Fair*, the *Address to the Deil*, *The Twa Herds*, *The Ordination*, *Holy Willie*, *The Kirk's Alarm*, the Epistles *To the Unco Guid* and *To John Goldie*—see Vols. i. and ii. (Text and Notes). There is no record of an appearance on the stool with Paton; but the circumstances of this his initial difficulty appear to be set

Then, too, he was full of rhymes, and they must out of him: his call had come, and he fell to obeying it with unexampled diligence. More than all, perhaps, he had the temperament of the *viveur*—the man who rejoices to live his life; and his appetites had been intensified, his gift of appreciation made abnormal (so to say), by a boyhood and an adolescence of singular hardship and quite exceptional continence. It is too late in the world's history to apologise for the primordial instinct; and to do so at any time were sheer impertinence and unreasoning ingratitude. To apologise in the case of a man who so exulted in its manifestations and results, and who so valiantly, not to say riotously, insisted on the fact of that exultation, as Robert Burns, were also a rank and frank absurdity. On this point he makes doubt impossible. The 'white flower of a blameless life' was never a button-hole for *him*:[1] his utterances, published and unpublished,

---

forth in the *Epistle to Rankine* (i. 155) and the *Reply to a Trimming Epistle* (ii. 96), with the Notes thereto appended. All these read, considered, and digested, what interest remains in Burns's quarrel with the Kirk consists in the fact that, being a person naturally and invincibly opposed to the 'sour-featured Whiggism' on which the Stuarts had wrecked themselves, Burns was naturally and invincibly a Jacobite. His Jacobitism was, he said, 'by way of *vive la bagatelle*.' He told Ramsay of Auchtertyre that he owed it to the plundering and unhousing (1715) of his grandfather, who was gardener to Earl Marischal at Inverurie (*sic*). But it came to him mainly through Gavin Hamilton (who was Episcopalian by descent) and his own resentment of clerical tyranny.

[1] It is true that he wrote thus 'To a Young Friend':—

    'The sacred lowe o' weel-plac'd love,
      Luxuriantly indulge it;
    But never tempt th' illicit rove,
      Tho' naething should divulge it:

are there to show that he would have disdained the presumption that it ever could have been. And it is from Mauchline, practically, that, his affair with Betty Paton over and done with, and, to anticipate a little, his affair with Jean Armour left hanging in the wind, he starts on his career as amorist at large.

And now for a little narrative. In the November of 1784 Elizabeth Paton bore him a daughter: 'the First Instance,' so he wrote above his *Welcome*, 'that entitled him to the Venerable Appellation of Father.' The mother is described as 'very plain-looking,' but of 'an exceedingly handsome figure'; 'rude and uncultivated to a great degree,' with a 'strong masculine understanding, and a thorough, though unwomanly, contempt for any sort of refinement'; withal, 'so active, honest, and independent a creature' that Mrs. Burns would have had Robert marry her, but 'both my aunts and Uncle Gilbert opposed it,' in the belief that 'the faults of her character would soon have disgusted him.' There had been no promise on his part; and though the

> I waive the quantum o' the sin,
> The hazard of concealing;
> But, och! it hardens a' within,
> And petrifies the feeling!'

But there is plenty to show that the writer was a great deal better at preaching than at practice. And he owns as much himself in his own epitaph:—

> 'Is there a man, whose judgment clear
> Can others teach the course to steer,
> Yet runs, himself, life's mad career
> Wild as the wave?—
> Here pause—and, thro' the starting tear,
> Survey this grave.'

reporter (his niece, Isabella Begg) has his own sister's warrant—(Mrs. Begg, by the way, was rather what her brother, in a mood of acute fraternal piety, might possibly have called 'a bletherin' b—tch ')—for saying that ' woman never loved man with a more earnest devotion than that poor woman did him,' he in nowise sentimentalised about her. She is identified with none of his songs; and while there is a pleasant reference to her in the *Welcome* :—

'Thy mither's person, grace, and merit':—

she is recognisably the 'paitrick' of the *Epistle to Rankine,* she is certainly the heroine of *The Fornicator,* she probably does duty in the *Reply to a Trimming Epistle,* none of which pieces shows the writer's 'penchant à l'adorable,' *etc.,* to advantage. No doubt, they were addressed to men. No doubt, too, they were, first and last, satirical impeachments of the Kirk : impeachments tinctured with the peasant's scorn of certain existing circumstances, and done with all the vigour and the *furia* which one particular peasant—a peasant who could see through shams and was intolerant of them—could with both hands bestow. And that the women did not resent their share in such things is shown by the fact that such things got done. It was 'the tune of the time' —in the peasant-world at least. Still, as Diderot says somewhere or other :—' On aime celle à qui on le donne, on est aimé de celle à qui on le prend.' And one can't help regretting that there are few or none but derisive references to Betty Paton in her lover's work.

IV

Of vastly greater importance than his mistresses, at this or any period of his life, is the entity, which, with an odd little touch of Eighteenth Century formality, he loved to call his Muse. That entity was now beginning to take shape and substance as a factor in the sum of the world's happiness; and the coming of that other entity in whose existence he took so high a pride and so constant a delight—I mean 'the Bard'—was but a matter of time. Burns had been ever a rhymester; and Burns, who, as Stevenson observed, and as the Notes to these Volumes have shown, 'was always ready to borrow the hint of a design, as though he had some difficulty in commencing,' had begun by borrowing his style, as well as divers hints of designs, from stall-artists and neighbour-cuckoos. But, once emancipated, once a man, once practically assured of the primal concerns of life, once conscious that (after all) he might have the root of the matter in him, the merely local poet begins to waver and dislimn, and the Burns of *Poor Mailie* (written at Lochlie) and the *Epistle to Davie* reigns — intermittently, perhaps, but obviously—in his stead. It is all over with stall-artists and neighbour-cuckoos. Poor Fergusson's book [1]

---

[1] Robert Fergusson (1750-1774) was certainly a prime influence in Burns's poetical life. Nevertheless—or shall I say consequently?—he has had less than justice from the most of Burns's Editors. Yet in his way he was so remarkable a creature that there can be no question but in his death, at four-and-twenty, a great loss was inflicted on Scottish literature. He had intelligence and an eye, a right touch of humour, the gifts of invention

has fallen into his hands, and (as he says in his ridiculous way) has 'caused him to string anew his wildly-sounding rustic lyre with emulating vigour.' At last the hour of the Vernacular Muse has come; and he is hip to haunch with such adepts in her mystery as the Sempills, and Hamilton of Gilbertfield, and Allan Ramsay, and Robert Fergusson, and the innominates whose verses, decent or not, have lived in his ear since childhood : catching their tone and their sentiment; mastering their rhythms; copying their methods; considering their effects in the one true language of his mind.[1] He could write

and observation and style, together with a true feeling for country and city alike; and his work in the Vernacular (his English verse is rubbish), with its easy expressiveness, its vivid and unshrinking realism, and a merit in the matter of character and situation which makes it—not readable only, but—interesting as art, at the same time that it is valuable as history, is nothing less than memorable: especially in view of the miserable circumstances—(the poor lad was a starveling scrivener, and died, partly of drink, in the public madhouse)—in which it was done. Burns, who learned much from Fergusson, was an enthusiast in his regard for him; bared his head and shed tears over 'the green mound and the scattered gowans' under which he found his exemplar lying in Canongate Churchyard; got leave from the managers to put up a headstone at his own cost there, and wrote an epitaph to be inscribed upon it, one line of which—

'No storied urn nor animated bust,'

is somehow to be read in Gray's *Elegy in a Country Churchyard*. Fergusson was as essentially an Edinburgh product—(the old Scots capital: gay, squalid, drunken, dirty, lettered, venerable: lives in his verses much as Burns knew it twelve years after his death)—as the late R. L. S. himself; and, while I write, old memories come back to me of the admiring terms: terms half-playful, half-affectionate: in which the later artist was wont to speak of his all but forgotten ancestor.

[1] I do not forget that Dugald Stewart noted the correctness of his speech and the success with which he avoided the use of

deliberate English, and, when he wanted to be not
so much sincere as impressive and 'fine,' he wrote
English deliberately, as the worse and weaker part
of his achievement remains to prove. He could
even write English, as Jourdain talked prose, 'without knowing it'—as we know from *Scots Wha
Hae*. He read Pope, Shenstone, Beattie, Goldsmith, Gray, and the rest, with so much enthusiasm
that one learned Editor has made an interesting
little list of pilferings from the works of these distinguished beings. But, so far as I can see, he
might have lived and died an English-writing Scot,
and nobody been a thrill or a memory the better
for his work. It is true that much of the *Saturday
Night* and the *Vision* and the *Mountain Daisy* is
written in English;[1] but one may take leave to

Scotticisms. But in his day Scots was, not an accent but, a living
tongue; and he certainly could not have talked at Mauchline and
at Dumfries as he did in a more or less polite and Anglified
Edinburgh.

[1] He contrives a compromise, to admirable purpose, too, in
Tam o' Shanter: which is written partly in English and partly in
the Vernacular. But (1) *Tam o' Shanter* is in a rhythmus classical
in Scotland since the time of Barbour's *Bruce*; (2) the English
parts of *Tam o' Shanter* are of no particular merit as *poetry*—that
is, 'the only words in the only order'; and (3) the best of *Tam
o' Shanter* is in the Vernacular alone. Contrast, for instance,
the diabolical fire and movement and energy of these lines:—

> 'They reeled, they set, they cross'd, they cleekit,
> Till ilka carlin swat and reekit,
> And coost her duddies to the wark,
> And linket at it in her sark':—

with another famous—perhaps too famous—passage:—

> 'But pleasures are like poppies spread:
> You seize the flower, its bloom is shed,' *etc.*

In the second the result is merely Hudibrastic. In the first the

wonder if these pieces, with so much else of Burns's own, would have escaped the 'iniquity of Oblivion,' had they not chanced, to their good fortune, to be companioned with *Halloween*, and *Holy Willie*, and *The Farmer to His Auld Mare*, and a score of masterpieces besides, in which the Vernacular is carried to the highest level—in the matter of force and fire, and brilliancy of diction, and finality of effect, to name but these—it has ever reached in verse.[1] Let this be as it may : there can be no question that when Burns wrote English he wrote what, on his own confession, was practically a foreign

suggestion—of mingled fury and stink and motion and heat and immitigable ardour—could only have been conveyed by the Vernacular Burns.

[1] It was Wordsworth's misfortune that, being in revolt against Augustan ideals and a worn-out poetic slang, he fell in with Burns, and sought to make himself out of common English just such a vocabulary as Burns's own. For he forgot that the Vernacular, in which his exemplar achieved such surprising and delectable results, had been a *literary* language for centuries when Burns began to work in it—that Burns, in fact, was handling with consummate skill a tool whose capacity had been long since proved by Ramsay and Fergusson and the greater men who went before them ; and, having no models to copy, and no verbal inspiration but his own to keep him straight, he came to immortal grief, not once but many times. It is pretended, too, that in the matter of style Burns had a strong influence on Byron. But had he ? Byron praises Burns, of course ; but is there ever a trace of Burns the lyrist in the Byron songs? Again, the Byron of *Childe Harold* and the tales was as it were a Babel in himself, and wrote Scott *plus* Coleridge *plus* Moore *plus* Beattie and Pope and the Augustan Age at large ; while the Byron of *Beppo* and the *Vision* and *Don Juan* approves himself the master of a style of such infernal brilliancy and variety, of such a capacity for ranging heaven-high and hell-deep, that it cannot without absurdity be referred to anything except the fact that he also was a born great writer.

tongue—a tongue in which he, no more than Fergusson or Ramsay, could express himself to any sufficing purpose; but that, when he used the dialect which he had babbled in babyhood, and spoken as boy and youth and man—the tongue, too, in which the chief exemplars and the ruling influences of his poetical life had wrought—he at once revealed himself for its greatest master since Dunbar.[1] More, much more, than that: his bearings once found, he marked his use of it by the discovery of a quantity hitherto unknown in literature. Himself, to wit: the amazing compound of style and sentiment with gaiety and sympathy, of wit and tender-

---

[1] For that is what it comes to in the end. He may seem to have little to do with Catholic and Feudal Scotland, and as little with the Scotland of the Early Reformation and the First Covenant. Also, it is now impossible to say if he knew any more of Scott and Dunbar and the older makers (Davie Lindsay and Barbour excepted) than he found in *The Ever Green*, which Ramsay garbled out of *The Bannatyne MS.*, if he were read in Pinkerton (1786), or if he got much more out of Gawain Douglas than the verse which serves as a motto to *Tam o' Shanter*: though a letter to Cleghorn shows that he certainly possessed a copy of that poet before 1796. The Scotland he represents, and of which his verses are the mirror, is the Scotland out of which the 'wild Whigs' crushed the taste for everything but fornication and theology and such expressions of derision and revolt as *Jenny M'Craw* and *Errock Brae*: the Scotland whose literary beginnings date, you'd fancy, not from Henryson, not from Dunbar and Douglas and the Lyon King-at-Arms, but from Sempill of Beltrees and the men who figure in the three issues of Watson's *Choice Collection*. But Ramsay and his fellows were a revival—not a new birth. The Vernacular School is one and indivisible. There are breaks in the effect; but the tradition remains unbroken. And Burns, for all his comparative modernity, descends directly from, and is, in fact, the last of that noble line which begins with Robert Henryson.

ness with radiant humour and an admirable sense of art, which is Robert Burns.

He could write ill, and was capable of fustian. But, excepting in his 'Epigrams' and 'Epitaphs' and in his imitations of poets whose methods he did not understand, he was nearly always a great writer, and he was generally (to say the least) incapable of fustian in the Vernacular. In essaying the effects of Pope and Shenstone and those other unfamiliars, he was like a man with a personal hand set to imitate a writing-master's copy: he made as good a shot as he could at it, but there was none of himself in the result. It was otherguess work when he took on the methods and the styles in which his countrymen had approved themselves: these he could compass so well that he could far surpass his exemplars technically, and could adequately express the individual Burns besides. The *Death and Dying Words of Poor Mailie* (written at Lochlie, and therefore very early work) trace back to Gilbertfield's *Bonnie Heck*; but the older piece is realistic in purpose and brutal in effect, while in the later—to say nothing of the farce in Hughoc—the whole philosophy of life of a decent mother-ewe is imagined with delightful humour, and set forth in terms so kindly in spirit and so apt in style, that the *Death and Dying Words* is counted one of the imperishables in English letters. Contrast, again, the *Elegy*, written some time after the *Death and Dying Words*, on this immortal beast, with its exemplars in Watson and Ramsay:—

'He was right nacky in his way,
An' eydent baith be night and day;

>   He wi' the lads his part could play
>   When right sair fleed,
>   He gart them good bull-sillar pay ;
>   But now he's dead. . . .'
>
> 'Wha'll jow Ale on my drouthy Tongue,
> To cool the heat of Lights and Lung?
> Wha'll bid me, when the Kaile-bell's rung,
>   To Buird me speed? . . .
> Wha'll set me by the Barrel-bung?
>   Since Sanny's dead? . . .'
>
> He was good Company at Jeists,
> And wanton when he came to Feasts ;
> He scorn'd the Converse of great Beasts
>   [F]or a Sheep's-head ;
> He leugh at Stories about Ghaists—
>   Blyth Willie's dead ':—

and you shall find the difference still more glaring. Cleverness apart—cleverness and the touch of life, the element of realism—the Laments for Hab Simson and Sanny Briggs, for John Cowper and Luckie Wood and the Writer Lithgow,[1] are merely squalid and cynical; while in every line the *Elegy,* in despite of realism and the humorous tone and intent

---

[1] All five, together with Ramsay's on Luckie Spence (an Edinburgh bawd) and *Last Words of a Wretched Miser,* should be read for the sake of their likeness, and at the same time their unlikeness, to not a little in Burns, and in illustration of the truth that the Vernacular tradition was one of humorous, and even brutal realism. I have cited R. L. S. in connexion with Fergusson. He had a far higher esteem for that maker than he had for that maker's ancestor, Allan Ramsay. Yet he quoted to me one day a stanza from the *John Cowper,* a certain phrase in which—a phrase obscenely significant of death—was, we presently agreed, as good an example of 'the Squalid-Picturesque' as could be found out of Villon.

(essential to the models and therefore inevitable in the copy) is the work of a writer of genius, who is also a generous human being.[1] Very early work, again, are *Corn Rigs* and *Green Grow the Rashes*; in suggestion, inspiration, technical quality, both are unalterably Scots; and in both the effect of mastery and completeness is of those that defy the touch of Time. To compare these two and any two of Burns's songs in English, or pseudo-English, is to realise that the poet of these two should never have ventured outside the pale of his supremacy. English had ten thousand secrets which he knew not, nor could ever have known, except imperfectly; for he recked not of those innumerable traditions, associations, connotations, surprises, as it were ambitions, which make up the romantic and the literary life of words — even as he was penetrated and possessed by the sense of any such elements as may have existed in the Vernacular. Thus, if he read Milton, it was largely, if not wholly, with a view to getting himself up as a kind of Tarbolton Satan. He was careless, so I must contend, of Shakespeare. With such knowledge as he could glean from song-books, he was altogether out of touch with the Elizabethans and the Carolines. Outside the Vernacular, in fact, he was a rather

---

[1] His suppression of such an old-fashioned touch in the first draft as this one:—

'Now Robin greetan chows the hams
Of Mailie dead':—

is significant. It is quite in the vein of *Bonnie Heck*, as indeed are the first four stanzas. But it would have ruined the *Elegy* as the world has known it since 1786.

unlettered Eighteenth Century Englishman, and the models which he must naturally prefer before all others were academic, stilted, artificial, and unexemplary to the highest point. It may be that I read the verse of Burns, and all Scots verse, with something of that feeling of 'preciousness' which everybody has, I take it, in reading a language, or a dialect, not his own : the feeling which blinds one to certain sorts of defect, and gives one an uncritical capacity for appreciating certain sorts of merit. However this be, I can certainly read my mother-tongue ; and most Englishmen—with, I should imagine, many Scots—will agree with me in the wish that Burns, for all the brilliant compromise between Scots and English which is devised and done in *Tam o' Shanter* and elsewhere, had never pretended to a mastery which assuredly he had not, nor in his conditions ever could have had.

I have stressed this point because I wish to stress another, and with a view to making clear, and to setting in its proper perspective, the fact that, genius apart, Burns was, no miracle but, a natural development of circumstance and time. The fact is patent enough to all but them that, for a superstition's sake, insist on ignoring history, and decline to recognise the unchanging processes of natural and social Law. Without the achievement of Æschylus, there can be no such perfection as Sophocles : just as, that perfection achieved, the decline of Tragedy, as in Euripides, is but a matter of time. But for the Middle Ages and the reaction against the Middle Ages there could have been no Ronsard, no Rabelais, no Montaigne in France. Had there been no Surrey and no Marlowe, no Chaucer and no Ovid (to name no more than these in a hundred influences), who shall take on himself to say the shape in which we now should be privileged to regard the greatest artist that ever expressed himself in speech? It is in all departments of human energy as in the eternal round of nature. There can be no birth where there is no preparation. The sower must take his seedsheet, and go afield into ground prepared for his ministrations; or there can be no harvest. The Poet springs from a compost of ideals and experiences and achievements, whose essences he absorbs and assimilates, and in whose absence he could not be the Poet. This is especially true of Burns. He was the last of a school. It culminated in him, because he had more genius, and genius of a finer, a rarer, and a more generous quality, than all his immediate ancestors put together. But he cannot fairly be said to have contributed anything to it except himself. He invented none of its forms; its spirit was not of his originating; its ideals and standards of perfection were discovered, and partly realised, by other men; and he had a certain timidity, as it were a *fainéantise*, in conception—a kind of unreadiness in initiative—which makes him more largely dependent upon his exemplars than any great poet has ever been. Not only does he take whatever the Vernacular School can give in such matters as tone, sentiment, method, diction, phrase; but also, he is content to run in debt to it for suggestions as regards ideas and for models in style. Hamilton of Gilbertfield and Allan Ramsay conventionalise the Rhymed Epistle; and he accepts the convention as it left their hands, and produces epistles in rhyme which are glorified Hamilton-Ramsay. Fergusson writes *Caller Water*, and *Leith Races*, and *The Farmer's Ingle*, and *Planestanes and Causey*, and the *Ode to the Gowdspink*; and he follows suit with *Scotch Drink*, and the *Saturday Night*, and *The Holy Fair*, and *The Brigs of Ayr*, and the *Mouse* and the *Mountain Daisy*. Sempill of Beltrees starts a tradition with *The Piper of Kilbarchan*; and his effect is plain in the elegies on Tam Samson and Poor Mailie. Ramsay sees a Vision, and tinkers old, indecent songs, and writes comic tales in glib octo-syllabics; and instinctively and naturally Burns does all three. It is as though some touch of rivalry were needed to put him on his mettle:[1] as though, instead of writing and caring for himself alone—(as Keats and Byron did, and Shelley: new men all, and founders of dynasties, not final expressions of sovranty)—to be himself he must still be emulous of some one

---

[1] It was with '*emulating* vigour' that he strung his 'wildly-sounding rustic lyre'; and he read Ramsay and Fergusson not 'for servile imitation' but 'to kindle at their flame.' Another instance, or rather another suggestion, from himself, and I have done. It 'exalted,' it 'enraptured' him 'to walk in the sheltered side of a wood, or high plantation, in a cloudy winter day,' and hear the wind roaring in the trees. Then was his 'best season for devotion,' for then was his mind 'rapt up in a kind of enthusiasm to Him who . . . "walks on the wings of the wind."' The 'rapture' and the 'exaltation' are but dimly and vaguely reflected in his *Winter*. But if some ancestor had tried to express a kindred feeling, then had *Winter* been a masterpiece.

else. This is not written as a reproach: it is stated as a fact. On the strength of that fact one cannot choose but abate the old, fantastic estimate of Burns's originality. But originality (to which, by the way, he laid no claim) is but one element in the intricately formed and subtly ordered plexus, which is called genius; and I do not know that we need think any the less of Burns for that it is not predominant in him. Original or not, he had the Vernacular and its methods at his fingers' ends. He wrote the heroic couplet (on the Dryden-Pope convention) clumsily, and without the faintest idea of what it had been in Marlowe's hands, without the dimmest foreshadowing of what it was presently to be in Keats's; he had no skill in what is called 'blank verse'—by which I mean the metre in which Shakespeare triumphed, and Milton after Shakespeare, and Thomson and Cowper, each according to his lights, after Shakespeare and Milton; he was a kind of hob-nailed Gray in his use of choric strophes and in his apprehension of the ode. But he entered into the possession of such artful and difficult stanzas as that of Montgomerie's *Banks of Helicon* and his own favourite sextain as an heir upon the ownership of an estate which he has known in all its details since he could know anything. It was fortunate for him and for his book, as it was fortunate for the world at large—as, too, it was afterwards to be fortunate for Scots song—that he was thus imitative in kind and thus traditional in practice. He had the sole ear of the Vernacular Muse; there was not a tool in her budget of which he was not master; and he took his place, the moment he moved for it, not so much, perhaps, by reason of his uncommon capacity [1] as, because he discovered himself to his public in the very terms—of diction, form, style, sentiment even — with which that public was familiar from of old, and in which it was waiting and longing to be addressed.

It was at Mossgiel that the enormous possibilities in Burns were revealed to Burns himself; and it was at Mossgiel that he did nearly all his best and strongest work. The revelation once made, he stayed not in his course, but wrote masterpiece after masterpiece, with a rapidity, an assurance, a command of means, a brilliancy of effect, which make his achievement one of the most remarkable in English letters. To them that can rejoice in the Vernacular his very titles are enough to recall a little special world of variety and character and delight: the world, in fact, where you can take your choice among lyrical gems like *Corn Rigs* and *Green Grow the Rashes* and *Mary Morison* and masterpieces of satire like *Holy Willie* and the *Address to the Unco Guid*. To this time belong *The Jolly Beggars* and *Halloween* and *The Holy Fair*; to this time the *Louse* and the *Mouse*, the *Auld Mare* and the *Twa Dogs*; to this time,

---

[1] In the same way Byron sold four or five editions of the *English Bards*, because it was written on a convention which was as old as Bishop Hall, and had been used by every satirist from the time of that master down to Mathias and Gifford. If he had cast his *libellus* into the octaves of *Don Juan*, the strong presumption is that it would have fallen still-born from the press. Other cases in point are Blake, Wordsworth, Shelley, Keats, and Browning: the manner of each was new, and not all have reached the general yet.

Scotch Drink and the *Address to the Deil*, the *Earnest Cry* and the *Mountain Daisy*, the *Epistles* to Smith and Rankine and Sillar and Lapraik, the *Elegies* on Tam Samson and the never-to-be-forgotten Mailie, the *Reply* to a Tailor and the *Welcome* and the *Saturday Night*. In some, as *The Ordination*, *The Holy Tulyie*, and, despite an unrivalled and inimitable picture of drunkenness, *Hornbook* itself, with others in a greater or less degree, the interest, once you have appreciated the technical quality as it deserves, is very largely local and particular.[1] In others, as the *Saturday Night* and *The Vision* (after the first stanzas of description), it is also very largely sentimental; and in both these it is further vitiated by the writer's 'falling to his English,' to a purpose not exhilarating to the student of Shakespeare and Milton and Herrick. But all this notwithstanding, and notwithstanding quite a little crowd of careless rhymes, the level of excellence is one that none but the born great writer can maintain. Bold, graphic, variable, expressive, packed with observations and ideas, the phrases go ringing and glittering on through verse after verse, through stave after stave, through poem after poem, in a way that makes the reading of this peasant a

---

[1] There is a sense in which the most are local—are parochial even. In *Holy Willie* itself the type is not merely the Scots Calvinistic pharisee: it is a particular expression of that type; the thing is a local satire introducing the 'kail and potatoes' of a local scandal. Take, too, *The Holy Fair*: the circumstances, the manners, the characters, the experience—all are local. Apply the test to almost any—not forgetting the *Tam o' Shanter* which is the top of Burns's achievement—and the result is the same.

peculiar pleasure for the student of style.[1] And if, with an eye for words and effects in words, that student have also the faculty of laughter, then are his admiration and his pleasure multiplied ten-fold. For the master-quality of Burns, the quality which has gone, and will ever go, the furthest to make him universally and perennially acceptable—acceptable in Melbourne (say) a hundred years hence as in Mauchline a hundred years syne—is humour. His sentiment is sometimes strained, obvious, and deliberate—as might be expected of the poet who foundered two pocket-copies of that very silly and disgusting book, *The Man of Feeling*; and it

---

[1] It is not, remember, for 'the love of lovely words,' not for such perfections of human utterance as abound in Shakespeare:—

'Gilding pale streams with heavenly alchemy':—

in Milton:—

'Now to the moon in wavering morrice move':—

in Keats:—

'And hides the green hill in an April shroud':—

in Herrick:—

'Ye have been fresh and green,
Ye have been filled with flowers,
And ye the walks have been
Where maids have spent their hours':—

that we revert to Burns. Felicities he has—felicities innumerable; but his forebears set themselves to be humorous, racy, natural, and he could not choose but follow their lead. The Colloquial triumphs in his verse as nowhere outside the *Vision* and *Don Juan*; but for Beauty we must go elsewhither. He has all manner of qualities: wit, fancy, vision of a kind, nature, gaiety, the richest humour, a sort of homespun verbal magic. But, if we be in quest of Beauty, we must e'en ignore him, and 'fall to our English': of whose secrets, as I've said, he never so much as suspected the existence, and whose supreme capacities were scaled from him until the end.

often rings a little false, as in much of the *Saturday Night*. But his humour—broad, rich, prevailing, now lascivious or gargantuan and now fanciful or jocose, now satirical and brutal and now instinct with sympathy, is ever irresistible. Holy Willie is much more vigorously alive in London, and Sydney, and Cape Town to-day than poor drunken old Will Fisher was in the Mauchline of 1785. That 'pagan full of pride,' the vigilant, tricksy, truculent, familiar, true-blue Devil lives ever in Burns's part pitying and fanciful, part humorous and controversial presentment; but he has long since faded out of his strongholds in the Kirk:—

> 'But fare-ye-weel, Auld Nickie-Ben,
> O, wad ye tak' a thocht, an' men',
> Ye aiblins micht—I dinna ken—
>   Still hae a stake!
> I'm wae to think upon yon den,
>   Ev'n for your sake.'

Lockhart, ever the true Son of the Manse, was so misguided—so mansified, to coin a word—as to wish that Burns had written a *Holy Fair* in the spirit and to the purpose of *The Cotter's Saturday Night*. But the bright, distinguishing qualities of *The Holy Fair* are humour and experience and sincerity; the intent of the *Saturday Night* is idyllic and sentimental, as its effect is laboured and unreal; and I, for my part, would not give my *Holy Fair*, still less my *Halloween* or my *Jolly Beggars*—observed, selected, excellently reported—for a wilderness of *Saturday Nights*. It is not hard to understand that (given the *prestance* of its author) the *Saturday Night*

was doomed to popularity from the first :[1] being of
its essence sentimental and therefore pleasingly un-
true, and being, also of its essence, patriotic—an
assertion of the honour and the glory and the piety
of Scotland. But that any one with an eye for fact
and an ear for verse should prefer its tenuity of
inspiration and its poverty of rhythm and diction
before the sincere and abounding humour and the
notable mastery of means, before the plenitude of
life and the complete accord of design and effect,
by which *Halloween,* and *The Holy Fair,* and nine-
tenths of the early pieces in the Vernacular are
distinguished, appears inexplicable. In these Burns
is an artist and a poet : in the *Saturday Night* he
is neither one nor other. In these, and in *Tam
o' Shanter,* the Scots School culminates : as English
Drama, with lyrical and elegiac English, culminates
in *Othello* and the *Sonnets,* in *Antony and Cleopatra*
and the *Adonis* and *The Rape of Lucrece* : more
gloriously far than the world would ever have
wagered on its beginnings. It is the most individual asset in the heritage bequeathed by 'the
Bard'; and still more, perhaps,[2] than the Songs,

---

[1] And such popularity ! 'Poosie Nansie's'—(thus writes a
friend, even as these sheets are passing through the press)—'or
rather a house on the site of Poosie Nansie's, is, as you know,
still a tavern. There is a large room (for parties) at the back.
And what, think you, is the poem that, printed and framed and
glazed, is hung in the place of honour on its walls ? "*The Jolly
Beggars*—naturally ?" Not a bit of it. *The Cotter's Saturday
Night* ! Surrounded, too, by engravings depicting its choicest
moments and its most affecting scenes.'

[2] I say, 'perhaps,' because Burns, among the general at least,
is better sung than read. But if the Songs, his own and those
which are effects of a collaboration, be the more national, the

it stamps and keeps him the National Poet. The world it pictures—the world of 'Scotch morals, Scotch Religion, and Scotch drink'—may be ugly or not (as refracted through his temperament, it is *not*). Ugly or not, however, it was the world of Burns; to paint it was part of his mission; it lives for us in his pictures; and many such attempts at reconstruction as *The Earthly Paradise* and *The Idylls of the King* will 'fade far away, dissolve,' and be quite forgotten, ere these pictures disfeature or dislimn. He had the good sense to concern himself with the life he knew. The way of realism [1] lay

---

Poems are the greater, and it is chiefly to the Poems that Burns is indebted for his place in literature.

[1] It is claimed for him, with perfect truth, that he went straight to Nature. But the Vernacular makers seldom did anything else. An intense and abiding consciousness of the common circumstances of life was ever the distinguishing note of Scots Poetry. It thrills through Henryson, through Dunbar and the Douglas of certain 'Prologus' to *Eneados*, through Lindsay and Scott, through the nameless lyrist of *Peeblis at the Play* and *Christ's Kirk on the Green*, through much of *The Bannatyne MS.*, the Sempill of the *Tulchene Bischope*, the Montgomerie of the *Flyting* with Polwarth and of certain sonnets:—

'Raw reid herring reistit in the reik.'

It is even audible in the *Guid and Godlie Ballats*; and after the silence it is heard anew in the verse which was made despite the Kirk, and in the verse which proceeded from that verse—the verse, that is, of Ramsay and Fergusson and Burns. This vivid and curious interest in facts is, as I think, a characteristic of the 'perfervid ingyne.' Compare, for instance, Pitscottie and Knox on the murder of Cardinal Beaton. The one is something naïve, the other as it were Shakespearean; but in both the element of particularity is vital to the complete effect. These are two instances only; but I could easily give two hundred. (See *post* p. 323, Note 1.) To return to Burns and his treatment of weather (say) and landscape. His verse is full of realities:—

broad-beaten by his ancestors, and was natural to
his feet; he followed it with vision, with humour,
with 'inspiration and sympathy,' and with art;
and in the sequel he is found to have a place of his
own in the first flight of English poets after Milton,
Chaucer, Shakespeare.

V

I take it that Burns was not more multifarious in
his loves than most others in whom the primordial
instinct is of peculiar strength. But it was written
that English literature—the literature of Chaucer,
Shakespeare, Fielding—should be turned into a
kind of schoolgirls' playground; so that careful
Editors have done their best to make him even as
themselves, and to fit him with a suit of practical
and literary morals, which, if his own verse and
prose mean anything, he would have refused, with
all the contumely of which his 'Carrick lips' were

> 'When lyart leaves bestrow the yird,
>   Or, wavering like the bauckie-bird,
>   Bedim cauld Boreas' blast;
>   When hailstanes drive wi' bitter skyte. . . .'
>
> 'The burn stealing under the lang, yellow broom. . . .'
> 'When, tumbling brown, the burn comes down. . . .'
> 'The speedy gleams the darkness swallowed. . . .'
> 'Yon murky cloud is foul with rain. . . .'
> 'November chill blaws loud wi' angry sugh':—

all exactly noted and vividly recorded (a very instructive instance
is the 'burnie' stanza in *Halloween*; for he had, they say, a
peculiar delight in running water). But for great, imaginative
impressions:—

> 'Those green-robed senators of mighty woods,
>   Tall oaks branch-charmèd by the earnest stars':—

you turn to other books than his.

capable, to wear. Nothing has exercised their ingenuity, their talent for chronology, their capacity for invention (even), so vigorously as the task of squaring their theory of Burns with the story of his marriage and the legend of his Highland Lassie. Now is the moment to deal with both.

Elizabeth Paton's child was born in the November of 1784. In the April of that year, a few weeks after the general settlement at Mossgiel, he made the acquaintance of Armour the mason's daughter, Jean. She was a handsome, lively girl; the acquaintance ripened into love on both sides; and in the end, after what dates approve a prolonged and serious courtship, Armour fell with child. Her condition being discovered, Burns, after some strong revulsions of feeling against—not Jean, I hope, but—the estate of marriage, gave her what he presently had every reason to call 'an unlucky paper,' recognising her as his wife; and, had things been allowed to drift in the usual way, the world had lacked an unforgotten scandal and a great deal of silly writing. This, though, was not to be. Old Armour—('a bit mason body, who used to snuff a guid deal, and gey af'en tak' a bit dram')—is said to have 'hated' Burns: so that he would 'reyther hae seen the Deil himsel' comin' to the hoose to coort his dochter than him.' Thus a contemporary of both Armour and Burns; and in any case Armour knew Burns for a needy and reckless man, the father of one by-blow, a rebel at odds with the Orthodox, of whom, in existing circumstances, it would be vain to ask a comfortable living. So he first obliged Jean to give up

Etching by WILLIAM HOLE

LINCLUDEN

the 'unlucky paper,' with a view to unmaking any engagement it might confirm,[1] and then sent her to Paisley, to be out of her lover's way. In the meanwhile Burns himself was in straits, and had half-a-dozen designs in hand at once. Mossgiel was a failure; he had resolved to deport himself to the West Indies; he had made up his mind to print, and the Kilmarnock Edition was setting, when Jean was sent into exile. Worst of all, he seems to have been not very sure whether he loved or not. When he knew that he and she had not eluded the Inevitable, he wrote to James Smith that 'against two things—staying at home and owning her conjugally'—he was 'fixed as fate.' 'The first,' he says, 'by heaven I will not do!' Then, in a burst of Don-Juanism—Don-Juanism of the kind that protests too much to be real—'the last, by hell I will never do.' Follows a gush of sentimentalism (to Smith), which is part nerves and part an attempt—as the run on the g's and the w's shows —at literature :—' A good God bless you, and make you happy, up to the warmest weeping wish of parting friendship.' And this is succeeded by a message to the poor, pregnant creature, of whom, but two lines before, he has sworn 'by hell' that he will never make her honest :—' If you see Jean, tell her

[1] I take it that the paper was 'unlucky,' because it became a weapon in old Armour's hands, and was the means of inflicting on the writer the worst and the most painful experience of his life. At the same time there seems to be no doubt that it made Jean Mrs. Burns, so that, consciously or not, Auld (who probably had a strong objection to the marriage) was guilty of an illegal act in certifying Burns a bachelor. Burns, in fact, was completely justified in his anger with the Kirk and in the scorn with which he visited the tyranny of her ministers.

I will meet her, so help me God in my hour of need.' This scrap is undated, but it must have been written before 17th February 1786, when he wrote thus to Richmond:—' I am extremely happy with Smith; he is the only friend I have *now* in Mauchline.' Well, he *does* meet Jean; and, his better nature getting the upper hand, the 'unlucky paper' is written. Then on the 20th March he writes thus to Muir:—' I intend to have a gill between us or a mutchkin stoup,' for the reason that it 'will be *a great comfort and consolation*':—which seems to show that Jean has repudiated him some time between the two letters. Before the 2nd April, on which day the Kirk-Session takes cognisance of the matter, Jean has gone to Paisley; the 'unlucky paper' is cancelled (apparently about the 14th April, the names were cut out with a penknife); so that Don Juan finds himself *planté-là*, and being not really Don Juan—(as what sentimentalist could be?)—he does not affect Don Juan any more. The prey has turned upon the hunter; the deserter becomes the deserted, the privilege of repudiation, 'by hell' or otherwise, has passed to the other side. The man's pride, inordinate for a peasant, is cut to the quick; and his unrivalled capacity for 'battering himself into an affection' or a mood has a really notable opportunity for display. In love before, he is ten times more in love than ever; he feels his loss to desperation; he becomes the disappointed lover—even the true-souled, generous, adoring victim of a jilt:—

> ' A jillet brak his heart at last
> That's owre the sea.'

In effect, his position was sufficiently distracting. He had made oath that he would *not* marry Jean; then he had practically married her; then he found that nobody wanted her married to him—that, on the contrary, he was the most absolute 'detrimental' in all Ayrshire; when, of course, the marriage became the one thing that made his life worth living. He tried to persuade old Armour to think better of his resolve, and, failing, ran 'nine parts and nine tenths out of ten stark staring mad.' Also he wrote the *Lament*, in which he told his sorrows to the moon[1] (duly addressing that satellite as 'O thou pale Orb'), and took her publicly into his confidence, in the beautiful language of Eighteenth Century English Poetry, and painted what is in the circumstances a really creditable picture of the effects upon a simple Bard of 'a faithless woman's broken vow.' Further, he produced *Despondency* in the same elegant lingo; and, in *Despondency*, having called for ' the closing tomb,' and pleasingly praised 'the Solitary's lot,'—

' Who, all-forgetting, all-forgot
  Within his humble cell—
The cavern, wild with tangling roots—
Sits o'er his newly gathered fruits,
  Beside his crystal well!' *etc.*—

he addressed himself to Youth and Infancy in these affecting terms:—

---

[1] Is it worth noting that, later, when he comes to sing of Mary Campbell, his confidant is no longer the Moon but the Morning Star?

'O enviable early days,
　When dancing thoughtless Pleasure's maze,
　　To care, to guilt unknown!
How ill exchang'd for riper times,
　To feel the follies or the crimes
　　Of others, or my own!
Ye tiny elves that guiltless sport,
　Like linnets in the bush,
Ye little know the ills ye court,
　When manhood is your wish!
　　The losses, the crosses
　　　That active man engage;
　　The fears all, the tears all
　　　Of dim declining Age!'[1]

Moreover, he took occasion to refer to Jean (to David Brice; 12th June 1786) as 'poor, ill-advised, ungrateful Armour'; vowed that he could 'have no nearer idea of the place of eternal punishment' than 'what I have felt in my own breast on her

---

[1] I cannot attach any great importance to these exercises in Poetic English. Burns wrote to a very different purpose when he wrote from his heart and in his native tongue:—

'Had we never loved sae kindly . . .'
'Of a' the airts the wind can blaw
　I dearly like the west':—

and so on, and so on. Still, there can be no doubt that they mean something. At any rate they are designed to be impressive and 'fine'; and probably the Bard believed in them to the extent to which he was satisfied with his achievement in what must certainly have seemed to him real poetry. None of your Vernacular (that is), but downright, solid, unmistakable English Verse: verse which might stand beside the works of Beattie and Shenstone and Thomson and the 'elegantly melting Gray.' That life departed them long since is plain. But it is just as plain that they meant something to Burns, for (apparently) he took much pains with them, saw not their humorous aspect, and included them in his first (Kilmarnock) Volume.

account'; and finally confessed himself to this purpose:—'I have tried often to forget her: I have run into all kinds of dissipation and riot . . . to drive her out of my head, but all in vain.' Long before this, however—as early, it would seem, as some time in March—his 'maddening passions, roused to tenfold fury,' having done all sorts of dreadful things, and then 'sunk into a lurid calm,' he had 'subsided into the time-settled sorrow of the sable widower,' and had lifted his 'grief-worn eye to look for—another wife.' In other words, he had pined for female society, and had embarked upon those famous love-passages with Highland Mary.

Little that is positive is known of Mary Campbell except that she once possessed a copy of the Scriptures (now very piously preserved at Ayr), and that she is the subject of a fantasy, in bronze, at Dunoon. But to consider her story is, almost inevitably, to be forced back upon one of two conclusions:—either (1) she was something of a lightskirts; or (2) she is a kind of Scottish Mrs. Harris. The theory in general acceptance—what is called the Episode Theory—is that she was 'an innocent and gentle Highland nursery-maid' (thus, after Chambers, R. L. S.) 'in the service of a neighbouring family' (Gavin Hamilton's); that she consoled Burns—*mais pour le bon motif*—for Jean's desertion; that they agreed to marry; that, on her departure for the West to prepare for the event, 'Ayr, gurgling, kissed his pebbled shore,' and they exchanged vows and Bibles; and that she died, of a malignant fever, some few months after her return to Greenock. Another identifies her (on Richmond's authority) with a serving-maid in Mauchline, who was the mistress of a Montgomerie, and had withal such a hold upon Burns that for a brief while he was crazy to make her his wife; and some have thought that this may be the Mary Campbell who, according to the Dundonald Session Records, fathered a child on one John Hay. This last hypothesis is, of course, most hateful to the puzzle-headed puritans who cannot, or will not, believe, despite the fact that the world has always teemed with Antonies, each of them mad for his peculiar Cleopatra, that Burns, particularly in his present straits, might very well have been enamoured of a gay girl to the point of marriage. So, for the consolation of these, there has been devised a third, according to which her name was either Mary Campbell or something unknown; but, whatever she was called, she was so far and away the purest and sweetest of her sex —the one 'white rose,' in fact, which grew up among 'the passion flowers' of the Bard's career —that she must, had she married him, have entirely 'rectified' his character, and have transformed him into a pattern Kirk-of-Scotland puritan of the puritans. On the other hand, it has become obvious to some whole-hearted devotees of the Marian Ideal that a 'young person' of this sort could scarce have been of so coming a habit as to skip with alacrity into Jean's old shoes, and— shutting her innocent eyes to the fact that Burns, a man notoriously at war with the Kirk and the seducer of two unmarried women, was at the same time at his wits' end for cash—consent to cast in her lot with his at a moment's notice and with never a sign from the family she was to enter. If she could do that, plainly she could not, except on strong positive testimony, be made to do duty as a white rose among passion-flowers; or if, on some unknown and inenarrable hypothesis, she could, then, says one of the devout, 'the conduct of Burns was that of a scoundrel.' This is absurd! So of late (1896-97) there has come into being a wish to believe that either Mary Campbell preceded Armour in the Bard's affections, or the Highland Lassie never existed at all, but was a creature of Burns's brain: an ideal of womanhood to which his thought ascended from the mire of this world—(the world of Ellisland, and Jean, and the children, and the songs in Johnson's *Museum*)—as Dante's to his Beatrice of dream. Given Burns's own habit and the habit of the Scots peasant woman, there is still no earthly reason for rejecting the Episode Theory—even were rejection possible—however seriously it reflect upon the morals of the parties concerned. But it is fair to add that the subject is both complicated and obscure. Burns's own references to his Highland Lassie are deliberately insignificant and vague: for once in his life he was reticent. His statement that she went home to prepare for their marriage is heavily discounted by the fact that he did not introduce her to his family as his betrothed, in nowise prepared for marriage on his own account, never dreamed, except in sporadic copies of verse, of taking her to the West Indies, and was all the while so desperately enamoured of Jean that not by any amount of self-indulgence could he rid his breast of her: by the fact, too, that, if his thought went back to the Highland Lassie in after years, his report of the journey is strongly tinctured with remorse.[1] Currie's statement is that 'the banks of Ayr formed the scene of youthful passions . . . the history of which it would be improper to reveal,' *etc.* Gilbert Burns, after noting that Nanie Fleming's charms were 'sexual'—'which indeed was the characteristic of the greater part of his (Robert's) mistresses'—is careful, perhaps with an eye on the heroine of *Thou Ling'ring Star,* to record the statement that Robert, at least, 'was no platonic lover, whatever he might pretend or suppose of himself to the contrary.' There is Richmond's statement, as reported by Train. There is the Mary Campbell of the Dundonald Register. There is the certainty that relations there were between Burns and a Mary Campbell. There is the strong probability that Mary Campbell and the Highland Lassie were one and the same person. There is Burns's own witness to the circumstance that they met and parted under extremely suspicious conditions. That, really, is all. Yet, on the strength of a romantic impulse on the part of Robert Chambers, the heroine-in-chief of Burns's story is not the loyal and patient soul whom he appreciated as the fittest to be his wife he 'd ever met: not the Jean who endured his affronts, and mothered his children (her own and another's), and took the rough and the smooth,

---

[1] He sent *Thou Ling'ring Star* to Mrs. Dunlop in a letter dated 8th November 1789. In acknowledging it, the lady noted its remorseful cast, and hoped it didn't set forth a personal experience. There is nothing to show that he gave her any particulars, or essayed to disabuse her of the idea that remorse there well might be.

the best and the worst of life with him, and wore his name for well-nigh forty years after his death as her sole title to regard. On the contrary, that heroine-in-chief is a girl of whom scarce anything definite is known, while what may be reasonably suspected of her, though natural and feminine enough, is so displeasing to some fanatics, that, for Burns's sake (not hers) they would like to mythologise her out of being; or, at the least, to make her as arrant an impossibility as the tame, proper, figmentary Burns, the coinage of their own tame, proper brains, which they have done their best to substitute for the lewd, amazing peasant of genius,[1] the inspired faun, whose voice has gone ringing through the courts of Time these hundred years and more, and is far louder and far clearer now than when it first broke on the ear of man.

Stevenson was an acute and delicate critic at many points; but he wrote like a novelist—like Thackeray, say, of Fielding and Sterne—when he wrote of Armour as a 'facile and empty-headed girl,' and insisted, still possessed by Chambers's vain imaginings, that she was first and last in love with another man. In truth the facility was on the other side. In 1784 Burns is willing to marry Betty Paton, and writes thus to Thomas Orr:—'I am very glad Peggy [Thomson] is off my hand, as I am at present embarrassed enough without her.' In 1785 he is courting Jean Armour, and very early in 1786 Jean is in the family way, and 'by hell' she shall never be his wife. But some time in March

---

[1] 'Peculiarly like nobody else' (R. B. to Arnot, April 1786).

Jean is sent to Paisley; and the 'maddening passions,' *etc.*, set to work; and he can no more 'se consoler de son départ' than Calypso could for that of Ulysses. So in a hand's turn he becomes the stricken deer, and, as we have seen, protests (to the Moon) that to marry Jean, and wear 'The promised father's tender name' are his sole ambitions. As Jean does not return, however, he seeks (and finds) such comfort as he may in exchanging vows and Bibles and what Chamfort called 'fantaisies' with Mary Campbell. On the 12th-13th May he writes *The Court of Equity*—a task the strangest conceivable for a lover, whether rejoicing or distraught. On the 14th 'Ayr gurgling kisses his pebbled shore,' and 'The flowers spring wanton to be pressed,' and Highland Mary leaves for the West to make these famous preparations. On the 15th May he dates (at least) the *Epistle to a Young Friend* :—

'The sacred lowe o' weel-placed love
    Luxuriantly indulge it,' *etc.* :—

and, as for some time past, he is still the gallant, howbeit in jest, of Betty Miller: till on the 9th June 'poor ill-advised Armour' returns to Mauchline; and on the 12th he writes that 'for all her part in a certain black affair' he 'still loves her to distraction,' and, with a view to forgetting her has 'run into all kinds of dissipation and riot . . . but in vain.' On the 28th June he appears before 'the Poacher Court,' acknowledges paternity, and is 'promised a certificate as a single man': on condition that he do penance before the congregation on three successive Sundays. On the 9th July, the occasion of his first appearance, he has 'a foolish hankering fondness' for Jean, but, calling on her and being put to the door, he remarks that she does not 'show that penitence that might have been expected'; so, on the 22nd, he executes a deed by which he makes over all his property to the 'wee image of his bonie Betty,' to the exclusion of whatever might come of his affair with the recusant. Then, on the 30th (old Armour having, meanwhile, got a warrant against him, and sent him into hiding [1]), he adjures Richmond—(who, he knows, will 'pour an execration' on Jean's head)—to 'spare the poor, ill-advised girl for my sake'; and on the 14th August he calls on Heaven to 'bless the Sex,' for that 'I feel there is still happiness for me among them.' Against this panorama of tumult and variety and adventure, enlarged in Edinburgh, and enriched at Ellisland and in Dumfries, there are to set the years of simple abnegation, magnanimity, and devotion with which the 'facile and empty-headed girl' repaid the husband of her choice. The conclusion is obvious. The Novelist turned Critic is still the Novelist. Consciously or not, he develops preferences, for, consciously or not, he must still create.[2] Stevenson's preferences were

---

[1] No doubt he retired on information sent by Jean.

[2] Thus Stevenson, who himself liked 'dressing a part' (so to speak), was persuaded that Burns did likewise, and accepted bodily that absurd, fantastic story (told by two Englishmen), in which the Bard, in a fox-skin cap and an enormous coat, and girt with a Highland broadsword, is seen angling from a Nithside rock. Jean denied it, and said that Robert (who hated field-sports, as we know) never angled in his life. But the Novelist was roused; and all that was ignored.

with Rab Mossgiel. And the result was a grave—but not, I hope, a lasting—injustice to an excellent and very womanly woman and a model wife.[1]

As to Highland Mary, one of two conclusions: (1) Either she was a paragon; or (2) she was not. In the first case, her story has yet to be written, and written on evidence that is positive and irrefutable. In the second, the bronze at Dunoon bears abiding witness to the existence (at a certain time) of what can only be described as a national delusion.

VI

By this time the end of Mauchline, and of much besides, was nearer than Burns knew. Probably sent to press in the May of 1786, the Kilmarnock Volume was published at the end of July.[2] Most of, if not

---

[1] On the 3rd September Jean lay in of twins. They were presently taken by their respective grandmothers, to whom, I doubt not, they gave great joy: as in that and other stages of society the appearance of the third generation, whether its right to exist be legal or not, does always. Burns announced the event as only Burns could, by sending *Nature's Law*:—

'Kind Nature's care had given him share
Large of the flaming current,' *etc.*:—

to Gavin Hamilton; a 'God bless the little dears'; with a snatch of indecent song, to Richmond, and a really heartfelt and affecting bit of prose on the subject of paternity to Robert Muir.

[2] One effect of its publication was to secure him the friendship of Mrs. Dunlop (ii. 352-3). It is evident from this lady's letters that her interest in him could scarce have been warmer had he been her son. She prized his correspondence as beyond rubies, and as a rule he was slower to reply than she (once, being hurt by his silence, she told him she wouldn't write again till he asked

all, the numbers contained in it were probably familiar to the countryside. Some had certainly been received with 'a roar of applause'; Burns, who was not the man to hide his light under a bushel (his temperament was too radiant and too vigorous for that), was given to multiplying his verses in MS. copies for friends; he had been 'read into fame' by Aiken the lawyer: so that *Poems, Chiefly in the Scottish Dialect* was, in a sense, as 'well advertised' as book could be. Its triumph was not less instant than well-deserved :[1] the first issue, six hundred copies strong, was exhausted in a month ('tis said that not one could be spared for Mossgiel). But Burns himself, according to himself, and he was ever punctiliously exact and scrupulous on the score of money, was but £20 in

---

her, and, failing to draw him, within a week she is found begging his pardon for her petulance). She made him many gifts—apparently in money and in kind—gifts at New Year and other times, and accepted gifts from him (once he sent her a keg of old brandy). Her influence made ever for decency, and it may well have been on her remonstrances, which were strong, that he finally resolved to remove some of the coarser phrases in his earlier editions. Her last (extant) letter is dated 11th January 1795. For some unexplained reasons she ceased from writing several months before the January of 1796. It may have been that she heard of him as often in drink, or that she was told of the affair at Woodley Park. In any case she esteemed him so highly, and admired him so lavishly, that 'tis quite impossible to believe the breach in the correspondence due to any fault of hers.

[1] 'Old and young,' says Heron, 'high and low, grave and gay, learned or ignorant, all were alike delighted, agitated, transported. I was at that time resident in Galloway, contiguous to Ayrshire: and I can well remember, how that even the plough-boys and maid-servants would have gladly bestowed the wages which they earned the most hardly, and which they wanted to purchase necessary clothing, if they might but secure the works of Burns.'

pocket by it; the Kilmarnock printer declined to strike off a second impression, with additions, unless he got the price of the paper (£27) in advance; and for some time it seemed that there was nothing but Jamaica for the writer, Local Bard and Local Hero though he were: so that he looked to have sailed in mid-August, and again on the 1st September, and at some indeterminate date had 'conveyed his chest thus far on the road to Greenock,' and written that solemn and moving song—far and away the best, I think, and the sincerest thing he left in English —*The Gloomy Night is Gathering Fast.* It was to be the 'last effort' of his 'Muse in Caledonia.' But, for one or another reason, his departure was ever deferred; and, though on the 30th October (some ten days, it is surmised, after the death of Mary Campbell), he was still writing that, 'ance to the Indies he was wonted,' he'd certainly contrive to 'mak' the best o' life Wi' some sweet elf,' on the 18th November, 'I am thinking for my Edinburgh expedition on Monday or Tuesday come s'ennight.' In effect, an 'Edinburgh expedition' was natural and inevitable. Ballantine of Ayr is said to have suggested the idea of such an adventure; Gilbert and the family are said to have applauded it. But as early as the 4th September the excellent Blacklock—(in 'a letter to a friend of mine which overthrew all my schemes')—had called—'for the sake of the young man'—for a second edition, 'more numerous than the former': inasmuch as 'it appears certain that its intrinsic merit, and the exertions of the author's friends, might give it a more universal circulation than anything of the kind which has been published within my memory.' Thus Blacklock; and the 'friend of mine,' which was Lawrie, the minister of Loudoun, had communicated Blacklock's letter to the person most concerned in Blacklock's suggestion. Bold, proud, intelligent *au possible*, strongly possessed too (so he says, and so I believe) by the genius of paternity, Burns the Man, who had a very becoming opinion of Burns the Bard, and could fairly appreciate that worthy's merits, must certainly have seen that in Edinburgh he had many chances of succeeding at the very point where the Kilmarnock printer failed him. I do not doubt, either, that he was tired of being the Local Poet, the Local Satirist, the Local Wit, the Local Lothario (even), and eager to essay himself on another and a vaster stage than Mauchline; for, if he hadn't been thus tired and thus eager, he wouldn't have been Robert Burns. The fighting spirit, the genius of emulation, is so strong in us all that a man of temperament and brains must assert himself, and get accepted at his own (or another) valuation, exactly as a cock must crow. And I love to believe that Burns, being immitigably of this metal, entered upon his adventure—(27th November: on a borrowed nag, with not much money, a letter of introduction to Dalrymple of Orangefield, and a visiting list consisting entirely in Dugald Stewart and Richmond the lawyer's clerk)—with the joyous heart and the stiff neck of one who knows himself a man among men, and whose chief ambition is to 'drink delight of battle with his peers'—if he can find them.

He reached the capital on the 28th November,

and was hospitably entertained by Richmond—to the extent, indeed, of a bedfellow's share in the clerk's one little room in Baxter's Place, Lawnmarket. Through Dalrymple of Orangefield he got access to Lord Glencairn and others: among them Harry Erskine, Dean of Faculty, and that curious, irascible, pompous ass, the Earl of Buchan, and Creech the publisher, who had been Glencairn's tutor, and who advertised the Edinburgh Edition on the 14th December. He was everywhere received as he merited, and he made such admirable use of his vogue that, five days before Creech's advertisement was printed, he could tell his friend and patron, Gavin Hamilton, that he was rapidly qualifying for the position of Tenth Worthy and Eighth Wise Man of the World. He saw everybody worth seeing, and talked with everybody worth talking to; he was made welcome by 'heavenly Burnett' and her frolic Grace of Gordon, and welcome by the ribald, scholarly, hard-drinking wits and jinkers of the Crochallan Fencibles, for whose use and edification he made the unique and precious collection now called *The Merry Muses of Caledonia*; he moved and bore himself as easily at Dugald Stewart's as in Baxter's Place, in Creech's shop, with Henry Mackenzie and Gregory and Blair, as at that extraordinary meeting of the St Andrew's Lodge, where, at the Grand Master's bidding, the Brethren assembled drank the health of 'Caledonia and Caledonia's Bard—Brother Burns': a toast received with 'multiplied honours and repeated acclamations.' To look at, 'he was like a farmer dressed to dine with the laird'; his manners were 'rustic, not clownish'; he had 'a sort of dignified plainness and simplicity.' Then, 'his address to females was always extremely deferential, and always'—this on the authority of the Duchess of Gordon—'with a turn to the pathetic or humorous, which engaged their attention particularly.' For the rest, 'I never saw a man in company with his superiors in station and information more perfectly free from either the reality or the affectation of embarrassment.' Thus, long afterwards, Sir Walter, who noted also, boy as he was, 'the strong expression of sense and shrewdness in all his lineaments,' and who, long afterwards, had never seen such an eye as Burns's 'in a human head, though I have seen the most distinguished men'— (Byron among them; and Byron's eye was one of Byron's points)—'of my time.' It is not wonderful, perhaps, that Burns, with his abounding temperament, his puissant charm, his potency in talk, his rare gifts of eye and voice,[1] should have strongly affected Edinburgh Society, brilliant in its elements and distinguished in its effect as it was. There has been no Burns since Burns; or history would pretty certainly have repeated itself. What is really wonderful is the way in which Burns kept his head in Edinburgh Society, and stood prepared for the inevitable reaction. Through all the 'thick, strong, stupefying incense smoke' (and there was certainly a very great deal of it), he held a steady eye upon his future. He saw most clearly that the

---

[1] Thus Maria Riddell:—'His voice alone could improve upon the magic of his eye. Sonorous, replete with the finest modulations,' *etc.* It will be remembered that children used to speak of Byron as 'the gentleman with the beautiful voice.'

life of a nine-days' wonder is at most nine days, and that now was his time or never. But if he expected preferment, he was neither extravagantly elated in anticipation, nor unduly depressed by disappointment; and, for all his self-consciousness—('And God had given his share')—he was not too platonic to disdain the favours of at least one servant-girl (he was arrested, August 1787, on a warrant *In meditatione fugæ*), nor too punctilious to make love to 'a Lothian farmer's daughter, a very pretty girl, whom I've almost persuaded to accompany me to the West Country, should I ever return,' *etc.*, nor too philosophical not to regret his Jean, and reflect (in this very letter to Gavin Hamilton) that he'd never 'meet so delicious an armful again.'

In the long-run his magnanimity suffered a certain change. The peasant at work scarce ever goes wrong; but abroad and idle he is easily spoiled, and soon. Edinburgh was a triumph for Burns; but it was also a misfortune. It was a centre of conviviality—a city of clubs and talk and good-fellowship, a city of harlotry and high jinks, a city (above all) of drink :—

> 'Whare couthy chiels at e'enin meet,
> Their bizzin craigs and mou's to weet :
> An' blythely gar auld Care gae by
> Wi' blinket and wi' bleering eye':—

a dangerous place for a peasant to be at large in, especially a peasant of the conditions and the stamp of Burns. He was young, he was buckishly given, and he was—Burns. He had, as certain numbers in *The Merry Muses* witness, an entirely admirable talent of a kind much favoured by our liberal ancestors. To hear him talk was ever a privilege; while to hear him make such use as he might of this peculiar capacity cannot but have constituted an unique experience. After all, a gift's a gift, and a man must use the gifts he has. No reasonable being can question that Burns used this one of his.[1] In those days he could scarce be buckish —or even popular—and do other. Even in the country, says Heron, in his loose yet lofty way, 'the

[1] This is noted neither in praise nor in dispraise. It is noted to show that Burns was essentially a man of his time: as how, peasant of genius that he was, could he be anything else? Our fathers loved sculduddery, and Burns, who came from Carrick —where, as Lockhart has remarked, the Vernacular was spoken with peculiar gaiety and vigour—was the best gifted of them all in this respect by virtue of his genius, his turn of mind, his peasanthood, and his wonderful capacity for talk. Josiah Walker notes of Burns that his conversation was 'not more licentious' than the conversation heard at the tables of the great; Lockhart regrets that he can give but few of Burns's *mots*, for the reason that the most of those preserved and handed down were unquotable. It was a trick of the time, and long after—(remember Colonel Newcome's indignant retreat before old Costigan) —so that Lord Cork of *The Bumper Toast*, and Captain Morris at Carlton House and Burns among the Crochallan Fencibles are but expressions of the same fashion in humour, the same tendency in the human mind to apprehend and rejoice in the farce of sex. I do not know that Burns and M'Queen of Braxfield (Stevenson's Weir of Hermiston) ever met. But it was said of M'Queen that he had never read anything but sculduddery and law; and to Ramsay of Auchtertyre, in whom Sir Walter found some elements of Monkbarns, the two men seemed cast in the same mould. Burns, in any case, was a man of the later Eighteenth Century (he sent one of his best-known *facetiæ* to Graham of Fintry, with a view to correcting some illiberal report about his politics); and to take him out of it, and essay to make him a smug, decent, Late-Victorian journalist is, as I think, to essay a task at once discreditable in aim and impossible of execution.

votaries of intemperate joys, with persons to whom he was recommended by licentious wit . . . had begun to fasten on him, and to seduce him to embellish the gross pleasures of their looser hours with the charms of his wit and fancy.' These temptations —(he was known, be it remembered, for the ribald of *The Fornicator* and *The Court of Equity* as well as for the poet of the *Mountain Daisy* and the *Saturday Night*)—he was by no means incapable of putting by. Mr. Arthur Bruce, indeed, 'a gentleman of great worth and discernment,' assured Heron that he had 'seen the Poet steadily resist such solicitations and allurements to convivial enjoyment, as scarcely any other person could have withstood.' But—thus this author: intelligent, not unfriendly on the whole, on the whole competent—'the bucks of Edinburgh accomplished . . . that in which the boors of Ayrshire [1] had failed. After residing some months in Edinburgh he began to estrange himself, not altogether, but in some measure, from the society of his graver friends. . . . He *suffered* himself to be surrounded by a race of miserable beings who were proud to tell that they had been in company with Burns, and had seen Burns as loose and as foolish as themselves.' [2] One result of this condescension was this: always the

---

[1] This appears to be a polite description, by a staunch (though drunken) Churchman, of those desperate spirits, Gavin Hamilton and Robert Aiken.

[2] I give all this for what it is worth. Heron himself was something of a wastrel. Yet he had a clerical habit and a clerical bias which made him easily censorious in the case of so hardened and so militant an anti-cleric as the Bard. He was personally acquainted, however, with that hero; and his little biography (1797) is neither unintelligent nor ill-written.

best man in the room, 'the cock of the company, as Heron puts it, 'he began to contract something of new arrogance in conversation'; till in the long-run 'he could scarcely refrain from indulging in similar freedom and dictatorial decision of talk, even in the presence of persons [1] who could less patiently endure his presumption.' Heron's detail is vague—not to say indefinite; his effect may be misleading. But, as I said, the peasant at large—the peasant without hard work to keep him straight—must, almost of necessity, run to waste. And it is plain that, treading thus closely on the heels of 'the dissipation and riot,' the 'mason-meetings, drinking-matches, and other mischief,' of the year before, the distractions and the triumphs of Edinburgh continued the work which the mistakes and follies of Dumfries were to finish ten years after.

At last, however, the First Edinburgh Edition appeared (21st April 1787). The issue ran to 2800 copies, and 1500 of these were subscribed in advance. What Burns got for it is matter of doubt. Creech informed Heron that it was £1100—which is a plain untruth; Chambers says £500; Burns himself told Mrs. Dunlop (25th March 1789) that he expected to clear some £440 to £450. (Other impressions were called for in the course of the year, but the Bard had sold his copyright, and had no interest in them.) Whatever the amount,[2] Creech

---

[1] Heron himself, no doubt. He 'had the tongues,' and thought himself the better man.

[2] At the instancing of Henry Mackenzie, Creech paid Burns (23rd April 1787) a hundred guineas for the copyright of the *Poems*, besides subscribing five hundred copies. The Caledonian Hunt subscribed another hundred; and Burns sent seventy to

was a slow paymaster; and, as Edinburgh was bad for Burns, and Creech was responsible for Burns's detention in Edinburgh, it is impossible not to regret that Burns had not another publisher. Burns in effect, his Second Edition once published, had nothing to do but pocket his receipts,[1] and be gone. This,

---

Ballantine for 'a proper person' in Ayr, and wrote from Dunse (17th May) to acknowledge the receipt, from Pattison, the Paisley bookseller, of 'Twenty-two pounds, seven shillings sterling, payment in full, after carriage deducted for ninety copies' more. Twenty-four copies went to the Earl and Countess of Glencairn, twenty to Prentice of Conington Mains, forty to Muir of Kilmarnock, twenty-one to Her Grace of Gordon, forty-two to the Earl of Eglintoun, and a certain number to the Scots Benedictionaries at Maryborough and Ratisbon, and the Scots Colleges at Douay, Paris, and Valladolid. The subscription price was five, the price to non-subscribers six, shillings: the extra shilling being (Burns to Pattison, *ut sup.*) 'Creech's profit.'

[1] Heron 'had reason to believe that he had consumed a much larger proportion of these gains than prudence could approve; while he superintended the impression, paid his court to his patrons, and wasted the full payment of the subscription money.' In effect, it is hard to see how, coming to Edinburgh with next to nothing in his pocket (the £20 from Wilson could not have gone very far), he could otherwise have lived. It would have been natural enough for him to have accepted gratuities, for the Age of Patronage was still afoot, and relief in this kind would have come as easily (to say the least) to the 'ploughing poet,' howbeit he was the proudest and in some respects the most punctilious of men, as to any other. I find it hard to believe that there were none. But there is no record of any; and a letter (unpublished) of this period in acknowledgment of a gift of money from Mrs. Dunlop is almost painful in its embarrassment of gratitude and discomfort. On the whole, I take it that, however cheaply he lived in Edinburgh, he must of necessity have had to discount his profits, though not to anything like the extent suggested by Heron. Moreover, it is like enough that he spent a certain amount upon his Tours, and it is certain that Mossgiel was a dead loss to him.

however, was what Creech could not let him do: so that he went and came, and came and went, and it was not until the March of 1789 that the two men squared accounts.[1]

The Edition floated, comes a jaunt to the Border (begun 5th May) with Robert Ainslie. Then, by the 9th June, Burns is back at Mauchline, a much richer and a vastly more important person than he left it: able to lend his brother £180; reconciled, too, with Jean and her people, but disgusted, or feigning himself disgusted (for, after the repudiation, he is ever the superior and the injured party in regard to Jean), with the 'mean, servile compliance' with which his advances are met. Follows a tour to the West Highlands, which seems to be largely an occasion for drink and talk; and in July you find him back at Mauchline, boasting how he, 'an old hawk at the sport,' has brought 'a certain lady'—(unknown)—'from her aerial towerings, pop, down at my foot, like Corporal Trim's hat': despite which Jean is presently with child by him for the second time. In August he is at Edinburgh, intent on a settlement with Creech, but on the 25th he starts for the Highland tour with his friend Nicol.[2] After a couple of excursions more—

---

[1] Of the work he did about this time the best is to be found in the *Haggis* and the *Epistles* to Creech and the Guidwife of Wauchope House. What is very much more to the purpose is that he made Johnson's acquaintance, and at once began contributing to the *Musical Museum*.

[2] Heron describes Nicol as a man who 'in vigour of intellect, and in wild yet generous impetuosity of passion, remarkably resembled ... Burns'; who 'by the most unwearied and extraordinary professional toil, in the midst of as persevering dissipa-

one to Ayrshire, to look at certain holdings—he is resolved on quitting Edinburgh, settlement or no settlement, to farm or go to the Indies, as circumstances shall dictate. But it is written that his life shall have another disputable episode and the world an immortal scrap of song :—

> ' Had we never loved sae kindly,
> Had we never loved sae blindly,
> Never met or never parted,
> We had ne'er been broken-hearted.'

So in the beginning of December he falls in with Mrs. M'Lehose; he instantly proposes to 'cultivate her friendship with the enthusiasm of religion'; and the two are languishing in Arcady in the twinkling of a cupid's wing.

She was a handsome, womanly creature—' of a somewhat voluptuous style of beauty' : a style the Bard appreciated—lively but devout, extremely sentimental yet inexorably dutiful : a grass widow with children—nine times in ten a lasting safeguard—

---

tion . . . won and accumulated an honourable and sufficient competence'; and who died of 'a jaundice, with a complication of other complaints, the effects of long-continued intemperance.' Burns admired Nicol, named a son after him, and immortalised him as the 'Willie' who 'brew'd a peck o' maut.' He had a generous heart and a brutal temper, with plenty of brains, a great contempt for custom and the Kirk, and what Lockhart calls 'a rapturous admiration of Burns's genius.' The violent vulgarity of his behaviour at Castle Gordon is typical of the man. He bought a little property not far from Ellisland, and, what with pride and vanity and republican independence (so called) and an immitigable turn for liquor, was certainly as bad a neighbour as the Bard could possibly have had.

and the strictest notions of propriety—a good enough defence for a time; but young (she was the Bard's own age), clever, 'of a poetical fabric of mind,' and all the rest. The upsetting of a hackney coach disabled Burns from calling on her for some weeks. But he wrote her letters, and she answered them; and he was Sylvander, and she signed herself Clarinda; and they addressed each other in verse as well as prose; and she said it could never be; and he said that at least he must know her heart was his; and Religion was her 'balm in every woe'; and he gave her his ideas of Deity; and, when they could meet, Clarinda was ever afraid lest she had let Sylvander go too far; and Sylvander, for his part, was monstrous eloquent about 'Almighty Love'—(he was sometimes dreadfully like his favourite Man of Feeling) —and was 'ready to hang himself' about 'a young Edinburgh widow.' Widow she was not; but her husband, who cared not a snap of the fingers for her, was away in the West Indies; and it may perhaps have suited her lover—who never, so far as is known, was trained to the compromises and the obsequiencies of adultery—to soothe his conscience by making believe that the affair was at the most a simple everyday amour. Clarinda was of another make. In the prime of life, deserted, sentimental, a tangle of simple instincts and as simple pieties, she had the natural woman's desire for a lover and the religious woman's resolve to keep that lover's passion within bounds. It is scarce questioned that she succeeded: though there is a legend that a certain gallant and insinuating little lyric:—

'O May, thy morn was ne'er sae sweet
 As the mirk night o' December.
For sparkling was the rosy wine,
 And secret was the chamber!
And dear was she I winna name
 But I will aye remember!'—

commemorates, not only their final meeting (December 6th, 1791) but also, the triumph of the Bard.[1] In any event she was plainly an excellent creature, bent on keeping herself honest and her lover straight; and it is impossible to read her letters to Sylvander without a respect, a certain admiration even, which have never been awakened yet by the study of Sylvander's letters to her. For Sylvander's point of view, as M'Lehose was still alive, and an open intrigue with a married woman would have been ruin, only one inference is possible: that he longed for the shepherd's hour to strike for the chime's sake only; so that, when he thought of his future, as he must have done anxiously and often, he cannot ever have thought

---

[1] Both *Ae Fond Kiss* and *O May, thy Morn* were sent to Clarinda after the final parting; but the legend is all-too obviously an effect of the very common human sentiment in deference to which so many novels end happily. For the rest, Sir Walter Scott wrote thus on the fly-leaf of a copy of the very scarce Belfast Edition (1806) of the *Letters Addressed to Clarinda by Robert Burns*, now at Abbotsford:—'Clarinda was a Mrs. Meiklehose, wife of a person in the West Indies, from whom she lived separate but without any blemish, I believe, on her reputation. I don't wonder that the Bard changed her "thrice unhappy name" for the classical sound of Clarinda. She was a relative of my friend the late Lord Craig, at whose house I have seen her, old, charmless and *devote*. There was no scandal attached to her philandering with the Bard, though the Lady ran risques, for Burns was anything but platonic in his amours,' *etc.*

of it as Clarinda's, even though in a moment of peculiar exaltation he swore to keep single till that wretch, the wicked husband, died.[1]

Very early in 1788, Jean—brought, she also, some time in the preceding summer 'pop, down at my feet, like Corporal Trim's hat'—was expelled her parents' house and took refuge at Tarbolton Mill. There Burns found her on his return, and thence he removed her to a house in 'Mauchline toun,' to the particular joy, a short while after, of Saunders Tait:—

> 'The wives they up their coats did kilt,
> And through the streets so clean did stilt,
> Some at the door fell wi' a pelt
>   Maist broke their leg,
> To see the Hen, poor wanton jilt!
>   Lay her fourth egg.' [2]

Follows what is perhaps the most perplexing sequence of circumstances in a perplexing life. To Clarinda, who knew of the affair with Armour, pitied

---

[1] M'Lehose outlived him many years.

[2] Some stanzas later in *B—rns's Hen Clockin in Mauchline*, Saunders (who has been likening Jean to a ship) thus notes her state:—
> 'Now she is sailing in the Downs,
> Calls at the ports of finest towns,
> *To buy bed hangings and galloons*':

and comments with fury on the fact that she's got, not only 'twa packs o' human leather,' but also
> 'A fine cap and peacock feather,
> And wi't she's douce,
> With a grand besom made of heather,
> To sweep her house.'

It is worth noting that he winds up his lampoon by accusing the gossips at the lying-in of talking scandal of the rankest and reading *The Holy Fair*!

the victim—(this does *not* mean that she wished her married to Burns)—and had sped her shepherd on his homeward way with 'twa wee sarkies' for the victim's little boy: a mistress, be it remembered, to whom he had written (14th February) in such terms as these:—'I admire you, I love you as a woman beyond any one in the circle of creation': —he wrote, a few days after his arrival at Mauchline, that he had 'this morning' (23rd February 1788) 'called for a certain woman,' and been 'disgusted with her,' so that he could not 'endure her.' Though his heart 'smote him for the profanity,' he sought to compare the two; and ''twas setting the expiring glimmer of a farthing taper beside the cloudless glory of the meridian sun.' 'Here,' the Old Hawk continues, '*here* was tasteless insipidity, vulgarity of soul, and mercenary fawning. *There*, polished good sense, Heaven-born genius, and the most generous, the most delicate, the most tender passion.' This to the contrary, it needs no great knowledge of life, and still less of Burns and Armour, to divine what happened; and it needs as little of Burns at this point in his career to see why he ended his confession to Clarinda thus:—'I have done with her, and she with me.' Eight days after this (3rd March 1788), in a letter to Ainslie, some parts of it too 'curious' for a Victorian page, he tells a different story.[1] 'Jean,' says he,

[1] The letter is best described as a Crochallanism—as something written by one Fencible for the edification of another Fencible, and dealing with its subject in right Fencible style and from the correct Fencible point of view. I am afraid that, like the aforesaid letter to Clarinda, it was designed as what Ainslie himself, then unregenerate, might have called 'a d——d bite.'

'I found banished like a martyr—forlorn, destitute, and friendless; all for the good old cause. I have reconciled her to her fate: I have reconciled her to her mother:[1] I have taken her a room: I have taken her to my arms: I have given her a mahogany bed: I have given her a guinea; and I have'—but here Scott Douglas's garbling begins, and Burns's inditing ends; and the original must be read, or the reader will never wholly understand what manner of man the writer was. Then comes an avowal so disconcerting that I cannot choose but disbelieve it, and conclude that it was made for some special purpose. 'But,' says the Old Hawk, 'but, as I always am, on every occasion—I have been prudent and cautious to an astounding degree; I swore her, privately and solemnly, never to attempt any claim on me as a husband, even though anybody should persuade her she had such a claim, which she had not,[2] neither during my life nor after my death. She did all this like a good girl, and . . .' The rest is unquotable. At first consideration, the spectacle of the Bard keeping 'the wish'd, the trysted hour,' with a settled purpose of 'prudence and caution' in his mind, and as it were the materials for swearing in his pocket, in no wise makes for enlightenment. On reflection, however, it becomes evident that Burns wrote thus to Ainslie, whom he had asked to call on Clarinda in his absence, simply that Ainslie might quote her his report of a second (and an entirely superfluous) act of

---

[1] Was reconciliation possible without a second offer of marriage? I doubt it.
[2] This is literally true: the 'unlucky paper' was destroyed.

repudiation on Jean's part:[1] to the end, as I cannot doubt, of using the fact for all it was worth, when he himself appeared upon the scene. That this is at least a possible theory is shown by the terms in which he tells (7th March) the story of his reconciliation to Brown:[2]—'I found Jean with her cargo very well laid in. . . . I have turned her into a convenient harbour where she may lie snug till she unload, and have taken the command myself, not ostensibly, but for a time in secret.' This can only mean that he purposes to marry the girl. For all that, though, he still has hopes of a practical issue to his Edinburgh affair; for in his next letter (writ the same day) to Clarinda, who has reproached him for silence, and at the same time owned that she counts 'all things (Heaven excepted) but lost, that I may win and keep you,' 'Was it not blasphemy, then,' he asks, 'against your own charms and against my feelings, to suppose that a short fortnight could abate my passion!' With a vast deal more to the same purpose. Three days after, he starts again for Edinburgh, and plunges deeper in desire than ever for his 'dearest angel' (so he calls her on the 17th March), the 'dearest partner of his soul' (four days after). 'Oh Clarinda' (same date), 'what do I owe to Heaven for blessing me with such

---

[1] There was no need of oaths from Jean: her lover had had his bachelor's certificate in his pocket for months. And such swearing as there was—*was it not all on the other side?*

[2] It is important to note the difference in manner and tone and suggestion between Burns to Brown and Burns to Ainslie. Burns writes to Brown as friend to friend; to Ainslie as Fencible to Fencible—much, in fact, as Swiveller, President of the Glorious Apollos, to Chuckster, Vice of the same sublime Society.

a piece of exalted excellence as you!' He must leave for Ellisland, *viâ* Mauchline, on the 24th; and 'Will you open,' he asks, 'with satisfaction and delight a letter'—('twas all to be limited to letters soon)—'from a man who loves, who has loved you, and who will love you to death, through death, and for ever!' They are to meet the next night, and he is to watch—(right Arcady, this!)—her lighted window:—''Tis the star that guides me to Paradise.' And for him 'the great relish to all is—that Honor —that Innocence—that Religion, are the witnesses and guarantees of our happiness.' Follows a bit of the Bible adapted to their peculiar case; and with an 'Adieu, Clarinda! I am going to remember you in my prayers,' the Old Hawk stoops to his perch for the night. Nothing is known of the last engagement; but apparently the citadel remains inviolate, for the leaguer is raised next day, and the besieger draws off his forces by way of Glasgow. Thence he writes to Brown (26th March) that 'these eight days' he has been 'positively crazed.' And by the 7th April he has made Jean Armour his wife.

An amazing-love story? True. But that love-story it was—that Burns was first and last enamoured of the woman he made his wife—is shown, I think, by the fact that to all intents and purposes he married her twice over. As for Clarinda, well ...! Clarinda complicates and exhilarates the interest to this extent at least: that if words mean anything, and the Bard be judged by those he wrote, the Bard, had Clarinda been indeed a widow, might at a given moment have found himself incapable of making Jean an honest woman. And had he followed his fancy, not his heart? How had the two Arcadians fared? 'Tis for some future Chambers to divine and say.

VII

Meanwhile he had taken Ellisland, a farm in Dumfriesshire, of Miller of Dalswinton: with an allowance from his landlord, a worthy and generous man, of £300, for a new steading and outhouses. His marriage at last made formal and public (it seems to have been celebrated by Gavin Hamilton), on the 5th August 1788 the bride and bridegroom appeared before the Session, acknowledged its irregularity, demanded its ' solemn confirmation,' were sentenced to be rebuked, were 'solemnly engaged to adhere faithfully to one another as husband and wife all the days of their life,' and were finally ' absolved from any scandal ' on the old account. But the new steading was long a-building. It was not till the 6th November that Burns and Jean set up their rest in Dumfriesshire; and even so, they had to go, not to their own farmhouse—(it was not ready for them till the August of 1789)—but, to a place called ' The Isle,' about a mile away from it. Burns had taken Ellisland on the advice of a friendly expert;[1]

---

[1] 'A lease was granted to the poetical farmer' (thus Heron, who knew the country) 'at the annual rent which his own friends declared that the due cultivation of his farm might easily enable him to pay.' But those friends, being Ayrshiremen, 'were little acquainted with the soil, with the manures, with the markets, with the dairies, with the modes of improvement in Dumfriesshire'; they had estimated his rental at Ayrshire rates; so that, 'contrary to his landlord's intention,' he must pay more for Ellisland than Ellisland was worth. According to the elder Cunningham, Ellisland was a poet's choice, not a farmer's.

but he had had his doubts about the wisdom of 'guid auld Glen's' decision, and these were soon justified. For a time, however, he stuck to his work like a man: conversing much, it would seem, in his leisure with his neighbour, Glenriddell, and others, whose honoured guest he was, making and vamping songs, paying some heed to national and local politics, and finding time for letters not a few—among them a long and elaborate criticism on some worthless verses by that crazy creature, Helen Maria Williams.[1] But by the end of July 1789 he had resolved to turn his holding into a dairy farm to be run by Jean and his sisters, and to take up his Gaugership[2] in earnest; and on the 10th of August, some brief while after the completion of *The Kirk's Alarm*, he learned from Graham of Fintry (whom he had met, in 1787, at the Duke of Athole's, on his Second Highland Tour) that he was appointed Exciseman for that district of Dumfriesshire in which Ellisland is situate. The work was hard, for he had charge of ten parishes, and must ride two hundred miles a week to get his duty

---

[1] Burns was not only a reader himself: he was ever the cause of reading in others. One of his occupations at Ellisland was the foundation and the management of a book-club. He took the keenest interest in the work, was especially careful in selection, and, according to Glenriddell, did whatever must be done himself. Like his father, he believed in education; and, like his father, he did his best to educate his kind by all the means which lay to his hand. He held that the peasant could not but be the better for good reading; and he exerted himself to the utmost to give the peasant what seemed to him the best that could be had. That he did so is as honourable a circumstance as is found in his career.

[2] By Glencairn's interest he had been appointed to a place in the Excise as early as 1787.

done. But by the beginning of December, ' I have found,' he writes, 'the Excise business go a great deal smoother with me than I expected'; and that he 'sometimes met the Muses,' as he jogged through the Nithsdale hills, is shown by the fact that *The Whistle*, the excellent verses on Captain Grose (with whom he made acquaintance at Glenriddell's table), and *Thou Ling'ring Star*, with *Willie Brew'd*, that best of drinking-songs, and *The Five Carlines* (a notable piece of mimicry, if no more), all belong to the period of his probation, and were all written before the end of the year. Plainly, too, he was an officer at once humane and vigilant: since, while it is told of him that he could always wink when staring would mean blank ruin to some old unchartered alewife (say), his first year's 'decreet' —his share, that is, of the fines imposed upon his information—was worth some fifty or sixty pounds. Exercise and the open air are held good for a man's health; yet in the winter of 1789-90 this man suffered cruelly from his old ailment. As for verse, the *Elegy on Matthew Henderson* and *Tam o' Shanter* (1790) seem a poor year's output for the poet of those wonderful months at Mossgiel. But work for Johnson was going steadily on; so that the results of these barren-looking times are in a sort the best known of his titles to greatness and to fame. Thus he strove, and faltered, and achieved till 1791, by the beginning of which year he had realised that Ellisland was impossible; that he could not afford his rent, which (so he told Mrs. Dunlop) was raised that year by £20, and must depend entirely on his Excisemanship: when he asked for service in a port, and, by Mrs. Dunlop's interest, was transferred to 'a vacant side-walk' in Dumfries town. Thither, his landlord setting no manner of impediment in his way, and his crops and gear having been well and profitably sold,[1] he removed himself in December, and established his family in a little house in the Wee Vennel.

'Tis a circumstance to note that, beginning at Ellisland as the Burns of *Of A' the Airts*, some time before the end he was the Burns of *Yestreen I Had a Pint o' Wine*.[2] That is, he married Jean in the April of 1788, and some two years after he got Anne Park with child. Jean bore him his second son (in wedlock) the 9th April 1791; and Anne Park had been delivered of a daughter by him ten days before (31st March). Some say that she died in childbed, some that she lived to marry a soldier. Nobody knows, and, apparently, nobody cares, what became of her. *She* was no 'white rose' (with a legend). She was scarce a

---

[1] The standing crops were 'rouped' in the last week of August. They realised 'a guinea an acre above the average.' But such a riot of drunkenness was 'hardly ever seen in this country.' See Burns to Sloan (Scott Douglas, v. 394) for details and for a confession :—'You will easily guess how I enjoyed the scene; as I was no farther over than you used to see me':—which take you back to the Burns of *The Jolly Beggars*. The stock and gear 'were not sold till August' (Scott Douglas, v. 392). 'We did not come empty-handed to Dumfries,' Mrs. Burns told M'Diarmid. 'The Ellisland sale was a very good one. A cow in her first calf brought eighteen guineas, and the purchaser never rued his bargain. Two other cows brought good prices. They had been presented by Mrs. Dunlop of Dunlop.'

[2] I have read somewhere that the first quatrain—the flower of the song—is old; but I cannot verify the description.

'passion flower';[1] and though the Bard himself thought the ditty he made upon her one of his best, the 'episode' in which she played a principal part is not regarded with any special interest by his biographers. She was a tavern waitress, and he was the Bard; and she pleased him; and she lived, or died—it matters not which; and there's an end on't. The true interest consists, perhaps, in the magnanimity of Jean, who, lying-in a few days after the interloper, was somehow moved to receive the interloper's child, and to suckle it with her own. It is further to note that Anne Park is the last of Burns's mistresses who has a name. That she was not the last in fact you gather from Currie;[2] but this one is innominate. So far as is

---

[1] Chambers declares that, if Jean had not been away in Ayrshire, there would have been no Elizabeth Burns: which is surely the boldest apology for a husband's lapse, at the same time that it is the frankest admission of this particular husband's inability to cleave to his wife in absence, that has ever been offered to an admiring world. Scott Douglas knocks it on the head, and shows that Chambers's valour is greater than Chambers's sense of history, by proving that neither in the June nor the July of 1790 could Jean have been away.

[2] He has been roundly and deservedly reproved for the manner and the circumstances in which he published his report—(of an 'accidental complaint')—which, by the way, was started by Heron. For another piece of scandal, whether published or not I do not know—that at Dumfries the Bard walked openly with harlots—it is, of course, entirely unauthenticated; and I here refer to it but for the purpose of pointing out that, if it were true, the fact of such familiarities, however horrifying to respectable Dumfries, would sit lightly enough both on Burns the peasant and on Burns the poet of *The Jolly Beggars* and *My Auntie Jean Held to the Shore*: that, if it were true, the memory of Burns exchanging terms with the light-heels of the port were simply one to set beside the memory of Burton rejoicing in the watermen at the bridge-foot at Oxford.

known, the goddesses of the years to come, the
Chlorises and Marias and Jessies :—

> ' 'Tis sweeter for thee despairing
> Than aught in the world beside ' :—

are all platonic in practice, if not in idea. The
recipe for song-making was soon to be this :—' I put
myself in the regimen of adoring a fine woman,
and in proportion to the adorability of her charms,
in proportion you ' — Thomson — ' are delighted
with my verses.' It was a mistake, so far as the
world is concerned. But Burns made it ; and by
the time it was made, he probably knew no better.
In his last years, indeed, the irresponsible Faunus
of Mossgiel and Edinburgh becomes a kind of
sentimental sultan, who changes, or rewards, his
slaves of dream with a magnificence which, edi-
fying or not, is at least amusing. Thus, you find
him designing the publication of a book of songs,
with portraits of the beauties by whom they are
inspired ; Maria Riddell is expelled his lyrical
harem as with a fork, because she has offended
him ; Jean Lorimer, she of ' the lint-white locks '
—(' Bonie lassie, artless lassie ! ')—is the Chloris
of ditty after ditty, till of a sudden Chloris is a
disgusting name, and ' what you once mentioned
of "flaxen locks" is just '—so just, indeed, that
' they cannot enter into an elegant description
of beauty.' [1] This he discovers in the February

---

[1] Is it not all the Peasant and his womankind ? The
peasant's women are his equals. The sentiment of chivalry is not
included in his heritage ; and he treats his associates in that lot
of penury and toil which is his birthright as the 'predominant
partner,' the breadwinner, the provider of children, may : he

of 1796, in the July of which year he dies. And he keeps up his trick of throwing the lyric handkerchief till the end. All through his last illness he is tenderly solicitous about his wife, be it remembered; yet the deathbed songs for Jessie Lewars are the best of those closing years.

In the result, then, Ellisland was a mistake: not so much because it was a farm, as because it was not Burns's own.[1] He was essentially and unalterably a peasant; and as a peasant-poet, a crofter taking down the best verses ever dictated by the Vernacular Muse, he might, one would like to think, what with work in the fields, and work at his desk, and the strong, persuasive inducements of home, have attained to length of days and peace of mind and the achievement of still greater fame, at the same time that he realised the ideal which he has sublimated in some famous lines:—

> 'To mak' a happy fireside clime
> For weans and wife,
> That's the true pathos and sublime
> Of human life.'

Plainly, though, it could not be. He had too much genius, too much temperament, for it to be: with too much interest in life, which to him, however diverse and however variable his moods, meant,

---

punishes, that is, and he rewards. It is unlikely that this was Burns's practice with Jean; but assuredly it was his practice with the 'fine women' of his dreams.

[1] He would have liked the life well enough, he says, had he tilled his own acres. But to take care of another man's, at the cost, too, of a horrible and ever-recurring charge called rent—that was the devil!

largely, if not wholly, Wine and Woman and Song. Also, he had been too hardly used, too desperately driven in his youth, and too splendidly petted and pampered in his manhood, to endure with constancy the work by which the tenant-farmer has to earn his bread. He had seen his father fail at Mount Oliphant and Lochlie; and he had shared his brother's failure at Mossgiel. By no fault of his own, but owing to the circumstance that he had taken a holding out of which he could not make his rent, he failed himself at Ellisland; and though, in his case, there was small risk of 'a factor's snash,' he was infinitely too honest and too proud to take undue advantage of another man's bounty: so, to make ends meet, he turned gauger, and took charge of ten parishes, and rode two hundred miles a week in all weathers. It was a thing he'd always wanted to do, and, at the time he took to doing it, it was the only thing that could profitably be done by him. But his misfortune in having to do it was none the less for that. It took him from his home, it unsettled his better habits, it threw him back on Edinburgh and his triumphing experience as an idler and a Bard, it led him into temptation by divers ways. And when Pan, his goat-foot father—Pan, whom he featured so closely, in his great gift of merriment, his joy in life, his puissant appetites, his innate and never-failing humanity —would whistle on him from the thicket, he could not often stop his ears to the call. He was the most brilliant and the most popular figure in the district; he loved good-fellowship; he needed applause; he rejoiced in the proof of his own pre-eminence in talk—rejoiced, too, in the transcendentalising effect of liquor upon the talker,[1] as in the positive result of his name and fame, his *prestance* and his personality, upon adoring women. Is it not plain that Dumfries was inevitable? Or, rather, is it not plain that, first and last, the life was one logical, irrefragable sequence of preparations for the death? That Mount Oliphant and Lochlie led irresistibly to Mauchline, as Mauchline to Edinburgh, and Edinburgh to Ellisland, and Ellisland to the house in the Mill Vennel? And is not the lesson of it all that there is none so unfortunate as the misplaced Titan—the man too great for his circumstances? Speaking broadly, I can call none to mind who, in strength and genius and temperament, presents so close a general likeness to Burns as Mirabeau. Born a noble, and given an opportunity commensurate with himself, Burns would certainly have done such work as Mirabeau's, and done it at least as well. Born a Scots peasant, Mirabeau must, as certainly, have lived the life and died the death of Burns. In truth, it is only the fortune of war that we remember the one by his conduct of the Revolution, which called his highest capacities into action, while we turn to the other for his verses, which are the outcome (so Maria Riddell thought, and was not alone in thinking) of by no means his strongest gift.

---

[1] He complained (to Clarinda) long ere this of the 'savage hospitality' he could not choose but accept. And, in effect, he had the ill-luck to start drinking at a time when whisky, fire-new from the Highlands, was the fashionable tipple, and was fast superseding ale. Born a generation earlier, when ale and claret were the staple comforters, he had stood a better chance.

VIII

Whatever the sequel, it may fairly be said for Ellisland that Burns and Jean were happy there, and that it saw the birth of *Tam o' Shanter* and the perfecting, in the contributions to Johnson's *Museum*, of the Vernacular Song.[1] The last, as we know, was Burns's work; but he had assistants, and they did him yeoman service. He worked in song exactly as he worked in satire and the rest—on familiar, old-established bases; but he did so to a very much greater extent than in satire and the rest, and with a great deal more of help and inspiration from without. I have said that he contributed nothing to Vernacular Poetry except himself, but, his contribution apart, was purely Scots-Traditional; and this is especially true of his treatment of the Vernacular Song. What he found ready to his hand was, in brief, his country's lyric life. Scotland had had singers before him; and they, nameless now and forgotten save as factors in the sum of his achievement, had sung of life and the experiences of life, the tragedy of death and defeat, the farce and the romance of sex, the rapture and the fun of

---

[1] I say nothing of the numbers sent to Thomson. Very many are copied from the *Museum*, and the others need not here be discussed with even an approach to particularity. A point to note in connexion with the contributions both to the *Museum* and to *Scottish Airs* is that Burns was honourably and intensely proud of them. He regarded them as work done in the service of the Scotland whose 'own inspirèd Bard' he was, and neither asked money, nor would take it, for them. To think that he was writing for Thomson to the very end is to have at least one pleasant memory of Dumfries.

battle and drink, with sincerity always, and often, very often, with rich or rich-rank humour. Among them they had observed and realised a little world of circumstance and character; among them they had developed the folk-song, had fixed its type, had cast it into the rhythms which best fitted its aspirations, had equipped it with all manner of situations and refrains, and, above all, had possessed it of a great number of true and taking lyrical ideas. Any one who has tried to write a song will agree with me, when I say that a lyrical idea—by which I mean a rhythm, a burden, and a drift—once found, the song writes itself. It writes itself easily or with difficulty, it writes itself well or ill; but in the end it writes itself. In this matter of lyrical ideas Burns was fortunate beyond any of Apollo's sons. He had no need to quest for them . there they lay ready to his hand, and he had but to work his will with them. That they were there explains the wonderful variety of his humours, his effects, and his themes: that he could live and work up to so many among them is proof positive and enduring of the apprehensiveness of his humanity, his gift of right, far-ranging sympathy. It is certain that, had he not been, they had long since passed out of practical life into the Chelsea Hospital of some antiquarian publication. But it is also certain that, had they not been there for him to take and despoil and use, he would not have been — he could not have been—the master-lyrist we know. What he found was of quite extraordinary worth to him; what he added was himself, and his addition made the life of his find perennial. But, much as are the touch of genius and the stamp of art, they are not everything. The best of many nameless singers lives in Burns's songs; but that Burns lives so intense a lyric life is largely due to the fact that he took to himself, and made his own, the lyrical experience, the lyrical longing, the lyrical invention, the lyrical possibilities of many nameless singers. He was the last and the greatest of them all; but he could not have been the greatest by so very much as he seems, had these innominates not been, nor could his songs have been so far-wandered as they are, nor so long-lived as they must be, had these innominates not lived their lyric life before him. In other terms, the atmosphere, the style, the tone, the realistic method and design,[1] with much of the material and the humanity, of Burns's songs are inherited. Again and again his forefathers find him in lyrical ideas, in whose absence there must certainly—there cannot but have been—

---

[1] As I have said (see *ante*, pp. 278-9, Note 1), realism is the distinguishing note of the Vernacular School; and the folk-singers are not less curious in detail than their literary associates and forebears. Even that long sob of pain, *O, Waly, Waly,* has its elements of everyday life and circumstance:—

'My love was clad in the black velvet,
And I myself in cramasie':—

its references to St. Anton's Well and Arthur's Seat and the sheets that 'sall ne'er be pressed by me.' *Cf.*, too, that wonderful little achievement in romance, *The Twa Corbies:*—

'Ye'll sit on his white hause-bane,
And I'll pyke out his bonie blue een,
Wi' ae lock o' his gowden hair
We'll theek our nest when it grows bare.'

Cf., too, in other styles, *Toddlin Hame* and *Ellibanks and Ellibraes* and—well, any folk-song you care to try!

a blank in his work. They are his best models, and he does not always surpass them, as he is sometimes not even their equal.[1] And if his effect along certain lines and in certain specified directions be so intense and enduring as it is, the reason is that they are a hundred strong behind him, and that he has selected from each and all of them that which was lyrical and incorruptible. A peasant like themselves, he knew them as none else could ever know. He sympathised from within with their ambitions, their fancies, their ideals, their derisions, even as he was master, and something more, of their methods. And, while it is fair to say that what is best in them is sublimated and glorified by him, it is also fair to say that, but for them, he could never have approved himself the most exquisite artist in folk-song the world has seen.

It has been complained that, thus much of his claim to be original removed, he must henceforth shine in the lyrical heaven with a certain loss of magnitude and his splendour something dimmed. And this is so far true that the Burns of fact differs, and differs considerably and at many points, from

---

[1] Cf. *O, Waly, Waly* and *The Twa Corbies* and *Helen of Kirkconnel*; with *Toddlin Hame*, which Burns thought 'the first bottle-song in the world,' the old sets of *A Cock-Laird Fu' Cadgie* and *Fee Him, Father*, and, in yet another *genre*, *O, Were My Love*. Even in *The Merry Muses* Burns, who wrote a particular class of song with admirable gust and spirit, does no better work than some of the innominates—the poets of *Erroch Brae* and *Johnie Scott* and *Jenny M'Craw*, for example; while his redaction of *Ellibanks and Ellibraes*—('an old free-spoken song which celebrates this locality would be enough in itself to bring the poet twenty miles out of his way to see it')—is in no wise superior to the original.

the Burns of legend. The one is an effect of certain long-lived, inexorable causes; the other—that 'formidable rival of the Almighty,' who, deriving from nobody, and appearing from nowhere, does in ten years the work of half-a-dozen centuries—is an impossible superstition, as it were a Scottish Mumbo-Jumbo. The one comes, naturally and inevitably, at the time appointed, to an appointed end; but by no conceivable operation in the accomplishing of human destiny could the other have so much as begun to be. And, after all, however poignant the regret, and however wide-eyed and resentful the amazement of those who esteem a man's work on the same terms as they would a spider's, and value it in proportion as it does, or does not, come out of his own belly, enough remains to Burns to keep him easily first in the first flight of singers in the Vernacular, and to secure him, outside the Vernacular, the fame of an unique artist. I have said that, as I believe, his genius was at once imitative and emulous; and, so far as the Vernacular Song is concerned, to turn the pages of our Third Volume is to see that, speaking broadly, his function was not origination but treatment, and that in treatment it is that the finer qualities of his endowment are best expressed and displayed. His measures are high-handed enough; but they are mostly justified.[1] He never boggles at appropriation,[2]

---

[1] Not always. See Vol. iii. (p. 96 and Note) for an attempt to improve upon Ayton (or another), and *ante* (p. 42 and Note) for another to improve upon Carew. Both are failures; but only one is in the Vernacular, and neither owns a Vernacular original.

[2] Besides the folk-singers and the nameless lyrists of the song-books, he is found pilfering from Sedley, Garrick, Lloyd,

so that some of his songs are the oddest conceivable mixture of Burns, Burns's original, and somebody Burns has pillaged. Take, for instance, that arch and fresh and charming thing, *For the Sake of Somebody*. In the first place, 'Somebody' comes to Burns as a Jacobite catchword; and in the next, the lyrical idea is found in a poor enough botch by Allan Ramsay:—

> 'For the sake of Somebody,
> For the sake of Somebody,
> I could wake a winter's night
> For the sake of Somebody.'

This is pretty certainly older than *The Tea-Table Miscellany*, and has nothing whatever to do with the verses which the later minstrel has tagged it withal. But it is a right lyrical idea, and in the long-run a lyrical idea is a song. So thinks Burns; and you have but to compare the two sets to see the difference between master and journeyman at a glance. The old, squalid, huckstering little comedy of courtship:—

> 'First we'll buckle, then we'll tell,
> Let her flyte and syne come to . . .
> I'll slip hame and wash my feet,
> An' steal on linens fair and clean,
> Syne at the trysting place we'll meet,
> To do but what my dame has done':—

Ramsay, Fergusson, Theobald, Carew, Mayne, Dodsley, and Sir Robert Ayton (or another). See also our Notes (Vol. iii.) on *Duncan Davison*, on *Landlady*, *Count the Lawin*, on *Sweetest May*, on *The Winter it is Past*, on *We're A' Noddin*, to name but these; and, as a further illustration of his method, note that, according to Scott Douglas (MS. annotation), the first three lines of *Gat Ye Me* belong to old song No. I., the next five to Burns, and the last eight to old song No. II.

gives place to a thing to-day as comfortable to the ear and as telling to the heart as when Burns vamped it from Ramsay's vamp from somebody unknown. What is further to note is that not all the latest vamp is Burns *plus* Ramsay *plus* Innominate I. *plus* Jacobite catchword: inasmuch as the first line of Stanza II. is conveyed from an owlish lover in *The Tea-Table Miscellany*:—

' Ye powers that preside over virtuous love.'

Thus some solemn poetaster a good half-century at least ere Burns, and for over a hundred years ' Ye powers that smile on virtuous love' has lived as pure Burns, and as pure Burns is now passed into the language. Yet, despite the pilferings and the hints, it were as idle to pretend that *Somebody*, as it stands, is not Burns, as it were foolish to assert that Burns would have written *Somebody* without a certain unknown ancestor. Another flash of illustration comes from *It Was A' For Our Rightfu' King*: with its third stanza lifted clean from *Mally Stewart*, and set in a jewel of Burnsian gold, especially contrived and chased to set it off and make the lyric best of it. A third example is found in *A Red, Red Rose*, which, as we have shown (iii. 143 and Note), is a mosaic of rather beggarly scraps of English verse: just as Jonson's peerless *Drink To Me Only With Thine Eyes* is a mosaic contrived in scraps of conceited Greek prose. It is exquisitely done, of course; but, the beggarly scraps of verse away, could it ever have been done at all? And *Auld Lang Syne*? It passes for pure Burns; but was the phrase itself—the phrase which by his time had rooted itself in the very vitals of the Vernacular—was the phrase itself, I say, not priceless to him? Something or nothing may be due to Ramsay for his telling demonstration of the way in which it should *not* be used as a refrain. But what of that older maker and the line which Burns himself thought worth repeating, and which the world rejoices, and will long rejoice, to repeat with Burns :—

> '*Should auld acquaintance be forgot,*
> *An' never thocht upon?*'

Is there nothing of his cadence, no taste of his sentiment, no smack of his lyrical idea, no memory (to say the least) of his burden :—

> 'On old long syne, my jo,
> On old long syne,
> That thou canst never once reflect
> On old long syne' :—

in the later masterpiece? To say 'No' were surely to betray criticism. And *Ay Waukin, O*—should we, could we ever, have had it, had there been nobody but Burns to start the tune and invent the lyrical idea?

> 'O, wat, wat,
> O, wat and weary!
> Sleep I can get nane
> For thinkin o' my dearie.

> 'A' the night I wake,
> A' the day I weary,
> Sleep I can get nane
> For thinkin o' my dearie.'

Thus, it may be, some broken man, in hiding among the wet hags; some moss-trooper, drenched and

W. H. Bartlett

ST. MICHAEL'S CHURCHYARD, DUMFRIES
(The burial-place of Burns)

"Don't be afraid. I'll be more respected a hundred years after I am dead than I am at present."—R. B., July 1796.

prowling, with a shirtful of sore bones! Whoever he was, and whatever his calling and condition, he had at least one lyrical impulse, he has his part in a masterpiece by Burns, and his part is no small one.

I might multiply examples, and pile Pelion upon Ossa of proof. But to do so were simply to repeat the *Bibliographical* and the *Notes* to our Third Volume; and in this place I shall be better employed in pointing out that these double conceptions (so to speak), these achievements in lyrical collaboration, are for the most part the best known and the best liked of Burns's songs, and are, moreover, those among Burns's songs which show Burns the songsmith at his finest. The truth is that he wrote two lyric styles: (1) the style of the Eighteenth Century Song-Books,[1] which is a bad one, and in which

---

[1] He was trained in it from the first. In early youth he carried an English song-book about with him—wore it in his breeches-pocket, so to speak. This was *The Lark*: 'Containing a Collection of above Four Hundred and Seventy Celebrated English and Scotch Songs, None of which are contain'd in the other Collections of the same size, call'd *The Syren* and *The Nightingale*. With a Curious and Copious Alphabetical Glossary for Explaining the *Scotch* words. London. Printed (1746) for John Osborn at the Golden Ball in Pater Noster Row.' 'Tis a fat little book, and as multifarious a collection of Restoration and—especially—post-Restoration songs as one could wish to have. Antiquated political squibs; ballads, as *Chevy Chace*, with *Gilderoy*, the *Queen's Old Soldier*, and *Katherine Hayes*; a number of indecencies from D'Urfey's *Pills*; Scots folk-songs, like *Toddlin Hame* and *The Ewe Bughts*, and *O, Waly, Waly* and *John Ochiltree* and *The Blithesome Bridal*; current English ditties like *Old Sir Simon* and *Phillida Flouts Me*; a song of a Begging Soldier, whose vaunt, 'With my rags upon my bum,' is echoed in *The Jolly Beggars*; much Allan Ramsay; with scattered examples of Dryden, Dorset, Congreve, Alexander Scott, Brome, Prior, Wycherley, Rochester, Farquhar, Cibber—even Skelton; and a

he could be as vulgar, or as frigid, or as tame, as very much smaller men;[1] and (2) the style of the Vernacular Folk-Song, which he handled with that understanding and that mastery of means and ends which stamp the artist. To consider his experiments in the first is to scrape acquaintance with *Clarinda, Mistress of My Soul*, and *Turn Again, Thou Fair Eliza*, and *On A Bank of Flowers*, and *Sensibility, How Charming*, and *Castle Gordon*, and *A Big-Bellied Bottle*, and *Strathallan's Lament*, and *Raving Winds Around Her Blowing*, and *How Pleasant the Banks*, and *A Rosebud By My Early Walk*,[2] and many a thing besides, which, were it not known for the work of a

---

wilderness of commonplace ditties about love and drink. On the whole, an interesting collection. Particularly if you take it as an element in the education of the lyric Burns.

[1] Cf. *Their Groves of Sweet Myrtle* (Vol. iii. 252-3 and Note), among other things:—

'The slave's spicy forests and gold-bubbling fountains
The brave Caledonian views wi' disdain;
He wanders as free as the winds of his mountains,
Save Love's *willing fetters*—the chains o' his Jean.

Such achievements in what Mr. Meredith calls 'the Bathetic,' are less infrequent in Burns than could be wished.

[2] It is understood that *Scots Wha Hae* is an essay in the Vernacular (I gather, by the way, that it is one of the two or three pieces by 'the Immortal Exciseman nurtured ayont the Tweed' which are most popular in England). But, even so, one has but to contrast it with *Is There for Honest Poverty*, to recognise that in the one the writer's technical and lyrical mastery is complete, while in the other it is merely academic—academic as the lyrical and technical mastery of (say) *Rule Britannia*. Now, *Is There for Honest Poverty* is *calqué* on a certain disreputable folk-song; while *Scots Wha Hae* is for all practical purposes the work of an Eighteenth Century Scotsman writing in English, and now and then propitiating the fiery and watchful Genius of Caledonia by spelling a word as it is spelt in the Vernacular.

great poet, would long since have gone down into the limbo that gapes for would-be art. In the other are all the little masterpieces by which Burns the lyrist is remembered. He had a lead in *The Silver Tassie*[1] and in *Auld Lang Syne*, in *A Man's a Man* and *Duncan Davison*, in *A Waukrife Minnie* and *Duncan Gray* and *Finlay*, in *I Hae a Wife* and *It Was A' For Our Rightfu' King* and *A Red, Red Rose*, in *Macpherson's Lament*, and *Ay Waukin, O*, and *Somebody*, and *Whistle, and I'll Come to You*— in all, or very nearly all, the numbers which make his lyrical bequest as it were a little park apart— an unique retreat of rocks and sylvan corners and heathy spaces, with an abundance of wildings, and here and there a hawthorn brake where, to a sound of running water, the Eternal Shepherd tells his tale—in the spacious and smiling demesne of English literature. And my contention—that it is to Burns the artist in folk-song that we must turn for thorough contentment—is proved to the hilt by those lyrics in the Vernacular for which, so far as we know, he found no hint elsewhere, and in which, so far as we know, he expressed himself and none besides. He had no suggestions, it seems (but I would not like to swear), no catchwords, no lyrical material for *Tam Glen* and *Of A' the Airts*, for *Willie Brewed* and *Bonie Doon*, for *Last May a Braw Wooer* and *O, Wert Thou in the Cauld Blast*,[2]

---

[1] 'The first four lines are old,' he says, 'the rest is mine.' And, in effect, the quatrain is unique in his work.

[2] It is oddly and amusingly illustrative of Burns's trick of mosaic that a line in this charming song .
  'The brightest jewel in my crown ':—
comes bodily from—*The Court of Equity*!

and *Mary Morison*—to name no more. But, if they be directly referable to nobody but himself, they feature his whole ancestry. They are folk-songs writ by a peasant of genius, who was a rare and special artist; and they show that the closer he cleaved to folk-models, and the fuller and stronger his possession by the folk-influence, the more of the immortal Burns is there to-day.

Suggested or not, the songs of Burns were devised and written by a peasant, devising and writing for peasants. The emotions they deal withal are the simplest, the most elemental, in the human list, and are figured in a style so vivid and direct as to be classic in its kind. Romance there is none in them, for there was none in Burns [1]—'tis the sole point, perhaps, at which he was out of touch with the unrenowned generations whose flower and crown he was. But of reality, which could best and soonest

---

[1] None, or so little that if his Jacobitisms seem romantic, it is only by contrast with the realities in which they occur. The interest of even *It Was A' For Our Rightfu' King* is centred in the vamper's sympathy with, not the romantic situation:—

'He turned him richt and round about
Upon the Irish shore,' *etc.* :—

but with that living, breathing, palpitating 'actuality' of sentiment developed in both hero and heroine by the disastrous turn of circumstances :—

'Now a' is done that man can do,
And a' is done in vain ' :—

and the position created by those circumstances at the end :—

'But I hae parted from my love
Never to meet again ' :—

which places this lyric somewhere near the very top of homely and familiar song.

bring them home to the class in which their genius was developed, and to which themselves were addressed :—

' Grain de musc qui gît invisible
Au fond de leur éternité ' :—

there is enough to keep them sweet while the Vernacular is read. They are for all, or nearly all, the peasant's trades and crafts : so that the gangrel tinker shares them with the spinner at her wheel, the soldier with the ploughman, the weaver with the gardener and the tailor and the herd. Morals, experiences, needs, love and liquor, the rejoicing vigour and unrest of youth, the placid content of age—there is scarce anything he can endure which is not brilliantly, and (above all) sincerely and veraciously, set forth in them. That old-world Scotland, whose last and greatest expression was Burns, either has passed or is fast passing away. In language, manners, morals, ideals, religion, substance, capacity, the theory and practice of life—in all these the country of Burns has changed : in some, has changed ' beyond report, thought, or belief.' But that much of her which was known to her Poet is with us still, and is with us in these songs. For man and woman change not, but endure for ever : so that what was truly said a thousand years ago comes home as truth to-day, and will go home as truth when to-day is a thousand years behind. To the making of these things there went the great and generous humanity of Burns, with the humanity, less great but still generous and sincere, of those unknowns, whose namelessness was ever a regret to him.[1] They are art in their kind. And there is no reason why this 'little Valclusa fountain' should lack pilgrims, or run dry, for centuries.[2]

IX

I purpose to deal with the Dumfries period with all possible brevity. The story is a story of decadence; and, even if it were told in detail, would tell us nothing of Burns that we have not already heard or are not all-too well prepared to learn. In a little town, where everybody's known

---

[1] 'Are you not quite vexed to think that these men of genius, for such they certainly were, who composed our fine Scottish lyrics, should be unknown? It has given me many a heartache' (R. B. to Thomson, 19th November 1794). And see his *Journal* for a more heart-felt recognition still.

[2] They lived not long the limited life of Johnson's *Musical Museum* and Thomson's *Scottish Airs*. Thus, in a collection of North of England chap-books (c. 1810-20) which I owe to the kindness of the Earl of Crawford, I find at least two Burns 'Songsters'—(they are the same, but one is called 'The Ayrshire Bard's Songster,' the other something else)—both 'Printed by J. Marshall in the Old Fleshmarket,' Newcastle. In a third—a miscellany, this one—is *Scots Wha Hae*, 'As sung by Mr. Braham at the Newcastle Theatre Royal' (Carlyle thought this famous lyric should be 'sung by the throat of the whirlwind'; but it had better luck than *that*). The great Jew tenor further warbled a couple of stanzas of *The Winter It is Past* at a concert in the same city, when Miss Stephens was responsible for *Charlie He's My Darling*. In other chaps Burns is found rubbing shoulders with Moore and Campbell and Tom Dibdin, and a hundred others, among them Allan Ramsay. In these *Of A' the Airts* is sandwiched between *The Twopenny Postman* and the *Wedding at Ballyporeen*, while *Somebody* is kept in countenance by *Paddy Carey* and *The Wounded Hussar*. The most popular, perhaps, are *Of A' the Airts*, and *Scots Wha Hae*, and *Willie Brew'd*; but *On a Bank of Flowers* lacks not admirers.

to everybody, there is ever an infinite deal of scandal; and Burns was too reckless and too conspicuous not to become a peculiar cock-shy for the scandalmongers of Dumfries. In a little town, especially if it be a kind of provincial centre, there must of necessity be many people with not much to do besides talking and drinking; and Burns was ever too careless of consequences, as well as ever too resolute to make the most of the fleeting hour—it may be, too, was by this time too princely and too habitual a boon-companion—to refrain from drink and talk when drink and talk were to be had. In the sequel, also, it would seem that that old jealousy of his betters (to use the ancient phrase) had come to be a more disturbing influence than it had ever been before. He knew, none better, that, however brilliantly the poet had succeeded, the man was so far a failure as an investment, that, with bad health and a growing family, he had nothing to look forward to but promotion in the Excise; and his discontent with the practical outcome of his ambition and the working result of his fame was certainly not soothed, and may very well have been exacerbated, by his rather noisy sympathy with the leading principles of the French Revolution. He was too fearless and too proud to dissemble that sympathy, which was presently (1794) to find expression in one of his most vigorous and telling lyrics; he was, perhaps, too powerful a talker not to exaggerate its quality and volume; and, though it was common, in the beginning at least, to many Scotsmen, its expression got him, as was inevitable, into trouble with his superiors, and in the long-run was pretty certainly intensified, to the point at which resentment is translated into terms of indiscretion and imprudence, by the reflection, whether just or not,[1] that it had damaged his chances of promotion. That he fought against temptation is as plain as that he proved incapable of triumph, and that, as Carlyle has wisely and humanely noted, the best for him, certain necessary conditions being impossible, was to die. Syme,[2] who knew and loved him, said that he was 'burnt to a cinder' ere Death took him; we can see for ourselves that the Burns of the Kilmarnock Volume and the good things in the *Museum* had

---

[1] It seems to have been unjust. Pitt, though he loved the poetry of Burns, did nothing for him—was probably, indeed, too busy to think of doing anything once the page was read and the bottle done; and Fox, to whom Burns looked for advancement, was ever out of office, and could do nothing, even had he been minded to do something, which we are not told that he was. But the Bard had a sure stay in Graham of Fintry; and, though Glencairn was dead, and he was sometimes reprimanded (*et pour cause*), there is no reason to believe that he would have missed preferment had he lived to be open to it.

[2] It has been said, I believe, that Syme's evidence is worthless, inasmuch as it tends to discredit Burns. But one eye-witness, however dull and prejudiced (and Syme was neither one nor other), is worth a wilderness of sentimental historians; and Syme's phrase, howbeit it is so picturesque that it conveys what is, perhaps, too violent an impression, probably means no more than that Burns had damaged himself with drink. That much Burns admitted time and again; and Currie—who cannot but have got his information from Maxwell—remarks that for over a year before the end 'there was an evident decline of our Poet's personal appearance, and, though his appetite continued unimpaired, he was himself sensible that his constitution was sinking.' It was all, the doctor thought, the effect of alcohol on a difficult digestion and a sensitive nervous system; and, though he was something of a fanatic in this matter, I see no reason, as he was also an honest man, to question his diagnosis.

ceased to be some time before the end; there is evidence that some time before the end he was neither a sober companion nor a self-respecting husband. And the reflection is not to be put by, that he left the world at the right moment for himself and for his fame.

There is small doubt that the report of his misconduct was at best unkindly framed; there is none that certain among his apologists have gone a very great deal too far in the opposite direction. We may credit Findlater, for instance, but it is impossible, having any knowledge of the man, to believe in the kind of Exciseman-Saint of Gray: impeccable in all the relations of life and never the worse for liquor: even as it is impossible to believe in the *bourgeois* Burns of the latest apotheosis. As Lockhart says, the truth lies somewhere between the two extremes; and one is glad to agree with Lockhart. Even so, however, tradition, as reported by friends and enemies alike, runs stronger in his disfavour than it does the other way.[1] And, though we know that party feeling ran high in Dumfries, and that Burns—with his stiff neck, and his notable distinction, and his absolute gift of speech—did certainly damn

---

[1] 'We are raising a subscription (horrid word)'—(thus Sir Walter, to Morritt, 15th January 1814)—'for a monument to Burns, an honour long delayed, perhaps till some parts of his character were forgotten by those among whom he lived.' This was written within twenty years of Burns's death: when the grievance of the Revolution was lost in the shadow cast by the tremendous presence of Napoleon. And, if it be urged that Burns's offending against Toryism must have been rank indeed to be recalled thus bitterly and thus late, it may be retorted that by no possibility can it have been an hundredth part so indecent as

himself in the eyes of many by what, in the circumstances, must have seemed a suicidal intemperance of feeling and expression, we know also that, once extremely popular, he was presently cut by Dumfries society; that after a time his reputation was an indifferent one on other counts than politics; and that more than once—as in the case of Mrs. Riddell, and again, when he had to apologise for a toast no reasonable or well-bred man would have proposed in the presence of a King's officer, unless he were prepared to face the consequences—he behaved himself ill, according to the standard of good manners then and now. The explanation in these and other cases is that he was drunk; and, as matter of fact, drink and disappointment were pretty certainly responsible between them for the mingled squalor and gloom and pathos of the end. There is nothing like liquor to make a strong man vain of his strength and jealous of his prerogative—even while it is stealing both away; and there is nothing like disappointment to confirm such a man in a friendship for liquor. Last of all, there needs but little knowledge of character and life to see that to apologise for Burns is vain: that we must accept him frankly and without reserve for a peasant of genius perverted from his peasanthood, thrust into a place for which his peasanthood and his genius

---

the conduct of the Parliamentary Whigs during the life and long after the death of Pitt. Of all men living Burns was entitled to an opinion; of all men living he had the best gift of expression. Well, he had his opinion, and he used his gift; and Dumfries could not forgive him. It is again a question of circumstances. Fox and the rest were honoured Members of His Majesty's Opposition. Burns was only an exciseman.

alike unfitted him, denied a perfect opportunity, constrained to live his qualities into defects, and in the long-run beaten by a sterile and unnatural environment. We cannot make him other than he was, and, especially, we cannot make him a man of our own time: a man born tame and civil and unexcessive—'he that died o' Wednesday,' and had obituary notices in local prints. His elements are all-too gross, are all-too vigorous and turbulent for that. 'God have mercy on me,' he once wrote of himself, 'a poor damned, incautious, duped, unfortunate fool! the sport, the miserable victim of rebellious pride, hypochondriac imaginations, agonising sensibility and bedlam passions.' Plainly he knew himself as his apologists have never known him, nor will ever know.

That his intellectual and temperamental endowment was magnificent we know by the way in which he affected his contemporaries, and through the terms in which some of them—Robertson, Heron, Dugald Stewart, and, especially, Maria Riddell—recorded their impression of him; yet we know also that, for all its magnificence, or, as I prefer to think, by reason of its magnificence, it could not save him from defeat and shame. Where was the lesion? What was the secret of his fall? Lord Rosebery, as I believe, has hit the white in saying that he was 'great in his strength and great in his weaknesses.'[1] His master-qualities, this critic

---

[1] I note with pleasure that Lord Rosebery knows too much of life, and is too good a judge of evidence, to think of putting a new complexion on the facts of these last, unhappy years. But has he been explanatory enough? What, after all, but failure is possible for strength misplaced and misapplied?

very justly notes, were 'inspiration and sympathy.' But if I would add 'and character'—which, to be sure, is largely an effect of conditions—how must the commentary run? There is pride—the pride of Lucifer: what did it spare him in the end? There is well-nigh the finest brain conceivable; yet is there a certain curious intolerance of facts which obliges the owner of that brain, being a Government officer and seeing his sole future in promotion, to flaunt a friendship with roaring Jacobins like Maxwell and Syme, and get himself nicknamed a 'Son of Sedition,' and have it reported of him, rightly or not, that he has publicly avowed disloyalty at the local theatre.[1] There is a passionate regard for women; with, as Sir Walter noted, a lack of chivalry which is attested by those lampoons on living Mrs. Riddell and on dead Mrs. Oswald. There is the strongest sense of fatherhood, with the tenderest concern for 'weans and wife'; and there is that resolve for pleasure which not even these uplifting influences can check. There is a noble generosity of heart and temper; but there is so imperfect a sense of conduct, so practical and so habitual a faith in a certain theory:—

---

[1] I do not for an instant forget that here is more circumstance: that he was a true Briton at heart, and that in the beginning his Jacobinism was chiefly, if not solely, an effect of sympathy with a tortured people. But there are ways and ways of favouring an unpopular cause; and Burns's were alike defiant and unwise. Thus Maxwell was practically what most people then called a 'murderer'—of the French King; yet it was while, or soon after, the enormities of the Terror were at their worst, that he became a chief associate of Burns. To some this seems a 'noble imprudence.' Was it not rather pure incontinence of self?

> 'The heart ay 's the part ay
> That maks us richt or wrang' :—

that in the end you have a broken reputation, and death at seven or eight and thirty, is the effect of a variety of discrediting causes. Taking the precisian's point of view, one might describe so extraordinary a blend of differences as a bad, well-meaning man, and one might easily enough defend the description. But the precisian has naught to do at this grave-side; and to most of us now it is history that, while there was an infinite deal of the best sort of good in Burns, the bad in him, being largely compacted of such purely unessential defects as arrogance, petulance, imprudence, and a turn for self-indulgence, this last exasperated by the conditions in which his lot was cast, was not of the worst kind after all. Yet the bad was bad enough to wreck the good. The little foxes were many and active and greedy enough to spoil a world of grapes. The strength was great, but the weaknesses were greater; for time and chance and necessity were ever developing the weaknesses at the same time that they were ever beating down the strength. That is the sole conclusion possible. And to the plea, that the story it rounds is very pitiful, there is this victorious answer:—that the Man had drunk his life to the lees, while the Poet had fulfilled himself to the accomplishing of a peculiar immortality; so that to Burns Death came as a deliverer and a friend

W. E. H.

INDEX TO ESSAY

A Bard's Epitaph, 259.
A Big-Bellied Bottle (*No Churchman Am I*), 330.
A Cock-Laird Fu' Cadgie, 324.
Addison, 237.
Address to a Haggis, 276, 303.
Address to the Unco Guid, 257, 273.
Address to the Deil, 257, 274.
Ae Fond Kiss, and Then We Sever, 304, 306.
Aiken, Robert, 257, 293, 300.
Ainslie, Robert, 303, 308, 309, 310.
Alloway Cottage, 235.
A Poet's Welcome to His Love-begotten Daughter, 251, 259, 260, 274.
A Red Red Rose, 327, 331.
Armour, Jean, 280-292.
—— Reconciliation with, 303, 307.
Arnot, John, 289.
A Rosebud By My Early Walk, 330.
Auld, Rev. William, 281.
Auld Lang Syne, 327, 331.
Authors read by Burns, 240, 241, 263.
A Waukrife Minnie, 331.
Ayr, 242.
Ayton, Sir Robert, 325, 326.
Ay Waukin, O, 328, 331.

BACHELORS' CLUB, 246, 257.
Ballantyne, John, 294, 302.
Ballochmyle, Lass of, 248.
Barbour, 265.
Beattie, 263, 284.
Begbie, Ellison, 249.
Begg, Mrs., 260.
Birth, 233, 235.
Blacklock, Dr. Thomas, 294.
Blair, Dr. Hugh, 296.
Blake, 273.
Bonnie Heck, 266.
Border Tour, 303.
Braxfield, M'Queen of, 299.
Brice, David, 284.
Brown, Agnes (Mrs. William Burness), 235.
—— Richard, 249, 250, 310, 311.
Browning, 273.
Bruce, Arthur, 300.
Buchan, Earl of, 296.
Burness (or Burnes), William, 235-246, 253.
Burnet, Miss Elizabeth, 296.
Burns, Elizabeth, 316.
—— Gilbert, 237, 238, 240, 241, 247, 248, 254, 256, 288, 294.
BURNS, ROBERT—
  Birth, 233, 235.
  Character and Influence, 234.
  Parentage, 235.

344 INDEX TO ESSAY

BURNS, ROBERT—*continued :*—
Education and Favourite Authors, 236-242.
Mount Oliphant, 239-245.
Effects of Early Hardship, 243, 244.
Lochlie, 245-254.
Early Love Affairs, 247, 248, 249.
Attitude towards Women, 247.
Irvine, 249-253.
Love - begotten Daughter, 251, 259.
Death of his father, 253.
Mossgiel, 254-312.
As a Farmer, 256.
Anti-clerical Poems, 257.
Jacobitism, 258.
Temperament, 258.
Elizabeth Paton, 259.
Characteristics of his Poetry, 261-279.
Robert Fergusson and Vernacular Poets, Influence of, 262.
Vernacular and English Verse contrasted, 262-269.
Wordsworth and Byron, Influence on, 264.
Relation to his Predecessors, 269-279.
Masterpieces, 273.
Humour, 275.
Realism, 278.
Jean Armour and Mary Campbell, 279-292.
Kilmarnock Edition, 292.
Mrs. Dunlop's Influence, 292.
Edinburgh, 294-303.
Conversational Powers and Dissipation, 299, 300.

BURNS, ROBERT—*continued :*—
First Edinburgh Edition, 301.
Border Tour, 303.
Highland Tours, 303.
Johnson's *Musical Museum*, 303.
Reconciliation with Jean Armour, 303.
Mrs. M'Lehose (Clarinda), 304-312.
Relations with Jean Armour, 307-310.
Marriage, 311, 312.
Ellisland, 312-315.
Excise Appointment, 313, 319.
Sale at Ellisland and removal to Dumfries, 315.
Anne Park, 315, 316.
Chloris, 317.
Too great for his Circumstances, 320.
As a Song-writer, 321-334
Dumfries, 334-342.
Decadence and Failing Health, 335.
Intellectual and Temperamental Endowment, 339.
Jacobinism, 340.
Death, 341.
Byron, 234, 264, 271, 273, 275, 297.

CALEDONIAN HUNT, 301.
Campbell, Mary, 283, 285-292.
Carew, 325, 326.
Castle Gordon, 330.
Chambers, Robert, 285, 288, 301, 316.
Charlie He's my Darling, 334.
Chloris, 317.
Clarinda, 304-312, 320.

INDEX TO ESSAY 345

Clarinda, Mistress of My Soul, 330.
Cleghorn, Robert, 239.
Conversational Powers, 300.
Cork, Lord, 299.
Corn Rigs, 268, 273.
Cowper, 272.
Creech, William, 296, 301.
Crochallan Fencibles, 296, 299, 308.
Currie, Dr., 288, 316, 336.

DALRYMPLE, JAMES, of Orangefield, 295, 296.
Dalrymple Parish School, 241.
Death and Dr. Hornbook, 274.
Death, 318, 341.
Despondency, 283.
Dodsley, 326.
Douglas, Gawain, 265, 278.
Drink to Me Only With Thine Eyes, 327.
Dumfries, 315, 334-342.
Dunbar, William, 265, 278.
Duncan Davison, 326, 331.
Duncan Gray, 331.
Dunlop, Mrs., 288, 292, 301, 302, 314, 315.

EDINBURGH, BURNS IN, 294-303.
Edinburgh Edition, First, 301.
Education and Favourite Authors, 236-242.
Eglintoun, Earl of, 302.
Elegy on Captain Matthew Henderson, 314.
Ellibanks and Ellibraes, 323, 324.
Ellisland, 311, 312-315.
Epistle to a Young Friend, 258, 290.
—— *to Davie,* 261, 341.
—— *to Lapraik,* 274.

Epistle to James Smith, 274.
—— *to John Rankine,* 252, 258, 260, 274.
Epitaph on Robert Fergusson, 262.
Errock Brae, 265, 324.
Erskine, Harry, Dean of Faculty, 296.
Excise Appointment, 313.
—— —— Prospects of Promotion, 335.

Fee Him, Father, 324.
Fergusson, Provost of Ayr, 235, 245.
—— Robert, 261, 264, 271, 278, 326.
Findlater, Alexander, 337.
Finlay (Wha is That at My Bower Door?), 331.
Flax-dressing at Irvine, 249.
Fleming, Nanie, 288.
For the Sake of Somebody, 326, 331.
Fox, Charles James, 336, 338.
Freemasonry, 246.
French Revolution, Sympathy with, 335, 340.

GARRICK, 325.
Gat Ye Me, 326.
Glencairn, Lord, 296, 302, 313, 336.
Glenriddell, Riddell of, 313.
Goldsmith, 263.
Gordon, Duchess of, 296, 297.
Graham of Fintry, 299, 313, 336.
Gray, 262, 263, 272, 284.
Gray, Farquhar, 337.
Green Grow the Rashes, 268, 273.
Gregory, Dr., 296.
Grose, Captain, 314.

Halloween, 264, 273, 276, 277, 279.
Hamilton, Gavin, 257, 258, 285, 292, 296, 298, 300, 312.
Hamilton of Gilbertfield, 262, 266, 271.
Helen of Kirkconnel, 324.
Henryson, Robert, 265, 278.
Heron, Robert, Author of *Life of Burns*, 293, 299, 300, 301, 302, 312, 316, 339.
Herrick, 275.
Highland Tours, 303.
Holy Willie's Prayer, 257, 264, 273, 274, 276.
How Pleasant the Banks of the Clear Winding Devon, 330.
Hume, David, 234.
Hutcheson, Francis, 233, 234.

I Hae a Wife, 331.
Irvine, 249.
Is There For Honest Poverty, 330, 331.
It Was A' For Our Rightfu' King, 327, 331, 332.

JACOBINISM, 335, 340.
Jacobitism, 258, 332.
Jenny M'Craw, 265, 324.
Johnie Scott, 324.
Johnson's *Musical Muscum*, 303, 314, 321, 334.

KEATS, 271, 272, 273, 275.
Kilmarnock Edition, 281, 292.
Kirk of Scotland, 233, 234, 236, 257, 260, 281.
Kirkoswald, 244, 247.
Knox, John, 236, 278.

LAMENTS ON LUCKIE SPENCE AND OTHERS, 267.
Landlady, Count the Lawin, 326.

Last May a Braw Wooer, 331.
Lawrie, Rev. Dr., 295.
Lewars, Jessie, 318.
Lindsay, David, 265, 278.
Lloyd, 325.
Lochlie, 245-254.
Lockhart, 276, 299, 337.
Lorimer, Jean, 317.

M'DIARMID, 315.
Mackenzie, Henry, 275, 296, 301.
M'Lehose, Mrs. (Clarinda), 304-312, 320.
M'Lure (William Burness's landlord), 253.
M'Pherson's Lament, 331.
Mally Stewart, 327.
Marlowe, 272.
Marriage, 312.
Mary Morison, 273, 332.
Mauchline, 257, 303, 307.
Maxwell, Dr. William, 336, 340.
Mayne, 326.
Merry Muses of Caledonia, 296, 298, 324.
Miller, Betty, 290.
———, Patrick, of Dalswinton, 312.
Milton, 268, 272, 275.
Mirabeau, 320.
Montgomerie, 272, 278.
Moore, Letters to, 237, 240, 246, 250, 251.
Morris, Captain, 299.
Mossgiel, 254-312.
Mount Oliphant, 239-245.
Muir, Robert, 282, 292, 302.
Murdoch, John, Schoolmaster, 237-242.
My Auntie Jean Held to the Shore, 316.

INDEX TO ESSAY

Nature's Law, 292.
Nicol, William, 303.
No Churchman Am I (A Bigbellied Bottle), 256.

Of A' the Airts, 315, 331, 334.
Oliphant, Mount, 239-245.
O May, Thy Morn Was Ne'er Sae Sweet, 306.
On a Bank of Flowers, 330, 334.
On Captain Grose, 314.
On William Creech, 303.
Orr, Thomas, 289.
Oswald, Mrs., 340.
O Waly, Waly, 323, 324.
O Were my Love, 324.
O Wert Thou in the Cauld Blast, 331.

PARENTAGE, 235.
Park, Anne, 315.
Paton, Elizabeth, 249, 257, 259, 260, 280, 289, 291.
Peacock, Flax-dresser, Irvine, 249, 250.
Peasant, Scots, Character of, 252.
Peasant's, Scots, Condition of Life, 236.
Pinkerton, 265.
Pitscottie, Lindsay of, 278.
Pitt, William, 336, 338.
Poor Mailie's Elegy, 266, 271.
Poosie Nansie, 277.
Pope, 263, 266.

RAMSAY, ALLAN, 262, 265, 266, 267, 271, 278, 326, 328.
Ramsay of Auchtertyre, 258, 299.
Raving Winds Around Her Blowing, 330.
Reply to a Trimming Epistle, 252, 258, 260, 274.

Richmond, John, 257, 282, 285, 288, 291, 292, 295, 296.
Riddell, Maria, 297, 317, 320, 338, 339, 340.
Robertson the Historian, 339.
Rosebery, Earl of, 339.

ST. ANDREW'S LODGE, Edinburgh, 296.
Scotch Drink, 271, 274.
Scots Wha Hae, 263, 330, 334.
Scott, Alexander, 265, 278.
—— Sir Walter, 297, 306, 337, 340.
Scott Douglas, 315, 316.
Sedley, 325.
Sempills, The, 262, 265, 271, 278.
Sensibility How Charming, 330.
Shakespeare, 238, 268, 272, 275.
Shelley, 271, 273.
Shenstone, 263, 266, 284.
Sillar, David, 248.
Sloan, John, 315.
Smith, Adam, 234.
—— James, 281, 282.
Songs of Burns, 321-334.
Stevenson, R. L., 251, 262, 267, 285, 289, 291.
Stewart, Dugald, 262, 295, 296, 339.
Strathallan's Lament, 330.
Sweetest May, 326.
Sylvander, 305.
Syme, John, 336, 340.

TAIT, SAUNDERS, 248, 249, 254, 307.
Tam Glen, 331.
Tam o' Shanter, 263, 265, 269, 274, 277, 314, 321.
Tam Samson's Elegy, 271, 274.
Tarbolton Mill, 307.

The Author's Earnest Cry and Prayer, 274.
The Brigs of Ayr, 271.
The Bumper Toast, 299.
The Cotter's Saturday Night, 257, 263, 271, 274, 276, 300.
The Court of Equity, 257, 290, 300, 331.
The Death and Dying Words of Poor Mailie, 261, 266, 271, 274.
The Farmer to His Auld Mare, 264, 273.
The Five Carlins, 314.
The Fornicator, 252, 257, 260, 300.
The Gloomy Night is Gathering Fast, 294.
The Holy Fair, 257, 271, 273, 274, 276, 277, 307.
The Holy Tulyie, 274.
Their Groves of Sweet Myrtle, 330.
'The Isle,' 312.
The Jolly Beggars, 257, 273, 276, 277, 315, 316.
The Kirk's Alarm, 257, 313.
The Lament, 283.
The Lark, 329.
The Lass of Ballochmyle, 248.
Theobald, 326.
The Ordination, 257, 274.
The School for Love, 239.
The Silver Tassie, 331.
The Twa Corbies, 323, 324.
The Twa Dogs, 245, 273.
The Twa Herds, 257, 274.

The Vision, 263, 274.
The Whistle, 314.
The Winter It Is Past, 326, 334.
Thomson, George, 317, 321, 334.
—— James, 272, 284.
—— Peggy, 247, 289.
Thomson's *Scottish Airs*, 321.
Thou Ling'ring Star, 288, 314.
To a Louse, 273.
To a Mountain Daisy, 263, 271, 274, 300.
To a Mouse, 271, 273.
Toddlin Hame, 323, 324.
To John Goldie, 257.
To the Guidwife of Wauchope House, 303.
Turn Again, Thou Fair Eliza, 330.

VERNACULAR SCHOOL OF POETRY, 234, 261, 263-279, 321-334.

WALKER, JOSIAH, 299.
We're A' Noddin, 326.
West Indies, 281, 285, 287, 294.
Whistle and I'll Come To You, 331.
Williams, Helen Maria, 313.
Willie Brew'd a Peck o' Maut 304, 314, 331, 334.
Winter, 271.
Wordsworth, 264, 273.

Yestreen I Had a Pint o' Wine, 315.
Ye Banks and Braes o' Bonie Doon, 331.

SONGS OF BURNS

SET TO MUSIC.

(*From "Scots Minstrelsie," edited by* JOHN GREIC, Mus. Doc.)

INDEX.

	PAGE		PAGE
A Highland lad my love was born	38	My ain kind dearie, O!	46
A man's a man for a' that	24	My bonnie Mary	63
Ae fond kiss	33	My heart is a-breaking	42
Afton Water	83	My heart is sair, I daurna tell	26
Auld Rob Morris	28	My heart's in the Highlands	78
Behind yon hills where Lugar flows	58	My love she's but a lassie yet	12
Bonnie lassie, will ye go	5	My Nannie's awa'	66
Bonnie wee thing	68	My Nannie, O!	58
Braw, braw lads	20	Now in her green mantle	66
Ca' the yowes to the knowes	10	Of a' the airts	2
Comin' thro' the rye	22	O Mary, at thy window be	50
Corn rigs	80	O my love is like a red red rose	30
Duncan Gray	36	O! wert thou in the cauld blast	44
Doun the burn, Davie lad	94	O whistle, and I'll come to you	86
First when Maggie was my care	18	Scots wha hae	8
Flow gently, sweet Afton	83	Tam Glen	42
For the sake o' somebody	26	The Birks o' Aberfeldie	5
Gae bring to me a pint o' wine	63	The Deil's awa' wi' th' exciseman	52
Gin a body meet a body	22	There's auld Rob Morris	28
Green grow the rashes, O!	48	There's nought but care on every han'	48
Here's a health to ane I lo'e dear	76	There was a lad was born in Kyle	40
Highland Mary	55	When o'er the hill the eastern star	46
I'm ower young to marry yet	60	When trees did bud and fields were green	94
Is there for honest poverty	24	Whistle o'er the lave o't	18
It was upon a Lammas night	81	Willie brewed a peck o' maut	91
Jessie	76	Ye banks and braes	14
John Anderson, my jo	16	Ye banks and braes and streams around	55
Lassie wi' the lint-white locks	73		
Last May a braw wooer	70		
Mary Morison	50		

Of a' the Airts.

1st Sixteen lines by BURNS. See Note.
Air, "Miss Admiral Gordon's Strathspey."

Andante Affettuoso.

Key G.

Of a' the airts the wind can blaw, I dear-ly lo'e the west; For there the bon-nie las-sie lives, The lass that I lo'e best; Tho wild woods grow, and riv-ers row, Wi'

O blaw, ye west-lin winds, blaw saft A-mang the leaf-y trees; Wi' gen-tle gale frae hill and dale, Bring hame the lad-en bees; And bring the las-sie back to me That's

3

mon-y a hill be-tween; Baith day and night, my fan-cy's flight Is
aye sae neat and clean; Ae blink o' her wad ban-ish care, Sae

ev-er wi' my Jean. I see her in the dew-y flow'r, Sae
love-ly is my Jean! What sigh and vows a-mang the knowes Hae

love-ly, sweet and fair;— I hear her voice in ilk-a bird, Wi'
pass'd a-tween us twa!— How fain to meet, how wae to part, That

4

The Birks o' Aberfeldie.

Words written by BURNS in 1787.   Air from Playford's "Dancing Master," 1657.

Allegretto e con anima.

Bon-nie las-sie, will ye go,— Will ye go,— will ye go,—

Bon-nie las-sie will ye go To the birks o' Ab-er-fel-die?

Now simmer blinks on flow-'ry braes, And o'er the crystal streamlet plays: Come let us spend the lightsome days In the birks o' Aberfeldie. Bonnie lassie will ye go, Will ye go, will ye go,

The remaining verses begin at the sign.

2

While o'er their heads the hazels hing,
The little birdies blythely sing,
Or lightly flit on wanton wing,
   In the birks o' Aberfeldie.
            Bonnie lassie, &c.

3

The braes ascend like lofty wa's,
The foamin' stream deep roarin' fa's,
O'erhung wi' fragrant spreadin' shaws,
   The birks o' Aberfeldie.
            Bonnie lassie, &c.

4

The hoary cliffs are crown'd wi' flowers,
White o'er the linns the burnie pours,
And, rising, weets wi' misty showers
   The birks o' Aberfeldie.
            Bonnie lassie, &c.

5

Let fortune's gifts at random flee,
They ne'er shall draw a wish frae me,
Supremely blest wi' love and thee,
   In the birks o' Aberfeldie.
            Bonnie lassie, &c.

For the sake of variety, the accompaniment to the refrain, as given at the outset, may be substituted at the end of verses 2 and 4.

Scots wha ha'e.

Words by BURNS. Air, "Hey, tuttie tattie."

Maestoso.

Key B♭.

Scots, wha hae wi' Wal-lace bled! Scots, wham Bruce has aften led!—

Wel-come to your gor-y bed, Or to vic-to-rie!

2

Wha wad be a traitor knave?
Wha wad fill a coward's grave?
Wha sae base as be a slave?
　　Let him turn and flee!
Wha, for Scotland's king and law,
Freedom's sword will strongly draw,
Freeman stand, or freeman fa',
　　Let him on wi' me!

3

By oppression's woes and pains,
By our sons in servile chains,
We will drain our dearest veins,
　　But they shall be free.
Lay the proud usurpers low!
Tyrants fall in ev'ry foe!
Liberty's in ev'ry blow!
　　Let us do or dee!

Ca' the Yowes to the Knowes.

Words by BURNS. Air preserved by BURNS.

2
We'll gae down by Cluden side,
Through the hazels spreadin' wide,
O'er the waves that sweetly glide
    To the moon sae clearly.
        Ca' the yowes, &c.

3
Yonder Cluden's silent towers,
Where, at moonshine midnight hours,
O'er the dewy bendin' flowers
    Fairies dance sae cheerie,
        Ca' the yowes, &c.

4
Ghaist nor bogle shalt thou fear,
Thou'rt to love and heaven sae dear;
Nocht o' ill may come thee near,
    My bonnie dearie.
        Ca' the yowes, &c.

5
Fair and lovely as thou art,
Thou hast stown my very heart;
I can die, but canna part,
    My bonnie dearie.
        Ca' the yowes, &c.

My Love she's but a Lassie yet.

Words by BURNS.
Air. "Put up your dagger, Jamie."

Allegretto scherzando.

KeyB♭.

My— love she's but a las - sie yet, My love she's but a las - sie yet; We'll
Come draw a drap o' the best o't yet, Come draw a drap o' the best o't yet; Gae

let her stand a year or twa, She'll no— be half sae sauc-y yet. I—
seek for pleas-ure where ye will, But here I nev - er miss'd it yet. We're

rue the day I sought her O, I rue the day I sought her O; Wha
a' dry wi' the drink-in' o't, We're a' dry wi' the drinkin' o't; The

gets her need-na say he's woo'd, But he may, say he's bought her O!
minis-ter kiss'd the fid-dler's wife, An' could-na preach for think-in' o't!

Last Verse.
think-in' o't.

Ye Banks and Braes.
Solo or Duet.

Words by BURNS.
Air, "The Caledonian Hunt's Delight".

Andante cantabile.

Soprano.
Ye banks and braes o' bon-nie Doon, How can ye bloom sae fresh and fair? How can ye chant, ye lit-tle birds, and I sae wea-ry, fu' o' care? Ye'll

Tenor 8ves lower.
Ye banks and braes o' bon-nie Doon, How can ye bloom sae fresh and fair? How can ye chant, ye lit-tle birds, And I sae wea-ry, fu' o' care? Ye'll

15

Oft hae I rov'd by bonnie Doon,
  To see the rose and woodbine twine;
And ilka bird sang o' its love,
  And fondly sae did I o' mine.
Wi' lightsome heart I pu'd a rose,
  Fu' sweet upon its thorny tree;
And my fause lover stole my rose,
  But ah! he left the thorn wi' me.

John Anderson, My Jo.

Words written by BURNS in 1789.   Air founded upon a Melody in Skene M.S., circa 1630.

Andante.

Voice

Piano. *mp* *p* *rall.*

p *mp*

Key B♭ :l₁ |m₁ :l₁ |l₁ :t₁ |d :—|d :r.d |t₁ :—.l₁ |s₁ :fe₁ |s₁ :—|—:l₁
Lah is G John An-der-son, my jo, John, When we were first ac-quent, Your

p a tempo *mp*

poco cres. *mf*

|m₁ :l₁ |l₁ :t₁ |d :—|d :r |m :—.r |d :r |m :—|—:s
locks were like the rav - en, Your bon-nie brow was brent; But

poco cres. *mf*

2

John Anderson, my jo, John,
  We clamb the hill thegither,
And mony a canty day, John,
  We've had wi' ane anither;
Now we maun totter down, John,
  But hand in hand we'll go,
And we'll sleep thegither at the foot,
  John Anderson, my jo.

WHISTLE O'ER THE LAVE O'T.

Words by BURNS.

Air ascribed to John Bruce of Dumfries, 1720.
Most probably much older.

Moderato giocoso.

Key F.

First when Mag-gie was my care, Heav'n I thought was in her air; Now we're mar-ried, speir nae mair, But whis-tle o'er the lave o't. Meg was meek and Meg was mild,

Sweet and harm-less as a child; Wis - er men than me's be - guil'd, Sae

whistle o'er the lave o't.

2
How we live, my Meg and me.
How we love and how we gree,
I carena by how few may see;
   Sae, whistle o'er the lave o't.
Wha I wish were maggots' meat,
Dish'd up in her windin' sheet,
I could write—but Meg maun see't;
   Sae, whistle o'er the lave o't.

BRAW, BRAW LADS.

Words by BURNS.

Air, "Gala Water," originally known as "Comin thro' the Broom"

Adagio con moto.

Key D.

Braw, braw lads on Yar-row braes, Ye wan-der thro' the bloom-ing heath-er; But Yar-row braes, nor Et-trick shaws Can match the lads o'

2

But there is ane, a secret ane,
  Aboon them a' I lo'e him better
And I'll be his, and he'll be mine.
  The bonnie lad o' Gala Water.

3

Altho' his daddie was nae laird,
  And tho' I ha'e na meikle tocher:
Yet, rich in kindest, truest love,
  We'll tent our flocks by Gala Water.

4

It ne'er was wealth, it ne'er was wealth,
  That coft contentment, peace or pleasure;
The bands and bliss o' mutual love.
  O that's the chiefest warld's treasure!

COMIN' THRO' THE RYE.

Words as published by John Walter.
Opening lines by BURNS.

Air, "The Miller's Daughter."

Moderato.

Key G. | s₁ .,s₁ :s₁ ,m.—|r .,d :r ,m.—| s₁ .,s₁.—:l₁ .,s₁ |d :—.
Gin a bod-y meet a bod-y Com-in' thro' the rye,

| s₁ .,s₁ :s ,m |r .,d :r ,m.—| s₁ .,s₁ :l₁ .,s₁ |d :—
Gin a bod-y! kiss a bod-y, Need a bod-y cry?

| s ,m:d ,m.—|r .,d :r ,m.—| s ,m:d ,m ,s |l :—.l
Ilk-a las-sie has her lad-die, Nane, they say, hae I; Yet

23

a' the lads they smile at me, When com - in' thro' the rye.

2
Gin a body meet a body
  Comin' frae the well;
Gin a body kiss a body,
  Need a body tell?
Ilka lassie has her laddie,
  Ne'er a ane ha'e I;
But a' the lads they smile on me
  When comin' through the rye.

3
Gin a body meet a body
  Comin' frae the town;
Gin a body greet a body,
  Need a body frown?
Ilka lassie has her laddie,
  Nane, they say, ha'e I;
But a' the lads they lo'e me weel,
  An' what the waur am I?

The following is often sung as a last verse:—

4
Among the train there is a swain
  I dearly lo'e mysel';
But whaur his hame, or what his name,
  I dinna care to tell.
Ilka lassie has her laddie,
  Nane, they say, ha'e I;
But a' the lads they lo'e me weel
  An' what the waur am I?

A Man's a Man for a' That.

Words by BURNS.   Old Melody.

Key A.

Is there for hon-est po-ver-ty, That hangs his head and a' that? The cow-ard slave we pass him by; We dare be puir, for a' that! For a' that and a' that, Our toils ob-scure and a' that; The

2

What tho' on hamely fare we dine,
  Wear hodden-grey, and a' that;
Gi'e fools their silks, and knaves their wine,
  A man's a man for a' that:
For a' that, and a' that,
  Their tinsel show, and a' that;
The honest man, tho' e'er sae puir
  Is king o' men for a' that.

3

Ye see yon birkie, ca'd a lord,
  Wha struts, and stares, and a' that;
Though hundreds worship at his word,
  He's but a coof for a' that
For a' that, and a' that,
  His ribbon, star, and a' that;
The man o' independent mind,
  He looks and laughs at a' that.

4

A prince can mak' a belted knight,
  A marquis, duke, and a' that;
But an honest man's aboon his might,
  Guid faith! he maunna fa' that!
For a' that, and a' that,
  Their dignities, and a' that;
The pith o' sense, and pride o' worth,
Are higher ranks than a' that.

5

Then let us pray that come it may,
  As come it will, for a' that,
That sense and worth, o'er a' the earth,
  May bear the gree, and a' that:
For a' that, and a' that,
  It's coming yet, for a' that,
That man to man, the warld o'er,
  Shall brithers be for a' that.

For the Sake o' Somebody.

Words by BURNS. The popular version of an old Air.

Andante non troppo.

My heart is sair, I daur - na tell, My heart is sair for some - bod - y;

I could wake a win - ter night,— For the sake o' some - bod - y.

Oh — hon, for some- bod-y Oh — hey, for some - bod.-

I could range the world a - round, For the sake o' some - bod-y!

2

Ye powers that smile on virtuous love,
O sweetly smile on somebody!
Frae ilka danger keep him free,
And send me safe my somebody.
Oh-hon, for somebody!
Oh-hey, for somebody!
I wad do—what wad I not?—
For the sake o' somebody.

AULD ROB MORRIS.

Words by BURNS. Air from the Leyden M S.(about 1700),with modification.

Un poco Andante.

KeyE♭ :m :r |d :-.l :s, |l, d :-:d¹ .l |l .s :f.m :r .d |m :r :m .r
There's auld___ Rob Mor_ris, that wons in yon glen,___ He's

|d .r :d .l :s, |l, d :-:d¹ .l |l .s :f.m :r .m |d :-:f .m
king o'__ guid fel_lows, and__ wale o'__ auld men; He has

2

She's fresh as the morning, the fairest in May ;
She's sweet as the ev'ning amang the new hay ;
As blythe and as artless as the lamb on the lea,
And dear to my heart as the light to the e'e.

3

But O ! she's an heiress—auld Robin's a laird,
And my daddie has nought but a cot-house and yard ;
A wooer like me maunna hope to come speed ;
The wounds I must hide that will soon be my dead.

4

The day comes to me, but delight brings me nane,
The night comes to me, but my rest it is gane ;
I wander my lane, like a night-troubled ghaist,
And I sigh as my heart it wad burst in my breast.

5

O, had she but been o' a lower degree,
I then might ha'e hop'd she wad smil'd upon me :
O, how past descriving had then been my bliss,
As now my distraction no words can express !

O MY LOVE IS LIKE A RED, RED ROSE.

Words old; revised and extended by BURNS.

Air, modernised version of "Low down in the Broom."

Moderato.

Voice.

Piano.

Key C. { :s .m
O my

{ |d :-.d |r :m |d¹ :-.t |l :s | l :-.s |l :d¹ |r¹ :- |- :d¹.r¹.m¹ }
love is like a red, red rose, That's new-ly sprung in June; O my

{ |d :-.d |r :m |d¹ :-.t |l :s | l :-.s |l :t |d¹ :- |- :s }
love is like a me-lo-die That's sweet-ly play'd in tune. As

fair art thou my bon-nie lass, So deep in love am I; And I will love thee still my dear, Till a' the seas gang dry. Till a' the seas gang dry my love, Till a' the seas gang

2

Till a' the seas gang dry, my dear,
   And the rocks melt wi the sun;
O I will love thee still, my dear,
   While the sands o' life shall run.
But fare thee weel, my only love,
   And fare thee weel awhile!
And I will come again, my love,
   Tho' 'twere ten thousand mile!
'Though 'twere ten thousand mile, my love!
   Tho' 'twere ten thousand mile!
And I will come again, my love,
   Tho' 'twere ten thousand mile!

33

AE FOND KISS.

Words by BURNS. Old Melody.

Andantino espressivo.

War-ring sighs and groans I'll wage thee. Who shall say that for-tune grieves him, While the star of hope she leaves him? Me, nae cheer-ful twin-kle lights me, Dark de-spair a-round be

2

I'll ne'er blame my partial fancy,—
Naething could resist my Nancy;
But to see her was to love her,
Love but her, and love for ever.
Had we never lov'd sae kindly,
Had we never lov'd sae blindly,
Never met or never parted,
We had ne'er been broken-hearted.
      Ae fond kiss!

3

Fare thee weel, thou first and fairest!
Fare thee weel, thou best and dearest!
Thine be ilka joy and treasure,
Peace, enjoyment, love and pleasure!
Ae fond kiss, and then we sever;
Ae fareweel, alas, for ever!
Deep in heart-wrung tears I'll pledge thee,
Warring sighs and groans I'll wage thee.
      Ae fond kiss!

DUNCAN GRAY.
(Solo or Part Song.)

Words by BURNS, Dec., 1792.　　　　　　　　　　　　　　Air, *circa* 1700.

37

2
Duncan fleech'd, an' Duncan pray'd,—
　Ha, ha, the wooin' o't ;
Meg was deaf as Ailsa Craig,—
　Ha, ha, the wooin' o't.
Duncan sigh'd baith out an' in,
Grat his e'en baith blear'd an' blin',
Spak' o' loupin' o'er a linn,—
　Ha, ha, the wooin' o't.

3
Time and chance are but a tide,—
　Ha, ha, the wooin' o't ;
Slighted love is sair to bide,—
　Ha, ha, the wooin' o't.
"Shall I, like a fool," quo' he,
" For a haughty hizzie dee ?
She may gae to—France—for me !—
　Ha, ha, the wooin' o't."

4
How it comes let doctors tell,—
　Ha, ha, the wooin' o't ;
Meg grew sick as he grew hale,—
　Ha, ha, the wooin' o't.
Something in her bosom wrings,
For relief a sigh she brings ;
An' O ! her e'en, they spak' sic things,—
　Ha, ha, the wooin' o't.

5
Duncan was a lad o' grace,—
　Ha, ha, the wooin' o't ;
Maggie's was a piteous case,—
　Ha, ha, the wooin' o't.
Duncan couldna be her death,
Swelling pity smoor'd his wrath ;
Now they're crouse a ' canty baith,—
　Ha, ha, the wooin' o't.

A Highland Lad my Love was Born.
Solo or Solo with Chorus.

Words by BURNS.
Air, "The White Cockade".

A Highland lad my love was born, The Lawland laws he held in scorn, But he still was faithfu' to his clan, My gallant, braw John Highlandman.

2
With his philabeg and tartan plaid,
An' gude claymore doun by his side,
The ladies' hearts he did trepan—
My gallant braw John Highlandman.
    Sing hey, &c.

3
They banish'd him beyond the sea;
But, ere the bud was on the tree,
Adoun my cheeks the pearls ran—
Embracing my John Highlandman.
    Sing hey, &c.

4
But, oh! they catch'd him at the last,
An' bound him in a dungeon fast;
My curse upon them ev'ry one,
They've hang'd my braw John Highlandman!
    Sing hey, &c.

39

There was a Lad was born in Kyle.

Solo or Solo with Chorus.

Words by BURNS

Air, "O gin ye were dead, guidman."

Allegretto.

There was a lad was born in Kyle, But what-na day, o' what-na style, I doubt it's hard-ly worth the-while To be sae nice wi' Rob-in.

2
Our monarch's hindmost year but ane
Was five-and-twenty days begun,
'Twas then a blast o' Janwar' win'
    Blew hansel in on Robin.
        For Robin was a rovin' boy, &c.

3
The gossip keekit in his loof,—
Quo' she, "Wha lives will see the proof,
This waly boy will be nae coof,
    I think we'll ca' him Robin.
        For Robin was a rovin' boy, &c.

4
He'll hae misfortunes great and sma,
But aye a heart aboon them a';
He'll be a credit till us a',—
    We'll a' be proud o' Robin.
        For Robin was a rovin' boy, &c.

5
But sure as three times three mak' nine,
I see by ilka score and line,
This chap will dearly like our kin',—
    So leeze me on thee, Robin."
        For Robin was a rovin' boy, &c.

41

Tam Glen.

Words by BURNS.
Air; "The Muckin' o' Geordie's byre."

Moderato.

Key G. Lah is E.

My heart is a break-in', dear tit-tie! Some coun-sel un-to me come len'; To an-ger them a' is a pit-y, But what will I do wi' Tam Glen? I'm think-in' wi' sic a braw fal-low, In poor-tith I might mak' a

2

There's Lowrie, the laird o' Drumeller,
  "Gude day to you," coof, he comes ben;
He brags and he blaws o' his siller,
  But when will he dance like Tam Glen?
My minnie does constantly deave me,
  And bids me beware o' young men;
They flatter, she says, to deceive me—
  But wha can think sae o' Tam Glen?

3

My daddie says, gin I'll forsake him,
  He'll gie me gude hunder merks ten;
But, if it's ordained I maun tak' him,
  O wha will I get but Tam Glen?
Yestreen, at the valentines dealin',
  My heart to my mou' gied a sten';
For thrice I drew ane without failin',
  And thrice it was written—Tam Glen.

4

The last Halloween I was waukin'
  My drookit sark sleeve, as ye ken;
His likeness cam' up the house staukin',
  And the very gray breeks o' Tam Glen.
Come, counsel, dear tittie, don't tarry;
  I'll gie ye my bonnie black hen,
Gif ye will advise me to marry
  The lad I lo'e dearly, Tam Glen.

O! WERT THOU IN THE CAULD BLAST.

Words by BURNS.
Air, "Lochiel's awa' to France."

Moderato e con espressione.

O wert thou in the cauld blast, On yonder lea, on yonder lea, My plaidie to the angry airt, I'd shelter thee, I'd shelter thee: Or

2

Or were I in the wildest waste,
  Sae bleak and bare, sae bleak and bare,
The desert were a paradise,
  If thou were there, if thou wert there:
Or were I monarch of the globe,
  Wi' thee to reign, wi' thee to reign,
The brightest jewel o' my crown
  Wad be my Jean, wad be my Jean.

My Ain Kind Dearie, O!

Words written by BURNS in 1792.

Air, "The Lea Rig."

When owre the hill the east-ern star Tells bught-in' time is near, my jo, And owsen, frae the fur-rowd field, Return sae dowf and wea-ry O; Down

47

Lyrics under music:
by — the burn, where scent-ed birks wi' dew are hang-in' clear, my jo, I'll — meet thee on the lea - rig, My ain — kind — dear-ie, O!

2
In mirkest glen, at midnight hour,
I'd rove, and ne'er be eerie, O,
If thro' that glen I gaed to thee,
My ain kind dearie, O!
Altho' the night were ne'er sae wild,
And I were ne'er sae weary, O,
I'd meet thee on the lea-rig,
My ain kind dearie, O!

3
The hunter lo'es the mornin' sun.
To rouse the mountain deer, my jo;
At noon the fisher seeks the glen,
Along the burn to steer, my jo:
Gi'e me the hour o' gloamin' gray,
It mak's my heart sae cheerie, O,
To meet thee on the lea-rig,
My ain kind dearie, O!

Green grow the rashes, O.

Words by BURNS.
Air considerably anterior to 1740

Vivace.

Key E♭ {:d | d .d :m ,.r |m .d :d .m | r .r :l ,.se |l .r :r .m
There's nought but care on ev'ry han', In ev'ry hour that pass_es, O; What

{:f ,.m :f .l | s .m :d .m | r .f :m ,.r | d .l₁ :l₁
sig_ni_fies the life o' man, An' twere_na for the lass_es, O?

2

The warldly race may riches chase,
And riches still may fly them, O;
And though at last they catch them fast,
Their hearts can ne'er enjoy them, O.
    Green grow, &c.

3

Gi'e me a canny hour at e'en,
My arms about my dearie, O,
An' warldly cares an' warldly men
May a' gae tapsalteerie, O.
    Green grow, &c.

4

For you sae douce, wha sneer at this,
Ye're nought but senseless asses, O;
The wisest man the warld e'er saw,
He dearly lo'ed the lasses, O.
    Green grow, &c.

5

Auld Nature swears the lovely dears
Her noblest work she classes, O;
Her prentice han' she tried on man,
An' then she made the lasses, O.
    Green grow, &c.

MARY MORISON.

Words by BURNS.
Air, "The Miller."

Andantino e con tenerezza.

O Mary, at thy window be, It is the wish'd, the trysted hour; Those smiles and glances let me see, That make the miser's treasure poor. How blythely wad I

51

2

Yestreen when, to the trembling string,
　The dance gaed through the lighted ha,
To thee my fancy took its wing,—
　I sat, but neither heard nor saw:
Though this was fair, and that was braw,
　And yon the toast o' a' the town,
I sigh'd, and said, amang them a',
　"Ye are na Mary Morison."

3

O Mary, canst thou wreck his peace,
　Wha for thy sake wad gladly dee?
Or canst thou break that heart of his,
　Whase only faut is loving thee?
If love for love thou wilt na gi'e,
　At least be pity to me shown;
A thought ungentle canna be
　The thought o' Mary Morison.

The Deil's Awa' Wi' Th' Exciseman.
(Solo or Trio, Soprano, Alto & Tenor.)

Words by BURNS. Air, "The Hemp-dresser."

53

cise man; An' ilk a wife cries, "Auld Ma-houn, I wish ye luck o' the
cise man; An' ilk a wife cries, "Auld Ma-houn, I wish ye luck o' the
cise man; An' ilk a wife cries, "Auld Ma-houn, I wish ye luck o' the

prize, man." The deil's a-wa', the deil's a-wa', The deil's a-wa' wi' th' Ex-
prize, man." The deil's a-wa', the deil's a-wa', The deil's a-wa' wi' th' Ex-
prize, man." The deil's a-wa', the deil's a-wa', The deil's a-wa' wi' th' Ex-

2

We'll mak' our maut, we'll brew our drink,
　　We'll dance, an' sing, an' rejoice, man;
An' mony braw thanks to the muckle black de'il
　　That danc'd awa' wi' th' Exciseman.
　　　　The de'il's awa', &c.

3

There's threesome reels, there's foursome reels,
　　There's hornpipes and strathspeys, man;
But the ae best dance e'er cam' to the lan'
　　Was, "The de'il's awa' wi' th' Exciseman."
　　　　The de'il's awa', &c.

HIGHLAND MARY.

Words by BURNS.
Air, "Katherine Ogie."

Andante mesto.

poco rall.

a tempo

Key A♭.
Lah is F.

{ :l₁ ,s₁ | m₁ :l₁ ,t₁ | l₁ :— ,t₁ }
Ye banks and braes, and

{ d :t₁ ,l₁ | l₁ :t₁ .d | r :— m | r ,t₁ :l₁ ,t₁ }
streams a-round The cas - tle o' Mont-

{ s₁ :— ,l₁ | t₁ :l₁ .s | m₁ :l₁ ,t₁ | l₁ :— ,t₁ }
gom - - 'ry, Green be your woods; and

56

fair your flow'rs, Your waters nev - er

rall. *a tempo.*
drum - lie! There sim - mer first un -

fauld her robes, And there the lang - est

tar - ry! For there I took the

2

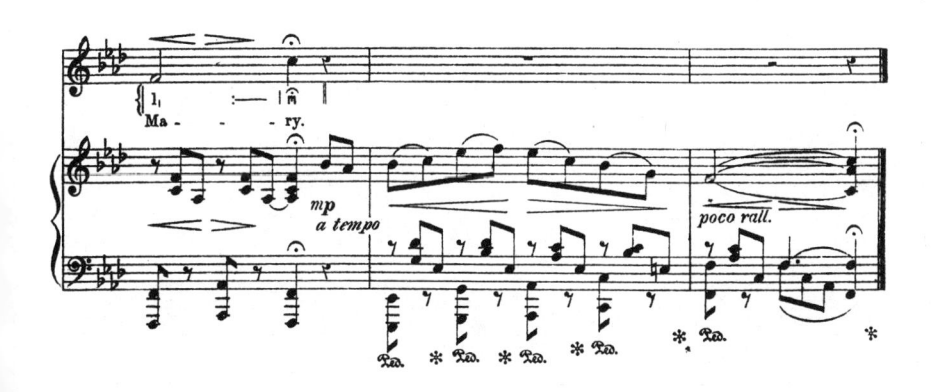

How sweetly bloomed the gay green birk,
   How rich the hawthorn's blossom,
As underneath their fragrant shade
   I clasped her to my bosom!
The golden hours, on angel-wings,
   Flew o'er me and my dearie;
For dear to me as light and life
   Was my sweet Highland Mary.

3

Wi' mony a vow and lock'd embrace,
   Our parting was fu' tender;
And, pledging aft to meet again,
   We tore ourselves asunder.
But, oh! fell death's untimely frost,
   That nipp'd my flower sae early!
Now green's the sod, and cauld's the clay
   That wraps my Highland Mary!

4

O pale, pale now, those rosy lips
   I aft ha'e kissed sae fondly!
And closed for aye the sparkling glance
   That dwelt on me sae kindly!
And mouldering now in silent dust
   The heart that lo'ed me dearly!
But still within my bosom's core
   Shall live my Highland Mary!

My Nannie, O.

Words by BURNS. Air from the "Orpheus Caledonius," 1725.

Andante espressivo.

Key E♭: :d.r | m :l, | m :r | d :t,.l, | l, :s | l d :-.r m,r :m.s
Lah is C. Be- hind yon hills where Lu- gar flows, 'Mang moors and moss- es

{ l :r.,m|r :d.r | m :f.,m|s :f.,m|r.d | r :m | d' :t | l :t,l.s m,.r :m.s
man- y, O, The win- try sun the day has clos'd, And I'll a- wa' to

{ l :l,.t,|l, :-.m,f | s :-.l | l.s :f.m | d' :s.l | s :d'.t
Nan- nie, O. The west- lin' wind blaws loud and shrill, The

2

My Nannie's charming, sweet and young,
  Nae artfu' wiles to win ye, O;
May ill befa' the flatt'ring tongue
  That wad beguile my Nannie, O!
Her face is fair, her heart is true,
  As spotless as she's bonnie, O;
The opening gowan, wat wi' dew,
  Nae purer is than Nannie, O.

3

A country lad is my degree,
  And few there be that ken me, O;
But what care I how few they be?
  I'm welcome aye to Nannie, O.
My riches a' 's my penny-fee,
  And I maun guide it cannie, O;
But warl's gear ne'er troubles me,—
  My thoughts are a' my Nannie, O

4

Our auld guidman delights to view
  His sheep and kye thrive bonnie, O;
But I'm as blythe that hauds his pleugh,
  And has nae care but Nannie, O.
Come weel, come wae, I care na by,
  I'll tak' what heaven will sen' me, O,
Nae ither care in life ha'e I
  But live, and love my Nannie, O.

I'M OWRE YOUNG TO MARRY YET.
(Solo, or Solo with Duet.)

Words partly by BURNS.
Strathspey Melody.

Allegretto con spirito.

I'm owre young, I'm owre young, I'm owre young to mar-ry yet; I'm owre young,'twad be a sin To tak' me frae my mammie yet.

61

I am my mammie's ae bairn, Nor o' my hame am wea-ry yet; And I wad ha'e ye learn, lads, That ye for me maun tar-ry yet.

Soprano. For I'm owre young, I'm owre young, I'm owre young to mar-ry yet; I'm

Contralto. For I'm owre young, I'm owre young, I'm owre young to mar-ry yet; I'm

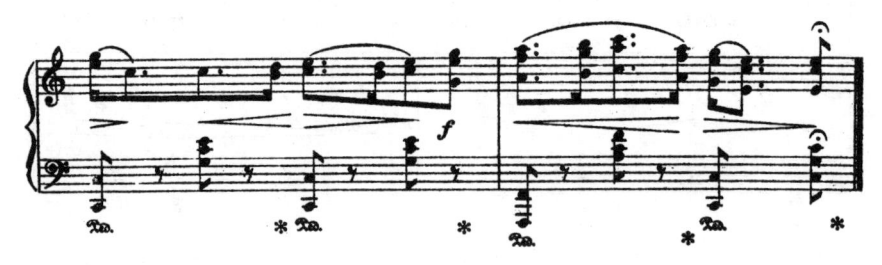

The remaining verses begin at the sign 𝄋.

2.
For I have had my ain way,
Nane daur to contradict me yet;
Sae soon to say I wad obey,—
In truth, I daurna venture yet.
    For I'm, &c.

3.
Fu' loud and shrill the frosty wind
Blaws through the leafless timmer, Sir;
But if ye come this gate again,
I'll aulder be gin simmer, Sir.
    For I'm, &c.

My Bonnie Mary.

(Solo, or Solo with Duet.)

Words by BURNS. Air credited to JAMES OSWALD, circa 1742.

Gae bring to me a pint o' wine, And fill it in a silver tassie, That I may drink, before I go, A service to my bonnie lassie. The boat rocks at the pier o'

Leith, Fu' loud the wind blaws frae the fer_ry; The ship rides by___ the Ber_wick Law, And I maun leave___ my bon_nie Ma_ry.

Tenor. (8ve lower.)
Gae bring to me a pint o' wine, And fill it in___ a sil_ver

Baritone. (8ve lower.)
Gae bring to me a pint o' wine, And fill it in___ a sil_ver

65

2.
The trumpets sound, the banners fly,
  The glitt'ring spears are ranked ready;
The shouts o' war are heard afar,
  The battle closes deep and bloody!
It's no the roar o' sea or shore
  Wad mak' me langer wish to tarry,
Nor shouts o' war that's heard afar,—
  It's leaving thee, my bonnie Mary.
    Gae bring to me, &c.

My Nannie's awa'.

Words by BURNS.

Air most probably modern.

Andante espressivo.

Key A. { :s₁ f₁ | m₁ -.f₁ :s₁ | s₁ :l₁ :d | m -.r :d | d :- :d }
Now in her green man_tle blythe Na_ture ar_rays, And

{ m -.r :d | d :l₁ :s₁ | l₁ :r -.r :r | :- :d }
lis _ tens the lamb_kins that bleat owre the braes, While

2.
The snaw-drap and primrose our woodlands adorn,
And violets bathe in the weet o' the morn;
They pain my sad bosom, sae sweetly they blaw!
‖:They mind me o' Nannie,— and Nannie's awa'.:‖

3.
Thou lav'rock, that springs frae the dews o' the lawn,
The shepherd to warn o' the grey-breakin' dawn,
And thou mellow mavis, that hails the night-fa'
‖:Give over for pity,— my Nannie's awa'.:‖

4.
Come, autumn, sae pensive, in yellow and grey,
And soothe me wi' tidings o' Nature's decay:
The dark, dreary winter, and wild drivin' snaw,
‖:Alane can delight me,— my Nannie's awa'.:‖

S. IV. h.

BONNIE WEE THING.

Words by BURNS.

Air from Oswald's "Caledonian Pocket Companion," *circa* 1755.

Un poco andante con espressione.

Bon-nie wee thing, can-nie wee thing, Love-ly wee thing, wert thou mine,

I wad wear thee in my bo-som, Lest my jew-el I should tine.

2

Bonnie wee thing, cannie wee thing,
   Lovely wee thing, wert thou mine,
I wad wear thee in my bosom,
   Lest my jewel I should tine.
Wit and grace, and love and beauty,
   In ae constellation shine!
To adore thee is my duty,
   Goddess of this soul o' mine.

Last May a Braw Wooer.

Words by BURNS. Air, "The Queen o' the Lothians."

Allegretto con spirito.

Key F.

Last May a braw woo-er cam' doun the lang glen, And sair wi' his love he did

71

deave me; I said there was nae-thing I hat-ed like men,— The deuce gae wi' him to be-lieve me, be-lieve me, The deuce gae wi' him to be-lieve me.

2

He spak' o' the darts o' my bonnie black een,
    And vow'd for my love he was deein';
I said he micht dee when he liket for Jean,—
      The guid forgi'e me for leein' for leein',
      The guid forgi'e me for leein'.

3

A weel-stockit mailin', himsel' o't the laird,
    And marriage aff hand, was his proffer;
I never loot on that I kenn'd it or cared,
      But thocht I micht ha'e a waur offer, waur offer,
      But thocht I micht ha'e a waur offer.

4

But what do you think? in a fortnight or less,
    The de'il's in his taste to gang near her!—
He's up the Gateslack to my black cousin Bess,—
      Guess ye how, the jaud! I could bear her, could bear her,
      Guess ye how, the jaud! I could bear her.

5

But a' the next week, as I fretted wi' care,
    I gaed to the tryst o' Dalgarnock;
And wha but my braw fickle wooer was there?
      Wha glower'd as if he'd seen a warlock, a warlock,
      Wha glower'd as if he'd seen a warlock.

6

Out owre my left shouther I gi'ed him a blink,
    Lest neighbours micht say I was saucy;
My wooer he caper'd as he'd been in drink,
      And vow'd that I was his dear lassie, dear lassie,
      And vow'd that I was his dear lassie.

7

I spier'd for my cousin, fu' couthie and sweet,
    Gin she had recover'd her hearin';
And how my auld shoon fitted her shauchled feet,—
      Guid sauf us! how he fell a-swearin', a-swearin',
      Guid sauf us! how he fell a-swearin'.

8

He begged for guid-sake I wad be his wife,
    Or else I wad kill him wi' sorrow;
Sae, e'en to preserve the puir body in life,
      I think I maun wed him to-morrow, to-morrow,
      I think I maun wed him to-morrow.

Lassie wi' the Lint-White Locks.
(**Solo, or Duet with Chorus.**)

Words written by BURNS in 1794.
Air, "Rothiemurchus Rant."

Affettuoso.

Lass-ie wi' the lint-white locks, Bon-nie lass-ie, art-less lass-ie;

Lass-ie wi' the lint-white locks, Bon-nie lass-ie, art-less lass-ie;

Wilt thou wi' me tent the flocks? Wilt thou be my dear-ie O?

Wilt thou wi' me tent the flocks? Wilt thou be my dear-ie O?

The remaining verses begin at the sign ✤.

2
And when the welcome simmer shower
Has cheer'd ilk drooping little flower,
We'll to the breathing woodbine bower
At sultry noon, my dearie, O.
Lassie wi', &c.

3
When Cynthia lights wi' silver ray
The weary shearer's hameward way,
Thro' yellow waving fields we'll stray,
And talk o' love, my dearie, O.
Lassie wi', &c.

4
And when the howling wintry blast
Disturbs my lassie's midnight rest,
Enclaspèd to my faithful breast,
I'll comfort thee, my dearie, O.
Lassie wi', &c.

75

JESSIE.

Words by BURNS.
Air from Johnson's "Museum" (1787-1803).

Andantino grazioso.

Here's a health to ane I lo'e dear, Here's a health to ane I lo'e dear; Thou art sweet as the smile when fond lov-ers meet, And soft as their part-ing tear, Jes-sie! Al-tho' thou maun nev-er be

77

2

I mourn through the gay gaudy day,
   As hopeless I muse on thy charms;
But welcome the dream o' sweet slumber,
   For then I am lock'd in thy arms, Jessie.
I guess by the dear angel smile,
   I guess by the love-rolling e'e;
But why urge the tender confession,
   'Gainst fortune's fell cruel decree, Jessie!

My Heart's in the Highlands.

Words mostly by BURNS.   Florid version of Gaelic Air, "Crochallan."

Andante espressivo.

Key E:

My heart's in the High-lands, my heart is not here, My heart's in the High-lands, a - chas - ing the deer; A - chas - ing the wild deer, and fol-low-ing the roe, My heart's in the High-lands wher-ev-er I go.

2

Farewell to the Highlands, farewell to the north,
The birth-place of valour, the country of worth,
Wherever I wander, wherever I rove,
The hills of the Highlands for ever I love.

3

Farewell to the mountains high cover'd with snow;
Farewell to the straths and green valleys below;
Farewell to the forests and wild-hanging woods;
Farewell to the torrents and loud-pouring floods.

4

My heart's in the Highlands, my heart is not here,
My heart's in the Highlands, a-chasing the deer;
A-chasing the wild deer, and following the roe,—
My heart's in the Highlands wherever I go.

CORN RIGS.

Words by BURNS.
Air considerably anterior to 1725.

81

tent-less heed, Till 'tween the late and ear-ly, O, Wi' sma' per-sua-sion she a-greed To see me thro' the bar-ley, O. Corn rigs and bar-ley rigs, Corn rigs are bon-nie, O: I'll ne'er for-get that hap-py night, A-mang the rigs wi'

2

The sky was blue, the wind was still,
    The moon was shining clearly, O;
I set her down wi' right guid-will,
    Amang the rigs o' barley, O.
I ken't her heart was a' my ain;
    I lov'd her most sincerely, O;
I kiss'd her owre and owre again,
    Amang the rigs o' barley, O.
        Corn rigs, &c.

3

I lock'd her in my fond embrace;
    Her heart was beating rarely, O;
My blessings on that happy place,
    Amang the rigs o' barley, O.
But by the moon and stars sae bright,
    That shone that hour sae clearly, O;
She aye shall bless that happy night,
    Amang the rigs o' barley, O.
        Corn rigs, &c.

4

I ha'e been blythe wi' comrades dear;
    I ha'e been merry drinkin', O;
I ha'e been joyfu' gath'rin' gear;
    I ha'e been happy thinkin', O.
But a' the pleasures e'er I saw,
    Though three times doubled fairly, O,–
That happy night was worth them a',
    Amang the rigs o' barley, O.
        Corn rigs, &c.

AFTON WATER.

Words by BURNS.
Melody by Alexander Hume, (1811-1859).

Andante con espressione.

Flow gent - ly, sweet Af - ton, a - mong thy green braes, Flow gent - ly, I'll sing thee a song in thy praise; My Ma - ry's a - sleep by thy

mur-mur - ing stream,— Flow gent - ly, sweet Af-ton, disturb not her dream. Thou stock - dove whose ech - o re-
sounds thro' the glen, Ye wild whist - ling black - birds in
yon thorn - y den, Thou

2

How lofty, sweet Afton, thy neighbouring hills,
Far-mark'd with the coursesof clear-winding rills!
There daily I wander as noon rises high,
My flocks and my Mary's sweet cot in my eye.
For pleasant thy banks and green valleys below;
Where wild in the woodlands the primroses blow;
Here oft as mild ev'ning creeps over the lea,
The sweet-scented birk shades my Mary and me.

3

Thy crystal stream, Afton, how lovely it glides,
And winds by the cot where my Mary resides,
How wanton thy waters her snowy feet lave,
As, gath'ring sweet flow'rets, she stems thy clear wave!
Flow gently, sweet Afton, among thy green braes,
Flow gently, sweet Afton, the theme of my lays;
My Mary's asleep by thy murmuring stream,—
Flow gently, sweet Afton, disturb not her dream.

O WHISTLE, AND I'LL COME TO YOU, MY LAD.
(Solo, or Solo with Chorus.)

Words by BURNS. Air by JOHN BRUCE, *circa* 1750.

Allegretto con spirito.

Key A.

O whis-tle, and I'll come to you, my lad; O whis-tle, and I'll come to you, my lad: Tho' fai-ther, and mith-er, and a' should gae mad, O whis-tle, and I'll come to you, my lad.

But war-i-ly tent when ye come to court me, And come na un-less the back

yett be a-jee; Syne up the back-stile, and let nae-bod-y see, And

88

The remaining verses begin at the sign 𝄋.

2

O whistle, and I'll come to you, my lad;
O whistle, and I'll come to you, my lad;
Though faither and mither and a' should gae mad,
O whistle, and I'll come to you, my lad.
At kirk or at market, whene'er ye meet me,
Gang by me as tho' that ye cared na a flie;
But steal me a blink o' your bonnie black e'e,
Yet look as ye were na lookin' at me,
Yet look as ye were na lookin' at me.
        O whistle, &c.

3

O whistle, and I'll come to you, my lad;
O whistle, and I'll come to you, my lad;
Though faither and mither and a' should gae mad,
O whistle and I'll come to you, my lad.
And whiles ye may lightlie my beauty a wee;
But court na anither, tho' jokin' ye be,
For fear that she wyle your fancy frae me,
For fear that she wyle your fancy frae me.
        O whistle, &c.

89

90

WILLIE BREW'D A PECK O' MAUT.
(Solo, or Solo with Chorus).

Words by BURNS.
Popular and modern air suggested by ALLAN MASTERTON'S melody, 1789.

Allegro moderato.

O Wil-lie brew'd a peck o' maut, And Rab and Al-lan cam' to pree; Three blyth-er hearts that lee-lang night, Ye wad-na fand in Christ-en-die.

2
Here are we met three merry boys,
Three merry boys I trow are we;
And mony a nicht we've merry been,
And mony mae we hope to be.
    We are nae fou', &c.

3
It is the moon—I ken her horn,
That's blinkin' in the lift sae hie;
She shines sae bricht to wyle us hame,
But by my sooth she'll wait a wee.
    We are nae fou', &c.

4
Wha first shall rise to gang awa',
A cuckold, coward loon is he;
Wha last beside his chair shall fa',
He is the king amang us three.
    We are nae fou', &c.

Chorus on following page.

92

*If the small notes in the first tenor part be taken, the small notes in the second tenor part must also be taken. The large notes in the one part are to be taken with the large notes in the other.
S.VI. g.

DOUN THE BURN, DAVIE, LOVE.

First three verses by ROBERT CRAWFORD, 1690–1733.
The other two by BURNS.

Air by JAMES HOOK, 1746–1827.

Key B. | d ,r | m ,r :d ,l, |-s₁,m₁-:r₁.d₁| m₁,s₁-:-s₁,d-|d -:r | m ,r :m ,s-|s₁,d-:f .m
When trees did bud, and fields were green, And broom bloom'd fair to

|m :-:fm r | :d ,r | m ,r :d,l, |-s₁,m₁-:-r₁.d₁| m₁,s₁-:-s₁,d-|d -:r
see; When Ma-ry was com-plete fif-teen, And

love laugh'd in her e'e; Blythe Davie's blinks her heart did move To speak her mind thus free, "Gang doun the burn, Davie, love, Doun the burn, Davie, love, Doun the burn, Davie, love, And I will follow thee. Doun the burn, Davie, love, Doun the burn, Davie, love,

2
Now Davie did each lad supass
That dwelt on yon burn side,
And Mary was the bonniest lass,
Just meet to be a bride.
      Blythe Davie's blinks, &c.

3
Her cheeks were rosy-red and white,
Her e'en were bonnie blue;
Her locks were like Aurora bright,
Her lips like hinney dew.
      Blythe Davie's blinks, &c.

4
As doun the burn they took their way,
And thro' the flow'ry dale,
His cheek to hers he aft did lay,
And love was aye the tale.
      Blythe Davie's blinks, &c.

5
"When, Mary, when shall we return,
Sic pleasure to renew?"
Quoth Mary, "Love, I like the burn,
And aye will follow you."
      Blythe Davie's blinks, &c.